ETHICS IN AMERICA

ETHICS IN AMERICA
SOURCE READER

SECOND EDITION

Edited by Lisa H. Newton, Ph.D.
Fairfield University

A College Television Course and Prime Time Television Series
Produced by Columbia University Seminars on Media and Society
An Annenberg/CPB Project

Major funding provided by the Annenberg/CPB Project with additional
support by EQUICOR-Equitable/HCA Corporation

PEARSON
Prentice
Hall

Upper Saddle River, New Jersey 07458

Library of Congress Cataloging-in-Publication Data
Ethics in America: source reader/[edited by] Lisa H. Newton.-- 2nd ed.
   p. cm.
  Includes bibliographical references (p.).
  ISBN 0-13-182625-5
  1. Ethics. 1. Newton, Lisa H. (date)
BJ1025.E85 2003
170—dc21   2002193132

Editorial Director: Charlyce Jones Owen
AVP, Director of Production and Marketing: Barbara Kittle
Senior Acquisitions Editor: Ross Miller
Assistant Editor: Wendy Yurash
Production Editor: Jan H. Schwartz
Manufacturing Manager: Mary Ann Gloriande
Manufacturing Buyer: Brian Mackey
Marketing Manager: Clair Bitting
Cover Design: Jayne Conte

Published by Pearson Education, Inc.
Upper Saddle River, New Jersey 07458

10 9 8 7 6 5 4 3 2 1

ISBN 0-13-182625-5

Pearson Education Ltd., *London*
Pearson Education Australia Pty. Ltd., *Sydney*
Pearson Education Singapore, Pte. Ltd.
Pearson Education North Asia Ltd., *Hong Kong*
Pearson Education Canada, Inc., *Toronto*
Pearson Educación de Mexico, S.A. de C.V.
Pearson Education—Japan, *Tokyo*
Pearson Education Malaysia, Pte. Ltd., *New Jersey*

Table of Contents

Preface

The volume in your hands is greatly expanded from the first edition, published in 1989. The expansion was undertaken on request by many who have used the book in their courses, and the reason was something of a surprise to me. It seems that this text is occasionally used, not just for a companion volume for the telecourse *Ethics in America,* but also on its own, as the text for an introductory level history of ethics course. But for that purpose, the selections were incomplete.

In the first edition I included only those works which were appealed to, explicitly or implicitly, by the panelists on the various discussions, and that means only works in the Western tradition. Further, only those works were included that had suggestions to make about how to solve ethical problems, to help students follow the actual reasoning of the panelists. Where the panelists' reasoning appealed (usually silently) to an ethical tradition, that tradition was included in the selections and the selections referenced in the *Study Guide,* the other companion volume. Only works so referenced were included in the *Source Reader.*

Now, that is one very exclusive principle of selection. Omitted were all religious traditions but our own, all Eastern thought of any kind, the entire nineteenth- and twentieth-century literature of doubt and ethical restructuring, and the contemporary movements of feminism, environmentalism, and other forms of multiculturalism (all movements that change the center of ethical consideration). If the text is to be used for a complete course in ethics, surely some selections must at least entertain the possibility of taking these literatures into account.

Accordingly, the second edition has expanded, to include selections from Islamic, Buddhist, and Confucian thought (attempts to put the *Bhagavad Gita* in some form that preserved the poetry were unsuccessful, so Hinduism is not included); also existentialism, feminism, and environmentalism. (A new selection on Fiduciary Duty, taken from the law, has also been added as a complement to the selection from Royce.) All the disclaimers that applied to the first edition still apply: you will get only a taste of these rich and fascinating authors, literature, and movements, the editor makes no claims to expertise on any of these authors in particular and certainly no claims to expertise on them all; you will be frustrated by the minimal selections provided; the only way you can relieve that frustration is by going in each case back to the original source. Go to it.

Introduction

THE REASON FOR THE READER

When you think about ethics, you do not think alone. Since human beings began to think at all, that is, as long as they have been human, questions of right and wrong have troubled them as they trouble us. We worry about these questions because of the type of creature we are: because we are social animals, we must operate with rules and social structures; because we are rational animals, we must worry about everything we do, including the rules and structures we have to live with. Ultimately, we will not accept any structure until it is ours—until we have created it or seen that it is good according to some standard of "good." But then that standard itself becomes an object of inquiry, question, and worry, and the name of that inquiry is "ethics."

Where questioning is inevitable, answering is irresistible. Since it became possible to preserve documents in writing, saints, sages, and other assorted experts have tried to answer the great questions of ethics: What makes an act right? What makes a human life good? What makes a state of affairs valuable, such that one should attempt to realize or preserve it? Their answers, the product of inquiry, have in turn been subjected to further critical inquiry, challenged, defended, refined, revised, resubmitted to the judgment of the literate thinkers of all the ages. The result of this process is a continuing dialogue, open to all who can read and think, a centuries-long conversation, which you are hereby invited to join.

Sometimes the conversation does not seem to be addressed to you, or at least to half of you, and perhaps a word should be said on that subject before we proceed. The Greeks assumed that only men—free male citizens, to be exact—could read and think, and addressed all their remarks to that tiny group of humans. From their assumptions, shared by the Jewish writers and, indeed, all their contemporaries, we evolved linguistic usage heavy on the masculine gender. *Man* is a social animal, I was taught, but *Man* is also a rational animal. We were taught the syllogism in the standard form: All *men* are mortal, Socrates is a *man*, therefore Socrates is mortal. More annoying to some of my colleagues, "he" is still the correct pronoun for the indefinite individual. Language persists long after the assumptions of male superiority are laid in the grave.

"Inclusive language," the movement to de-gender, sex-neutralize, the language of philosophical teaching, has never particularly appealed to me; there seem to be so many more important issues of justice to address, and so many more important forums in which to address them. Nevertheless, in the introductions and commentaries, I have attempted to avoid the most egregious of the male-oriented language (we will find "humans" being social and rational, for instance), and have attempted to spread the examples between the male and female gender. The authors, however—Aristotle and Aquinas and Thomas Hobbes—have been left in their original form with no attempt at modification or excuse. I decided long ago that whatever *he* might have thought of the matter, Aristotle was really addressing all intelligent people; I am an intelligent person; therefore Aristotle is addressing me. He addresses you, too. Whatever you think of his assumptions, may you enjoy his company.

THE DIVISION OF THE READER

The conversation about ethics does not proceed uniformly, but intensifies and dies out as the civilizations around it provide or deny the order, leisure, and facilities needed for systematic extended thought and the keeping of records. For convenience's sake, we shall focus our discussion not on chronological slices of philosophical time, but on four separate orientations that wax and wane, but coexist, throughout the history of philosophy:

- The pursuit of virtue, exemplified by Ancient Greece;
- Obedience to God, and religious tradition generally;
- The Deontological Tradition, Natural Law to John Rawls;
- The Hedonists and Utilitarians, Epicurus to John Stuart Mill.

At the conclusion of this survey, we append the Belmont Report, a document produced, believe it or not, by a committee appointed by the U.S. Congress, that has become the framework of the new and vital fields of practical or professional ethics—medical ethics, business ethics, and all the others.

- A final section, "Doubts and Experiments," records the rebellion against rational ethics embodied by Existentialism, Marxism, environmentalism, and feminism.

This division frankly acknowledges the overlaps in time among the traditions, by tracing each from ancient time to contemporary examples. It loses historical unity, but that may be an acceptable compromise for the conceptual coherence gained. Anomalies remain: there are some odd bedfellows (Epictetus, for example, and Thomas Aquinas, who rejected all pagans) and some lost souls (where shall we put Norman Vincent Peale?). But anomalies attend every division, and the one chosen for our purposes has at least the advantage of focusing attention on fundamentally different notions of human good—its possibility, its nature, and the means of its attainment.

These notions are all still very much with us today. They have not gone out of date. They inform our literature, the policy disputes of our legislatures, the editorials of our newspapers, and the air we breathe. To see them clearly, we must see them in the form in which they started, under the pens of the authors who first articulated them: but it should not surprise us to find contemporary inclusions for some of the ancient traditions. These cornerstones are still in place, and we still return to all of them to construct our arguments, policies, and systems, rediscovering each in turn as the others appear to be inadequate. (For example, when secular Utilitarianism does not seem to be adequate to the tasks before us, we may expect an upsurge of the Biblical tradition in the form of Christian Fundamentalism). Hence their inclusion, side by side for your inspection and evaluation, in hopes that you will be inspired to engage their thought directly with your own questions.

THE CONTENT AND FORM OF THE READER

A shelf of volumes could not include even all the currently influential writings on ethics. The embarrassment of riches on the subject renders absurd all efforts to have a single reader containing the most important ethical works available in the Western tradition. This particular reader, additionally, must contain selections that are relevant to the concepts explored in the telecourse, which span the whole subject matter of ethics. It must include selections of sufficient length, finally, to give a true representation of the author's thought and style. As editor of this reader, I faced the following options as to *content*:

1. I could choose to treat the writings as historical documents, emphasizing the significance that each writing had in the philosophical conversation of the writer's own time, preserving the context of controversy of that age, elucidating the meanings of the terms as understood by the writer and his contemporaries;
2. I could choose to treat the writers as contemporaries of mine, engaged in the timeless task of reflecting on the unchanging aspects of human nature—including the unchanging demand for knowledge of the best possible human life.

I chose Option 2. It is a familiar claim, that the Bible speaks to us in language we can understand; I do not find it any stranger to believe that, properly translated, Plato, Aristotle, Thomas Aquinas, and Immanuel Kant also speak to us. Human nature has not changed. They were concerned with the same creature with which we are familiar, and we can benefit from their often superior insights.

Similar choices arise as to *form*—length and style, for instance, of presentation:

1   The Great Books Option: I could create a shelf full of readers, with selections from all the important works of ethics in the Western tradition, long selections to give a fair sample of every author's work. But buying that collection would bankrupt you.

2   The Meet the Elite Option: I could include only a very few selections in a one-volume reader, again long selections to give fair samples of the works, and mention all the other works and authors in footnotes or chapter introductions. But if you'll meet most of these people only in footnotes, why bother with a reader at all?

3   I could use shorter selections of the works of most of the authors, retaining longer selections for only a crucial few, keeping the original words of the seminal works of ethics at the expense of context, rhythm, and often of style.

I chose option 3. Consider this: We have no archival responsibilities here, no responsibility to preserve the great writings for posterity. None of the great writers of ethics is out of print. Plato is easily available in several translations. Kant and Mill are out in paperback. Hobbes and Rawls are in any library. If you write the Gideon Society, they will send you a Bible for free. This book is meant to introduce you to the bare bones of the dialogue, and with luck, whet your appetite for the meat. From my point of view, the risk is ideal—the worst that can happen is that, frustrated with thin-sliced greatness and morsels of wisdom, you will consume this little reader at a sitting and, still hungry, get to the real sources, the original works, all readily accessible, to take on the authors for yourself.

But that, of course, would be the best that could happen.

ONE

The Greek Tradition

Several centuries before the birth of Christ, the ancient Greeks asked the hardest question of ethics: Why should we pay any attention at all to what is just, or right, or fair? Of course it's nice to be moral, nice for others, that is, and sometimes it makes us feel good about ourselves. But when the chips are down, and you can get away with it, aren't you much better off taking advantage of others whenever it helps your cause, and increasing your own pleasure, profit, and power without limit? Isn't that what the good life is all about?

Having asked the question, they put forward an answer, an answer that has galvanized Western philosophy ever since. You should live a good and just life in order to be happy. Much as it may surprise you, the life of gratified desire is in no way a happy life. Your worst enemies are not other people, but your own passions, and when you have brought your passions under control, you will be truly happy. Right now, the only happy man is the man who does the most for others—and that is the selfless philosopher.

I dislike admitting it, but that goes against the grain of my ordinary thinking. I know, intuitively, that I'd be happier if I had a big house, a yacht, a luxury car, lavish parties, power, all the possessions and privileges that belong to the Rich and Famous, whose Lifestyles we enjoy watching. The Greeks had much the same intuitions, but their philosophers did not agree. Do you?

Thucydides (Died ca. 401 B.C.)

Let's start with the Athenians, since Athens in the fourth and fifth centuries B.C. was the center of philosophy. The Athenians in this case, though, are in the middle of the Peloponnesian War. In the passage that follows, from Thucydides' history of that war, we find them dismissing all talk of "right" and "justice" in their proposal to reduce the island of Melos to slaughter or slavery—between which they will allow the Melian leaders to decide. The Melians protest that justice is on their side, but the Athenians are unyielding: the strong do what they will, the weak suffer what they must, and morality is irrelevant.

From Thucydides, *The Peloponnesian War*

The Athenians also made an expedition against the island of Melos. They had thirty of their own ships, six from Chios, and two from Lesbos; 1,200 hoplites, 300 archers, and twenty mounted archers, all from Athens; and about 1,500 hoplites from the allies and the islanders. . . . Now the generals Cleomedes, the son of Lycomedes, and Tisias, the son of Tisimachus, encamped with the above force in Melian territory and before doing any harm to the land, first of all sent representatives to negotiate. The Melians did not invite these representatives to speak before the people, but asked them to make the statement for which they had come in front of the governing body and the few.

The Athenian representatives then spoke as follows. . . . "We on our side will use no fine phrases saying, for example, that we have a right to our empire because we defeated the Persians, or that we have come against you now because of the injuries you have done us—a great mass of words that nobody would believe. And we ask you on your side not to imagine that you will influence us by saying that you, though a colony of Sparta, have not joined Sparta in the war, or that you have never done us any harm. Instead, we recommend that you should try to get what it is possible for you to get, taking into consideration what we both really do think; since you know as well as we do that, when these matters are discussed by practical people, the standard of justice depends on the equality of power to compel and that in fact the strong do what they have the power to do and the weak accept what they have to accept." . . .

Melians: So you would not agree to our being neutral, friends instead of enemies, but allies of neither side?

Athenians: No, because it is not so much your hostility that injures us; it is rather the case that, if we were on friendly terms with you, our subjects would regard that as a sign of weakness in us, whereas your hatred is evidence of our power.

Melians: Is that your subjects' idea of fair play—that no distinction should be made between people who are quite unconnected with you and people who are mostly your own colonists or else rebels whom you have conquered? . . .

Athenians: So far as right and wrong are concerned they think that there is no difference between the two, that those who still preserve their independence do so because they are strong, and that if we fail to attack them it is because we are afraid. . . .

Melians: It is difficult, and you may be sure that we know it, for us to oppose your power and fortune, unless the terms be equal. Nevertheless we trust that the gods will give us fortune as good as yours, because we are standing for what is right against what is wrong; and as for what we lack in power, we trust that it will be made up for by our alliance with the Spartans, who are bound, if for no other reason, then for honor's sake, and because we are their kinsmen, to come to our help. Our confidence, therefore, is not so entirely irrational as you think.

Athenians: So far as the favor of the gods is concerned, we think we have as much right to that as you have. Our aims and our actions are perfectly consistent with the beliefs men hold about the gods and with the principles which govern their own conduct. Our opinion of the gods and our knowledge of men lead us to conclude that it is a general and necessary law of nature to rule wherever one can. This is not a law that we made ourselves, nor were we the first to act upon it when it was made. We found it already in existence, and we shall leave it to exist forever among those who come after us. We are merely acting in accordance with it, and we know that anyone else with the same power as ours would be acting in precisely the same way. And therefore, as far as the gods are concerned, we see no good reason why we should fear to be at a disadvantage. But with regard to your views about Sparta and your confidence that she, out of a sense of honor, will come to your aid, we must say that we congratulate you on your simplicity but do not envy you your folly. In matters that concern themselves or their own constitution the Spartans are quite remarkably good; as for their relations with others, that is a long story, but it can be expressed shortly and clearly by saying that of all people we know the Spartans are most conspicuous for believing that what they like doing is honorable, and what suits their interests is just. And this kind of attitude is not going to be of much help to you in your absurd quest for safety at the moment.

You will therefore be showing an extraordinary lack of common sense if, after you have asked us to retire from this meeting, you still fail to reach a conclusion wiser than anything you have mentioned so far. Do not be led astray by a false sense of honor—a thing which often brings men to ruin when they are faced with an obvious danger that somehow affects their pride. For in many cases men have still been able to see the dangers ahead of them, but this thing called dishonor, this word, by its own force of seduction, has drawn them into a state where they have surrendered to an idea, while in fact they have fallen voluntarily into irrevocable disaster, in dishonor that is all the more dishonorable because it has come to them from their own folly rather than their misfortune. . . .

The Melians decide to fight, and the result is just as the Athenians predicted:

Siege operations were now carried on vigorously and, as there was also some treachery from inside, the Melians surrendered unconditionally to the Athenians, who put to death all the men of military age whom they took, and sold the women and children as slaves. Melos itself they took over for themselves, sending out later a colony of 500 men.

In the lines of the Athenians we find the briefest, and one of the clearest, expressions of the thesis that might alone makes "right." But the Greek ideal of the life of "excellence" or "virtue" stood against that thesis and in total opposition to it.

This ideal evolved from a very unphilosophical type—the figure of the strong nobleman in a feudal society. Against the vicissitudes of a life lived in constant danger from the barbarians, the Athenians of Homer's era of necessity developed a concept of the good human life as materially self-sufficient; the "good man" was the strong man who could handle himself well in all circumstances, protect himself and his own, be generous with friends, and justly terrible to enemies. In time, this aristocratic ideal evolved into one of spiritual as well as material self-sufficiency, and posited a new and philosophical ideal—the man whose soul, perfectly ordered, could survive unchanging through all the mischief the "strong" of this world could visit on the body.

The authors of this transformation, Plato and Aristotle, had a clear model of this man before them: Plato's teacher Socrates. Although he had lived a life of very modest external fortunes, he presented to his disciples an inspiring portrait of serenity and strength in his final days—in his arrest, trial, imprisonment, and death. In two of the early Platonic dialogues, the Apology *and the* Crito, *Plato gives us a picture of this man, his explanation of what he is and why he acts as he does, and his (somewhat surprising) insistence that the laws and the City in which he was raised deserve the credit for his victory.*

Plato (427 B.C.–347 B.C.)

Socrates was charged (by citizens Anytus, Meletus, and Lycon) with corrupting the youth and worshipping strange and foreign gods. The Apology *is his brief for his own defense at the trial. Socrates argues in these passages that he is no apostate or tempter, but a philosopher, dispatched by the oracle of Delphi (identified with the god Apollo) to question citizens unremittingly on the conduct of their lives. Socrates states that he has no intention of renouncing that mission out of fear of the mob.*

From Plato, *The Apology*

When the generals whom you chose to command me, Athenians, assigned me my station during the battles of Potidaea, Amphipolis, and Delium, I remained where they stationed me and ran the risk of death, like other men. It would be very strange conduct on my part if I were to desert my station now from fear of death or of any other thing when the god has commanded me—as I am persuaded that he has done—to spend my life in searching for wisdom, and in examining myself and others. That would indeed be a very strange thing. Then certainly I might with justice be brought to trial for not believing in the gods, for I should be disobeying the oracle, and fearing death and thinking myself wise when I was not wise. For to fear death, my friends, is only to think ourselves wise without really being wise, for it is to think that we know that we do not know. For no one knows whether death may not be the greatest good that can happen to man. But men fear it as if they knew quite well that it was the greatest of evils. And what is this but that shameful ignorance of thinking that we know what we do not know? In this matter, too, my friends, perhaps I am different from the multitude. And if I were to claim to be at all wiser than others, it would be because, not knowing very much about the other world, I do not think I know. But I do know very well that it is evil and disgraceful to do an unjust act, and to disobey my superior, whether man or god. I will never do what I know to be evil, and shrink in fear from what I do not know to be good or evil. . . . If you were therefore to say to me, "Socrates, this time we will not listen to Anytus. We will let you go, but on the condition that you give up this investigation of yours, and philosophy. If you are found following these pursuits again, you shall die." I say, if you offered to let me go on these terms, I should reply: "Athenians, I hold you in the highest regard and affection, but I will be persuaded by the god rather than you. As long as I have breath and strength I will not give up philosophy and exhorting you and declaring the truth to every one of you whom I meet, saying, as I am accustomed, 'My good friend, you are a citizen of Athens, a city which is very great and very famous for its wisdom and power. Are you not ashamed of caring so much for the making of money and for fame and prestige, when you neither think nor care about wisdom and truth and the improvement of your soul?'" If he disputes my words and says that he does care about these things, I shall not at once release him and go away: I shall question him and cross-examine him and test him. If I think that he has not attained excellence, though he says that he has, I shall reproach him for undervaluing the most valuable things, and overvaluing those that are less valuable. This I shall do to everyone whom I meet, young or old, citizen or stranger, but especially to citizens, since they are more closely related to me. This, you must recognize, the god has commanded me to do. And I think that no greater good has ever befallen you in the state than my service to the god. For I spend my whole life in going about and persuading you all to give your first and greatest care to the improvement of your souls, and not till you have done that to think of your bodies or your wealth. And I tell you that wealth does not bring excellence, but that wealth, and every other good thing which men have, whether in public or private, comes from excellence. If then I corrupt the youth by this teaching, these things must be harmful. But if any man says that I teach anything else, there is nothing in what he says. And therefore, Athenians, I say, whether you are persuaded by Anytus or not, whether you acquit me or not, I shall not change my way of life, no, not if I have to die for it many times. . . .

Unpersuaded that Socrates' service to the god is the best thing that ever happened to them, the citizens of Athens find him guilty. The custom of the court called then for prosecution and defense each to propose a penalty, between which the jury would vote. The prosecution proposes death. To the citizens' discomfiture, the defense proposes no real alternative penalty (exile would have been acceptable, but the defense proposed only a small fine), so the jury has no choice but to vote for death. Socrates resumes the conversation:

. . . when I was defending myself. I thought that I ought not to do anything unworthy of a free man because of the danger which I ran, and I have not changed my mind now. I would very much rather defend myself as I did, and die, than as you would have had me do, and live. Both in a lawsuit and in war, there are some things which neither I nor any other man may do in order to escape from death. In battle, a man often sees that he may at least escape from death by throwing down his arms and falling on his knees before the pursuer to beg for his life. And there are many other ways of avoiding death in every danger if a man is willing to say and to do anything. But, my friends, I think that it is a much harder thing to escape from wickedness than from death, for wickedness is swifter than death. And now I, who am old and slow, have been overtaken by the slower pursuer: and my accusers, who are clever and swift, have been overtaken by the swifter pursuer—wickedness. And now I shall go away, sentenced by you to death; they will go away, sentenced by truth to wickedness and injustice. And I abide by this award as well as they. Perhaps it was right for these things to be so. I think that they are fairly balanced.

And now I wish to prophesy to you, Athenians, who have condemned me. For I am going to die, and that is the time when men have most prophetic power. And I prophesy to you who have sentenced me to death that a far more severe punishment than you have inflicted on me will surely overtake you as soon as I am dead. You have done this thing, thinking that you will be relieved from having to give an account of your lives. But I say that the result will be very different. There will be more men who will call you to account. . . . And they will be harsher toward you than I have been, for they will be younger. . . . For if you think that you will restrain men from reproaching you for not living as you should, by putting them to death, you are very much mistaken. That way of escape is neither possible nor honorable. It is much more honorable and much easier not to suppress others, but to make yourselves as good as you can. This is my parting prophecy to you who have condemned me. . . .

With you who have acquitted me I should like to discuss this thing that has happened, while the authorities are busy, and before I go to the place where I have to die. . . . if we reflect in another way, we shall see that we may well hope that death is a good. For the state of death is one of two things: either the dead man wholly ceases to be and loses all consciousness or, as we are told, it is a change and a migration of the soul to another place. And if death is the absence of all consciousness, and like the sleep of one whose slumbers are unbroken by any dreams, it will be a wonderful gain. For if a man had to select that night in which he slept so soundly that he did not even dream, and had to compare with it all the other nights and days of his life, and then had to say how many days and nights in his life he had spent better and more pleasantly than this night, I think that a private person, nay, even the Great King of Persia himself, would find them easy to count, compared with the others. If that is the nature of death, I for one count it a gain. For then it appears that all time is nothing more than a single night. But if death is a journey to another place, and what we are told is true—that all who have died are there—what good could be greater than this, my judges? Would a journey not be worth taking, at the end of which, in the other world, we should be delivered from the pretended judges here and should find the true judges who are said to sit in judgment below? . . .

And you too, judges, must face death hopefully, and believe this one truth, that no evil can happen to a good man, either in life or after death. His affairs are not neglected by the gods; and what has happened to me today has not happened by chance. I am persuaded that it was better for me to die now, and to be released from trouble . . . And so I am not at all angry with my accusers or with those who have condemned me to die. Yet it was not with this in mind that they accused me and condemned me, but meaning to do me an injury. So far I may blame them.

Yet I have one request to make of them. When my sons grow up, punish them, my friends, and harass them in the same way that I have harassed you, if they seem to you to care for riches or for any other thing more than excellence. . . . And if you will do this, I myself and my sons will have received justice from you.

But now the time has come, and we must go away—I to die, and you to live. Which is better is known to the god alone.

> *Socrates is condemned to death, but no one really wants him to die. They just want him out of town, which is why he probably could have won the penalty vote had he proposed exile as an alternative to death. In point of fact, it is not too late for that choice. In days when Athenian law was only partially enforced against well-connected citizens, it was entirely possible to sneak someone out of jail on the promise that he would not be seen in the streets again. It is this proposal that his friend Crito brings to Socrates. Socrates will have none of it, for some interesting reasons: the man and citizen, he argues, are the creation of the City; they are its property (like slaves) and its children, and the individual has no right to assert individual rights against the City; further, one deals with the City as with a friend, and must keep one's agreements with it. This is the first appearance of what a later age will call "Social Contract Theory"; that theory emerges in more articulate form in the passages from* The Republic, *later in this chapter. The passage here, from the* Crito, *has "the laws and the commonwealth" of Athens appearing to Socrates to talk him out of escaping with Crito:*

From Plato, *Crito*

Socrates: Consider it in this way. Suppose the laws and the commonwealth were to come and appear to me as I was preparing to run away (if that is the right phrase to describe my escape) and were to ask, "Tell us, Socrates, what have you in your mind to do? What do you mean by trying to escape but to destroy us, the laws and the whole state, so far as you are able? Do you think that a state can exist and not be overthrown, in which the decisions of law are of no force, and are disregarded and undermined by private individuals?" How shall we answer questions like that, Crito? Much might be said, especially by an orator, in defense of the law which makes judicial decisions supreme. Shall I reply, "But the state has injured me by judging my case unjustly?" Shall we say that?

Crito: Certainly we will, Socrates.

Socrates: And suppose the laws were to reply, "Was that our agreement? Or was it that you would abide by whatever judgments the state should pronounce?" And if we were surprised by their words, perhaps they would say, "Socrates, don't be surprised by our words, but answer us; you yourself are accustomed to ask questions and to answer them. What complaint have you against us and the state, that you are trying to destroy us? Are we not, first of all, your parents? Through us your father took your mother and brought you into the world. Tell us, have you any fault to find with those of us that are the laws of marriage?" "I have none," I should reply. "Or have you any fault to find with those of us that regulate the raising of the child and the education which you, like others, received? Did we not do well in telling your father to educate you in music and athletics?" "You did," I should say. "Well, then, since you were brought into the world and raised and educated by us, how, in the first place, can you deny that you are our child and our slave, as your fathers were before you? And if this be so, do you think that your rights are on a level with ours? Do you think that you have a right to retaliate if we should try to do anything to you? You had not the same rights that your father had, or that your master would have had if you had been a slave. You had no right to retaliate if they ill-treated you, or to answer them if they scolded you, or to strike them back if they struck you, or to repay them evil with evil in any way. And do you think that you may retaliate in the case of your country and its laws? If we try to destroy you, because we think it just, will you in return do all that you can to destroy us, the laws, and your country, and say that in so doing you are acting justly—you, the man who really thinks so much of excellence? Or are you too wise to see that your country is worthier, more to be revered, more sacred, and held in higher honor both by the gods and by all men of understanding, than your father and your mother and all your other ancestors; and that you ought to reverence it, and to submit to it and to approach it more humbly when it is angry with you than you would approach your father; and either to do whatever it tells you to do or to persuade it to excuse you; and to obey in silence if it orders you to endure flogging or imprisonment, or if it sends you to battle to be wounded or to die? That is just. You must not give way, nor retreat, nor desert your station. In war, and in the court of justice, and everywhere, you must do whatever your state and your country tell you to do, or you must persuade them that their commands are unjust. But it is impious to use violence against your father and mother, and much more impious to use violence against your country." What answer shall we make, Crito? Shall we say that the laws speak the truth?

Crito: I think that they do.

Socrates: "Then consider, Socrates," perhaps they would say, "if we are right in saying that in attempting to escape you are attempting an injustice. We brought you into the world, we raised you, we educated you, we gave you and every other citizen a share of all the good things we could. Yet we proclaim that if any man of the Athenians is dissatisfied with us, he may take his goods and go away wherever he pleases; we give that privilege to every man who chooses to avail himself of it, so soon as he has reached manhood, and sees us, the laws, and the administration of our state. No one of us stands in his way or forbids him to take his goods and go wherever he likes, whether it be to an Athenian colony or to any foreign country, if he is dissatisfied with us and with the state. But we say that every man of you who remains here, seeing how we administer justice, and how we govern the state in other matters, has agreed, by the very fact of remaining here, to do whatsoever we tell him. And, we say, he who disobeys us acts unjustly on three counts; he disobeys us who are his parents, and he disobeys us who reared him, and he disobeys us after he has agreed to obey us, without persuading us that we are wrong. Yet we did not tell him sternly to do whatever we told him. We offered him an alternative; we gave him his choice either to obey us or to convince us that we were wrong; but he does neither.

"These are the charges, Socrates, to which we say that you will expose yourself if you do what you intend; and you are more exposed to these charges than other Athenians." And if I were to ask "Why?" they might retort with justice that I have bound myself by the agreement with them more than other Athenians. They would say, "Socrates, we have very strong evidence that you were satisfied with us and with the state. You would not have been content to stay at home in it more than other Athenians unless you had been satisfied with it more than they. You never went away from Athens to the festivals, nor elsewhere except on military service; you never made other journeys like other men; you had no desire to see other states or other laws; you were contented with us and our state; so strongly did you prefer us, and agree to be governed by us. And what is more, you had children in this city, you found it so satisfactory. Besides, if you had wished, you might at your trial have offered to go into exile. At that time you could have done with the state's consent what you are trying now to do without it. But then you gloried in being willing to die. You said that you preferred death to exile. And now you do not honor those words; you do not respect us, the laws, for you are trying to destroy us; and you are acting just as a miserable slave would act, trying to run away, and breaking the contracts and agreement which you made to live as our citizen. First, therefore, answer this question. Are we right, or are we wrong, in saying that you have agreed not in mere words, but in your actions, to live under our government?" What are we to say, Crito? Must we not admit that it is true?

Crito:	We must, Socrates.
Socrates:	Then they would say, "Are you not breaking your contracts and agreements with us?

And you were not led to make them by force or by fraud. You did not have to make up your mind in a hurry. You had seventy years in which you might have gone away if you had been dissatisfied with us, or if the agreement had seemed to you unjust. But you preferred neither Sparta nor Crete, though you are fond of saying that they are well governed, nor any other state, either of the Greeks or the Barbarians. You went away from Athens less than the blind and the crippled. Clearly you, far more than other Athenians, were satisfied with the state, and also with us who are its laws; for who would be satisfied with a state which had no laws? And now will you not abide by your agreement? If you take our advice, you will, Socrates; then you will not make yourself ridiculous by going away from Athens. . . .

"No, Socrates, be persuaded by us who have reared you. Think neither of children nor of life, nor of any other thing before justice, so that when you come to the other world you may be able to make your defense before the rulers who sit in judgment there. It is clear that neither you nor any of your friends will be happier, or more just, or more pious in this life, if you do this thing, nor will you be happier after you are dead. Now you will go away a victim of the injustice, not of the laws, but of men. But if you repay evil with evil, and injustice with injustice in this shameful way, and break your agreements and covenants with us, and injure those whom you should least injure, yourself and your friends and your country and us, and so escape, then we shall be angry with you while you live, and when you die our brothers, the laws in Hades, will not receive you kindly; for they will know that on earth you did all that you could to destroy us. Listen then to us, and let not Crito persuade you to do as he says."

Be sure, my dear friend Crito, that this is what I seem to hear, as the worshippers of Cybele seem, in their passion, to hear the music of flutes; and the sound of these arguments rings so loudly in my ears, that I cannot hear any other arguments. And I feel sure that if you try to change my mind you will speak in vain. Nevertheless, if you think that you will succeed, speak.

Crito: I have nothing more to say, Socrates.

Socrates: Then let it be, Crito, and let us do as I say, since the god is our guide.

The Greeks, as you see, were fond of bright contrasts. Thucydides' Athenians see no earthly reason why they should restrict their pursuit of self-interest—or heavenly reason, for that matter, since of the gods we know by tradition, as of men we know for a fact, that they rule wherever they can. Considerations of "justice" are to them only so many fine words, and present no obstacle to unlimited personal aggrandizement. Against this conclusion stands the portrait of the philosopher. By living just the sort of law-abiding, virtuous life held in contempt by Thucydides' Athenians, he has attained to such personal strength and serenity that he can in turn hold even his own public rejection and death in contempt.

Socrates died in 399 B.C. His friend and disciple Plato set up a school, the Academy, and started a career of teaching and writing. Some years later, Plato set his hand to a direct comparison of the two paths of life that confront each other in the Greek tradition. The Republic, *a book-length treatment of that conflict, is Plato's greatest work, possibly the greatest work of philosophy ever written. In it the questions above are put directly: What is it, really, to be a happy human being? Which is better, the life of self-interest— the pursuit of profit, pleasure, and power—or the philosopher's life, renouncing all material gain and living according to reason and the needs of the spirit? Can we prove that one way of life is happier than the other?*

Like his other works, Plato's Republic *is a "dialogue," a conversation among friends and acquaintances, set some years before Socrates' death. The characters in the opening conversation, besides Socrates, include Cephalus, a wealthy elder of the community, Cephalus' son Polemarchus, Thrasymachus (a young Sophist, or "wise man"), and Plato's brothers, Glaucon and Adeimantus. (Plato himself is not present.) Socrates, as usual, is asking most of the questions, and one of the questions he puts to Cephalus launches us into a discussion of the nature and value of "justice," or the moral life. He asks Cephalus,*

From Plato, *The Republic*

Tell me, what do you take to be the greatest advantage you have got from being wealthy?

One that perhaps not many people would take my word for [answered Cephalus]. I can tell you, Socrates, that, when the prospect of dying is near at hand, a man begins to feel some alarm about things that never troubled him before. He may have laughed at those stories they tell of another world and of punishments there for wrongdoing in this life; but now the soul is tormented by a doubt whether they may not be true. Maybe from the weakness of old age, or perhaps because, now that he is nearer to what lies beyond, he begins to get some glimpse of it himself—at any rate he is beset with fear and misgiving; he begins thinking over the past: is there anyone he has wronged? If he finds that his life has been full of wrongdoing, he starts up from his sleep in terror like a child, and his life is haunted by dark forebodings; whereas, if his conscience is clear, that "sweet Hope" that Pindar speaks of is always with him to tend his age. . . . Now in this, as I believe, lies the chief value of wealth, not for everyone, perhaps, but for the right-thinking man. It can do much to save us from going to that other world in fear of having cheated or deceived anyone even unintentionally or of being in debt to some god for sacrifice or to some man for money. Wealth has many other uses, of course; but, taking one with another, I should regard this as the best use that can be made of it by a man of sense.

You put your case admirably, Cephalus, said I. [Socrates is narrator of *The Republic*.] But take this matter of doing right: can we say that it really consists in nothing more nor less than telling the truth and paying back anything we may have received? Are not these very actions sometimes right and sometimes wrong? Suppose, for example, a friend who had lent us a weapon were to go mad and then ask for it back, surely anyone would say we ought not to return it. It would not be "right" to do so; nor yet to tell the truth without reserve to a madman.

No, it would not.

Right conduct, then, cannot be defined as telling the truth and restoring anything we have been trusted with.

Yes, it can, Polemarchus broke in, at least if we are to believe Simonides. Well, well, said Cephalus, I will bequeath the argument to you. It is time for me to attend to the sacrifice.

Your part, then, said Polemarchus, will fall to me as your heir.

By all means, said Cephalus with a smile; and with that he left us, to see to the sacrifice.

Then, said I, if you are to inherit this discussion, what is this saying of Simonides about right conduct which you approve?

That it is just to render every man his due. That seems to me a fair statement. It is certainly hard to question the inspired wisdom of a poet like Simonides; but what this saying means you may know, Polemarchus, but I do not. Obviously it does not mean what we were speaking of just now—returning something we have been entrusted with to the owner even when he has gone out of his mind. And yet surely it is his due, if he asks for it back?

Yes.

But it is wrong to give it back when he has gone mad?

True.

Simonides, then, must have meant something different from that when he said it was just to render a man his due.

Certainly he did; his idea was that, as between friends, what one owes to another is to do him good, not harm.

I see, said I; to repay money entrusted to one is not to render what is due, if the two parties are friends and the repayment proves harmful to the lender. That is what you say Simonides meant?

Yes, certainly.

And what about enemies? Are we to render whatever is their due to them?

Yes, certainly, what really is due to them; which means, I suppose, what is appropriate to an enemy—some sort of injury.

It seems, then, that Simonides was using words with a hidden meaning, as poets will. He really meant to define justice as rendering to everyone what is appropriate to him; only he called that his "due."

Well, why not?

But look here, said I. Suppose we could question Simonides about the art of medicine—whether a physician can be described as rendering to some object what is due or appropriate to it; how do you think he would answer?

That the physician administers the appropriate diet or remedies to the body.

And the art of cookery—can that be described the same way?

Yes; the cook gives the appropriate seasoning to his dishes.

Good. And the practice of justice?

If we are to follow those analogies, Socrates, justice would be rendering services or injuries to friends or enemies.

So Simonides means by justice doing good to friends and harm to enemies?

I think so.

And in matters of health who would be the most competent to treat friends and enemies in that way?

A physician.

And on a voyage, as regards the dangers of the sea?

A ship's captain.

In what sphere of action, then, will the just man be the most competent to do good or harm?

In war, I should imagine; when he is fighting on the side of his friends and against his enemies.

I see. But when we are well and staying on shore, the doctor and the ship's captain are of no use to us.

True.

Is it also true that the just man is useless when we are not at war?

I should not say that.

So justice has its uses in peace-time too?

Yes.

Like farming, which is useful for producing crops, or shoemaking, which is useful for providing us with shoes. Can you tell me for what purposes justice is useful or profitable in time of peace?

For matters of business, Socrates.

In a partnership, you mean?

Yes.

But if we are playing draughts, or laying bricks, or making music, will the just man be as good and helpful a partner as an expert draught-player, or a builder, or a musician?

No.

Then in what kind of partnership will he be more helpful?

Where money is involved, I suppose.

Except, perhaps, Polemarchus, when we are putting our money to some use. If we are buying or selling a horse, a judge of horses would be a better partner; or if we are dealing in ships, a shipwright or a sea captain.

I suppose so.

Well, when will the just man be specially useful in handling our money?

When we want to deposit it for safekeeping.

When the money is to lie idle, in fact?

Yes.

So justice begins to be useful only when our money is out of use?

Perhaps so.

And in the same way, I suppose, if a pruning knife is to be used, or a shield, or a lyre, then a vine-dresser, or a soldier, or a musician will be of service; but justice is helpful only when these things are to be kept safe. In fact justice is never of any use in using things; it becomes useful when they are useless.

That seems to follow.

If that is so, my friend, justice can hardly be a thing of much value. And here is another point. In boxing or fighting of any sort skill in dealing blows goes with skill in keeping them off, and the same doctor that can keep us from disease would also be clever at producing it by stealth; or again, a general will be good at keeping his army safe, if he can also cheat the enemy and steal his plans and dispositions. So a man who is expert in keeping things will always make an expert thief.

Apparently.

The just man, being good at keeping money safe, will also be good at stealing it.

That seems to be the conclusion, at any rate.

So the just man turns out to be a kind of thief. You must have learned that from Homer, who showed his predilection for Odysseus' grandfather Autolycus by remarking that he surpassed all men in cheating and perjury. Justice, according to you and Homer and Simonides, turns out to be a form of skill in cheating, provided it is to help a friend or harm an enemy. That was what you meant?

Good God, no, he protested, but I have forgotten now what I did mean. All the same, I do still believe that justice consists in helping one's friends and harming one's enemies.

> *The passage to this point is a fine example of Socratic Method—asking questions to get at the truth. All too often, as Polemarchus has just discovered, the truth of the matter is that we use words very carelessly. Even when we have a good general notion of what a word may mean, and "justice" certainly does mean, in general, "rendering every one his due," we may be very hard put to spell out what that means in practice, and why it means what it does. Polemarchus' problems here are typical of the goodhearted but intellectually fuzzy citizens with whom Socrates consorted.*
>
> *Well then, if the major effect of the questioning is to confuse the earnest but unsophisticated citizen, why do it? Why bother with all this precision? Because not all of the conversationalists were the sincere, if imprecise, seekers of the good represented by Polemarchus. The Sophists, professional teachers of rhetoric who hired out to advise on ethics, were very precise, and clever, and good at bewildering the citizens—in this case, with the aim of proving that the selfish life was, after all, the best.*
>
> *The next interlocutor in the dialogue, Thrasymachus, Sophist and student of Sophists, is invited to present his, and their, interpretation of "justice," or the moral life:*

Listen then, Thrasymachus began. What I say is that "just" or "right" means nothing but what is to the interest of the stronger party. Well, where is your applause? You don't mean to give it me.

I will, as soon as I understand, I said. I don't see yet what you mean by right being the interest of the stronger party. For instance, Polydamas, the athlete, is stronger than we are, and it is to his interest to eat beef for the sake of his muscles; but surely you don't mean that the same diet would be good for weaker men and therefore be right for us?

You are trying to be funny, Socrates. It's a low trick to take my words in the sense you think will be most damaging.... Don't you know ... that a state may be ruled by a despot, or a democracy, or an aristocracy? ... and that the ruling element is always the strongest? ... Well, then, in every case the laws are made by the ruling party in its own interest; a democracy makes democratic laws, a despot autocratic ones, and so on. By making these laws they define as "right" for their subjects whatever is for their own interest, and they call anyone who breaks them a "wrongdoer" and punish him accordingly. That is what I mean: in all states alike "right" has the same meaning, namely what is for the interest of the party established in power, and that is the strongest. So the sound conclusion is that what is "right" is the same everywhere: the interest of the stronger party.

Now I see what you mean, said I; whether it is true or not, I must try to make out. . . . I agree myself that right is in a sense a matter of interest; but when you add "to the stronger party," I don't know about that. I must consider.

Go ahead, then.

I will. Tell me this. No doubt you also think it is right to obey the men in power? I do.

Are they infallible in every type of state, or can they sometimes make a mistake?

Of course they can make a mistake.

In framing laws, then, they may do their work well or badly?

No doubt.

Well, that is to say, when the laws they make are to their own interest; badly, when they are not?

Yes.

But the subjects are to obey any law they lay down, and they will then be doing right?

Of course.

If so, by your account, it will be right to do what is not to the interest of the stronger party, as well as what is so.

What's that you are saying?

Just what you said, I believe: but let us look again. Haven't you admitted that the rulers, when they enjoin certain acts on their subjects, sometimes mistake their own best interests, and at the same time that it is right for the subjects to obey, whatever they may enjoin?

Yes, I suppose so.

Well, that amounts to admitting that it is right to do what is not to the interest of the rulers or the stronger party. They may unwittingly enjoin what is to their own disadvantage; and you say it is right for the others to do as they are told. In that case, their duty must be the opposite of what you said, because the weaker will have been ordered to do what is against the interest of the stronger. You with your intelligence must see how that follows. . . .

> *At this point Polemarchus enters the conversation, trying to clarify the matter for himself.*

Thrasymachus said it was right to do what you are told by the men in power: . . . he also said that what is to the interest of the stronger party is right; and, after making both these assertions, he admitted that the stronger sometimes command the weaker subjects to act against their interests. From all of which it follows that what is in the stronger's interest is no more right than what is not.

No, said Cleitophon; he meant whatever the stronger *believes* to be in his own interest. That is what the subject must do, and what Thrasymachus meant to define as right.

That was not what he said, rejoined Polemarchus.

No matter, Polemarchus, said I; if Thrasymachus says so now, let us take him in that sense. Now, Thrasymachus, tell me, was that what you intended to say—that right means what the stronger thinks is to his interest, whether it really is so or not?

Most certainly not, he replied. . . .

> *Advancing the most straightforward of cynical views, Thrasymachus has been (to his amazement) caught in a contradiction. Are you a bit confused by the colloquy? So was Thrasymachus, and that was the point. We need precise terminology and sophistication in argument, for the bad guys—the Sophists, delighted to tell you what you want to hear, for a fee—are doubly sophisticated and aimed at trapping you, should you disagree with them, into the wrong answer.*

> *Socrates continues along this line of questioning, slowly eliciting from Thrasymachus the admission that ruling must be errorless because it is an art, or craft, which does not contain in itself the mistakes the craftsman may make. (When the physician inadvertently doses me with bleach, he is not "practicing medicine.") But an art, or craft, is oriented not to the benefit of the practitioner, or the art itself, but to that of the subject matter—the potter's clay, the physician's patient, and the ruler's subjects. In the passages that follow, Plato expounds the selfless ethic of the artist, which we find today in professional and other fiduciary relationships—the ethic that governs the relationship between professional and client, trustee and beneficiary, guardian and ward. In considering the action to be taken, the fiduciary may consider only the benefit of the one for whom he acts, not himself, not his art.*

In itself, an art is sound and flawless, so long as it is entirely true to its own nature as an art in the strictest sense—and it is the strict sense that I want you to keep in view. Is not that true?

So it appears.

Then, said I, the art of medicine does not study its own interest, but the needs of the body, just as a groom shows his skill by caring for horses, not for the art of grooming. And so every art seeks, not its own advantage—for it has no deficiencies—but the interest of the subject on which it is exercised.

It appears so.

But surely, Thrasymachus, every art has authority and superior power over its subject.

To this he agreed, though very reluctantly.

So far as arts are concerned, then, no art ever studies or enjoins the interest of the superior or stronger party, but always that of the weaker over which it has authority.

Thrasymachus assented to this at last, though he tried to put up a fight. I then went on:

So the physician, as such, studies only the patient's interest, not his own. For as we agreed, the business of the physician, in the strict sense, is not to make money for himself, but to exercise his power over the patient's body; and the ship's captain, again, considered strictly as no mere sailor, but in command of the crew, will study and enjoin the interest of his subordinates, not his own.

He agreed reluctantly.

And so with government of any kind: no ruler, in so far as he is acting as ruler, will study or enjoin what is for his own interest. All that he says and does will be said and done with a view to what is good and proper for the subject for whom he practices his art.

> *Furious at his defeat, Thrasymachus abandons the attempt to* define *justice in such a way that might must, by definition, make right. Instead he makes an empirical claim: granted that the unjust man is not "right," he's still happier. He has the things that you and I want; he gets the better of every deal; he's living the lifestyle that everyone dreams of. Right or not, you're better off choosing injustice as your way of life. This cynical outburst is the initial statement of the problem of* The Republic.

At this point, when everyone could see that Thrasymachus's definition of justice had been turned inside out, instead of making any reply, he said:

Socrates, have you a nurse?

Why do you ask such a question as that? I said. . . .

Because she lets you go about sniffling like a child whose nose wants wiping. She hasn't even taught you to know a shepherd when you see one, or his sheep either.

What makes you say that?

Why, you imagine that a herdsman studies the interests of his flocks or cattle, tending and fattening up with some other end in view than his master's profit or his own; and so you don't see that, in politics, the genuine ruler regards his subjects exactly like sheep, and thinks of nothing else, night and day, but the good he can get out of them for himself. You are so far out in your notions of right and wrong, justice and injustice, as not to know that "right" actually means what is good for someone else, and to be "just" means serving the interest of the stronger who rules, at the cost of the subject who obeys; whereas injustice is just the reverse, asserting its authority over those innocents who are called just, so that they minister solely to their master's advantage and happiness, and not in the least degree to their own. Innocent as you are yourself, Socrates, you must see that a just man always has the worst of it. Take a private business: when a partnership is wound up, you will never find that the more honest of two partners comes off with the larger share; and in their relations to the state, when there are taxes to be paid, the honest man will pay more than the other on the same amount of property; or if there is money to be distributed, the dishonest will get it all. When either of them holds some public office, even if the just man loses in no other way, his private affairs at any rate will suffer from neglect, while his principles will not allow him to help himself from the public funds; not to mention the offense he will give to his friends and relations by refusing to sacrifice those principles to do them a good turn. Injustice has all the opposite advantages. I am speaking of the type I described just now, the man who can get the better of other people on a large scale: you must fix your eye on him, if you want to judge how much it is to one's own interest not to be just. You can see that best in the most consummate form of injustice, which rewards wrongdoing with supreme welfare and happiness and reduces its victims, if they won't retaliate in kind, to misery. That form is despotism, which uses force or fraud to plunder the goods of others, public or private, sacred or profane, and to do it in a wholesale way. If you are caught committing any one of these crimes on a small scale, you are punished and disgraced; they call it sacrilege, kidnapping, burglary, theft and brigandage. But if, besides taking their property, you turn all your countrymen into slaves, you will hear no more of those ugly names; your countrymen themselves will call you the happiest of men and bless your name, and so will everyone who hears of such a complete triumph of injustice; for when people denounce injustice, it is because they are afraid of suffering wrong, not of doing it. So true is it, Socrates, that injustice, on a grand enough scale, is superior to justice in strength and freedom and autocratic power, and "right," as I said at first, means simply what serves the interest of the stronger party; "wrong" means what is for the interest and profit of oneself.

> *At this point in* The Republic, *Socrates takes up Thrasymachus' challenge. Over the course of the next passages, he provides another round of confusion-a-la-Sophiste—and another technical refutation. The details of that argument are of no interest to us here. What is clear at the end is that the philosopher can beat the Sophist at his own game.*
>
> *But the question has not really been answered. Given that Thrasymachus can be foiled in his own match, is he, in the end, right, whether or not he knows how to argue with Socrates? Can it be shown that the easy victories of injustice over justice—in winding up partnerships and the like—are hollow, and not really in the interest of the cleverly unjust person? Glaucon and Adeimantus, Plato's brothers, set the problem in earnest at the outset of the second book of* The Republic, *requiring of Socrates a real and complete answer.*

I thought that, with these words, I was quit of the discussion; but it seems this was only a prelude. Glaucon, undaunted as ever, was not content to let Thrasymachus abandon the field.

Socrates, he broke out, you have made a show of proving that justice is better than injustice in every way. Is that enough, or do you want us to be really convinced?

Certainly I do, if it rests with me.

Then you are not going the right way about it. I want to know how you classify the things we call good. Are there not some which we should wish to have, not for their consequences, but just for their own sake, such as harmless pleasures and enjoyments that have no further result beyond the satisfaction of the moment?

Yes, I think there are good things of that description.

And also some that we value both for their own sake and for their consequences—things like knowledge and health and the use of our eyes?

Yes.

And a third class which would include physical training, medical treatment, earning one's bread as a doctor or otherwise—useful, but burdensome things, which we want only for the sake of the profit or other benefit they bring.

Yes, there is that third class. What then?

In which class do you place justice?

I should say, in the highest, as a thing which anyone who is to gain happiness must value both for itself and for its results.

Well, that is not the common opinion. Most people would say it was one of those things, tiresome and disagreeable in themselves, which we cannot avoid practicing for the sake of reward or a good reputation.

I know, said I; that is why Thrasymachus has been finding fault with it all this time and praising injustice. But I seem to be slow in seeing his point.

Listen to me, then, and see if you agree with mine. There was no need, I think, for Thrasymachus to yield so readily, like a snake you had charmed into submission; and nothing so far said about justice and injustice has been established to my satisfaction. I want to be told what each of them really is, and what effect each has, in itself, on the soul that harbours it, when all rewards and consequences are left out of account. So here is my plan, if you approve. I shall revive Thrasymachus' theory. First, I will state what is commonly held about the nature of justice and its origin; secondly, I shall maintain that it is always practiced with reluctance, not as good in itself, but as a thing one cannot do without; and thirdly, that this reluctance is reasonable, because the life of injustice is much the better life of the two—so people say. That is not what I think myself, Socrates; only I am bewildered by all that Thrasymachus and ever so many others have dinned into my ears; and I have never yet heard the case for justice stated as I wish to hear it. You, I believe, if anyone, can tell me what is to be said in praise of justice in and for itself; that is what I want. Accordingly, I shall set you an example by glorifying the life of injustice with all the energy that I hope you will show later in denouncing it and exalting justice in its stead. Will that plan suit you?

Nothing could be better, I replied. Of all subjects this is one on which a sensible man must always be glad to exchange ideas.

Good, said Glaucon. Listen then, and I will begin with my first point: the nature and origin of justice.

What people say is that to do wrong is, in itself, a desirable thing; on the other hand, it is not at all desirable to suffer wrong, and the harm to the sufferer outweighs the advantage to the doer. Consequently, when men have had a taste of both, those who have not the power to seize the advantage and escape the harm decide that they would be better off if they made a compact neither to do wrong nor to suffer it. Hence they began to make laws and covenants with one another; and whatever the law prescribed they called lawful and right. That is what right or justice is and how it came into existence;

it stands half-way between the best thing of all—to do wrong with impunity—and the worst, which is to suffer wrong without the power to retaliate. So justice is accepted as a compromise, and valued, not as good in itself, but for lack of power to do wrong; no man worthy of the name, who had that power, would ever enter into such a compact with anyone; he would be mad if he did. That, Socrates, is the nature of justice according to this account, and such the circumstances in which it arose.

The next point is that men practice it against the grain, for lack of power to do wrong. How true that is, we shall best see if we imagine two men, one just, the other unjust, given full license to do whatever they like, and then follow them to observe where each will be led by his desires. We shall catch the just man taking the same road as the unjust; he will be moved by self-interest, the end which it is natural to every creature to pursue as good, until forcibly turned aside by law and custom to respect the principle of equality.

Now, the easiest way to give them that complete liberty of action would be to imagine them possessed of the talisman found by Gyges, the ancestor of the famous Lydian. The story tells how he was a shepherd in the King's service. One day there was a great storm, and the ground where his flock was feeding was rent by an earthquake. Astonished at the sight, he went down into the chasm and saw, among other wonders of which the story tells, a brazen horse, hollow, with windows in its sides. Peering in, he saw a dead body, which seemed to be of more than human size. It was naked save for a gold ring, which he took from the finger and made his way out. When the shepherds met, as they did every month, to send an account to the King of the state of his flocks, Gyges came wearing the ring. As he was sitting with the others, he happened to turn the bezel of the ring inside his hand. At once he became invisible, and his companions, to his surprise, began to speak of him as if he had left them. Then, as he was fingering the ring, he turned the bezel outwards and became visible again. With that, he set about testing the ring to see if it really had this power, and always with the same result: according as he turned the bezel inside or out he vanished and reappeared. After this discovery he contrived to be one of the messengers sent to the court. There he seduced the Queen, and with her help murdered the King and seized the throne.

Now suppose there were two such magic rings, and one were given to the just man, the other to the unjust. No one, it is commonly believed, would have such iron strength of mind as to stand fast in doing right or keep his hands off other men's goods, when he could go to the market-place and fearlessly help himself to anything he wanted, enter houses and sleep with any woman he chose, set prisoners free and kill men at his pleasure, and in a word go about men with the powers of a god. He would behave no better than the other; both would take the same course. Surely this would be strong proof that men do right only under compulsion; no individual thinks of it as good for him personally, since he does wrong whenever he finds he has the power. Every man believes that wrongdoing pays him personally much better, and, according to this theory, that is the truth. Granted full license to do as he liked, people would think him a miserable fool if they found him refusing to wrong his neighbors or to touch their belongings, though in public they would keep up a pretense of praising his conduct, for fear of being wronged themselves. So much for that.

Finally, if we are really to judge between the two lives, the only way is to contrast the extremes of justice and injustice. We can best do that by imagining our two men to be perfect types, and crediting both to the full with the qualities they need for their respective ways of life. To begin with the unjust man: he must be like any consummate master of a craft, a physician or a captain, who, knowing just what his art can do, never tries to do more, and can always retrieve a false step. The unjust man, if he is to reach perfection, must be equally discreet in his criminal attempts, and he must not be found out, or we shall think him a bungler; for the highest pitch of injustice is to seem just when you are not. So we must endow our man with the full complement of injustice; we must allow him to have secured a spotless reputation for virtue while committing the blackest crimes; he must be able to retrieve any mistake, to defend himself with convincing eloquence if his misdeeds are denounced, and, when force is required, to bear down all opposition by his courage and strength and by his command of friends and money.

Now set beside this paragon the just man in his simplicity and nobleness, one who, in Aeschylus' words, "would be, not seem, the best." There must, indeed, be no such seeming; for if his character were apparent, his reputation would bring him honors and rewards, and then we should not know whether it was for their sake that he was just or for justice's sake alone. He must be stripped of everything but justice, and denied every advantage the other enjoyed. Doing no wrong, he must have the worst reputation for wrong-doing, to test whether his virtue is proof against all that comes of having a bad name: and under this lifelong imputation of wickedness, let him hold on his course of justice unwavering to the point of death. And so, when the two men have carried their justice and injustice to the last extreme, we may judge which is the happier.

My dear Glaucon, I exclaimed, how vigorously you scour these two characters clean for inspection, as if you were burnishing a couple of statues!

I am doing my best, he answered. Well, given two such characters, it is not hard, I fancy, to describe the sort of life that each of them may expect; and if the description sounds rather coarse, take it as coming from those who cry up the merits of injustice rather than from me. . . . They will tell you that our just man will be thrown into prison, scourged and racked, will have his eyes burnt out, and, after every kind of torment, be impaled. That will teach him how much better it is to seem virtuous than to be so. In fact those lines of Aeschylus I quoted are more fitly applied to the unjust man, who, they say, is a realist and does not live for appearances: "he would be, not seem" unjust, "reaping the harvest sown In those deep furrows of the thoughtful heart Whence wisdom springs." With his reputation for virtue, he will hold offices of state, ally himself by marriage to any family he may choose, become a partner in any business, and, having no scruples about being dishonest, turn all these advantages to profit. If he is involved in a lawsuit, public or private, he will get the better of his opponents, grow rich on the proceeds, and be able to help his friends and harm his enemies. Finally, he can make sacrifices to the gods and dedicate offerings with due magnificence, and, being in a much better position than the just man to serve the gods as well as his chosen friends, he may reasonably hope to stand higher in the favor of heaven. So much better, they say, Socrates, is the life prepared for the unjust by gods and men.

Here Glaucon ended, and I was meditating a reply, when his brother Adeimantus exclaimed:

Surely, Socrates, you cannot suppose that that is all there is to be said.

Why, isn't it? said I.

The most essential part of the case has not been mentioned, he replied. . . . If we want a clear view of what I take to be Glaucon's meaning, we must study the opposite side of the case, the arguments used when justice is praised and injustice condemned. When children are told by their fathers and all their pastors and masters that it is a good thing to be just, what is commended is not justice in itself but the respectability it brings. They are to let men see how just they are, in order to gain high positions and marry well and win all the other advantages which Glaucon mentioned, since the just man owes all these to his good reputation.

In this matter of having a good name, they go farther still: they throw in the favorable opinion of heaven, and can tell us of no end of good things with which they say the gods reward piety. There is the good old Hesiod, who says the gods make the just man's oak-trees "bear acorns at the top and bees in the middle; and their sheep's fleeces are heavy with wool," and a great many other blessings of that sort. And Homer speaks in the same strain: "As when a blameless king fears the gods and upholds right judgment; then the dark earth yields wheat and barley, and the trees are laden with fruit; the young of his flocks are strong, and the sea gives abundance of fish." Musaeus and his son Eumolpus enlarge in still more spirited terms upon the rewards from heaven they promise to the righteous. They take them to the other world and provide them with a banquet of the Blest, where they sit for all time carousing with garlands on their heads, as if virtue could not be more nobly recompensed than by an eternity of intoxication. Others, again, carry the rewards of heaven yet a stage farther: the pious man who keeps his oaths is to have children's children and to leave a posterity after him. When they have sung the praises of justice in that strain, with more to the same effect, they proceed to plunge the sinners and unrighteous men into a pool of mud in the world below, and set them to fetch water in a sieve. Even in this life, too, they give them a bad name, and make out that the unjust suffer all those penalties which Glaucon described as falling upon the good man who has a bad reputation: they can think of no others. That is how justice is recommended and injustice denounced. . . . You may say it is not so easy to be wicked without ever being found out. Perhaps not; but great things are never easy. Anyhow, if we are to reach happiness, everything we have been told points to this as the road to be followed. We will form secret societies to save us from exposure; besides, there are men who teach the art of winning over popular assemblies and courts of law; so that, one way or another, by persuasion or violence, we shall get the better of our neighbors without being punished. You might object that the gods are not to be deceived and are beyond the reach of violence. But suppose that there are no gods, or that they do not concern themselves with the doings of men; why should we concern ourselves to deceive them? Or, if the gods do exist and care for mankind, all we know or have ever heard about them comes from current tradition and from the poets who recount their family history, and these same authorities also assure us that they can be won over and turned from their purpose "by sacrifice and humble prayers" and votive offerings. We must either accept both these statements or neither. If we are to accept both, we had better do wrong and use part of the proceeds to offer sacrifice. By being just we may escape the punishment of heaven, but we shall be renouncing the profits of injustice; whereas by doing wrong we shall make our profit and escape punishment into the bargain, by means of those entreaties which win over the gods when we transgress and do amiss. But then, you will say, in the other world the penalty for our misdeeds on earth will fall either upon us or upon our children's children. We can counter that objection by reckoning on the great efficacy of mystic rites and the divinities of absolution, vouched for by the most advanced societies and by the descendants of the gods who have appeared as poets and spokesmen of heavenly inspiration.

What reason, then, remains for preferring justice to the extreme of injustice, when common belief and the best authorities promise us the fulfillment of our desires in this life and the next, if only we conceal our ill-doing under a veneer of decent behavior? The upshot is, Socrates, that no man possessed of superior powers of mind or person or rank or wealth will set any value on justice; he is more likely to laugh when he hears it praised. So even one who could prove my case false, and were quite sure that justice is best, far from being indignant with the unjust, will be very ready to excuse them. He will know that, here and there, a man may refrain from wrong because it revolts some instinct he is graced with or because he has come to know the truth; no one else is virtuous of his own will; it is only lack of spirit or the infirmity of age or some other weakness that makes men condemn the iniquities they have not the strength to practice. This is easily seen: give such a man the power, and he will be the first to use it to the utmost.

What lies at the bottom of all this is nothing but the fact from which Glaucon, as well as I, started upon this long discourse. We put it to you, Socrates, with all respect, in this way. All you who profess to sing the praises of right conduct, from the ancient heroes whose legends have survived down to the men of the present day, have never denounced injustice or praised justice apart from the reputation, honors, and rewards they bring; but what effect either of them in itself has upon its possessor when it dwells in his soul *unseen of gods or men,* no poet or ordinary man has ever yet explained. No one has proved that a soul can harbor no worse evil than injustice, no greater good than justice. Had all of you said that from the first and tried to convince us from our youth up, we should not be keeping watch upon our neighbors to prevent them from doing wrong to us, but everyone would keep a far more effectual watch over himself, for fear lest by wronging others he should open his doors to the worst of all evils.

That, Socrates, is the view of justice and injustice which Thrasymachus and, no doubt, others would state, perhaps in even stronger words. For myself, I believe it to be a gross perversion of their true worth and effect; but, as I must frankly confess, I have put the case with all the force I could muster because I want to hear the other side from you. You must not be content with proving that justice is superior to injustice; you must make clear what good or what harm each of them does to its possessor, taking it simply in itself and, as Glaucon required, leaving out of account the reputation it bears. . . . I might put up with others dwelling on those outward effects as a reason for praising the one and condemning the other; but from you, who have spent your life in the study of this question, I must beg leave to demand something better. You must not be content merely to prove that justice is superior to injustice, but explain how one is good, the other evil, in virtue of the intrinsic effect each has on its possessor, whether gods or men see it or not.

> *To answer this challenge, Socrates undertakes a long and painstaking argument. First we must discover the nature of the virtues in general, by developing an ideal state and finding the roles of the virtues within it. The virtues we seek are wisdom, courage, temperance, and justice: justice, the culminating virtue for the state, will be last. The virtues thus discovered can be assumed to be the same in the state and in the soul of the individual, so we can then proceed to inquire into the nature of the virtuous person. When we discover the notion of justice, we must proceed to determine its effect on the soul of its possessor, what sort of person it makes him; then we must ask, is that condition one of "happiness," that is, would a reasonable person prefer it?*
>
> *In the course of developing the notion of virtue as derived from the ideal state, Plato discovers first the need for survival, then the need for stable economic expectations, then the need for luxury, and then, as a consequence of that last need (or greed) the need for an army to protect and expand the material assets of the state. This scenario is grim, but leads him to hypothesize the existence of a standing force, and leads him into a brief and interesting commentary on the qualities of the good soldier.*

Book II

These guardians of our state, then, in as much as their work is the most important of all, will need the most complete freedom from other occupations and the greatest amount of skill and practice.

I quite agree.

And also a native aptitude for their calling.

Certainly.

So it is our business to define, if we can, the natural gifts that fit men to be guardians of a commonwealth, and to select them accordingly. It will certainly be a formidable task; but we must grapple with it to the best of our power.

Yes.

Don't you think then, said I, that, for the purpose of keeping guard, a young man should have much the same temperament and qualities as a wellbred watch-dog? I mean, for instance, that both must have quick senses to detect an enemy, swiftness in pursuing him, and strength, if they have to fight when they have caught him.

Yes, they will need all those qualities.

And also courage, if they are to fight well.

Of course.

And courage, in dog or horse or any other creature, implies a spirited disposition. You must have noticed that a high spirit is unconquerable. Every soul possessed of it is fearless and indomitable in the face of any danger.

Yes, I have noticed that.

So now we know what physical qualities our Guardian must have, and also that he must be of a spirited temper. . . .

> The Guardian class becomes the army. Later, when the elements of the state are
> fully set forth, they are described as embodying the courage not only of themselves, but of
> the state.

Book IV

Next there is courage. It is not hard to discern that quality or the part of the community in which it resides so as to entitle the whole to be called brave.

Why do you say so?

Because anyone who speaks of a state as either brave or cowardly can only be thinking of that part of it which takes the field and fights in its defense; the reason being, I imagine, that the character of the state is not determined by the bravery or cowardice of the other parts. . . . Courage, then, is another quality which a community owes to a certain part of itself. And its being brave will mean that, in this part, it possesses the power of preserving, in all circumstances, a conviction about the sort of things that it is right to be afraid of—the conviction implanted by the education which the law-giver has established. Is not that what you mean by courage?

I do not quite understand. Will you say it again?

I am saying that courage means preserving something.

Yes, but what?

The conviction, inculcated by lawfully established education, about the sort of things which may rightly be feared. . . . When I added "in all circumstances" I meant preserving it always and never abandoning it, whether under the influence of pain or of pleasure, of desire or of fear. If you like, I will give an illustration.

Please do.

You know how dyers who want wool to take a purple dye, first select the white wool from among all the other colors, next treat it very carefully to make it take the dye in its full brilliance, and only then dip it in the vat. Dyed in that way, wool gets a fast color, which no washing, even with soap, will rob of its brilliance; whereas if they choose wool of any color but white, or if they neglect to prepare it, you know what happens.

Yes, it looks washed-out and ridiculous.

That illustrates the result we were doing our best to achieve when we were choosing our fighting men and training their minds and bodies. Our only purpose was to contrive influences whereby they might take the color of our institutions like a dye, so that, in virtue of having both the right temperament and the right education, their convictions about what ought to be feared and on all other subjects might be indelibly fixed, never to be washed out by pleasure and pain, desire and fear, solvents more terribly effective than all the soap and fuller's earth in the world. Such a power of constantly preserving, in accordance with our institutions, the right conviction about the things which ought, or ought not, to be feared, is what I call courage. . . .

Justice, the crowning virtue, was the object of the expedition. The definition of justice is discovered by examining the constitution of that hypothetical city-state, and turns out to be, roughly, "each part doing its own job and not interfering with the others." As such, it is the virtue that permits the other virtues in the state—wisdom in the ruling class, courage in the military, temperance among the populace as a whole—to flourish and ensure the stability, safety, and prosperity of the nation. On the assumption, and note that it is an assumption, that the soul of the individual human being is identical in structure to the state, we now have an understanding of virtue in the soul: First, reason rules with wisdom; second, the spirited element ("will," in later philosophy) is strong and carries out unflinchingly the decisions of the reason; and third, the passions or appetites are healthy and disciplined, well under control. "Justice," then, will be the working together of these three parts to produce a balanced constitution overall. The discussion takes up at this point.

And so, after a stormy passage, we have reached the land. We are fairly agreed that the same three elements exist alike in the state and in the individual soul.

That is so.

Does it not follow at once that state and individual will be wise or brave by virtue of the same element in each and in the same way? Both will possess in the same manner any quality that makes for excellence.

That must be true.

Then it applies to justice: we shall conclude that a man is just in the same way that a state was just. And we have surely not forgotten that justice in the state meant that each of the three orders in it was doing its own proper work. So we may henceforth bear in mind that each one of us likewise will be a just person, fulfilling his proper function, only if the several parts of our nature fulfill theirs.

Certainly.

And it will be in the business of reason to rule with wisdom and forethought on behalf of the entire soul; while the spirited element ought to act as its subordinate and ally. The two will be brought into accord, as we said earlier, by that combination of mental and bodily training which will tune up one string of the instrument and relax the other, nourishing the reasoning part on the study of noble literature and allaying the other's wildness by harmony and rhythm. When both have been thus nurtured and trained to know their own true functions, they must be set in command over the appetites, which form the greater part of each man's soul and are by nature insatiably covetous. They must keep watch lest this part, by battening on the pleasures that are called bodily, should grow so great and powerful that it will no longer keep to its own work, but will try to enslave the others and usurp a dominion to which it has no right, thus turning the whole of life upside down. At the same time, those two together will be the best of guardians for the entire soul and for the body against all enemies from without: the one will take counsel, while the other will do battle, following its ruler's commands and by its own bravery giving effect to the ruler's designs. . . .

Now, is there any indistinctness in our vision of justice, that might make it seem somehow different from what we found it to be in the state?

I don't think so.

Because, if we have any lingering doubt, we might make sure by comparing it with some commonplace notions. Suppose, for instance, that a sum of money were entrusted to our state or to an individual of corresponding character and training, would anyone imagine that such a person would be specially likely to embezzle it?

No.

And would he not be incapable of sacrilege and theft, or of treachery to friend or country: never false to an oath or any other compact; the last to be guilty of adultery or of neglecting parents or the due service of the gods?

Yes.

And the reason for all this is that each part of his nature is exercising its proper function, of ruling or of being ruled.

Yes, exactly.

Are you satisfied, then, that justice is the power which produces states or individuals of whom that is true, or must we look further?

There is no need; I am quite satisfied. And so our dream has come true—I mean the inkling we had that, by some happy chance, we had lighted upon a rudimentary form of justice from the very moment when we set about founding our commonwealth. Our principle that the born shoemaker or carpenter had better stick to his trade turns out to have been an adumbration of justice; and that is why it has helped us. But in reality justice, though evidently analogous to this principle, is not a matter of external behavior, but of the inward self and of attending to all that is, in the fullest sense, a man's proper concern. The just man does not allow the several elements in his soul to usurp one another's functions; he is indeed one who sets his house in order, by self-mastery and discipline coming to be at peace with himself, and bringing into tune those three parts, like the terms in the proportion of a musical scale, the highest and lowest notes and the mean between them, with all the intermediate intervals. Only when he has linked these parts together in well-tempered harmony and has made himself one man instead of many, will he be ready to go about whatever he may have to do, whether it be making money and satisfying bodily wants, or business transactions, or the affairs of state. In all these fields when he speaks of just and honorable conduct, he will mean the behavior that helps to produce and to preserve this habit of mind; and by wisdom he will mean the knowledge which presides over such conduct. Any action which tends to break down this habit will be for him unjust; and the notions governing it he will call ignorance and folly.

That is perfectly true, Socrates. . . . Justice is produced in the soul, like health in the body, by establishing the elements concerned in their natural relations of control and subordination, whereas injustice is like disease and means that this natural order is inverted.

Quite so.

It appears, then, that virtue is as it were the health and comeliness and wellbeing of the soul, as wickedness is disease, deformity, and weakness.

True.

And also that virtue and wickedness are brought about by one's way of life, honorable or disgraceful.

That follows.

So now it only remains to consider which is the more profitable course: to do right and live honorably and be just, whether or not anyone knows what manner of man you are, or to do wrong and be unjust, provided that you can escape the chastisement which might make you a better man.

But really, Socrates, it seems to me ridiculous to ask that question now that the nature of justice and injustice has been brought to light. People think that all the luxury and wealth and power in the world cannot make life worth living when the bodily constitution is going to rack and ruin; and are we to believe that, when the very principle whereby we live is deranged and corrupted, life will be worth living so long as a man can do as he will, and wills to do anything rather than to free himself from vice and wrongdoing and to win justice and virtue?

Yes, I replied, it is a ridiculous question. . . .

> *Socrates says he's answered the question: All we have to do is look at the nature of justice, and the just man, and we will see that such a one must be happier than any-one not possessed of justice. Possibly so, but the task is still incomplete. The man of in-justice, set forth so vividly in the opening challenges of Glaucon and Adeimantus, must be described, not in his deeds, but in his internal nature. The discord of his ele-ments is more clearly seen on the broad canvas of the society in the constitution that mirrors injustice—or rather, since there are many types of injustice, the various con-stitutions that mirror their diseases. When the ultimately unjust man stands before us, we will be able to compare his characteristic constitution and soul with the mod-els of justice. The solution to the problem of* The Republic *lies in a comparison of the two with respect to the happiness of their lives.*

When we were studying moral qualities earlier, we began with the state, because they stood out more clearly there than in the individual. On the same principle we had better now take, in each case, the constitution first, and then, in the light of our results, examine the corresponding character. We shall start with the constitution dominated by motives of ambition—it has no name in common use that I know of, let us call it timarchy or timocracy—and then go on to oligarchy and democracy, and lastly visit a state under despotic government and look into the despot's soul. We ought then to be in a position to decide the question before us.

Yes, such a systematic review should give us the materials for judgment.

> *The best constitution, recall, is the one elaborated in the first books of* The Republic: *the aristocracy, the government by philosophically trained rulers, in which Plato discovered the virtues of state and soul. At this point in the work Plato runs down the characteristics of that "timarchy," which is the second-best constitution, correlating with it the knightly, honor-seeking man he calls the "timocrat." Then Socrates turns his attention to the third best type of constitution and person, the oligarchy; and the man best fitted for it, the tycoon/ruler called the "oligarch." As per his plan, Socrates first de-scribes the state run by the very wealthy for their own benefit, then turns his attention to the development and normal operation of the oligarchic soul:*

We have finished, then, with the constitution known as oligarchy, where power is held on a prop-erty qualification, and we may turn now to the history and character of the corresponding individual.

Yes, let us do so.

The transition from the timocratic type to the oligarchical happens somewhat in this way. The ti-mocratical man has a son, who at first emulates his father and follows in his steps. Then suddenly he sees him come up against society, like a ship striking a sunken rock, and founder with all his posses-sions; he may have held some high office or command and then have been brought to trial by inform-ers and put to death or banished or outlawed with the loss of all his property.

All this might well happen.

The son is terror-stricken at the sight of this ruin, in which his own fortunes are involved. At once that spirit of eager ambition which hitherto ruled in his heart is thrust headlong from the throne. Humbled by poverty, he turns to earning his living and, little by little, through hard work and petty sav-ings, scrapes together a fortune. And now he will install another spirit on the vacant throne, the money-loving spirit of sensual appetite, like an eastern monarch with diadem and golden chain and scimitar girt at his side. At its footstool, on either hand, will crouch the two slaves he has forced into subjection: Reason, whose thought is now confined to calculating how money may breed more money, and Ambition, suffered to admire and value nothing but wealth and its possessors and to excel in nothing but the struggle to gain money by any and every means.

Such is the oligarch. His soul, out of order, is committed to an inherently insatiable quest—ever higher numbers in the bank book, the bonus, the inventory of material possessions. The just man can be satisfied: Enough wisdom and justice are enough, and the appetites never seek beyond what wisdom will counsel and justice will allot. But the oligarchic man, ruled by a limitless appetite, dooms himself to gnawing hunger forever.

New unhappiness is found when we move on to the democratic state and soul. At first it all sounds pleasant enough:

Now what is the character of this new regime? Obviously the way they govern themselves will throw light on the democratic type of man.

No doubt.

First of all, they are free. Liberty and free speech are rife everywhere; anyone is allowed to do what he likes.

Yes, so we are told.

That being so, every man will arrange his own manner of life to suit his pleasure. The result will be a greater variety of individuals than under any other constitution. So it may be the finest of all, with its variegated pattern of all sorts of characters. Many people may think it the best, just as women and children might admire a mixture of colors of every shade in the pattern of a dress. At any rate if we are in search of a constitution, here is a good place to look for one. A democracy is so free that it contains a sample of every kind; and perhaps anyone who intends to found a state, as we have been doing, ought first to visit this emporium of constitutions and choose the model he likes best. He will find plenty to choose from. Here, too, you are not obliged to be in authority, however competent you may be, or to submit to authority, if you do not like it; you need not fight when your fellow citizens are at war, nor remain at peace when they do, unless you want peace; and though you may have no legal right to hold office or sit on juries, you will do so all the same if the fancy takes you. A wonderfully pleasant life, surely, for the moment.

For the moment, no doubt.

There is a charm, too, in the forgiving spirit shown by some who have been sentenced by the courts. In a democracy you must have seen how men condemned to death or exile stay on and go about in public, and no one takes any more notice than he would of a spirit that walked invisible. There is so much tolerance and superiority to petty considerations; such a contempt for all those fine principles we laid down in founding our commonwealth, as when we said that only a very exceptional nature could turn out a good man, if he had not played as a child among things of beauty and given himself only to creditable pursuits. A democracy tramples all such notions under foot; with a magnificent indifference to the sort of life a man has led before he enters politics, it will promote to honor anyone who merely calls himself the people's friend.

Magnificent indeed.

These then, and such as these, are the features of a democracy, an agreeable form of anarchy with plenty of variety and an equality of a peculiar kind for equals and unequals alike.

All that is notoriously true. . . .

Thus the democratic state is composed of a wide variety of people vying for attention and influence, with no ordering principle. Plato continues with a discussion of the appropriate soul:

There are appetites which cannot be got rid of, and there are all those which it does us good to fulfill. Our nature cannot help seeking to satisfy both these kinds; so they may fairly be described as necessary. On the other hand, "unnecessary" would be the right name for all appetites which can be got rid of by early training and which do us no good and in some cases do harm. Let us take an example of each kind, so as to form a general idea of them. The desire to eat enough plain food—just bread and meat to keep in health and good condition—may be called necessary. In the case of bread the necessity is twofold, since it not only does us good but is indispensable to life, whereas meat is only necessary in so far as it helps keep us in good condition. Beyond these simple needs the desire for a whole variety of luxuries is unnecessary. . . . When a young man, bred, as we were saying, in a stingy and uncultivated home, has once tasted the . . . pleasures in all their multitudinous variety, then the oligarchical constitution of his soul begins to turn into a democracy. The corresponding revolution was effected in the state by one of the two factions calling in the help of partisans from outside. In the same way one of the conflicting sets of desires in the soul of this youth will be reinforced from without by a group of kindred passions; . . . In the end, they seize the citadel of the young man's soul, finding it unguarded by the trusty sentinels which keep watch over the minds of men favored by heaven. Knowledge, right principles, true thoughts, are not at their post; and the place lies open to the assault of false and presumptuous notions. . . . In the internal conflict they gain the day; modesty and self-control, dishonored and insulted as the weaknesses of an unmanly fool, are thrust out into exile; and the whole crew of unprofitable desires take a hand in banishing moderation and frugality, which, as they will have it, are nothing but churlish meanness. . . .

In his life thenceforward he spends as much time and pains and money on his superfluous pleasures as on the necessary ones. If he is lucky enough not to be carried beyond all bounds, the tumult may begin to subside as he grows older. Then perhaps he may recall some of the banished virtues and cease to give himself up entirely to the passions which ousted them; and now he will set all his pleasures on a footing of equality, denying to none its equal rights and maintenance, and allowing each in turn, as it presents itself, to succeed, as if by the chance of the lot, to the government of his soul until it is satisfied. When he is told that some pleasures should be sought and valued as arising from desires of a higher order, others chastised and enslaved because the desires are base, he will shut the gates of the citadel against the messengers of truth, shaking his head and declaring that one appetite is as good as another and all must have their equal rights. So he spends his days indulging the pleasure of the moment, now intoxicated with wine and music, and then taking to a spare diet and drinking nothing but water; one day in hard training, the next doing nothing at all, the third apparently immersed in study. Every now and then he takes a part in politics, leaping to his feet to say or do whatever comes into his head. Or he will set out to rival someone he admires, a soldier it may be, or, if the fancy takes him, a man of business. His life is subject to no order or restraint, and he has no wish to change an existence which he calls pleasant, free and happy.

That well describes the life of one whose motto is liberty and equality.

Yes, and his character contains the same fine variety of pattern that we found in the democratic state; it is as multifarious as that epitome of all types of constitution. Many a man, and many a woman too, will find in it something to envy. So we may see in him the counter-part of democracy, and call him the democratic man.

We may.

From this point we move to the fourth type of unjust man, the despot, worst of all.

Last comes the man of despotic character. It remains to ask how he develops from the democratic type, what he is like, and whether his life is one of happiness or of misery.

Yes. . . .

Among the unnecessary pleasures and desires, some, I should say, are unlawful. . . . in every one of us, even those who seem most respectable, there exist desires, terrible in their untamed lawlessness, which reveal themselves in dreams. Do you agree?

I do.

Remember, then, our account of the democratic man, how his character was shaped by his early training under a parsimonious father, who respected only the businesslike desires, dismissing the unnecessary ones as concerned with frivolous embellishments. Then, associating with more sophisticated people who were a prey to those lawless appetites we have just described, he fell into their ways, and hatred of his father's miserliness drove him into every sort of extravagance. . . . Now imagine him grown old in his turn, with a young son bred in his ways, who is exposed to the same influences, drawn towards the utter lawlessness which his seducers call perfect freedom, while on the other side his father and friends lend their support to the compromise. When those terrible wizards who would conjure up an absolute ruler in the young man's soul begin to doubt the power of their spells, in the last resort they contrive to engender in him a master passion, to champion the mob of idle appetites which are for dividing among themselves all available plunder—a passion that can only be compared to a great winged drone. . . . Then at last this passion, as leader of the soul, takes madness for the captain of its guard and breaks out in frenzy; if it can lay hold upon any thoughts or desires that are of good report and still capable of shame, it kills them or drives them forth, until it has purged the soul of all sobriety and called in the partisans of madness to fill the vacant place.

That is a complete picture of how the despotic character develops.

Is not this the reason why lust has long since been called a tyrant? A drunken man, too, has something of this tyrannical spirit; and so has the lunatic who dreams that he can lord it over all mankind and heaven besides. Thus, when nature or habit or both have combined the traits of drunkenness, lust, and lunacy, then you have the perfect specimen of the despotic man.

Quite true. . . .

If there are a few such characters in a country where most men are law-abiding, they will go elsewhere to join some despot's bodyguard or serve as mercenaries in any war that is toward. In quiet times of peace, they stay at home and commit crimes on a small scale, as thieves, burglars, pickpockets, temple robbers, kidnappers; or, if they have a ready tongue, they may take to selling their services as informers and false witnesses.

Such crimes will be a small matter, you mean, so long as the criminals are few in number.

Small is a relative term; and all of them put together do not, as they say, come within sight of the degradation and misery of society under a despot. When the number of such criminals and their hangers-on increases and they become aware of their strength, then it is they who, helped by the folly of the common people, create the despot out of that one among their number whose soul is itself under the most tyrannical despotism.

Yes, such a state of mind would naturally be his best qualification.

All goes smoothly if men are ready to submit. But the country may resist; and then, just as he began by calling his father and mother to order, so now he will discipline his once loved fatherland . . . and see that it shall live in subjection to the new-found partisans he has called in to enslave it. So this man's desires come to their fulfillment.

Yes, that is true.

In private life, before they gain power, men of this stamp either consort with none but parasites ready to do them any service, or, if they have a favor to beg, they will not hesitate themselves to cringe and posture in simulated friendliness, which soon cools off when their end is gained. So, throughout life, the despotic character has not a friend in the world; he is sometimes master, sometimes slave, but never knows true friendship or freedom. There is no faithfulness in him; and, if we were right in our notion of justice, he is the perfect example of the unjust man.

Certainly.

> *With the unjust man now as clearly in our vision as the just one, we are ready for the comparison of the just and unjust lives with respect to happiness, and the final answer to Thrasymachus.*

To sum up, then: this worst type of man is he who behaves in waking life as we said men do in their dreams. The born despot who gains absolute power must come to this, and the longer he lives as a tyrant, the more this character grows upon him.

Inevitably, said Glaucon, who now took his turn to answer.

Now shall we find that the lowest depth of wickedness goes with the lowest depth of unhappiness, and that the misery of the despot is really in proportion to the extent and duration of his power, though the mass of mankind may hold many different opinions?

Yes, that much is certain.

It is true, is it not? that each type of individual—the despotic, the democratic and so on—resembles the state with the corresponding type of constitution, and will be good and happy in a corresponding degree.

Yes, of course.

In point of excellence, then, how does a state under a despotism compare with the one governed by kings, such as we first described?

They are at opposite extremes: the best and the worst.

I shall not ask which is which, for that is obvious. Is your estimate the same with respect to their degrees of happiness or misery? We must not let our eyes be dazzled by fixing them only on the despot himself and some few of his supporters; we should not decide until we have looked into every corner and inspected the life of the whole community.

That is a fair demand. Everyone must see that a state is most wretched under a despot and happiest under a true king.

And in judging between the corresponding individuals, is it not equally fair to demand the verdict of one who is not dazzled, like a child, by the outward pomp and parade of absolute power, but whose understanding can enter into a man's heart and see all that goes on within? Should we not all do well to listen to such a competent judge, if he had also lived under the same roof and witnessed the despot's behavior, not only in the emergencies of public life, but towards intimates in his own household, where he can best be seen stripped of his theatrical garb? We might then ask for a report on the happiness or misery of the despot as compared with the rest of the world.

Yes, that would be perfectly fair. . . .

To begin with the state: is it free under a despot, or enslaved?

Utterly enslaved.

And yet you see it contains some who are masters and free men.

Yes, a few; but almost the whole of it, including the most respectable part, is degraded to a miserable slavery.

If the individual, then, is analogous to the state, we shall find the same order of things in him: a soul laboring under the meanest servitude, the best elements in it being enslaved, while a small part, which is also the most frenzied and corrupt, plays the master. Would you call such a condition of the soul freedom or slavery?

Slavery, of course.

And just as a state enslaved to a tyrant cannot do what it really wishes, so neither can a soul under a similar tyranny do what it wishes as a whole. Goaded on against its will by the sting of desire, it will be filled with confusion and remorse. Like the corresponding state, it must always be poverty-stricken, unsatisfied, and haunted by fear. Nowhere else will there be so much lamentation, groaning, and anguish as in a country under a despotism and in a soul maddened by the tyranny of passion and lust. It cannot be otherwise.

These, I think, were the considerations that made you judge such a state to be the most unhappy of all.

Was I not right?

Certainly. But in view of the same facts, what would you say of the despotic type of individual?

That he is by far the most miserable of men.

There I think you are wrong. You will perhaps agree that there is a still lower depth of misery, to be found in a man of this temperament who has not the good fortune to remain in a private station but is thrust by circumstance into the position of an actual despot.

Judging by what we have said already, I should think that must be true.

Yes; but this is the most important of all questions, the choice between a good and an evil life; and we must be content with nothing short of a reasoned conviction. Am I right in thinking that some light may be gained from considering those wealthy private individuals who own a large number of slaves? In that respect they are like the despot, though his subjects are still more numerous. Now, as you know, they do not live in terror of their servants.

No; what have they to fear?

Nothing. But do you see why?

Yes, it is because the individual is protected by the whole community.

True; but imagine a man owning fifty or more slaves, miraculously caught up with his wife and children and planted, along with all his household goods and servants, in some desert place where there were no freemen to come to his rescue. Would he not be horribly afraid that his servants would make away with him and his family? He would be driven to fawn upon some of the slaves with liberal promises and give them their freedom, much against his will. So he would become a parasite, dependent on his own henchmen.

That would be his only way to escape destruction.

Moreover, the place he was transported to might be surrounded by neighbors who would not tolerate the claims of one man to lord it over others, but would retaliate fiercely on anyone they caught in such an attempt.

In that case he would be in still more desperate straits, hemmed in on all sides by enemies.

Is that not a picture of the prison to which the despot is confined? His nature is such as we have described, infested with all manner of fears and lusts. However curious he may be, he alone can never travel abroad to attend the great festivals which every freeman wants to witness, but must live like a woman ensconced in the recesses of his house, envying his countrymen who can leave their homes to see what is worth seeing in foreign lands. You spoke just now of the despotic character, illgoverned in his own soul, as the most miserable of men; but these disadvantages I have mentioned add to his wretchedness when he is driven by ill luck out of his private station to become an actual despot and undertake to rule others when he is not his own master. You might as well force a paralytic to leave the sheltered life of an invalid and spend his days in fighting or in trials of physical strength.

Quite true, Socrates; that is a fair comparison.

So the despot's condition, my dear Glaucon, is supremely wretched, even harder than the life you pronounced the hardest of all. Whatever people may think, the actual tyrant is really the most abject slave, a parasite of the vilest scoundrel. Never able to satisfy his desires, he is always in need, and, to an eye that sees a soul in its entirety, he will seem the poorest of the poor. His condition is like that of the country he governs, haunted throughout life by terrors and convulsed with anguish. Add to this what we said before, that power is bound to exaggerate every fault and make him ever more envious, treacherous, unjust, friendless, impure, harboring every vice in his bosom, and hence only less of a calamity to all about him than he is to himself.

No man of sense will dispute that.

Then the time has come for you, as the final judge in this competition, to decide who stands first in point of happiness and to arrange in order all our five types of character, the kingly, the timocratic, the oligarchic, the democratic, the despotic.

That decision is easy. In respect both of goodness and of happiness I range them in the order in which they have entered the lists.

Shall we hire a herald, then, or shall I myself proclaim that, in the judgment of the son of Ariston, the happiest man is he who is first in goodness and justice, namely the true king who is also king over himself; and the most miserable is that lowest example of injustice and vice, the born despot whose tyranny prevails in his own soul and also over his country.

Yes, you may proclaim that.

May I add that it would make no difference if the true character of both should remain unknown to heaven and to mankind?

You may.

Aristotle (384–322 B.C.)

In Plato we have the ideal: *The happiest life is the life of the philosopher, detached from material goods and ambitions, caring for friends and family but not to the point of letting their desires sway him from the proper course of action, most at home in the tranquil and unchanging world of ideas. In all of this he is surely right, after a fashion. I agree, I guess, that he has succeeded in proving that I should abandon the pursuit of pleasure, profit, and power, and live only for the truth. But agreeing with his argument (and admiring the example of the ideal life) is one thing; translating that ideal into the constantly changing day-by-day moral turmoil of our lives is something else altogether. Further, even the philosopher must be discontent with the structure of justification left to us in Plato's Dialogues; isn't there some more systematic way of connecting moral ideals to the patterns of the world we see around us?*

In Plato's student Aristotle we have the real: *Starting from human beings and human activities as we know them, Aristotle develops a framework for understanding them that is equally valid for the growth of an acorn into an oak tree, the development of a kitten into a fierce hunter, or the education of a baby into a solid citizen—or a philosopher. The elements of the scheme can be picked out of the following passages, but it might help if we summarized them as follows:*

Each thing starts as matter *without apparent* form; *the form is there, in the matter—the oak is "in" the acorn, the human being is "in" the fertilized egg, but only as a guiding principle, which will tell the thing how to grow from that point on. More interesting, he thinks the* polis, *or city-state, the Greek form of the political association, is "in" the very first attempts of human beings to associate and establish a rule of social life for themselves. To get from this beginning to its perfection—the actualization of its potential—the growing thing has to interact with the world in which it lives; to do so, it needs assorted pushes and pulls, also dictated by its nature. The pushes, or agencies that act on the thing, include the nourishment it takes in, the rewards and punishments it gets, and all the shaping influences of the world over which it has no choice or control. The pulls, or goals toward which creatures aim in their growth and development, are the ends toward which, consciously or unconsciously, they must move by reason of what they are—their essence, or indwelling form. It was clear to Aristotle that these four principles of explanation were necessary to show how anything—a house or a nation, as well as a plant or an animal—became what it should be. He called them the four causes of anything for which a cause is sought: the Material Cause or matter from which the thing is made (hunks of wood for the house, people for the nation), the Formal Cause or form, the Efficient Cause or agencies of change, and the Final Cause or goal toward which it tends.*

In the passages that follow, Aristotle considers the nature and end of humankind, the nature of virtue (excellence), the kinds of virtue and the ways that they may be attained. After a consideration of the various kinds of virtue—moral and intellectual, social and individual—the volume concludes with a final discussion and definition of human happiness.

From Aristotle, *Nicomachean Ethics*

Book I

1. Every art and every inquiry, and similarly every action and pursuit, is thought to aim at some good; and for this reason the good has rightly been declared to be that at which all things aim.... Now, as there are many actions, arts, and sciences, their ends also are many; the end of the medical art is health, that of shipbuilding a vessel, that of strategy victory, that of economics wealth. But where such arts fall under a single capacity—as bridle-making and the other arts concerned with the equipment of horses fall under the art of riding, and this and every military action under strategy, in the same way other arts fall under yet others—in all of these the ends of the master arts are to be preferred to all the subordinate ends; for it is for the sake of the former that the latter are pursued....

2. If, then, there is some end of the things we do, which we desire for its own sake (everything else being desired for the sake of this), and if we do not choose everything for the sake of something else (for at that rate the process would go on to infinity, so that our desire would be empty and vain), clearly this must be the good and the chief good. Will not the knowledge of it, then, have a great influence on life? Shall we not, like archers who have a mark to aim at, be more likely to hit upon what is right? If so, we must try, in outline at least, to determine what it is, and of which of the sciences or capacities it is the object. It would seem to belong to the most authoritative art and that which is most truly the master art. And politics appears to be of this nature; for it is this that ordains which of the sciences should be studied in a state, and which each class of citizens should learn and up to what point they should learn them; and we see even the most highly esteemed of capacities to fall under this, e.g. strategy, economics, rhetoric; now, since politics uses the rest of the sciences, and since, again, it legislates as to what we are to do and what we are to abstain from, the end of this science must include those of the others, so that this end must be the good for man. For even if the end is the same for a single man and for a state, that of the state seems at all events something greater and more complete whether to attain or to preserve; though it is worthwhile to attain the end merely for one man, it is finer and more godlike

to attain it for a nation or for city states. These, then, are the ends at which our inquiry aims, since it is political science, in one sense of that term.

3. Our discussion will be adequate if it has as much clearness as the subject matter admits of, for precision is not to be sought for alike in all discussions. . . . Now fine and just actions, which political science investigates, admit of much variety and fluctuation of opinion, so that they may be thought to exist only by convention, and not by nature. And goods also give rise to a similar fluctuation because they bring harm to many people; for before now men have been undone by reason of their wealth, and others by reason of their courage. We must be content, then, in speaking of such subjects and with such premises to indicate the truth roughly and in outline, and in speaking about things which are only for the most part true and with premises of the same kind to reach conclusions that are no better. In the same spirit, therefore, should each type of statement be *received*; for it is the mark of an educated man to look for precision in each class of things just so far as the nature of the subject admits; it is evidently equally foolish to accept probable reasoning from a mathematician and to demand from a rhetorician scientific proofs.

Now each man judges well the things he knows, and of these he is a good judge. And so the man who has been educated in a subject is a good judge of that subject, and the man who has received an all-round education is a good judge in general. Hence a young man is not a proper hearer of lectures on political science; for he is inexperienced in the actions that occur in life, but its discussions start from these and are about these; and further, since he tends to follow his passions, his study will be vain and unprofitable, because the end aimed at is not knowledge but action. And it makes no difference whether he is young in years or youthful in character, the defect does not depend on time, but on his living, and pursuing each successive object, as passion directs. For to such persons, as to the incontinent, knowledge brings no profit; but to those who desire and act in accordance with a rational principle knowledge about such matters will be of great benefit.

These remarks about the student, the sort of treatment to be expected, and the purpose of the inquiry, may be taken as our preface.

4. Let us resume our inquiry and state, in view of the fact that all knowledge and every pursuit aims at some good, what it is that we say political science aims at and what is the highest of all goods achievable by action. . . .

After some discussion of contemporary teachings, Aristotle returns to his subject:

7. Let us again return to the good we are seeking, and ask what it can be. It seems different in different actions and arts; it is different in medicine, in strategy, and in the other arts likewise. What then is the good of each? Surely that for whose sake everything else is done. In medicine this is health, in strategy victory, in architecture a house, in any other sphere something else, and in every action and pursuit the end; for it is for the sake of this that all men do whatever else they do. Therefore, if there is an end for all that we do, this will be the good achievable by action. . . .

Since there are evidently more than one end, and we choose some of these . . . for the sake of something else, clearly not all ends are final ends; but the chief good is evidently something final. Therefore, if there is only one final end, this will be what we are seeking, and if there are more than one, the most final of these will be what we are seeking. Now we call that which is in itself worthy of pursuit more final than that which is worthy of pursuit for the sake of something else, and that which is never desirable for the sake of something else more final than the things that are desirable both in themselves and for the sake of that other thing, and therefore we call final without qualification that which is always desirable in itself and never for the sake of something else.

Now such a thing happiness, above all else, is held to be; for this we choose always for itself and never for the sake of something else, but honor, pleasure, reason, and every virtue we choose indeed for themselves . . . , but we choose them also for the sake of happiness, judging that by means of them we shall be happy. Happiness, on the other hand, no one chooses for the sake of these, nor, in general, for anything other than itself. . . .

Presumably, however, to say that happiness is the chief good seems a platitude, and a clearer account of what it is, is still desired. This might perhaps be given, if we could first ascertain the function of man. For just as for a flute-player, a sculptor, or any artist, and, in general, for all things that have a function or activity, the good and the "well" is thought to reside in the function, so would it seem to be for man, if he has a function. Have the carpenter, then, and the tanner certain functions or activities, and has man none? Is he born without a function? Or as eye, hand, foot, and in general each of the parts evidently has a function, may one lay it down that man similarly has a function apart from all these? What then can this be? Life seems to be common even to plants, but we are seeking what is peculiar to man. Let us exclude, therefore, the life of nutrition and growth. Next there would be a life of perception, but it also seems to be common even to the horse, the ox, and every animal. There remains, then, an active life of the element that has a rational principle; of this, one part has such a principle in the sense of being obedient to one, the other in the sense of possessing one and exercising thought. And, as "life of the rational element" also has two meanings, we must state that life in the sense of activity is what we mean; for this seems to be the more proper sense of the term. Now if the function of man is an activity of soul which follows or implies a rational principle, and if we say . . . the function of a *good* man [is] the good and noble performance of [this], and if any action is well performed when it is performed in accordance with the appropriate excellence [or virtue]: if this is the case, human good turns out to be activity of soul in accordance with virtue, and if there are more than one virtue, in accordance with the best and most complete.

But we must add "in a complete life." For one swallow does not make a summer, nor does one day, and so too one day, or a short time, does not make a man blessed and happy. . . .

Now for most men their pleasures are in conflict with one another because these are not by nature pleasant, but the lovers of what is noble find pleasant the things that are by nature pleasant; and virtuous actions are such, so that these are pleasant for such men as well as in their own nature. Their life, therefore, has no further need of pleasure as a sort of adventitious charm, but has its pleasure in itself. For, besides what we have said, the man who does not rejoice in noble actions is not even good; since no one would call a man just who did not enjoy acting justly, nor any man liberal who did not enjoy liberal actions; and similarly in all other cases. If this is so, virtuous actions must be in themselves pleasant. But they are also *good* and *noble,* and have each of these attributes in the highest degree, since the good man judges well about these attributes; his judgment is such as we have described. Happiness then is the best, noblest, and most pleasant thing in the world. . . .

Yet evidently . . . it needs the external goods as well, for it is impossible, or not easy, to do noble acts without the proper equipment. In many actions we use friends and riches and political power as instruments; and there are some things the lack of which takes the lustre from happiness, as good birth, goodly children, beauty; for the man who is very ugly in appearance or ill-born or solitary and childless is not very likely to be happy, and perhaps a man would be still less likely if he had thoroughly bad children or friends or had lost good children or friends by death . . . . happiness seems to need this sort of prosperity in addition; for which reason some identify happiness with good fortune, though others identify it with virtue. . . .

Book II

1. Virtue, then, being of two kinds, intellectual and moral, intellectual virtue in the main owes both its birth and its growth to teaching (for which reason it requires experience and time), while moral virtue comes about as the result of habit, whence also its name *ethike* is one that is formed by a slight variation from the word *ethos* (habit). From this it is also plain that none of the moral virtues

arises in us by nature; for nothing that exists by nature can form a habit contrary to its nature. For instance the stone which by nature moves downwards cannot be habituated to move upwards, not even if one tries to train it by throwing it up ten thousand times; nor can fire be habituated to move downwards, nor can anything else that by nature behaves in one way be trained to behave in another. Neither by nature, then, nor contrary to nature do the virtues arise in us; rather, we are adapted by nature to receive them, and are made perfect by habit.

Again, of all the things that come to us by nature we first acquire the potentiality and later exhibit the activity (this is plain in the case of the senses; for it was not by often seeing or often hearing that we got these senses, but on the contrary we had them before we used them, and did not come to have them by using them); but the virtues we get by first exercising them, as also happens in the case of the arts as well. For the things we have to learn before we can do them, we learn by doing them, e.g., men become builders by building and lyre-players by playing the lyre; so too we become just by doing just acts, temperate by doing temperate acts, brave by doing brave acts.

This is confirmed by what happens in states; for legislators make the citizens good by forming habits in them; and this is the wish of every legislator, and those who do not effect it miss their mark, and it is in this that a good constitution differs from a bad one.

Again, it is from the same causes and by the same means that every virtue is both produced and destroyed, and similarly every art; for it is from playing the lyre that both good and bad lyre players are produced. And the corresponding statement is true of builders and of all the rest; men will be good or bad builders as a result of building well or badly. For if this were not so, there would have been no need of a teacher, but all men would have been born good or bad at their craft. This, then, is the case with the virtues also; by doing the acts that we do in our transactions with other men we become just or unjust, and by doing the acts that we do in the presence of danger, and being habituated to feel fear or confidence, we become brave or cowardly. The same is true of appetites and feelings of anger; some men become temperate and good-tempered, others self-indulgent and irascible, by behaving in one way or the other in the appropriate circumstances. Thus, in one word, states of character arise out of like activities. This is why the activities we exhibit must be of a certain kind; it is because the states of character correspond to the differences between these. It makes no small difference, then, whether we form habits of one kind or of another from our very youth; it makes a very great difference, or rather all the difference.

2. Since, then, the present inquiry does not aim at theoretical knowledge like the others (for we are inquiring not in order to know what virtue is, but in order to become good, since otherwise our inquiry would have been of no use), we must examine the nature of actions, namely how we ought to do them; for these determine also the nature of the states of character that are produced. . . . First, then, let us consider this, that it is the nature of such things to be destroyed by defect and excess, as we see in the case of life and health (for to gain light on things imperceptible we must use the evidence of sensible things); both excessive and defective exercise destroys the strength, and similarly drink or food which is above or below a certain amount destroys the health, while that which is proportionate both produces and increases and preserves it. So too is it, then, in the case of temperance and courage and the other virtues. For the man who flies from and fears everything and does not stand his ground against anything becomes a coward, and the man who fears nothing at all but goes to meet every danger becomes rash; and similarly the man who indulges in every pleasure and abstains from none becomes self-indulgent, while the man who shuns every pleasure, as boors do, becomes in a way insensible; temperance and courage, then, are destroyed by excess and defect, and preserved by the mean.

But not only are the sources and causes of their origination and growth the same as those of their destruction, but also the sphere of their actualization will be the same; for this is also true of the things which are more evident to sense, e.g., of strength; it is produced by taking much food and undergoing much exertion, and it is the strong man that will be most able to do these things. So too is it with the virtues; by abstaining from pleasures we become temperate, and it is when we have become so that we are most able to abstain from them; and similarly too in the case of courage; for by being habituated to despise things that are terrible and to stand our ground against them we become brave, and it is when we have become so that we shall be most able to stand our ground against them.

3. We must take as signs of states of character the pleasure or pain that ensues on acts, for the man who abstains from bodily pleasures and delights in this very fact is temperate, while the man who is annoyed at it is self-indulgent, and he who stands his ground against things that are terrible and delights in this or at least is not pained is brave, while the man who is pained is a coward. For moral excellence is concerned with pleasures and pains; it is on account of the pleasure that we do bad things, and on account of the pain that we abstain from noble ones. Hence we ought to have been brought up in a particular way from our very youth, as Plato says, so as both to delight in and to be pained by the things that we ought; for this is the right education. . . .

4. The question might be asked, what we mean by saying that we must become just by doing just acts, and temperate by doing temperate acts; for if men do just and temperate acts, they are already just and temperate, exactly as, if they do what is in accordance with the laws of grammar and of music, they are grammarians and musicians. . . .

Actions, then, are called just and temperate when they are such as the just or temperate man would do; but it is not the man who does these that is just or temperate, but the man who also does them as just and temperate men do them. It is well said, then, that it is by doing just acts that the just man is produced, and by doing temperate acts the temperate man; without doing these no one would have even a prospect of becoming good.

But most people do not do these, but take refuge in theory and think they are being philosophers and will become good in this way, behaving somewhat like patients who listen attentively to their doctors, but do none of the things they are ordered to do. As the latter will not be made well in body by such a course of treatment, the former will not be made well in soul by such a course of philosophy. . . .

6. We must, however, not only describe virtue as a state of character, but also say what sort of state it is. We may remark, then, that every virtue or excellence both brings into good condition the thing of which it is the excellence and makes the work of that thing be done well; e.g., the excellence of the eye makes both the eye and its work good; for it is by the excellence of the eye that we see well. Similarly the excellence of the horse makes a horse both good in itself and good at running and at carrying the rider and at awaiting the attack of the enemy. Therefore, if this is true in every case, the virtue of man also will be the state of character which makes a man good and which makes him do his own work well. . . .

Virtue, then, is a state of character concerned with choice, lying in a mean, i.e., the mean relative to us, this being determined by a rational principle, and by that principle by which the man of practical wisdom would determine it. Now it is a mean between two vices, that which depends on excess and that which depends on defect; and again it is a mean because the vices respectively fall short of or exceed what is right in both passions and actions, while virtue both finds and chooses that which is intermediate. Hence in respect of its substance and the definition which states its essence virtue is a mean, with regard to what is best and right an extreme.

Book III

1. Since virtue is concerned with passions and actions, and on voluntary passions and actions praise and blame are bestowed, on those that are involuntary pardon, and sometimes also pity, to distinguish the voluntary and the involuntary is presumably necessary for those who are studying

the nature of virtue, and useful also for legislators with a view to the assigning both of honors and punishments.

Those things, then, are thought involuntary, which take place under compulsion or owing to ignorance; and that is compulsory of which the moving principle is outside, being a principle in which nothing is contributed by the person who is acting or is feeling the passion, e.g. if he were to be carried somewhere by a wind, or by men who had him in their power.

But with regard to the things that are done from fear of greater evils or for some noble object (e.g. if a tyrant were to order one to do something base, having one's parents and children in his power, and if one did the action they were to be saved, but otherwise would be put to death), it may be debated whether such actions are involuntary or voluntary. Something of the sort happens also with regard to the throwing of goods overboard in a storm; for in the abstract no one throws good away voluntarily, but on condition of its securing the safety of himself and his crew any sensible man does so. Such actions, then, are mixed, but are more like voluntary actions; for they are worthy of choice at the time when they are done, and the end of an action is relative to the occasion. Both the terms, then, "voluntary" and "involuntary," must be used with reference to the moment of action. Now the man acts voluntarily; for the principle that moves the instrumental parts of the body in such actions is in him, and the things of which the moving principle is in a man himself are in his power to do or not to do. Such actions, therefore, are voluntary, but in the abstract perhaps involuntary; for no one would choose any such act in itself.

For such actions men are sometimes even praised, when they endure something base or painful in return for great and noble objects gained; in the opposite case they are blamed, since to endure the greatest indignities for no noble end or for a trifling end is the mark of an inferior person. On some actions praise indeed is not bestowed, but pardon is, when one does what he ought not under pressure which overstrains human nature and which no one could withstand. . . .

What sort of acts, then, should be called compulsory? We answer that without qualification actions are so when the cause is in the external circumstances and the agent contributes nothing. But the things that in themselves are involuntary, but now and in return for these gains are worthy of choice, and whose moving principle is in the agent, are in themselves involuntary, but now and in return for these gains voluntary. They are more like voluntary acts, for actions are in the class of particulars, and the particular acts here are voluntary. What sort of things are to be chosen, and in return for what, it is not easy to state; for there are many differences in the particular cases.

But if some one were to say that pleasant and noble objects have a compelling power, forcing us from without, all acts would be for him compulsory; for it is for these objects that all men do everything they do. And those who act under compulsion and unwillingly act with pain, but those who do acts for their pleasantness and nobility do them with pleasure; it is absurd to make external circumstances responsible, and not oneself, as being easily caught by such attractions, and to make oneself responsible for noble acts but the pleasant objects responsible for base acts. The compulsory, then, seems to be that whose moving principle is outside, the person compelled contributing nothing. . . .

Since that which is done under compulsion or by reason of ignorance is involuntary, the voluntary would seem to be that of which the moving principle is in the agent himself, he being aware of the particular circumstances of the action. Presumably acts done by reason of anger or appetite are not rightly called involuntary. For in the first place, on that showing none of the other animals will act voluntarily, nor will children; and secondly, is it meant that we do not do voluntarily any of the acts that are due to appetite or anger, or that we do the noble acts voluntarily and the base acts involuntarily? Is not this absurd, when one and the same thing is the cause? . . .

3. Do we deliberate about everything, and is everything a possible subject of deliberation, or is deliberation impossible about some things? We ought presumably to call not what a fool or a madman would deliberate about, but what a sensible man would deliberate about, a subject of deliberation. Now about eternal things no one deliberates, e.g., about the material universe or the incommensurability of the diagonal and the side of a square. But no more do we deliberate about the things that involve movement but always happen in the same way, whether of necessity or by nature or from any other cause, e.g., the solstices and the risings of the stars; nor about things that happen now in one way, now in another, e.g., droughts and rains; nor about chance events, like the finding of treasure. But we do not deliberate even about all human affairs; for instance, no Spartan deliberates about the best constitution for the Scythians. For none of these things can be brought about by our own efforts.

We deliberate about things that are in our power and can be done; and these are in fact what is left. For nature, necessity, and chance are thought to be causes, and also reason and everything that depends on man. Now every class of men deliberates about the things that can be done by their own efforts. And in the case of exact and self-contained sciences there is no deliberation, e.g., about the letters of the alphabet (for we have no doubt how they should be written), but the things that are brought about by our own efforts, but not always in the same way, are the things about which we deliberate, e.g., questions of medical treatment or of money-making. . . .

We deliberate not about ends but about means. For a doctor does not deliberate whether he shall heal, nor an orator whether he shall persuade, nor a statesman whether he shall produce law and order, nor does any one else deliberate about his end. They assume the end and consider how and by what means it is to be attained; and if it seems to be produced by several means they consider by which it is most easily and best produced, while if it is achieved by one only they consider how it will be achieved by this and by what means this will be achieved, till they come to the first cause, which in the order of discovery is last. For the person who deliberates seems to investigate and analyze in the way described as though he were analyzing a geometrical construction (not all investigation appears to be deliberation—for instance mathematical investigations—but all deliberation is investigation), and what is last in the order of analysis seems to be first in the order of becoming. . . .

The same thing is deliberated upon and is chosen, except that the object of choice is already determinate, since it is that which has been decided upon as a result of deliberation that is the object of choice. For every one ceases to inquire how he is to act when he has brought the moving principle back to himself and to the ruling part of himself; for this is what chooses. This is plain also from the ancient constitutions, which Homer represented; for the kings announced their choices to the people. The object of choice being one of the things in our own power which is desired after deliberation, choice will be deliberate desire of things in our own power, for when we have decided as a result of deliberation, we desire in accordance with our deliberation.

4. . . . For each state of character has its own ideas of the noble and the pleasant, and perhaps the good man differs from others most by seeing the truth in each class of things, being as it were the norm and measure of them. In most things the error seems to be due to pleasure; for it appears a good when it is not. We therefore choose the pleasant as a good, and avoid pain as an evil.

5. The end, then, being what we wish for, the means what we deliberate about and choose, actions concerning means must be according to choice and voluntary. Now the exercise of the virtues is concerned with means. Therefore virtue also is in our own power, and so too vice. For where it is in our power to act it is also in our power not to act, and *vice versa,* so that, if to act, where this is noble, is in our power, not to act, which will be base, will also be in our power. Now if it is in our power to do noble or base acts, and likewise in our power not to do them, and this was what being good or bad meant, then it is in our power to be virtuous or vicious. . . .

Witness seems to be borne to this both by individuals in their private capacity and by legislators themselves; for these punish and take vengeance on those who do wicked acts (unless they have acted under compulsion or as a result of ignorance for which they are not themselves responsible), while they honor those who do noble acts, as though they meant to encourage the latter and deter the former. But no one is encouraged to do the things that are neither in our power nor voluntary; it is assumed that there is no gain in being persuaded not to be hot or in pain or hungry or the like, since we shall experience these feelings none the less. Indeed, we punish a man for his very ignorance, if he is thought responsible for the ignorance, as when penalties are doubled in the case of drunkenness; for the moving principle is in the man himself, since he had the power of not getting drunk and his getting drunk was the cause of his ignorance. And we punish those who are ignorant of anything in the laws that they ought to know and that is not difficult, and so too in the case of anything else that they are thought to be ignorant of through carelessness; we assume that it is in their power not to be ignorant, since they have the power of taking care.

But perhaps a man is the kind of man not to take care. Still they are themselves by their slack lives responsible for becoming men of that kind, and men make themselves responsible for being unjust or self-indulgent, in the one case by cheating and in the other by spending their time in drinking bouts and the like; for it is activities exercised on particular objects that make the corresponding character. This is plain from the case of people training for any contest or action; they practice the activity the whole time. Now not to know that it is from the exercise of activities on particular objects that states of character are produced is the mark of a thoroughly senseless person. Again, it is irrational to suppose that a man who acts unjustly does not wish to be unjust or a man who acts self-indulgently to be self-indulgent. But if *without* being ignorant a man does the things which will make him unjust, he will be unjust voluntarily. Yet it does not follow that if he wishes he will cease to be unjust and will be just. For neither does the man who is ill become well on those terms. We may suppose a case in which he is ill voluntarily, through living incontinently and disobeying his doctors. In that case it was *then* open to him not to be ill, but not now, when he has thrown away his chance, just as when you have let a stone go it is too late to recover it; but yet it was in your power to throw it, since the moving principle was in you. So, too, to the unjust and to the self-indulgent man it was open at the beginning not to become men of this kind, and so they are unjust and self-indulgent voluntarily; but now that they have become so it is not possible for them not to be so. . . .

With regard to the virtues in *general* we have stated their genus in outline, viz., that they are means and that they are states of character, and that they tend, and by their own nature, to the doing of the acts by which they are produced, and that they are in our power and voluntary, and act as the right rule prescribes. But actions and states of character are not voluntary in the same way; for we are masters of our actions from the beginning right to the end, if we know the particular facts, but though we control the beginning of our states of character the gradual progress is not obvious, any more than it is in illnesses; because it was in our power, however, to act in this way or not in this way, therefore the states are voluntary. . . .

The conclusion is gently reached, but inescapable: we are as responsible for our habitually tawdry lives as for single acts, we are responsible for our moral characters and may justly be condemned for inadequate ones.

> *Aristotle continues to consider specific virtues, of which the most important is "justice," treated in Book V of the* Nicomachean Ethics. *Aristotle first explains that he does not mean by this term, as Plato did, "virtue entire," or the state of the soul in its best condition. Instead, he is after a much more limited virtue, having to do with fairness and the pursuit of gain, subject to the law, much more as we use the term today.*

Book V

2. But at all events what we are investigating is the justice which is a *part* of virtue; for there is a justice of this kind, as we maintain. Similarly it is with injustice in the particular sense that we are concerned.

That there is such a thing is indicated by the fact that while the man who exhibits in action the other forms of wickedness acts wrongly indeed, but not graspingly (e.g., the man who throws away his shield through cowardice or speaks harshly through bad temper or fails to help a friend with money through meanness), when a man acts graspingly he often exhibits none of these vices—no, nor all together, but certainly wickedness of some kind (for we blame him) and injustice. There is, then, another kind of injustice which is a part of injustice in the wide sense, and a use of the word "unjust" which answers to a part of what is unjust in the wide sense of "contrary to the law." Again, if one man commits adultery for the sake of gain and makes money by it, while another does so at the bidding of appetite though he loses money and is penalized for it, the latter would be held to be self-indulgent rather than grasping, but the former is unjust, but not self-indulgent, evidently, therefore, he is unjust by reason of his making gain by his act. Again, all other unjust acts are ascribed invariably to some particular kind of wickedness, e.g., adultery to self-indulgence, the desertion of a comrade in battle to cowardice, physical violence to anger; but if a man makes gain, his action is ascribed to no form of wickedness but injustice. Evidently, therefore, there is apart from injustice in the wide sense another, "particular," injustice which shares the name and nature of the first, because its definition falls within the same genus; for the significance of both consists in a relation to one's neighbor, but the one is concerned with honor or money or safety . . . and its motive is the pleasure that arises from gain: . . .

The unjust has been divided into the unlawful and the unfair . . . the unfair and the unlawful are not the same, but are different as a part is from its whole (for all that is unfair is unlawful, but not all that is unlawful is unfair) . . . for practically the majority of the acts commanded by the law are those which are prescribed from the point of view of virtue taken as a whole; for the law bids us practice every virtue and forbids us to practice any vice. And the things that tend to produce virtue taken as a whole are those of the acts prescribed by the law which have been prescribed with a view to education for the common good. . . .

Of particular justice and that which is just in the corresponding sense, (A) one kind is that which is manifested in distributions of honor or money or the other things that fall to be divided among those who have a share in the constitution (for in these it is possible for one man to have a share either unequal or equal to that of another), and (B) one is that which plays a rectifying part in transactions between man and man. . . .

3. (A) We have shown that both the unjust man and the unjust act are unfair or unequal; . . . but this is the origin of quarrels and complaints—when either equals have and are awarded unequal shares, or unequals equal shares. Further, this is plain from the fact that awards should be "according to merit," for all men agree that what is just in distribution must be according to merit in some sense, though they do not all specify the same sort of merit, but democrats identify it with the status of freeman, supporters of oligarchy with wealth (or with noble birth), and supporters of aristocracy with excellence. . . .

This, then is what the just is—the proportional; the unjust is what violates the proportion. Hence one term becomes too great, the other too small, as indeed happens in practice; for the man who acts unjustly has too much, and the man who is unjustly treated too little, of what is good. . . . This, then, is one species of the just.

(B) The remaining one is the rectificatory, which arises in connection with transactions both voluntary and involuntary. This form of the just has a different specific character from the former. For the justice which distributes common possessions is always in accordance with the kind of proportion mentioned above (for in the case also in which the distribution is made from the common funds of a partnership it will be according to the same ratio which the funds put into the business by the partners bear to one another): and the injustice opposed to this kind of justice is that which violates the proportion. But the justice in transactions between man and man is a sort of equality indeed, and the injustice a sort of inequality: not according to that kind of proportion, however, but according to arithmetical proportion. For it makes no difference whether a good man has defrauded a bad man or a bad man a good one, nor whether it is a good or a bad man that has committed adultery; the law looks only to the distinctive character of the injury, and treats the parties as equal, if one is in the wrong and the other is being wronged, and if one inflicted injury and the other has received it. Therefore, this kind of injustice being an inequality, the judge tries to equalize it; for in the case also in which one has received and the other has inflicted a wound, or one has slain and the other been slain, the suffering and the action have been unequally distributed, but the judge tries to equalize things by means of the penalty, taking away from the gain of the assailant. . . . This is why, when people dispute, they take refuge in the judge; and to go to the judge is to go to justice; for the nature of the judge is to be a sort of animate justice; and they seek the judge as an intermediate, and in some states they call judges mediators, on the assumption that if they get what is intermediate they will get what is just. . . .

5. Some think that reciprocity is without qualification just, as the Pythagoreans said; for they defined justice without qualification as reciprocity. Now "reciprocity" fits neither distributive nor rectificatory justice—yet people *want* even the justice of Rhadamanthus to mean this: "Should a man suffer what he did, right justice would be done"—for in many cases reciprocity and rectificatory justice are not in accord, e.g., (1) if an official has inflicted a wound, he should not be wounded in return, and if some one has wounded an official, he ought not to be wounded only but punished in addition. Further (2) there is a great difference between a voluntary and an involuntary act. But in associations for exchange this sort of justice does hold men together—reciprocity in accordance with a proportion and not on the basis of precisely equal return. For it is by proportionate requital that the city holds together. Men seek to return either evil for evil—and if they cannot do so, think their position mere slavery—or good for good—and if they cannot do so there is no exchange, but it is by exchange that they hold together. . . .

> The entirety of Book V of the Nicomachean Ethics *is devoted to justice, treated for the most part, as above, very abstractly, almost as a function of mathematics. In Chapter Six of the Book, Aristotle reaches what he sees as the actual origin and necessary condition of justice—the* polis *or political association. Justice in the abstract has to do with rules of the mean or intermediate, proportions, and balances; justice in the political sense has to do with the way men govern men, and the conditions of living a life in which education toward excellence is possible. This chapter is the source of our national preference, and the preference of every democracy, for a government of laws, not of men.*

Now we have previously stated how the reciprocal is related to the just; but we must not forget that what we are looking for is not only what is just without qualification but also political justice. This is found among men who share their life with a view to self-sufficiency, men who are free and either proportionately or arithmetically equal, so that between those who do not fulfill this condition there is no political justice but justice in a special sense and by analogy. For justice exists only between men whose mutual relations are governed by law; and law exists for men between whom there is injustice; for legal justice is the discrimination of the just and the unjust.

> *Political justice cannot exist, for example, between man and dog, or freeman and slave, for their statuses are not just unequal—they are incommensurable. Hence it is possible to be cruel to a dog, or slave, but never to be unjust to one—at least not in this sense of justice.*

And between men between whom there is injustice there is also unjust action (though there is not injustice between all between whom there is unjust action), and this is assigning too much to oneself of things good in themselves and too little of things evil in themselves. This is why we do not allow a *man* to rule, but *rational principle,* because a man behaves thus in his own interests and becomes a tyrant. The magistrate on the other hand is the guardian of justice, and, if of justice, then of equality also. And since he is assumed to have no more than his share, if he is just (for he does not assign to himself more of what is good in itself, unless such a share is proportional to his merits—so that it is for others that he labors, and it is for this reason that men, as we stated previously, say that justice is "another's good"), therefore a reward must be given him, and this is honor and privilege; but those for whom such things are not enough become tyrants.

The justice of a master and that of a father are not the same as the justice of citizens, though they are like it; for there can be no injustice in the unqualified sense towards things that are one's own, but a man's chattel, and his child until it reaches a certain age and sets up for itself, are as it were part of himself, and no one chooses to hurt himself (for which reason there can be no injustice towards oneself). Therefore the justice or injustice of citizens is not manifested in these relations; for [that justice is] according to law, and between people naturally subject to law, and these . . . are people who have an equal share in ruling and being ruled.

> *Book X returns us to the subject of happiness, last seen in Book I, and homes in finally on the best life that a human can live.*

7. If happiness is activity in accordance with virtue, it is reasonable that it should be in accordance with the highest virtue; and this will be that of the best thing in us. Whether it be reason or something else that is this element which is thought to be our natural ruler and guide and to take thought of things noble and divine, whether it be itself also divine or only the most divine element in us, the activity of this in accordance with its proper virtue will be perfect happiness . . . this activity is contemplative.

Now this would seem to be in agreement both with what we said before and with the truth. For, firstly, this activity is the best (since not only is reason the best thing in us, but the objects of reason are the best of knowable objects); and, secondly, it is the most continuous, since we can contemplate truth more continuously than we can do anything. And we think happiness has pleasure mingled with it, but the activity of philosophic wisdom is admittedly the pleasantest of virtuous activities; at all events the pursuit of it is thought to offer pleasures marvelous for their purity and their enduringness, and it is to be expected that those who know will pass their time more pleasantly than those who inquire. And the self-sufficiency that is spoken of must belong most to the contemplative activity. For while a philosopher, as well as a just man or one possessing any other virtue, needs the necessaries of life, when they are sufficiently equipped with things of that sort the just man needs people towards whom and with whom he shall act justly, and the temperate man, the brave man, and each of the others is in the same case, but the philosopher, even when by himself, can contemplate truth, and the better the wiser he is; he can perhaps do so better if he has fellow-workers, but still he is the most self-sufficient. And this activity alone would seem to be loved for its own sake; for nothing arises from it apart from the contemplating, while from practical activities we gain more or less apart from the action. And happiness is thought to depend on leisure; for we are busy that we may have leisure, and make war that we may live in peace. . . . But the activity of reason, which is contemplative, seems both to be superior in serious worth and to aim at no end beyond itself, and to have its pleasure proper to itself (and this augments the activity), and the self-sufficiency, leisureliness, unweariedness (so far as this is possible for man), and all the other attributes ascribed to the supremely happy man are evidently those connected with this activity, it follows that this will be the complete happiness of man. . . .

But such a life would be too high for man; for it is not in so far as he is man that he will live so, but in so far as something divine is present in him; and by so much as this is superior to our composite nature is its activity superior to that which is the exercise of the other kind of virtue. If reason is divine, then, in comparison with man, the life according to it is divine in comparison with human life. But we must not follow those who advise us, being men, to think of human things, and, being mortal, of mortal things, but must, so far as we can, make ourselves immortal, and strain every nerve to live in accordance with the best thing in us; for even if it be small in bulk, much more does it in power and worth surpass everything. This would seem, too, to be each man himself, since it is the authoritative and better part of him. It would be strange, then, if he were to choose not the life of his self but that of something else. And what we said before will apply now; that which is proper to each thing is by nature best and most pleasant for each thing; for man, therefore, the life according to reason is best and pleasantest, since reason more than anything else is man. This life therefore is also the happiest. . . .

But that perfect happiness is a contemplative activity will appear from the following consideration as well. We assume the gods to be above all beings blessed and happy; but what sort of actions must we assign to them? Acts of justice? Will not the gods seem absurd if they make contracts and return deposits, and so on? Acts of a brave man, then, confronting dangers and running risks because it is noble to do so? Or liberal acts? To whom will they give? It will be strange if they are really to have money or anything of the kind. And what would their temperate acts be? Is not such praise tasteless, since they have no bad appetites? If we were to run through them all, the circumstances of action would be found trivial and unworthy of gods. Still, every one supposes that they live and therefore that they are active; we cannot suppose them to sleep like Endymion. Now if you take away from a living being action, and still more production, what is left but contemplation? Therefore the activity of God, which surpasses all others in blessedness, must be contemplative; and of human activities, therefore, that which is most akin to this must be most of the nature of happiness. . . .

But, being a man, one will also need external prosperity; for our nature is not self-sufficient for the purpose of contemplation, but our body also must be healthy and must have food and other attention. Still, we must not think that the man who is to be happy will need many things or great things, merely because he cannot be supremely happy without external goods; for self-sufficiency and action do not involve excess, and we can do noble acts without ruling earth and sea; for even with moderate advantages one can act virtuously . . . for the life of the man who is active in accordance with virtue will be happy. Solon, too, was perhaps sketching well the happy man when he described him as moderately furnished with externals but as having done (as Solon thought) the noblest acts, and lived temperately; for one can with but moderate possessions do what one ought. . . . For if the gods have any care for human affairs, as they are thought to have, it would be reasonable both that they would delight in that which was best and most akin to them (i.e. reason) and that they should reward those who love and honor this most, as caring for things which are dear to them and acting both rightly and nobly. And that all these attributes belong most of all to the philosopher is manifest. He, therefore, is the dearest to the gods. And he who is that will presumably be also the happiest; so that in this way too the philosopher will more than any other be happy.

9. . . . Now if arguments were in themselves enough to make men good, they would justly, as Theognis says, have won very great rewards, and such rewards should have been provided; but as things are, while they seem to have power to encourage and stimulate the generous-minded among our youth, and to make a character which is gently born, and a true lover of what is noble, ready to be possessed by virtue, they are not able to encourage the many to nobility and goodness. For these do not by nature obey the sense of shame, but only fear, and do not abstain from bad acts because of their baseness but through fear of punishment; living by passion they pursue their own pleasures and the means to them, and avoid the opposite pains, and have not even a conception of what is noble and truly pleasant, since they have never tasted it. What argument would remold such people? It is hard, if not impossible, to remove by argument the traits that have long since been incorporated in the character; and perhaps we must be content if, when all the influences by which we are thought to become good are present, we get some tincture of virtue.

Now some think that we are made good by Nature, others by habituation, others by teaching. Nature's part evidently does not depend on us, but as a result of some divine causes is present in those who are truly fortunate; while argument and teaching, we may suspect, are not powerful with all men, but the soul of the student must first have been cultivated by means of habits for noble joy and noble hatred, like earth which is to nourish the seed. For he who lives as passion directs will not hear argument that dissuades him, nor understand it if he does; and how can we persuade one in such a state to change his ways? And in general passion seems to yield not to argument but to force. The character, then, must somehow be there already with a kinship to virtue, loving what is noble and hating what is base.

But it is difficult to get from youth up a right training for virtue if one has not been brought up under right laws; for to live temperately and hardily is not pleasant to most people, especially when they are young. For this reason their nurture and occupations should be fixed by law; for they will not be painful when they have become customary. But it is surely not enough that when they are young they should get the right nurture and attention; since they must, even when they are grown up, practice and be habituated to them, we shall need laws for this as well, and generally speaking to cover the whole of life; for most people obey necessity rather than argument, and punishments rather than the sense of what is noble. . . .

The highest life, the pure life of contemplation, is the life of the philosopher. But this life is unattainable without the previous attainment of moral virtue. Virtue is impossible without correct early training, but equally requires good laws through the whole of life. Then the proper setting for the moral life is the good polis, and those concerned to make people good must engage in the legislative life of that setting.

And surely he who wants to make men, whether many or few, better by his care must try to become capable of legislating, if it is through laws that we can become good. For to get any one whatever—any one who is put before us—into the right condition is not for the first chance comer; if any one can do it, it is the man who knows, just as in medicine and all other matters which give scope for care and prudence.

Must we not, then, next examine whence or how one can learn how to legislate? Is it, as in all other cases, from statesmen? . . . Or is a difference apparent between statesmanship and the other sciences and arts? . . .

Now our predecessors have left the subject of legislation to us unexamined; it is perhaps best, therefore, that we should ourselves study it, and in general study the question of the constitution, in order to complete to the best of our ability our philosophy of human nature. . . .

And the whole of Aristotle's Politics *follows from this point. We include here only selections from the first two chapters of the first Book of the* Politics.

From Aristotle, *Politics*

1. Every state is a community of some kind, and every community is established with a view to some good; for mankind always act in order to obtain that which they think good. But, if all communities aim at some good, the state or political community, which is the highest of all, and which embraces all the rest, aims at good in a greater degree than any other, and at the highest good.

Some people think that the qualifications of a statesman, king, householder and master are the same, and that they differ, not in kind, but only in the number of their subjects. For example, the ruler over a few is called a master; over more, the manager of a household; over a still larger number, a statesman or king, as if there were no difference between a great household and a small state. The distinction which is made between the king and the statesman is as follows: When the government is personal, the ruler is a king, when, according to the rules of the political science, the citizens rule and are ruled in turn, then he is called a statesman.

But all this is a mistake; for governments differ in kind, as will be evident to anyone who considers the matter according to the method which has hitherto guided us. As in other departments of science, so in politics, the compound should always be resolved into the simple elements or least parts of the whole. We must therefore look at the elements of which the state is composed, in order that we may see in what the different kinds of rule differ from one another, and whether any scientific result can be attained about each one of them.

2. He who thus considers things in their first growth and origin, whether a state or anything else, will obtain the clearest view of them. In the first place there must be a union of those who cannot exist without each other; namely, of male and female, that the race may continue (and this is a union which is formed, not of deliberate purpose, but because, in common with other animals and with plants, mankind have a natural desire to leave behind them an image of themselves), and of natural ruler and subject, that both may be preserved. For that which can foresee by the exercise of mind is by nature intended to be lord and master, and that which can with its body give effect to such foresight is a subject, and by nature a slave; hence master and slave have the same interest. . . .

Out of these two relationships between man and woman, master and slave, the first thing to arise is the family, and Hesiod is right when he says—"First house and wife and an ox for the plough," for the ox is the poor man's slave. The family is the association established by nature for the supply of men's everyday wants, and the members of it are called by Charondas "companions of the cupboard," and by Epimenides the Cretan, "companions of the manger." But when several families are united, and the association aims at something more than the supply of daily needs, the first society to be formed is the village. And the most natural form of the village appears to be that of a colony from the family, composed of the children and grandchildren, who are said to be "suckled with the same milk." And this is the reason why Hellenic states were originally governed by kings; because the Hellenes were under royal rule before they came together, as the barbarians still are. Every family is ruled by the eldest, and therefore in the colonies of the family the kingly form of government prevailed because they were of the same blood. As Homer says: "Each one gives law to his children and to his wives." For they lived dispersedly, as was the manner in ancient times. Wherefore men say that the gods have a king, because they themselves either are or were in ancient times under the rule of a king. For they imagine, not only the forms of the gods, but their ways of life to be like their own.

When several villages are united in a single complete community, large enough to be nearly or quite self-sufficing, the state comes into existence, originating in the bare needs of life, and continuing in existence for the sake of a good life. And therefore, if the earlier forms of society are natural, so is the state, for it is the end of them, and the nature of a thing is its end. For what each thing is when fully developed, we call its nature, whether we are speaking of a man, a horse, or a family. Besides, the final cause and end of a thing is the best, and to be self-sufficing is the end and the best.

Hence it is evident that the state is a creation of nature, and that man is by nature a political animal. And he who by nature and not by mere accident is without a state, is either a bad man or above humanity; he is like the "Tribeless, lawless, hearthless one," whom Homer denounces—the natural outcast is forthwith a lover of war; he may be compared to an isolated piece at draughts.

Now, that man is more of a political animal than bees or any other gregarious animals is evident. Nature, as we often say, makes nothing in vain, and man is the only animal whom she has endowed with the gift of speech. And whereas mere voice is but an indication of pleasure or pain, and is therefore found in other animals (for their nature attains to the perception of pleasure and pain and the intimation of them to one another, and no further), the power of speech is intended to set forth the expedient and inexpedient, and therefore likewise the just and the unjust. And it is a characteristic of man that he alone has any sense of good and evil, of just and unjust, and the like, and the association of living beings who have this sense makes a family and a state.

Further, the state is by nature clearly prior to the family and to the individual, since the whole is of necessity prior to the part; for example, if the whole body be destroyed, there will be no foot or hand, except in an equivocal sense, as we might speak of a stone hand; for when destroyed the hand will be no better than that. But things are defined by their working and power; and we ought not to say that they are the same when they no longer have their proper quality, but only that they have the same name. The proof that the state is a creation of nature and prior to the individual is that the individual, when isolated, is not self-sufficing: and therefore he is like a part in relation to the whole. But he who is unable to live in society, or who has no need because he is sufficient for himself, must be either a beast or a god: he is no part of a state. A social instinct is implanted in all men by nature, and yet he who first founded the state was the greatest of benefactors. For man, when perfected, is the best of animals, but, when separated from law and justice, he is the worst of all: since armed injustice is the more dangerous, and he is equipped at birth with arms, meant to be used by intelligence and virtue, which he may use for the worst ends. Wherefore, if he have not virtue, he is the most unholy and the most savage of animals, and the most full of lust and gluttony. But justice is the bond of men in states, for the administration of justice, which is the determination of what is just, is the principle of order in political society.

Religious Traditions

Ethicists tend to tread warily around religion, for it has a way of violating the basic rules for practicing ethics (see *Ethics in America: Study Guide*, Chapter 1): it refuses to modify itself in response to reasoned objections, and it denies the validity of alternative religious experience. Yet religion has more influence on the ethical behavior of contemporary humans than all the philosophy in history. If we are interested in ethical practice, then, we had better be aware of the religious traditions that guide our citizens.

Our citizens, while we're on the subject, have changed. The last decades have seen an enormous influx of new residents to our shores, not for the first time. As the waves of immigration of the nineteenth/early twentieth centuries brought Jews and Catholics to Protestant America, so the waves of the twentieth/early twenty-first centuries are bringing waves of Muslims and of practitioners of Eastern religious traditions to Judeo-Christian America. Religious teachings now include new entries from the East and from the world of Islam, and so they are included here.

The Bible

The Biblical tradition in ethics is the oldest that we deal with, and certainly the most familiar. Associated with "religion," cult, irrational beliefs, and infallible teachings, it tends to be included only peripherally in history of philosophy or ethical theories courses, at least until the major philosophers—St. Augustine and St. Thomas Aquinas—combine the beliefs of Christianity with the insights of Plato and Aristotle (respectively) to form the core of medieval philosophy. Such sideline treatment I take to be a bad mistake in teaching ethics. The Bible is not (at least until late in the New Testament) a repository of sophisticated philosophical thought. It is a repository of ethical directives, however, and those directives have been taken very seriously from the beginnings of the Western tradition.

From hundreds of years before the birth of Christ until this day, the Commandments and all the rules that follow from them have been taken as literal directions for living, by a very large number of people. Whole communities and nations have adopted the teachings of the Jewish Law or the Christian Way as models for ethical behavior. Thousands practice, or attempt to practice, the life of obedience and devotion taught in the Bible. How many thousands, or hundreds, or tens, attempt to live according to the teachings of Plato or Immanuel Kant? Ethics, as Aristotle taught us, consists of practice as much as thought, and we neglect widely practiced teachings at our peril.

Philosophers avoid the Bible not only because religion is an emotionally charged and politically sensitive issue, but also because of the Bible's peculiarly non-philosophical form of ethical justification. The authors of the Bible occasionally explain their conclusions on matters of morals by a narrative ("For I am the Lord your God Who brought you out of Egypt"), or back them up with threats ("And in anger and wrath I will execute vengeance upon the nations that did not obey,") or, at other times, present them without any justification at all. None of these methods qualifies as valid in the academic halls of the "logic of justification" and the "is-ought" distinction. Yet the very power and endurance of these pronouncements, embedded in our culture as they are, ensure their centrality in contemporary philosophy. They guarantee that when one of the most precise of contemporary philosophers, the late John Rawls of Harvard University, tested his conclusions against "our ethical intuitions," these are the intuitions he tested against.

The Judaeo-Christian tradition is, fundamentally, a story. The story begins at the creation of Time and ends at the end of Time. To understand what Jews and Christians are is to know that story. To be a Jew or a Christian is to believe that that story is true, or at least the part of the story that applies to you. We will not have the space to tell the whole story: the creation of the world and everything in it, the Fall of Man, the Flood, the Covenant, the generations of the Patriarchs, Egypt, Exodus, the settling of the Promised Land, all the trials and battles of Israel, Judges, Kings, Prophets, and wanderings, and the birth and life of Christ, teachings, death, resurrection, and the travels and teachings of the Apostles. Rather, we will concentrate only on those portions of the story with clear implications for a moral commitment in this life. We have selected particularly those passages with a bearing on how we ourselves might live, since those who adopt this tradition as their own take it to be as applicable today as it ever was.

According to the Bible, there was a time when morality was not necessary—when man lived naked and innocent, and had no notion of sin or evil, hence no notion of right conduct or good. Our tale, the tale of ethics, begins at the point where the subject of morality arises suddenly from the ground—or swings down from the Tree, depending on which artist you follow.

Genesis

Chapters 2 and 3:

The Lord God took the man and put him in the garden of Eden to till it and keep it. And the Lord God commanded the man, saying, "You may freely eat of every tree of the garden; but of the tree of the knowledge of good and evil you shall not eat, for in the day that you eat of it you shall die...."

Now the serpent was more subtle than any other wild creature that the Lord God had made. He said to the woman, "Did God say, 'You shall not eat of any tree of the garden'?" And the woman said to the serpent, "We may eat of the fruit of the trees of the garden, but God said, 'You shall not eat of the fruit of the tree which is in the midst of the garden, neither shall you touch it, lest you die.'" But the serpent said to the woman, "You will not die. For God knows that when you eat of it your eyes will be opened, and you will be like God, knowing good and evil." So when the woman saw that the tree was good for food, and that it was a delight to the eyes, and that the tree was to be desired to make one wise, she took of its fruit and ate; and she also gave some to her husband, and he ate. Then the eyes of both were opened, and they knew that they were naked; and they sewed fig leaves together and made themselves aprons.

And they heard the sound of the Lord God walking in the garden in the cool of the day, and the man and his wife hid themselves from the presence of the Lord God among the trees of the garden. But the Lord God called to the man, and said to him, "Where are you?" And he said, "I heard the sound of thee in the garden, and I was afraid, because I was naked; and I hid myself." He said, "Who told you that you were naked? Have you eaten of the tree of which I commanded you not to eat?" The man said, "The woman whom thou gavest to be with me, she gave me fruit of the tree, and I ate." Then the Lord God said to the woman, "What is this that you have done?" The woman said, "The Serpent beguiled me, and I ate." The Lord God said to the serpent,

"Because you have done this, cursed are you above all cattle, and above all wild animals; upon your belly you shall go, and dust you shall eat all the days of your life. I will put enmity between you and the woman, and between your seed and her seed; he shall bruise your head, and you shall bruise his heel."

To the woman he said, "I will greatly multiply your pain in childbearing; in pain you shall bring forth children, yet your desire shall be for your husband, and he shall rule over you."

And to Adam he said, "Because you have listened to the voice of your wife, and have eaten of the tree of which I commanded you, 'You shall not eat of it,' cursed is the ground because of you; in toil you shall eat of it all the days of your life; thorns and thistles it shall bring forth to you; and you shall eat the plants of the field. In the sweat of your face you shall eat bread till you return to the ground, for out of it you were taken; you are dust, and to dust you shall return."

> *Sin, once discovered, only gets worse. Note, in the following passage, a repetition of the most striking fact of the first passage: having sinned by disobeying God's command, the man instantly knows his guilt and the justice of his swift punishment. If the Jews of this tradition ever asked, as did the earliest Greeks, "Why should I bother to be moral?" we have no record of it.*

Genesis

Chapter 4:

Now Adam knew Eve his wife, and she conceived and bore Cain, saying, "I have gotten a man with the help of the Lord." And again, she bore his brother, Abel. Now Abel was a keeper of sheep, and Cain a tiller of the ground. In the course of time Cain brought to the Lord an offering of the fruit of the ground, and Abel brought of the firstlings of his flock and of their fat portions. And the Lord had regard for Abel and his offering, but for Cain and his offering he had no regard. So Cain was very angry, and his countenance fell. The Lord said to Cain, "Why are you angry, and why has your countenance fallen? If you do well, will you not be accepted? And if you do not do well, sin is couching at the door; its desire is for you, but you must master it."

Cain said to Abel his brother, "Let us go out to the field." And when they were in the field, Cain rose up against his brother Abel, and killed him. Then the Lord said to Cain, "Where is Abel your brother?" He said, "I do not know; am I my brother's keeper?" And the Lord said, "What have you done? The voice of your brother's blood is crying to me from the ground. And now you are cursed from the ground, which has opened its mouth to receive your brother's blood from your hand. When you till the ground, it shall no longer yield to you its strength; you shall be a fugitive and a wanderer on the earth." Cain said to the Lord, "My punishment is more than I can bear. Behold, thou has driven me this day away from the ground; and from thy face I shall be hidden; and I shall be a fugitive and a wanderer on the earth, and whoever finds me will slay me."

> *The story of the tribe of Israel really begins with the Covenant, the contract between God and the Jews. God selects Abram, a descendant of Noah's son Shem, to be the founder of the Israelites, for no apparent reason. The initiation of the Covenant is a direct command: "Now the Lord said to Abram, 'Go from your country and your kindred and your father's house to the land that I will show you,'" followed by an unsolicited promise, "And I will make of you a great nation, and I will bless you, and make your name great, so that you will be a blessing. I will bless those who bless you, and him who curses you I will curse; and by you all the families of the earth shall bless themselves." (Genesis, Chapter 12). A legalist might object that such an address does not contain the elements of a real contract. But Abram promptly trusts and obeys the Lord, and that is the point. Later, the Covenant is made more formal and specific:*

Genesis

Chapter 17:

When Abram was ninety-nine years old the Lord appeared to Abram, and said to him, "I am God Almighty; walk before me, and be blameless. And I will make my covenant between me and you, and will multiply you exceedingly." Then Abram fell on his face, and God said to him, "Behold, my covenant is with you, and you shall be the father of a multitude of nations. No longer shall your name be Abram, but your name shall be Abraham, for I have made you the father of a multitude of nations. . . . And I will give to you, and your descendants after you, the land of your sojournings, all the land of Canaan, for an everlasting possession; and I will be their God."

And God said to Abraham, "As for you, you shall keep my covenant, you and your descendants after you throughout their generations. This is my covenant, which you shall keep, between me and you and your descendants after you: Every male among you shall be circumcised. You shall be circumcised in the flesh of your foreskins, and it shall be a sign of the covenant between me and you. . . . So shall my covenant be in your flesh an everlasting covenant."

> *The aged Abraham and his equally aged wife Sarah are blessed, miraculously, with a son, Isaac. Soon thereafter follows one of the most famous, and puzzling, stories in the Bible. Can it fit into any humane scheme of rational ethics?*

Genesis

Chapter 22:

God tested Abraham, and said to him, . . ."Take your son, your only son Isaac, whom you love, and go to the land of Moriah, and offer him there as a burnt offering upon one of the mountains of which I shall tell you." So Abraham rose early in the morning, saddled his ass, and took two of his young men with him, and his son Isaac; and he cut the wood for the burnt offering, and arose and went to the place of which God had told him. On the third day Abraham lifted up his eyes and saw the place afar off. Then Abraham said to his young men, "Stay here with the ass; I and the lad will go yonder and worship, and come again to you." And Abraham took the wood of the burnt offering, and laid it on Isaac his son; and he took in his hand the fire and the knife. So they went both of them together. And Isaac said . . . "Behold, the fire and the wood; but where is the lamb for a burnt offering?" Abraham said, "God will provide himself the lamb for a burnt offering, my son." So they went both of them together.

When they came to the place of which God had told him, Abraham built an altar there, and laid the wood in order, and bound Isaac his son, and laid him on the altar, upon the wood. Then Abraham put forth his hand, and took the knife to slay his son. But the angel of the Lord called to him from heaven, and said, ". . . Do not lay your hand on the lad or do anything to him; for now I know that you fear God, seeing you have not withheld your son, your only son, from me." And Abraham lifted up his eyes and looked, and behold, behind him was a ram, caught in a thicket by his horns; and Abraham went and took the ram, and offered it up as a burnt offering instead of his son.

> *Having offered up the ram, Abraham named the place, "The Lord Will Provide," and the angel of the Lord called to Abraham a second time, and related that the Lord was so impressed by Abraham's obedience that he would "indeed bless you, and I will multiply your descendants as the stars of heaven and as the sand which is on the seashore," and there will be many military victories. But why the agonizing test of faith? The story of the gratuitous test of an old man's faith is repeated in the book of Job, not included in this collection; the inescapable conclusion is that the Judaeo-Christian tradition is as shot through with paradox as the Greek tradition is with rationality.*
>
> *The story continues through the generations of the Patriarchs into the Egyptian sojourn, which ends violently when the Egyptians stop being gracious hosts and start being slavers and tyrants. Then the Lord appears to Moses and, after the failure of some preliminary moves to obtain voluntary release, renews the promises of the Covenant:*

Exodus

Chapter 6:

And God said to Moses, "I am the Lord. I appeared to Abraham, to Isaac, and to Jacob . . . I also established my covenant with them, to give them the land of Canaan, the land in which they dwelt as sojourners. Moreover I have heard the groaning of the people of Israel whom the Egyptians hold in bondage and I have remembered my covenant. Say therefore to the people of Israel, I am the Lord, and I will bring you out from under the burdens of the Egyptians, and I will deliver you from their bondage, and I will redeem you with an outstretched arm and with great acts of judgment, and I will take you for my people, and I will be your God; and you shall know that I am the Lord your God, who has brought you out from under the burdens of the Egyptians. And I will bring you into the land which I swore to give to Abraham, to Isaac, and to Jacob. I will give it to you for a possession. I am the Lord."

> *They do get out of Egypt, as the Lord parts the Red Sea for the escaping Jews and drowns Pharaoh's pursuing army in the reunion of the waves. But gratitude to the Lord and serene piety never came easily to the Israelites; complaints began very soon (Exodus*

16:2–3): "And the whole congregation of the people of Israel murmured against Moses and Aaron in the wilderness, and said to them, 'Would that we had died by the hand of the Lord in the land of Egypt, when we sat by the fleshpots and ate bread to the full; for you have brought us out into this wilderness to kill this whole assembly with hunger.'" Bread sent from God satisfies the hunger for the moment, but eventually, to unify the people, there will have to be a law, so Moses ascends Mount Sinai, at the command of the Lord, to receive laws for his people. These laws become the basis of the Biblical ethic from now on:

Exodus

Chapter 20:

And God spoke all these words, saying, "I am the Lord your God, who brought you out of the land of Egypt, out of the house of bondage.

You shall have no other gods before me.

You shall not make for yourself a graven image, or any likeness of anything that is in heaven above, or that is in the earth beneath, or that is in the water under the earth; you shall not bow down to them or serve them; for I the Lord your God am a jealous God, visiting the iniquity of the fathers upon the children to the third and the fourth generation of those who hate me, but showing steadfast love to thousands of those who love me and keep my commandments.

You shall not take the name of the Lord your God in vain: for the Lord will not hold him guiltless who takes his name in vain.

Remember the Sabbath day, to keep it holy. Six days you shall labor, and do all your work; but the seventh day is a Sabbath to the Lord your God; in it you shall not do any work, you, or your son, or your daughter, your manservant, or your maidservant, or your cattle, or the sojourner who is within your gates; for in six days the Lord made heaven and earth, the sea, and all that is in them, and rested the seventh day; therefore the Lord blessed the Sabbath day and hallowed it.

Honor your father and your mother, that your days may be long in the land which the Lord your God gives you.

You shall not kill.

You shall not commit adultery.

You shall not steal.

You shall not bear false witness against your neighbor.

You shall not covet your neighbor's house; you shall not covet your neighbor's wife, or his manservant, or his maidservant, or his ox, or his ass, or anything that is your neighbor's."

Now when all the people perceived the thunderings and the lightnings and the sound of the trumpet and the mountain smoking, the people were afraid and trembled; and they stood afar off, and said to Moses, "You speak to us, and we will hear; but let not God speak to us, lest we die." And Moses said to the people, "Do not fear, for God has come to prove you, and that the fear of him may be before your eyes, that you may not sin."

The Commandments are very general; the needs of the Israelites for order among a disorderly people were very great. Immediately the Lord, through the mouth of Moses, sets out statutes and ordinances, laws applying to specific situations, to rule the people.

*These ordinances form an interesting contrast to the abstract considerations of "justice"
in (for example) Book V of Aristotle's* Nicomachean Ethics. *These are concrete, clear,
applicable, very harsh, very fair, and have formed our sense of what is just and fair to the
present day.*

Exodus

Chapters 21–23:

(The passages are in quotation marks because God is talking to Moses)

"Whoever strikes a man so that he dies shall be put to death. But if he did not lie in wait for him, but God let him fall into his hand, then I will appoint for you a place to which he may flee. But if a man willfully attacks another to kill him treacherously, you shall take him from my altar, that he may die.

"Whoever strikes his father or his mother shall be put to death.

"Whoever steals a man, whether he sells him or is found in possession of him, shall be put to death.

"Whoever curses his father or his mother shall be put to death.

"When men quarrel and one strikes the other with a stone or with his fist and the man does not die but keeps his bed, then if the man rises again and walks abroad with his staff, he that struck him shall be clear; only he shall pay for the loss of his time, and shall have him thoroughly healed. . . .

"When men strive together, and hurt a woman with child, so that there is a miscarriage, and yet no harm follows, the one who hurt her shall be fined, according as the woman's husband shall lay upon him; and he shall pay as the judges determine. If any harm follows, then you shall give life for life, eye for eye, tooth for tooth, hand for hand, foot for foot, burn for burn, wound for wound, stripe for stripe.

"When a man strikes the eye of his slave, male or female, and destroys it, he shall let the slave go free for the eye's sake. If he knocks out the tooth of his slave, male or female, he shall let the slave go free for the tooth's sake.

"When an ox gores a man or a woman to death, the ox shall be stoned, and its flesh shall not be eaten; but the owner of the ox shall be clear. But if the ox has been accustomed to gore in the past, and its owner has been warned but has not kept it in, and it kills a man or a woman, the ox shall be stoned, and its owner also shall be put to death. . . .

"When a man leaves a pit open, or when a man digs a pit and does not cover it, and an ox or an ass falls into it, the owner of the pit shall make it good; he shall give money to its owner, and the dead beast shall be his.

"When one man's ox hurts another's, so that it dies, then they shall sell the live ox and divide the price of it; and the dead beast also they shall divide. Or if it is known that the ox has been accustomed to gore in the past, and its owner has not kept it in, he shall pay ox for ox, and the dead beast shall be his. . . .

"When a man causes a field or vineyard to be grazed over, or lets his beast loose and it feeds in another man's field, he shall make restitution from the best in his own field and in his own vineyard. . . ."

*But civil order is not sufficient to rule this people, for this is a holy people, set apart
by God for his own, that He might dwell among them. These people are consecrated, and
must keep themselves apart from all impurity. The laws of* Leviticus, *book of the priests,
make this clear.*

Leviticus

Chapters 11, 17, 18, 19:

And the Lord said to Moses and Aaron, "Say to the people of Israel, These are the living things which you may eat among all the beasts that are on the earth. Whatever parts the hoof and is cloven-footed and chews the cud, among the animals, you may eat. . . .

"These you may eat, of all that are in the waters. Everything in the waters that has fins and scales, whether in the seas or in the rivers, you may eat. But anything in the seas or the rivers that has not fins and scales, of the swarming creatures in the waters and of the living creatures that are in the waters, is an abomination to you. . . .

"Every swarming thing that swarms upon the earth is an abomination; it shall not be eaten. Whatever goes on its belly, and whatever goes on all fours, or whatever has many feet, all the swarming things that swarm upon the earth, you shall not eat; for they are an abomination. You shall not make yourselves abominable with any swarming thing that swarms; and you shall not defile yourselves with them, lest you become unclean. For I am the Lord your God; consecrate yourselves therefore, and be holy, for I am holy. You shall not defile yourselves with any swarming thing that crawls upon the earth. For I am the Lord who brought you up out of the land of Egypt, to be your God; you shall therefore be holy, for I am holy.

"This is the law pertaining to beast and bird and every living creature that moves through the waters and every creature that swarms upon the earth, to make a distinction between the unclean and the clean and between the living creature that may be eaten and the living creature that may not be eaten. . . ."

And the Lord said to Moses, . . . "If any man of the house of Israel or of the strangers that sojourn among them eats any blood, I will set my face against that person who eats blood, and will cut him off from among his people. For the life of the flesh is in the blood; and I have given it for you upon the altar to make atonement for your souls; for it is the blood that makes atonement, by reason of the life. . . . And every person that eats what dies of itself or what is torn by beasts, whether he is a native or a so-journer, shall wash his clothes, and bathe himself in water, and be unclean until the evening; then he shall be clean. But if he does not wash them or bathe his flesh, he shall bear his iniquity. . . .

"None of you shall approach any one near of kin to him to uncover nakedness. I am the Lord. You shall not uncover the nakedness of your father, which is the nakedness of your mother; she is your mother, you shall not uncover her nakedness. . . .

"You shall not approach a woman to uncover her nakedness while she is in her menstrual uncleanness. And you shall not lie carnally with your neighbor's wife, and defile yourself with her.

"You shall not give any of your children to devote them by fire to Molech, and so profane the name of your God; I am the Lord. You shall not lie with a male as with a woman; it is an abomination. And you shall not lie with any beast and defile yourself with it, neither shall any woman give herself to a beast to lie with it; it is perversion.

"Do not defile yourselves by any of these things, for by all these the nations I am casting out before you defiled themselves; and the land became defiled, so that I punished its iniquity, and the land vomited out its inhabitants. But you shall keep my statutes and my ordinances and do none of these abominations, either the native or the stranger who sojourns among you. . . ."

And the Lord said to Moses, "Say to all the congregation of the people of Israel, You shall be holy; for I the Lord your God am holy. . . .

"When you reap the harvest of your land, you shall not reap your field to its very border, neither shall you gather the gleanings after your harvest. And you shall not strip your vineyard bare, neither shall you gather the fallen grapes of your vineyard; you shall leave them for the poor and for the so-journer: I am the Lord your God.

"You shall not steal, nor deal falsely, nor lie to one another. And you shall not swear by my name falsely, and so profane the name of your God: I am the Lord.

"You shall not oppress your neighbor or rob him. The wages of a hired servant shall not remain with you all night until the morning. You shall not curse the deaf or put a stumbling block before the blind, but you shall fear your God: I am the Lord.

"You shall do no injustice in judgment; you shall not be partial to the poor or defer to the great, but in righteousness shall you judge your neighbor. You shall not go up and down as a slanderer among your people, and you shall not stand forth against the life of your neighbor: I am the Lord.

"You shall not hate your brother in your heart, but you shall reason with your neighbor, lest you bear sin because of him. You shall not take vengeance or bear any grudge against the sons of your own people, but you shall love your neighbor as yourself: I am the Lord. . . ."

One point should be noticed right now. Whatever we may say in general about the "evolution" of the Judaeo-Christian ethic from an ethic of strict judgment to an ethic of love, all the elements associated with the later form are here in Leviticus, *third of the books of Moses. "Love your neighbor as yourself" has been part of the commands since the earliest formulation of the moral law of this tradition. Under the harsh conditions of desert wandering, these spiritual commands may be lost among the dietary rules and rules for treating leprosy, but they are an integral part of the teaching from the outset.*

The teaching is summed up in Moses' last sermon, given as the Israelites approach the Promised Land.

Deuteronomy

Chapters 4, 7, 10, and 30:

"And now, O Israel, give heed to the statutes and the ordinances which I teach you, and do them; that you may live, and go in and take possession of the land which the Lord, the God of your fathers, gives you. You shall not add to the word which I command you, nor take from it; that you may keep the commandments of the Lord your God which I command you. . . . Behold, I have taught you statutes and ordinances, as the Lord my God commanded me, that you should do them in the land which you are entering to take possession of it. Keep them and do them, for that will be your wisdom and your understanding in the sight of the peoples, who, when they hear all these statutes, will say, 'Surely this great nation is a wise and understanding people.' For what great nation is there that has a god so near to it as the Lord our God is to us, whenever we call upon him? And what great nation is there, that has statutes and ordinances so righteous as all this law which I set before you this day?

"Only take heed, and keep your soul diligently, lest you forget the things which your eyes have seen, and lest they depart from your heart all the days of your life; make them known to your children and your children's children. . . .

"For you are a people holy to the Lord your God; the Lord your God has chosen you to be a people for his own possession, out of all the peoples that are on the face of the earth. It was not because you were more in number than any other people that the Lord set his love upon you and chose you, for you were the fewest of all peoples; but it is because the Lord loves you, and is keeping the oath which he swore to your fathers, that a Lord has brought you out with a mighty hand, and redeemed you from the house of bondage, from the hand of Pharaoh king of Egypt. Know therefore that the Lord your God is God, the faithful God who keeps covenant and steadfast love with those who love him and keep his commandments, to a thousand generations, and requites to their face those who hate him, by destroying them; he will not be slack with him who hates him, he will requite him to his face. You shall therefore be careful to do the commandment, and the statutes, and the ordinances, which I command you this day. . . .

"And now, Israel, what does the Lord your God require of you, but to fear the Lord your God, to walk in all his ways, to love him, to serve the Lord your God with all your heart and with all your soul, and to keep the commandments and statutes of the Lord, which I command you this day for your good? Behold, to the Lord your God belong heaven and the heaven of heavens, the earth with all that is in it; yet the Lord set his heart in love upon your fathers and chose their descendants after them, you above all peoples, as at this day. Circumcise therefore the foreskin of your heart, and be no longer stubborn. For the Lord your God is God of gods and Lord of lords, the great, the mighty, and the terrible God, who is not partial and takes no bribe. He executes justice for the fatherless and the widow, and loves the sojourner, giving him food and clothing. Love the sojourner, therefore; for you were sojourners in the land of Egypt. You shall fear the Lord your God; you shall serve him and cleave to him, and by his name you shall swear. He is your praise; he is your God, who has done for you these great and terrible things which your eyes have seen. Your fathers went down to Egypt seventy persons; and now the Lord your God has made you as the stars of heaven for multitude. . . .

"For this commandment which I command you this day is not too hard for you, neither is it far off. It is not in heaven, that you should say, 'Who will go up for us to heaven, and bring it to us, that we may hear it and do it?' Neither is it beyond the sea, that you should say, 'Who will go over the sea for us, and bring it to us, that we may hear it and do it?' But the word is very near you; it is in your mouth and in your heart, so that you can do it. . . .

"I call heaven and earth to witness against you this day, that I have set before you life and death, blessing and curse; therefore choose life, that you and your descendants may live, loving the Lord your God, obeying his voice, and cleaving to him; for that means life to you and length of days, that you may dwell in the land which the Lord swore to your fathers, to Abraham, to Isaac, and to Jacob, to give them. . . ."

> *The teaching is absolutely simple. Keep the statutes and ordinances, change nothing, obey all, and you will live. The Lord commands them not only to move into the Promised Land, but also (Numbers 33:50–56) to kill any people they find already living there; it is to be their land alone. But even as Moses prepares for his death, the Lord tells him that as soon as the people cross the river Jordan into the Promised Land of Israel, they will start breaking the laws, whoring after strange gods, forgetting the commands given to their fathers: (Deuteronomy 32:20) "For when I have brought them into the land flowing with milk and honey, which I swore to give their fathers, and they have eaten and are full and grown fat, they will turn to other gods and serve them, and despise me and break my covenant."*
>
> *And so the Lord punished them with exiles and famines, yet sent them, now and again, excellent kings who built cities and temples and restored the boundaries of the Land. Always the Lord sent prophets: ordinary citizens picked from the people, who were advised of their appointments in dreams, much to their surprise and often to their dismay. The prophets were sent among the Israelites to remind them that they were a people set apart by God to do justice and to care for each other; that the Lord was great in mercy to those who feared him and terrible in vengeance to those who would not; and that their complacency in injustice was as terrible as outright offense. Amos, a shepherd from the small Judaean village of Tekoa, was one of the most eloquent of these prophets:*

Amos

Books 2, 5, and 8:

Thus says the Lord: "For three transgressions of Moab, and for four, I will not revoke the punishment; because he burned to lime the bones of the king of Edom. So I will send a fire upon Moab, and it shall devour the strongholds of Kerioth, and Moab shall die amid uproar, amid shouting and the sound of the trumpet; I will cut off the ruler from its midst, and will slay all its princes with him," says the Lord.

Thus says the Lord: "For three transgressions of Judah, and for four, I will not revoke the punishment; because they have rejected the law of the Lord, and have not kept his statutes, but their lies have led them astray, after which their fathers walked. So I will send a fire upon Judah, and it shall devour the strongholds of Jerusalem."

Thus says the Lord: "For three transgressions of Israel, and for four, I will not revoke the punishment; because they sell the righteous for silver, and the needy for a pair of shoes; they that trample the head of the poor into the dust of the earth, and turn aside the way of the afflicted; a man and his father go in to the same maiden, so that my holy name is profaned; they lay themselves down beside every altar upon garments taken in pledge; and in the house of their God they drink the wine of those who have been fined. Yet I destroyed the Amorite before them, whose height was like the height of the cedars, and who was as strong as the oaks; I destroyed his fruit above, and his roots beneath. Also I brought you up out of the land of Egypt, and led you forty years in the wilderness, to possess the land of the Amorite. And I raised up some of your sons for prophets, and some of your young men for Nazirites. Is it not indeed so, O people of Israel?" says the Lord.

"But you made the Nazirites drink wine, and commanded the prophets, saying, 'You shall not prophesy.' Behold, I will press you down in your place, as a cart full of sheaves presses down. Flight shall perish from the swift, and the strong shall not retain his strength, nor shall the mighty save his life; he who handles the bow shall not stand, and he who is swift of foot shall not save himself, nor shall he who rides the horse save his life; and he who is stout of heart among the mighty shall flee away naked in that day," says the Lord. . . .

Seek the Lord and live, lest he break out like fire in the house of Joseph, and it devour, with none to quench it for Bethel, O you who turn justice to wormwood, and cast down righteousness to the earth!

He who made the Pleiades and Orion, and turns deep darkness into the morning, and darkens the day into night, who calls for the waters of the sea, and pours them out upon the surface of the earth, the Lord is his name, who makes destruction flash forth against the strong, so that destruction comes upon the fortress.

They hate him who reproves in the gate, and they abhor him who speaks the truth. Therefore because you trample upon the poor and take from him exactions of wheat, you have built houses of hewn stone, but you shall not dwell in them; you have planted pleasant vineyards, but you shall not drink their wine.

For I know how many are your transgressions, and great are your sins—you who afflict the righteous, who take a bribe, and turn aside the needy in the gate. . . .

"I hate, I despise your feasts, and I take no delight in your solemn assemblies. Even though you offer me your burnt offerings and cereal offerings, I will not accept them, and the peace offerings of your fatted beasts, I will not look upon. Take away from me the noise of your songs; to the melody of your harps I will not listen. But let justice roll down like waters, and righteousness like an ever-flowing stream. . . ."

Thus the Lord God showed me: behold a basket of summer fruit. And he said, "Amos, what do you see?" And I said, "A basket of summer fruit." Then the Lord said to me, "The end has come upon my people Israel; I will never again pass by them. The songs of the temple shall become wailings in that day," says the Lord God, "the dead bodies shall be many; in every place they shall be cast out in silence."

Hear this, you who trample upon the needy, and bring the poor of the land to an end, saying, "When will the new moon be over, that we may sell grain? And the Sabbath, that we may offer wheat for sale, that we may make the ephah small and the shekel great, and deal deceitfully with false balances, that we may buy the poor for silver and the needy for a pair of sandals, and sell the refuse of the wheat?"

The Lord has sworn by the pride of Jacob: "Surely I will never forget any of their deeds. Shall not the land tremble on this account, and every one mourn who dwells in it, and all of it rise like the Nile, and be tossed about and sink again, like the Nile of Egypt?" "And on that day," says the Lord God, "I will make the sun go down at noon, and darken the earth in broad daylight. I will turn your feasts into mourning, and all your songs into lamentation; I will bring sackcloth upon all loins, and baldness on every head; I will make it like the mourning for an only son, and the end of it like a bitter day...."

In the Book of Micah, the message is the same: turn away, Israel, from the ways of injustice that you have picked up among the foreigners, and return to the simple ways of the Lord. If you do not, the punishment of the Lord is dreadful; but in the end, it is the intention of the Lord to restore you to your land where you should live in peace. Micah also has some prophecies of historical note, of the destruction of Jerusalem and the coming of a Shepherd Ruler from Bethlehem.

Micah

Chapters 3 through 7:

3. ... Hear this, you heads of the house of Jacob and rulers of the house of Israel, Who abhor justice and pervert all equity, who build Zion with blood and Jerusalem with wrong. Its heads give judgment for a bribe, its priests teach for hire, its prophets divine for money; yet they lean upon the Lord and say, "Is not the Lord in the midst of us? No evil shall come upon us."

Therefore because of you Zion shall be plowed as a field, Jerusalem shall become a heap of ruins, and the mountain of the house a wooded height.

4. It shall come to pass in the latter days that the mountain of the house of the Lord shall be established as the highest of the mountains, and shall be raised up above the hills; and peoples shall flow to it, and many nations shall come, and say: "Come, let us go up to the mountain of the Lord, to the house of the God of Jacob; that he may teach us his ways and we may walk in his paths."

For out of Zion shall go forth the law, and the word of the Lord from Jerusalem. He shall judge between many peoples, and shall decide for strong nations afar off; and they shall beat their swords into plowshares, and their spears into pruning hooks; nation shall not lift up sword against nation, neither shall they learn war any more; but they shall sit every man under his vine and under his fig tree, and none shall make them afraid; for the mouth of the Lord of hosts has spoken....

5. Now you are walled about with a wall; siege is laid against us; with a rod they strike upon the cheek the ruler of Israel. But you, O Bethlehem Ephrathah, who are little to be among the clans of Judah, From you shall come forth for me one who is to be ruler in Israel, whose origin is from of old, from ancient days. Therefore he shall give them up until the time when she who is in travail has brought forth; then the rest of his brethren shall return to the people of Israel.

And he shall stand and feed his flock in the strength of the Lord, in the majesty of the name of the Lord his God. And they shall dwell secure, for now he shall be great to the ends of the earth. . . .

6. ". . . With what shall I come before the Lord, and bow myself before God on high? Shall I come before him with burnt offerings, with calves a year old? Will the Lord be pleased with thousands of rams, with ten thousands of rivers of oil? Shall I give my first-born for my transgression, the fruit of my body for the sin of my soul?"

He has showed you, O man, what is good; and what does the Lord require of you but to do justice, and to love kindness, and to walk humbly with your God?

7. . . . Who is a God like thee, pardoning iniquity, and passing over transgression for the remnant of his inheritance? He does not retain his anger for ever because he delights in steadfast love. He will again have compassion upon us, he will tread our iniquities under foot.

Thou wilt cast all our sins into the depths of the sea. Thou wilt show faithfulness to Jacob and steadfast love to Abraham, as thou hast sworn to our fathers from the days of old.

> *The foregoing passages make it clear that the framework of the Judaeo-Christian ethic, mercy and steadfast love as well as justice, was well in place by the birth of Christ. Yet in Christian teaching a new note appears, not changing the Law so much as extending it to matters internal and spiritual. The Sermon on the Mount, presented to nameless crowds shortly after the beginning of Jesus' ministry, provides a summary of Jesus' teaching:*

The Gospel According to Matthew

Chapters 5 and 7:

5. Seeing the crowds, he went up on the mountain, and when he sat down his disciples came to him. And he opened his mouth and taught them, saying:

Blessed are the poor in spirit, for theirs is the kingdom of heaven.

Blessed are those who mourn, for they shall be comforted.

Blessed are the meek, for they shall inherit the earth.

Blessed are those who hunger and thirst for righteousness, for they shall be satisfied.

Blessed are the merciful, for they shall obtain mercy.

Blessed are the pure in heart, for they shall see God.

Blessed are the peacemakers, for they shall be called the sons of God.

Blessed are those who are persecuted for righteousness' sake, for theirs is the kingdom of heaven.

Blessed are you when men revile you and persecute you and utter all kinds of evil against you falsely on my account. Rejoice and be glad, for your reward is great in heaven, for so men persecuted the prophets who were before you.

You are the salt of the earth; but if salt has lost its taste, how shall its saltness be restored? It is no longer good for anything except to be thrown out and trodden under foot by men.

You are the light of the world. A city set on a hill cannot be hid. Nor do men light a lamp and put it under a bushel, but on a stand, and it gives light to all in the house. Let your light so shine before men, that they may see your good works and give glory to your Father who is in heaven.

Think not that I have come to abolish the law and the prophets; I have come not to abolish them but to fulfill them. For truly, I say to you, till heaven and earth pass away, not an iota, not a dot, will pass from the law until all is accomplished. Whoever then relaxes one of the least of these commandments and teaches men so, shall be called least in the kingdom of heaven; but he who does them and teaches them shall be called great in the kingdom of heaven. For I tell you, unless your righteousness exceeds that of the scribes and Pharisees, you will never enter the kingdom of heaven.

You have heard that it was said to the men of old, "You shall not kill; and whoever kills shall be liable to judgment." But I say to you that every one who is angry with his brother shall be liable to judgment; whoever insults his brother shall be liable to the council, and whoever says, "You fool!" shall be liable to the hell of fire. So if you are offering your gift at the altar, and there remember that your brother has something against you, leave your gift there before the altar and go; first be reconciled to your brother, and then come and offer your gift. Make friends quickly with your accuser, while you are going with him to court, lest your accuser hand you over to the judge, and the judge to the guard, and you be put in prison; truly, I say to you, you will never get out till you have paid the last penny.

You have heard that it was said, "You shall not commit adultery." But I say to you that every one who looks at a woman lustfully has already committed adultery with her in his heart. If your right eye causes you to sin, pluck it out and throw it away; it is better that you lose one of your members than that your whole body be thrown into hell. And if your right hand causes you to sin, cut it off and throw it away; it is better that you lose one of your members than that your whole body go into hell.

It was also said, "Whoever divorces his wife, let him give her a certificate of divorce." But I say to you that every one who divorces his wife, except on the ground of unchastity, makes her an adulteress; and whoever marries a divorced woman commits adultery.

Again you have heard that it was said to the men of old, "You shall not swear falsely, but shall perform to the Lord what you have sworn." But I say to you, Do not swear at all, either by heaven, for it is the throne of God, or by the earth, for it is his footstool, or by Jerusalem, for it is the city of the great King. And do not swear by your head, for you cannot make one hair white or black. Let what you say be simply "Yes" or "No"; anything more than this comes from evil.

You have heard that it was said, "An eye for an eye and a tooth for a tooth." But I say to you, Do not resist one who is evil. But if any one strikes you on the right cheek, turn to him the other also; and if any one would sue you and take your coat, let him have your cloak as well, and if any one forces you to go one mile, go with him two miles. Give to him who begs from you, and do not refuse him who would borrow from you.

You have heard that it was said, "You shall love your neighbor and hate your enemy." But I say to you, Love your enemies and pray for those who persecute you, so that you may be the sons of your Father who is in heaven; for he makes his sun rise on the evil and on the good, and sends rain on the just and on the unjust. For if you love those who love you, what reward have you? Do not even the tax collectors do the same? And if you salute only your brethren, what more are you doing than others? Do not even the Gentiles do the same? You, therefore, must be perfect, as your heavenly Father is perfect.

6. Beware of practicing your piety before men in order to be seen by them; for then you will have no reward from your Father who is in heaven.

Thus, when you give alms, sound no trumpet before you, as the hypocrites do in the synagogues and in the streets, that they may be praised by men. Truly, I say to you, they have their reward. But when you give alms, do not let your left hand know what your right hand is doing, so that your alms may be in secret; and your Father who sees in secret will reward you.

And when you pray, you must not be like the hypocrites; for they love to stand and pray in the synagogues and at the street corners, that they may be seen by men. Truly, I say to you, they have their reward. But when you pray, go into your room and shut the door and pray to your Father who is in secret: and your Father who sees in secret will reward you.

And in praying, do not heap up empty phrases as the Gentiles do: for they think that they will be heard for their many words. Do not be like them, for your Father knows what you need before you ask him. Pray then like this: "Our Father who art in heaven, Hallowed be thy name. Thy kingdom come. Thy will be done on earth as it is in heaven. Give us this day our daily bread, And forgive us our debts, As we also have forgiven our debtors; And lead us not into temptation, But deliver us from evil."

For if you forgive men their trespasses, your heavenly Father also will forgive you; but if you do not forgive men their trespasses, neither will your Father forgive your trespasses.

And when you fast, do not look dismal, like the hypocrites, for they disfigure their faces that their fasting may be seen by men. Truly, I say to you, they have their reward. But when you fast, anoint your head and wash your face, that your fasting may not be seen by men but by your Father who is in secret; and your Father who sees in secret will reward you.

Do not lay up for yourselves treasures on earth, where moth and rust consume and where thieves break in and steal, but lay up for yourselves treasures in heaven, where neither moth nor rust consumes and where thieves do not break in and steal. For where your treasure is, there will your heart be also. . . .

No one can serve two masters; for either he will hate the one and love the other, or he will be devoted to the one and despise the other. You cannot serve God and mammon.

Therefore I tell you, do not be anxious about your life, what you shall eat or what you shall drink, nor about your body, what you shall put on. Is not life more than food, and the body more than clothing? Look at the birds of the air: they neither sow nor reap nor gather into barns, and yet your heavenly Father feeds them. Are you not of more value than they? And which of you by being anxious can add one cubit to his span of life? And why are you anxious about clothing? Consider the lilies of the field, how they grow; they neither toil nor spin; yet I tell you, even Solomon in all his glory was not arrayed like one of these. But if God so clothes the grass of the field, which today is alive and tomorrow is thrown into the oven, will he not much more clothe you, O men of little faith? Therefore do not be anxious, saying "What shall we eat?" or "What shall we drink?" or "What shall we wear?" For the Gentiles seek all these things; and your heavenly Father knows that you need them all. But seek first his kingdom and his righteousness, and all these things shall be yours as well.

Therefore do not be anxious about tomorrow, for tomorrow will be anxious for itself. Let the day's own trouble be sufficient for the day.

7. Judge not, that you be not judged. For with the judgment you pronounce you will be judged, and the measure you give will be the measure you get. Why do you see the speck that is in your brother's eye, but do not notice the log that is in your own eye? Or how can you say to your brother, "Let me take the speck out of your eye," when there is a log in your own eye? You hypocrite, first take the log out of your own eye, and then you will see clearly to take the speck out of your brother's eye. . . .

Ask, and it will be given you: seek, and you will find; knock, and it will be opened to you. For every one who asks receives, and he who seeks finds, and to him who knocks it will be opened. Or what man of you, if his son asks him for bread, will give him a stone? Or if he asks for a fish, will give him a serpent? If you then, who are evil, know how to give good gifts to your children, how much more will your Father who is in heaven give good things to those who ask him! So whatever you wish that men would do to you, do so to them, for this is the law and the prophets.

Enter by the narrow gate; for the gate is wide and the way is easy, that leads to destruction, and those who enter by it are many. For the gate is narrow and the way is hard, that leads to life, and those who find it are few. . . .

Every one then who hears these words of mine and does them will be like a wise man who built his house upon the rock; and the rain fell, and the floods came, and the winds blew and beat upon that house, but it did not fall, because it had been founded on the rock. And every one who hears these words of mine and does not do them will be like a foolish man who built his house upon the sand, and the rain fell, and the floods came, and the winds blew and beat against that house, and it fell; and great was the fall of it.

And when Jesus finished these sayings, the crowds were astonished at his teaching, for he taught them as one who had authority, and not as their scribes.

> *New in these passages is the strain of antimaterialism: contempt for even the necessities of life and the assurance that "God will provide." This is a much more affluent Israel than wandered through the desert and fought off savage tribes; urbanized, this Israel supports scribes and teachers off the surplus of the land. But Jesus is uncompromising about the extent of the precept to leave material things behind. Asked by a rich young man (Matthew 19:16), "Teacher, what good deed must I do, to have eternal life?" Jesus first tells him to keep the Ten Commandments, and when he says he has done that since his youth, Jesus continues (19:21), "If you would be perfect, go, sell what you possess and give to the poor, and you will have treasure in heaven; and come, follow me." To his disciples, he goes on (19:23–24), "Truly, I say to you, it will be hard for a rich man to enter the kingdom of heaven. Again I tell you, it is easier for a camel to go through the eye of a needle than for a rich man to enter the kingdom of God." Pressed by his disciples, Jesus concedes that "with God all things are possible," so it may well be that any given rich man will be saved. Nevertheless, renunciation of all material goods is the best path, and those who, like his twelve followers, have left everything for the task of ministry will be preferred "in the new world" (19:29). "And every one who has left houses or brothers or sisters or father or mother or children or lands, for my name's sake, will receive a hundredfold, and inherit eternal life."*
>
> *What is not new in the Sermon is the emphasis on spiritual purity and justice. As with Amos and Micah, inward purity matters for Jesus far more than the strict observance of the outward signs, sacrifices, and rituals, which people perform merely to obtain social favor. In his ministry, Jesus was often called a "prophet"; confronted with the social-religious authorities of his day, he reacted much as Amos the shepherd:*

Chapter 23:

Then said Jesus to the crowds and to his disciples, "The scribes and the Pharisees sit on Moses' seat; so practice and observe whatever they tell you, but not what they do; for they preach, but do not practice. They bind heavy burdens, hard to bear, and lay them on men's shoulders; but they themselves will not move them with their finger. They do all their deeds to be seen by men; for they make their phylacteries broad and their fringes long, and they love the place of honor at feasts and the best seats in the synagogues, and salutations in the market places, and being called rabbi by men. But you are not to be called rabbi, for you have one teacher, and you are all brethren. And call no man your father on earth, for you have one Father, who is in heaven. Neither be called masters, for you have one master, the Christ. He who is greatest among you shall be your servant; whoever exalts himself will be humbled, and whoever humbles himself will be exalted.

"But woe to you, scribes and Pharisees, hypocrites! because you shut the kingdom of heaven against men; for you neither enter yourselves, nor allow those who would enter to go in. Woe to you, scribes and Pharisees, hypocrites! for you traverse sea and land to make a single proselyte, and when he becomes a proselyte, you make him twice as much a child of hell as yourselves . . .

"Woe to you, scribes and Pharisees, hypocrites! for you tithe mint and dill and cumin, and have neglected the weightier matters of the law, justice and mercy and faith; these you ought to have done, without neglecting the others. You blind guides, straining out a gnat and swallowing a camel!

"Woe to you, scribes and Pharisees, hypocrites! for you cleanse the outside of the cup and of the plate, but inside they are full of extortion and rapacity. . . . Woe to you, scribes and Pharisees, hypocrites! for you are like whitewashed tombs, which outwardly appear beautiful, but within they are full of dead men's bones and all uncleanness. So you also outwardly appear righteous to men, but within you are full of hypocrisy and iniquity.

"Woe to you, scribes and Pharisees, hypocrites! for you build the tombs of the prophets and adorn the monuments of the righteous, saying, 'If we had lived in the days of our fathers, we would not have taken part with them in shedding the blood of the prophets.' Thus you witness against yourselves, that you are the sons of those who murdered the prophets. Fill up, then, the measure of your fathers. You serpents, you brood of vipers, how are you to escape being sentenced to hell? . . .

"O Jerusalem, Jerusalem, killing the prophets and stoning those who are sent to you! How often would I have gathered your children together as a hen gathers her brood under her wings, and you would not! Behold, your house is forsaken and desolate. For I tell you, you will not see me again, until you say, 'Blessed is he who comes in the name of the Lord.'"

Not a new teaching of the Judaeo-Christian ethic, but surely a new emphasis, is found in Jesus' teaching on love. The ancient "Love your neighbor as yourself" seems to have been a teaching of civility, general consideration, and neighborliness, necessary for a going community of people who were not strangers to each other. But Jesus extends this love to the stranger, and indeed to anyone in need:

The Gospel According to Luke

10:25:

And behold, a lawyer stood up to put him to the test, saying, "Teacher, what shall I do to inherit eternal life?" He said to him, "What is written in the law? How do you read?" And he answered, "You shall love the Lord your God with all your heart, and with all your soul, and with all your strength, and with all your mind; and your neighbor as yourself." And he said to him, "You have answered right; do this, and you will live."

But he, desiring to justify himself, said to Jesus, "And who is my neighbor?" Jesus replied,

"A man was going down from Jerusalem to Jericho, and he fell among robbers, who stripped him and beat him, and departed, leaving him half dead. Now by chance, a priest was going down that road; and when he saw him he passed by on the other side. So likewise a Levite, when he came to the place and saw him, passed by on the other side. But a Samaritan, as he journeyed, came to where he was; and when he saw him, he had compassion, and went to him and bound up his wounds, pouring on oil and wine; then he set him on his own beast and brought him to an inn, and took care of him. And the next day he took out two denarii and gave them to the innkeeper, saying, 'Take care of him; and whatever more you spend, I will repay you when I come back.' Which of these three, do you think, proved neighbor to the man who fell among the robbers?" He said, "The one who showed mercy on him." And Jesus said to him, "Go and do thou likewise."

In fact, the teaching of love calls for a profound respect for each other as individuals, extending from geographical neighbors to strangers to enemies, and replaces (or at least precedes) any judgment of other individuals. This amounts to a Biblical foundation for the modern command to respect the rights and the autonomy of the individual human being just because *that person is a human being, regardless of tribe, sect, color, or persuasion. So grounded, this command operates at a much deeper level than the mere injunction to observe legal protections of individual liberties; on the contrary, it is a continual impetus in our law to extend those rights and liberties. As such, it informs our political system to this day. Jesus' teaching concerning love is found in its most original and moving form in his final reflections before his death, just after the treacherous apostle Judas departs to betray him, in the book of John:*

From the Gospel According to John

Chapters 13–15:

When he had gone out, Jesus said, "Now is the Son of man glorified, and in him God is glorified; if God is glorified in him, God will also glorify him in himself, and glorify him at once. Little children, yet a little while I am with you. You will seek me; and as I said to the Jews so now I say to you, Where I am going you cannot come. A new commandment I give to you, that you love one another; even as I have loved you, that you also love one another. By this all men will know that you are my disciples, if you have love for one another. . . .

"Let not your hearts be troubled; believe in God, believe also in me. In my Father's house are many rooms; if it were not so, would I have told you that I go to prepare a place for you? And when I go and prepare a place for you, I will come again and will take you to myself, that where I am you may be also. And you know the way where I am going." Thomas said to him, "Lord, we do not know where you are going; how can we know the way?" Jesus said to him, "I am the way, and the truth, and the life; no one comes to the Father, but by me. If you had known me, you would have known my Father also; henceforth you know him and have seen him. . . .

"If you love me, you will keep my commandments. And I will pray the Father, and he will give you another Counselor, to be with you forever, even the Spirit of truth, whom the world cannot receive, because it neither sees him nor knows him; you know him, for he dwells with you, and will be in you. . . .

"This is my commandment, that you love one another as I have loved you. Greater love has no man than this, that a man lay down his life for his friends. You are my friends if you do what I command you. No longer do I call you servants, for the servant does not know what his master is doing, but I have called you friends, for all that I have heard from my Father I have made known to you. You did not choose me, but I chose you and appointed you that you should go and bear fruit and that your fruit should abide; so that whatever you ask the Father in my name, he may give it to you. This I command you, to love one another. . . ."

> *Shortly thereafter, Jesus dies. Christians believe that he rose again the following Sunday, and a good deal of the world's history in the West follows from that belief. The historical influence begins with the Apostles' decision, first, to go abroad, strengthened by the Holy Spirit (the Counselor referred to in the last speech) and preach Christian doctrine—Christ crucified, risen, and coming again—and second, not to limit their teaching to an audience of "the lost sheep of Israel," as Jesus generally had.*
>
> *The prophets came only to remind the Israelites of their derelictions vis-a-vis their Covenant; Jesus came only, he said, to save those same Israelites. But in the very early*

years of the Church, its leader, the apostle Simon Peter, had a strange vision, in which it seemed to him that the Lord gave him permission to eat foods that the Jewish practice had, since the Exodus from Egypt (and as recorded in Leviticus*), called "unclean." Then he was asked to visit the house of a centurion, Cornelius, in Caesarea. Cornelius was not a Jew; could Peter enter the house? That, he decided, was what the vision was about, and set out to visit Cornelius.*

Acts

Chapter 10:

And on the following day they entered Caesarea. Cornelius was expecting them and had called together his kinsmen and close friends. When Peter entered, Cornelius met him and fell down at his feet and worshiped him. But Peter lifted him up, saying, "Stand up; I too am a man." And as he talked with him, he went in and found many persons gathered; and he said to them, "You yourselves know how unlawful it is for a Jew to associate with or to visit any one of another nation; but God has shown me that I should not call any man common or unclean. So when I was sent for, I came without objection. I ask then why you sent for me." And Cornelius said, "Four days ago, about this hour, I was keeping the ninth hour of prayer in my house; and behold, a man stood before me in bright apparel, saying 'Cornelius, your prayer has been heard and your alms have been remembered before God. Send therefore to Joppa and ask for Simon who is called Peter; he is lodging in the house of Simon, a tanner, by the seaside.' So I sent to you at once, and you have been kind enough to come. Now therefore we are all here present in the sight of God, to hear all that you have been commanded by the Lord."

And Peter opened his mouth and said: "Truly I perceive that God shows no partiality, but in every nation any one who fears him and does what is right is acceptable to him. You know the word which he sent to Israel, preaching good news of peace by Jesus Christ (he is Lord of all), the word which was proclaimed throughout all Judea, beginning from Galilee after the baptism which John preached: how God anointed Jesus of Nazareth with the Holy Spirit and with power; how he went about doing good and healing all that were oppressed by the devil, for God was with him. And we are witnesses to all that he did both in the country of the Jews and in Jerusalem. They put him to death by hanging him on a tree; but God raised him on the third day and made him manifest; not to all the people but to us who were chosen by God as witnesses, who ate and drank with him after he rose from the dead. And he commanded us to preach to the people, and to testify that he is the one ordained by God to be judge of the living and the dead. To him all the prophets bear witness that everyone who believes in him receives forgiveness of sins through his name."

While Peter was still saying this, the Holy Spirit fell on all who heard the word. And the believers from among the circumcised who came with Peter were amazed, because the gift of the Holy Spirit had been poured out even on the Gentiles. For they heard them speaking in tongues and extolling God. Then Peter declared, "Can any one forbid water for baptizing these people who have received the Holy Spirit just as we have?" And he commanded them to be baptized in the name of Jesus Christ. . . .

About this time, the infant Church picked up its greatest teacher, missionary, theoretician, and above all correspondent. An ex-persecutor of Christians, a Jew trained as a rabbi, Saul of Tarsus took the name "Paul," "Little One," after his violent conversion on the road to Damascus. Paul founded Christian churches all over the Roman world. As a Roman citizen, he had easy passage through that world, and kept in touch with his congregations through instructional letters, some of which have come down to us. A fitting concluding selection for the ethical tradition is Paul's exposition of the Christian commandment of love, for the benefit of the Church at Corinth:

I Corinthians

Chapter 13:

If I speak in the tongues of men and of angels, but have not love, I am a noisy gong or a clanging cymbal. And if I have prophetic powers, and understand all mysteries and all knowledge, and if I have all faith, so as to remove mountains, but have not love, I am nothing. If I give away all I have, and if I deliver my body to be burned, but have not love, I gain nothing.

Love is patient and kind; love is not jealous or boastful; it is not arrogant or rude. Love does not insist on its own way; it is not irritable or resentful; it does not rejoice at wrong, but rejoices in the right. Love bears all things, believes all things, hopes all things, endures all things.

Love never ends; as for prophecies, they will pass away, as for tongues, they will cease; as for knowledge, it will pass away. For our knowledge is imperfect and our prophecy is imperfect; but when the perfect comes, the imperfect will pass away. When I was a child, I spoke like a child, I thought like a child, I reasoned like a child; when I became a man, I gave up childish ways. For now we see in a mirror dimly, but then face to face. Now I know in part; then I shall understand fully, even as I have been fully understood. So faith, hope, love abide, these three; but the greatest of these is love.

Islam

The central message of Judaism is the Law, and the rich tradition that accompanies it; the central message of Christianity is Love, and the inclusiveness of its message of salvation. The central message of Islam is submission to God and God's word.

Christianity, in contrast to Judaism, became an evangelistic religion, attempting to convert the nations to become believers and apostles. In its rapid expansion and missionary zeal, it became the official religion under the Roman Emperor Constantine, the majority religion in Europe, and, to its shame, the persecutor of its parent Judaism. It conquered Europe, but the Arabian peninsula—that vast region, mostly desert, bounded by the Tigris and Euphrates on the North, the Red Sea on the West, the Indian Ocean on the South, and the Persian Gulf on the East—it left alone. That is where Islam began.

For the springs that had nourished Judaism and Christianity still flowed, and became the inspiration, in the seventh century A.D., for one more Prophet of the Book. Mohammed, a merchant in the caravan trade and reputedly a descendant of Ishmael, Abraham's other son, was approached by the angel Gabriel while meditating in a cave and told to "read." He could not read. The angel told him to read anyway, and the "reading" of the illiterate holy man became the Qur'an (or Koran, in variant spelling). The vision he had was of a new teaching, to bring all peoples together in submission to God. "Islam" means submission, "Muslim" is one who submits—to God. Inspired by the command to spread the teaching, Mohammed moved in A.D. 622 from his home in Mecca to Medina, the first "hejira" from which all later pilgrimages derive. The people of Medina accepted his teaching, and so began the expansion of Islam across the Middle East and eventually West across the entire Mediterranean world and East as far as the Pacific. Its teachings were simplicity itself. The Muslim must believe in God (Allah) and Mohammed as his messenger, must pray five times a day, must fast during the month of Ramadan, must make a pilgrimage to Mecca if possible, and must give alms to the poor. From humble beginnings, Islam has spread over much of the world, commanding the loyalty of up to 900 million people, primarily in Asia.

One aspect of Islam that sets it firmly apart from the other two religions of the Book, Judaism and Christianity, is its deliberate independence from the critical intellectual traditions of Greek philosophy. Both Judaism and Christianity, as far back as we can trace them, tolerated and encouraged philosophical debate on the interpretations and applications of their faiths. A delightful, if chaotic, history of clashing interpretations has made the Judeo-Christian tradition a strong and flexible foundation for ethical reasoning, even as it produces a rainbow of colors of Jewish belief and Christian denomination. There is only one Islam (although groups vary in the stringency of their observation of the law). Debate is not welcome. It is to be lived, not voted on. The passage that follows conveys the strength of belief that sustains the civilization of the Prophet:

From Abu'l A'la Mawdudi, *The Islamic Law and Constitution*

With certain people it has become a sort of fashion to somehow identify Islam with one or the other system of life in vogue at the time. So at this time also there are people who say that Islam is a democracy, and by this they mean to imply that there is no difference between Islam and the democracy as in vogue in the West. Some others suggest that Communism is but the latest and revised version of Islam and it is in the fitness of things that Muslims imitate the Communist experiment of Soviet Russia. Still some others whisper that Islam has the elements of dictatorship in it and we should revive the cult of "obedience to the Amir" (the leader). All these people, in this misinformed and misguided zeal to serve what they hold to be the cause of Islam, are always at great pains to prove that Islam contains within itself the elements of all types of contemporary social and political thought and action. Most of the people who indulge in this prattle have no clear idea of the Islamic way of life. They have never made nor try to make a systematic study of the Islamic political order—the place and nature of democracy, social justice, and equality in it. Instead they behave like the proverbial blind men who gave altogether contradictory descriptions of an elephant because one had been able to touch only its tail, the other its legs, the third its belly and the fourth its ears only. Or perhaps they look upon Islam as an orphan whose sole hope for survival lies in winning the patronage and the sheltering care of some dominant creed. That is why some people have begun to present apologies on Islam's behalf. As a matter of fact, this attitude emerges from an inferiority complex, from the belief that we as Muslims can earn no honor or respect unless we are able to show that our religion resembles the modern creeds and it is in agreement with most of the contemporary ideologies. These people have done a great disservice to Islam; they have reduced the political theory of Islam to a puzzle, a hotchpotch. They have turned Islam into a juggler's bag out of which can be produced anything that holds a demand! Such is the intellectual plight in which we are engulfed. Perhaps it is a result of this sorry state of affairs that some people have even begun to say that Islam has no political or economic system of its own and anything can fit into its scheme.

In these circumstances it has become essential that a careful study of the political theory of Islam should be made in a scientific way, with a view to grasp its real meaning, nature, purpose and significance.

Such a systematic study alone can put an end to this confusion of thought and silence those who out of ignorance proclaim that there is nothing like Islamic political theory, Islamic social order and Islamic culture. I hope it will also bring to the world groping in darkness the light that it urgently needs, although it is not yet completely conscious of such a need. . . .

First Principle of Islamic Political Theory

The belief in the Unity and the sovereignty of Allah is the foundation of the social and moral system propounded by the Prophets. It is the very starting-point of the Islamic political philosophy. The basic principle of Islam is that human beings must, individually and collectively, surrender all rights of over-lordship, legislation and exercising of authority over others. No one should be allowed to pass orders or make commands *in his own right* and no one ought to accept the obligation to carry out such commands and obey such orders. None is entitled to make laws on his own authority and none is obliged to abide by them. This right vests in Allah alone:

> The Authority rests with none but Allah. He commands you not to surrender to any one save Him. This is the right way (of life). (*Qur'an 12:40*)

> They ask: "have we also got some authority?" Say: "all authority belongs to God alone." (*3:154*)

> Do not say wrongly with your tongues that this is lawful and that is unlawful. (*16:116*) Whoso does not establish and decide by that which Allah has revealed, such are disbelievers. (*5:44*)

According to this theory, sovereignty belongs to Allah. He alone is the law-giver. No man, even if he be a Prophet, has the right to order others *in his own right* to do or not to do certain things. The Prophet himself is subject to God's commands:

> I do not follow anything except what is revealed to me. (*6:50*)

Other people are required to obey the Prophet because he enunciates not his own but God's commands:

> We sent no messenger save that he should be obeyed by Allah's command. (*4:64*)

> They are the people to whom We gave the Scripture and Command and Prophethood. (*6:90*)

> It is not (possible) for any human being to whom Allah has given the Scripture and the Wisdom and the Prophethood that he should say to people: Obey me instead of Allah. Such a one (could only say): be solely devoted to the Lord. (*3:79*)

Thus the main characteristics of an Islamic state that can be deduced from these express statements of the Holy Qur'an are as follows:

1. No person, class or group, not even the entire population of the state as a whole, can lay claim to sovereignty. God alone is the real sovereign; all others are merely His subjects;
2. God is the real law-giver and the authority of absolute legislation vests in Him. The believers cannot resort to totally independent legislation nor can they modify any law which God has laid down, even if the desire to effect such legislation or change in Divine laws is unanimous; and
3. An Islamic state must, in all respects, be founded upon the law laid down by God through His Prophet. The government which rims such a state will be entitled to obedience in its capacity as a political agency set up to enforce the laws of God and only in so far as it acts in that capacity. If it disregards the law revealed by God, its commands will not be binding on the believers.

The Islamic State

The preceding discussion makes it quite clear that Islam, speaking from the view-point of political philosophy, is the very antithesis of secular Western democracy. The philosophical foundation of Western democracy is the sovereignty of the people. In it, this type of absolute powers of legislation—of the determination of values and of the norms of behavior—rest in the hands of the people. Law-making is their prerogative and legislation must correspond to the mood and temper of their opinion. If a particular piece of legislation is desired by the masses, howsoever ill-conceived it may be from a religious and moral viewpoint, steps have to be taken to place it on the statute book; if the people dislike any law and demand its abrogation, howsoever just and rightful it might be, it has to be expunged forthwith. This is not the case in Islam. On this count, Islam has no trace of Western democracy. Islam, as already explained, altogether repudiates the philosophy of popular sovereignty and rears its polity on the foundations of the sovereignty of God and the vicegerency (*Khilafah*) of man.

A more apt name for the Islamic polity would be the "kingdom of God" which is described in English as a "theocracy." But Islamic theocracy is something altogether different from the theocracy of which Europe has had a bitter experience wherein a priestly class, sharply marked off from the rest of the population, exercises unchecked domination and enforces laws of its own making in the name of God, thus virtually imposing its own divinity and godhood upon the common people. Such a system of government is satanic rather than divine. Contrary to this, the theocracy built up by Islam is not ruled by any particular religious class but by the whole community of Muslims including the rank and file. The entire Muslim population runs the state in accordance with the Book of God and the practice of His Prophet. If I were permitted to coin a new term, I would describe this system of government as a "theo-democracy," that is to say a divine democratic government, because under it the Muslims have been given a limited popular sovereignty under the suzerainty of God. The executive under this system of government is constituted by the general will of the Muslims who have also the right to depose it. All administrative matters and all questions about which no explicit injunction is to be found in the *shari'ah* are settled by the consensus of opinion among the Muslims. Every Muslim who is capable and qualified to give a sound opinion on matters of Islamic law, is entitled to interpret the law of God when such interpretation becomes necessary. In this sense the Islamic polity is a democracy. But, as has been explained above, it is a theocracy in the sense that where an explicit command of God or His Prophet already exists, no Muslim leader or legislature, or any religious scholar can form an independent judgment, not even all the Muslims of the world put together have any right to make the least alteration in it.

Before proceeding further, I feel that I should put in a word of explanation as to why these limitations and restrictions have been placed upon popular sovereignty in Islam, and what is the nature of these limitations and restrictions. It may be said that God has, in this manner, taken away the liberty of the human mind and intellect instead of safeguarding it as I was trying to prove. My reply is that God has retained the right of legislation in His own hand not in order to deprive man of his natural freedom but to safeguard that very freedom. His purpose is to save man from going astray and inviting his own ruin.

One can easily understand this point by attempting a little analysis of the so-called Western secular democracy. It is claimed that this democracy is founded on popular sovereignty. But everybody knows that the people who constitute a state do not all of them take part either in legislation or in its administration. They have to delegate their sovereignty to their elected representatives so that the latter may make and enforce laws on their behalf. For this purpose, an electoral system is set up. But as a divorce has been effected between politics and religion, and as a result of this secularization, the society and particularly its politically active elements have ceased to attach much or any importance to morality and ethics. And this is also a fact that only those persons generally come to the top who can dupe the masses by their wealth, power, and deceptive propaganda. Although these representatives come into power by the votes of the common people, they soon set themselves up as an independent authority and assume the position of overlords (*ilahs*). They often make laws not in the best interest of the people who raised them to power but to further their own sectional and class interests. They impose their will on the people by virtue of the authority delegated to them by those over whom they rule. This is the situation which besets people in England, America and in all those countries which claim to be the haven of secular democracy.

Even if we overlook this aspect of the matter and admit that in these countries laws are made according to the wishes of the common people, it has been established by experience that the great mass of the common people are incapable of perceiving their own true interests. It is the natural weakness of man that in most of the affairs concerning his life he takes into consideration only some one aspect of reality and loses sight of other aspects. His judgments are usually one-sided and he is swayed by emotions and desires to such an extent that rarely, if ever, can he judge important matters with the impartiality and objectivity of scientific reason. Quite often he rejects the plea of reason simply because it conflicts with his passions and desires. I can cite many instances in support of this contention but to avoid prolixity I shall content myself with giving only one example: the Prohibition Law of America. It had been rationally and logically established that drinking is injurious to health, produces deleterious effects on mental and intellectual faculties and leads to disorder in human society. The American public accepted these facts and agreed to the enactment of the Prohibition Law. Accordingly the law was passed by the majority vote. But when it was put into effect, the very same people by whose vote it had been passed, revolted against it. The worst kinds of wine were illicitly manufactured and consumed, and their use and consumption became more widespread than before. Crimes increased in number, and eventually drinking was legalized by the vote of the same people who had previously voted for its prohibition. This sudden change in public opinion was not the result of any fresh scientific discovery or the revelation of new facts providing evidence against the advantages of prohibition, but because the people had been completely enslaved by their habit and could not forgo the pleasures of self-indulgence. They delegated their own sovereignty to the evil spirit in them and set up their own desires and passions as their *ilahs* (gods) at whose call they all went in for the repeal of the very law they had passed after having been convinced of its rationality and correctness. There are many other similar instances which go to prove that man is not competent to become an absolute legislator. Even if he secures deliverance from the service of other *ilahs*, he becomes a slave to his own petty passions and exalts the devil in him to the position of a supreme Lord. Limitations on human freedom, provided they are appropriate and do not deprive him of all initiative are absolutely necessary in the interest of man himself.

That is why God has laid down those limits which, in Islamic phraseology, are termed "divine limits." These limits consist of certain principles, checks and balances and specific injunctions in different spheres of life and activity, and they have been prescribed in order that man may be trained to lead a balanced and moderate fife. They are intended to lay down the broad framework within which man is free to legislate, decide his own affairs and frame subsidiary laws and regulations for his conduct. These limits he is not permitted to overstep and if he does so, the whole scheme of his fife will go awry.

Take for example man's economic life. In this sphere God has placed certain restrictions on human freedom. The right to private property has been recognized, but it is qualified by the obligation to pay *Zakah* (poor dues) and the prohibition of interest, gambling and speculation. A specific law of inheritance for the distribution of property among the largest number of surviving relations on the death of its owner has been laid down and certain forms of acquiring, accumulating and spending wealth have been declared unlawful. If people observe these just limits and regulate their affairs within these boundary walls, on the one hand their personal liberty is adequately safeguarded and, on the other, the possibility of class war and domination of one class over another, which begins with capitalist oppression and ends in working-class dictatorship, is safely and conveniently eliminated.

Similarly in the sphere of family life, God has prohibited the unrestricted intermingling of the sexes and has prescribed *Pardah* [practices secluding women, such as veiling], recognized man's guardianship of woman, and clearly defined the rights and duties of husband, wife and children. The laws of divorce and separation have been clearly set forth, conditional polygamy has been permitted and penalties for fornication and false accusations of adultery have been prescribed. He has thus laid down limits which, if observed by man, would stabilize his family life and make it a haven of peace and happiness. There would remain neither that tyranny of male over female which makes family life an inferno of cruelty and oppression, nor that satanic flood of female liberty and license which threatens to destroy human civilization in the West.

In like manner, for the preservation of human culture and society God has, by formulating the law of *Qisydsy* (Retaliation) commanding to cut off the hands for theft, prohibiting winedrinking, placing limitations on uncovering of one's private parts and by laying down a few similar permanent rules and regulations, closed the door of social disorder forever. I have no time to present to you a complete list of all the divine limits and show in detail how essential each one of them is for maintaining equilibrium and poise in life. What I want to bring home to you here is that through these injunctions God has provided a permanent and immutable code of behavior for man, and that it does not deprive him of any essential liberty nor does it dull the edge of his mental faculties. On the contrary, it sets a straight and clear path before him, so that he may not, owing to his ignorance and weaknesses which he inherently possesses, lose himself in the maze of destruction and instead of wasting his faculties in the pursuit of wrong ends, he may follow the road that leads to success and progress in this world and the hereafter. If you have ever happened to visit a mountainous region, you must have noticed that in the winding mountain paths which are bounded by deep caves on the one side and lofty rocks on the other, the border of the road is barricaded and protected in such a way as to prevent travellers from straying towards the abyss by mistake. Are these barricades intended to deprive the wayfarer of his liberty? No, as a matter of fact, they are meant to protect him from destruction; to warn him at every bend of the dangers ahead and to show him the path leading to his destination. That precisely is the purpose of the restrictions which God has laid down in His revealed Code. These limits determine what direction man should take in life's journey and they guide him at every turn and pass and point out to him the path of safety which he should steadfastly follow.

As I have already stated, this code, enacted as it is by God, is unchangeable. You can, if you like, rebel against it, as some Muslim countries have done. But you cannot alter it. It will continue to be unalterable till the last day. It has its own avenues of growth and evolution, but no human being has any right to tamper with it. Whenever an Islamic State comes into existence, this code would form its fundamental law and will constitute the mainspring of all its legislation. Everyone who desires to remain a Muslim is under an obligation to follow the Qur'an and the Sunnah which must constitute the basic law of an Islamic State.

> *We verily sent Our messengers with clear proofs, and revealed with them the Scripture and the Balance, that mankind may observe right measure; and We revealed iron, wherein is mighty power and (many) uses for mankind. (57:25)*

In this verse steel symbolizes political power and the verse also makes it clear that the mission of the Prophets is to create conditions in which the mass of people will be assured of social justice in accordance with the standards enunciated by God in His Book which gives explicit instructions for a well-disciplined mode of life. In another place God has said:

(Muslims are) those who, if We give them power in the land, establish the system of salah (worship) and Zakah (poor dues) and enjoin virtue and forbid evil and inequity. (22:41)

You are the best community sent forth to mankind; you enjoin the Right conduct and forbid the wrong; and you believe in Allah. (3:110)

It will readily become manifest to anyone who reflects upon these verses that the purpose of the state visualized by the Holy Qur'an is not negative but positive. The object of the state is not merely to prevent people from exploiting each other, to safeguard their liberty and to protect its subjects from foreign invasion. It also aims at evolving and developing that well-balanced system of social justice which has been set forth by God in His Holy Book. Its object is to eradicate all forms of evil and to encourage all types of virtue and excellence expressly mentioned by God in the Holy Qur'an. For this purpose political power will be made use of as and when the occasion demands; all means of propaganda and peaceful persuasion will be employed; the moral education of the people will also be undertaken; and social influence as well as the force of public opinion will be harnessed to the task. . . .

Buddhism

Siddhartha Guatama was born a Nepalese prince, about 563 B.C. and raised in luxury. Traveling outside the palace as a young man, he saw human misery—pain, disease, hunger—and was deeply touched by it. When he was 29 years old he decided to seek the solution of human suffering through meditation and fasting. He studied with the wise men, he starved himself and practiced other austerities, but nothing worked until he decided to sit under a tree without moving until he received some sign of truth. That worked. He attained "enlightenment"; thereafter he was known as "the Buddha," or "the Enlightened One" (and the tree under which he sat became known as the "Bo-Tree," or "Tree of Enlightenment"). The wisdom he had received was that freedom from suffering came only in nirvana, *freedom or release, a mental state in which suffering was no more. Thereafter he taught that all could reach* nirvana *and should strive to attain it, and he developed a series of mental exercises designed to help to reach it. He founded an order of monks to practice and carry out his teaching, and continued active until he died at the age of 80 in 483 B.C., before Socrates was born. His teaching is summarized in* The Four Noble Truths.

The Four Noble Truths

The Buddha is speaking:

17. "Again, monks, a monk abides contemplating mind-objects as mind-objects in respect of the Four Noble Truths. How does he do so? Here, a monk knows as it really is: 'This is suffering'; he knows as it really is: 'This is the origin of suffering'; he knows as it really is: 'This is the cessation of suffering'; he knows as it really is: 'This is the way of practice leading to the cessation of suffering.'

18. "And what, monks, is the Noble Truth of Suffering? Birth is suffering, aging is suffering, death is suffering, sorrow, lamentation, pain, sadness and distress are suffering. Being attached to the unloved is suffering, being separated from the loved is suffering, not getting what one wants is suffering. In short, the five aggregates of grasping are suffering. . . .

"And how, monks, in short, are the five aggregates of grasping suffering? They are as follows: the aggregate of grasping that is form, the aggregate of grasping that is feeling, the aggregate of grasping that is perception, the aggregate of grasping that is the mental formations, the aggregate of grasping that is consciousness. These are, in short, the five aggregates of grasping that are suffering. ["Form" seems to refer to the physical body, "feelings" to the data of the senses, "perception" to the consciousness of sensation, "mental formations" to the dispositions to action that arise from sensations, and "consciousness" to the sum total of all of the above.] And that, monks, is called the Noble Truth of Suffering.

19. "And what, monks, is the Noble Truth of the Origin of Suffering? It is that craving which gives rise to rebirth, bound up with pleasure and lust, finding fresh delight now here, now there: that is to say sensual craving, craving for existence, and craving for non-existence.

"And where does this craving arise and establish itself? Wherever in the world there is anything agreeable and pleasurable, there this craving arises and establishes itself.

"And what is there in the world that is agreeable and pleasurable? The eye in the world is agreeable and pleasurable, the ear . . ., the nose . . ., the tongue . . ., the body . . ., the mind in the world is agreeable and pleasurable, and there this craving arises and establishes itself. Sights, sounds, smells, tastes, tangibles, mind-objects in the world are agreeable and pleasurable, and there this craving arises and establishes itself.

"The craving for sights, sounds, smells, tastes, tangibles, mind-objects in the world is agreeable and pleasurable, and there this craving arises and establishes itself.

"Thinking of sights, sounds, smells, tastes, tangibles, mind-objects in the world is agreeable and pleasurable, and there this craving arises and establishes itself. "Pondering on sights, sounds, smells, tastes, tangibles and mind-objects in the world is agreeable and pleasurable, and there this craving arises and establishes itself. And that, monks, is called the Noble Truth of the Origin of Suffering.

20. "And what, monks, is the Noble Truth of the Cessation of Suffering? It is the complete fading-away and extinction of this craving, its forsaking and abandonment, liberation from it, detachment from it. And how does this craving come to be abandoned, how does its cessation come about? . . .

21. "And what, monks, is the Noble Truth of the Way of Practice Leading to the Cessation of Suffering? It is just this Noble Eightfold Path, namely:—Right View, Right Thought; Right Speech, Right Action, Right Livelihood; Right Effort, Right Mindfulness, Right Concentration.

"And what, monks, is Right View? It is, monks, the knowledge of suffering, the knowledge of the origin of suffering, the knowledge of the cessation of suffering, and the knowledge of the way of practice leading to the cessation of suffering. This is called Right View.

"And what, monks, is Right Thought? The thought of renunciation, the thought of non-ill-will, the thought of harmlessness. This, monks, is called Right Thought.

"And what, monks, is Right Speech? Refraining from lying, refraining from slander, refraining from harsh speech, refraining from frivolous speech. This is called Right Speech.

"And what, monks, is Right Action? Refraining from taking life, refraining from taking what is not given, refraining from sexual misconduct. This is called Right Action.

"And what, monks, is Right Livelihood? Here, monks, the Ariyan disciple, having given up wrong livelihood, keeps himself by right livelihood.

"And what, monks, is Right Effort? Here, monks, a monk rouses his will, makes an effort, stirs up energy, exerts his mind and strives to prevent the arising of unarisen evil unwholesome mental states. He rouses his will . . . and strives to overcome evil unwholesome mental states that have arisen. He rouses his will . . . and strives to produce unarisen wholesome mental states. He rouses his will, makes an effort, stirs up energy, exerts his mind and strives to maintain wholesome mental states that have arisen, not to let them fade away, to bring them to greater growth, to the full perfection of development. This is called Right Effort.

"And what, monks, is Right Mindfulness? Here, monks, a monk abides contemplating body as body, ardent, clearly aware and mindful, having put aside hankering and fretting for the world; he abides contemplating feelings as feelings . . .; he abides contemplating mind as mind . . .; he abides contemplating mind-objects as mind-objects, ardent, clearly aware and mindful, having put aside hankering and fretting for the world. This is called Right Mindfulness.

"And what, monks, is Right Concentration? Here, a monk, detached from sense-desires, detached from unwholesome mental states, enters and remains in the first *jhana* [*jhana*, or *dhyana*, is a heightened state of awareness that occurs in meditation], which is with thinking and pondering, born of detachment, filled with delight and joy. And with the subsiding of thinking and pondering, by gaining inner tranquillity and oneness of mind, he enters and remains in the second *jhana*, which is without thinking and pondering, born of concentration, filled with delight and joy. And with the fading away of delight, remaining imperturbable, mindful and clearly aware, he experiences in himself the joy of which the Noble Ones say: "Happy is he who dwells with equanimity and mindfulness," he enters the third *jhana*. And, having given up pleasure and pain, and with the disappearance of former gladness and sadness, he enters and remains in the fourth *jhana*, which is beyond pleasure and pain, and purified by equanimity and mindfulness. This is called Right Concentration. And that, monks, is called the way of practice leading to the cessation of suffering."

> *Aflame with the denunciations of Amos, Micah, and Jesus, the Western reader may find the Buddha's reaction to the pain and suffering of the world somewhat disappointing. The monks are urged to act with vigor, and concentration, and rouse their wills, and make every effort—to keep impure thoughts from their minds? How's that going to help the poor? Yet we will see this reaction to the sinful world (often called "quietism") again in the Western monastic tradition, given philosophical form in the Stoics.*
>
> *Beyond the unfamiliar withdrawal from our customary activism, some of the Buddha's teachings are simply mysterious. That "Eightfold Path" is more suggestive than indicative, and probably leaves most of us in confusion. The next passage, a commentary on the Fourth Noble Truth by a Buddhist scholar from Sri Lanka, the Rev. Dr. Walpola Rahula, is an essay at clarification.*

From Walpola Rahula, *What the Buddha Taught*

"The Fourth Noble Truth"

The Fourth Noble Truth is that of the Way leading to the Cessation of *Dukkha* [suffering] (*Dukkhanirodhagdminfpatipadaariyasacca*). This is known as the "Middle Path" (*Majjhima Patipada*), because it avoids two extremes: one extreme being the search for happiness through the pleasures of the senses, which is "low, common, unprofitable and the way of the ordinary people"; the other being the search for happiness through self-mortification in different forms of asceticism, which is "painful, unworthy and unprofitable." Having himself first tried these two extremes, and having found them to be useless, the Buddha discovered through personal experience the Middle Path "which gives vision and knowledge, which leads to Calm, Insight, Enlightenment, *Nirvana*." This Middle Path is generally referred to as the Noble Eightfold Path (*Ariya-Atthansgika-Magga*), because it is composed of eight categories or divisions: namely,

1. Right Understanding (*Samma ditthi*)
2. Right Thought (*Samma sanskappa*)

3. Right Speech (*Samma vaca*)
4. Right Action (*Samma kammanta*)
5. Right Livelihood (*Samma ajiva*)
6. Right Effort (*Samma vayama*)
7. Right Mindfulness (*Samma sati*)
8. Right Concentration (*Samma samadhi*)

Practically the whole teaching of the Buddha, to which he devoted himself during 45 years, deals in some way or other with this Path. He explained it in different ways and in different words to different people, according to the stage of their development and their capacity to understand and follow him. But the essence of those many thousand discourses scattered in the Buddhist Scriptures is found in the Noble Eightfold Path.

It should not be thought that the eight categories or divisions of the Path should be followed and practiced one after the other in the numerical order as given in the usual list above. But they are to be developed more or less simultaneously, as far as possible according to the capacity of each individual. They are all linked together and each helps the cultivation of the others.

These eight factors aim at promoting and perfecting the three essentials of Buddhist training and discipline: namely: (a) Ethical Conduct (*Sila*), (b) Mental Discipline (*Samadhi*) and (c) Wisdom (*Panna*). It will therefore be more helpful for a coherent and better understanding of the eight divisions of the Path, if we group them and explain them according to these three heads.

Ethical Conduct is built on the vast conception of universal love and compassion for all living beings, on which the Buddha's teaching is based. It is regrettable that many scholars forget this great ideal of the Buddha's teaching, and indulge in only dry philosophical and metaphysical divagations when they talk and write about Buddhism. The Buddha gave his teaching "for the good of the many, for the happiness of the many, out of compassion for the world" (*bahujanahitaya bahujanasukhaya lokanukampaya*).

According to Buddhism, for a man to be perfect there are two qualities that he should develop equally: compassion (*karuna*) on one side, and wisdom (*panna*) on the other. Here compassion represents love, charity, kindness, tolerance and such noble qualities on the emotional side, or qualities of the heart, while wisdom would stand for the intellectual side or the qualities of the mind. If one develops only the emotional, neglecting the intellectual, one may become a good-hearted fool; while to develop only the intellectual side neglecting the emotional may turn one into a hard-hearted intellect without feeling for others. Therefore, to be perfect one has to develop both equally. That is the aim of the Buddhist way of life: in it wisdom and compassion are inseparably linked together . . .

Now, in Ethical Conduct (*Sila*), based on love and compassion, are included three factors of the Noble Eightfold Path: namely, Right Speech, Right Action and Right Livelihood (Nos. 3, 4 and 5 in the list).

Right speech means abstention (1) from telling lies, (2) from backbiting and slander and talk that may bring about hatred, enmity, disunity and disharmony among individuals or groups of people, (3) from harsh, rude, impolite, malicious and abusive language, and (4) from idle, useless and foolish babble and gossip. When one abstains from these forms of wrong and harmful speech one naturally has to speak the truth, has to use words that are friendly and benevolent, pleasant and gentle, meaningful and useful. One should not speak carelessly: speech should be at the right time and place. If one cannot say something useful, one should keep "noble silence."

Right Action aims at promoting moral, honorable, and peaceful conduct. It admonishes us that we should abstain from destroying life, from stealing, from dishonest dealings, from illegitimate sexual intercourse, and that we should also help others to lead a peaceful and honorable life in the right way.

Right Livelihood means that one should abstain from making one's living through a profession that brings harm to others, such as trading in arms and lethal weapons, intoxicating drinks, poisons, killing animals, cheating, etc., and should live by a profession which is honorable, blameless and innocent of harm to others. One can clearly see here that Buddhism is strongly opposed to any kind of war, when it lays down that trade in arms and lethal weapons is an evil and unjust means of livelihood.

These three factors (Right Speech, Right Action and Right Livelihood) of the Eightfold Path constitute Ethical Conduct. It should be realized that the Buddhist ethical and moral conduct aims at promoting a happy and harmonious life both for the individual and for society. This moral conduct is considered as the indispensable foundation for all higher spiritual attainments. No spiritual development is possible without this moral basis.

Next comes Mental Discipline, in which are included three other factors of the Eightfold Path: namely, Right Effort, Right Mindfulness (or Attentiveness) and Right Concentration. (Nos. 6, 7 and 8 in the list).

Right Effort is the energetic will (1) to prevent evil and unwholesome states of mind from arising, and (2) to get rid of such evil and unwholesome states that have already arisen within a man, and also (3) to produce, to cause to arise, good and wholesome states of mind not yet arisen, and (4) to develop and bring to perfection the good and wholesome states of mind already present in a man.

Right Mindfulness (or Attentiveness) is to be diligently aware, mindful and attentive with regard to (1) the activities of the body (*kaya*), (2) sensations or feelings (*vedana*), (3) the activities of the mind (*citta*) and (4) ideas, thoughts, conceptions and things (*dhamma*).

The practice of concentration on breathing (*anapanasati*) is one of the well-known exercises, connected with the body, for mental development. There are several other ways of developing attentiveness in relation to the body-as modes of meditation.

With regard to sensations and feelings, one should be clearly aware of all forms of feelings and sensations, pleasant, unpleasant and neutral, of how they appear and disappear within oneself.

Concerning the activities of mind, one should be aware whether one's mind is lustful or not, given to hatred or not, deluded or not, distracted or concentrated, etc. In this way one should be aware of all movements of mind, how they arise and disappear.

As regards ideas, thoughts, conceptions and things, one should know their nature, how they appear and disappear, how they are developed, how they are suppressed, and destroyed, and so on.

These four forms of mental culture or meditation are treated in detail in the *Satipatthanasutta* (Setting-up of Mindfulness).

The third and last factor of Mental Discipline is Right Concentration leading to the four stages of *Dhyana*, generally called trance or *recueillement*. In the first stage of *Dhyana*, passionate desires and certain unwholesome thoughts like sensuous lust, ill-will, languor, worry, restlessness, and skeptical doubt are discarded, and feelings of joy and happiness are maintained, along with certain mental activities. In the second stage, all intellectual activities are suppressed, tranquillity and "one-pointedness" of mind developed, and the feelings of joy and happiness are still retained. In the third stage, the feeling of joy, which is an active sensation, also disappears, while the disposition of happiness still remains in addition to mindful equanimity. In the fourth stage of *Dhyana*, all sensations, even of happiness and unhappiness, of joy and sorrow, disappear, only pure equanimity and awareness remaining.

Thus the mind is trained and disciplined and developed through Right Effort, Right Mindfulness, and Right Concentration.

The remaining two factors, namely Right Thought and Right Understanding go to constitute Wisdom.

Right Thought denotes the thoughts of selfless renunciation or detachment, thoughts of love and thoughts of non-violence, which are extended to all beings. It is very interesting and important to note here that thoughts of selfless detachment, love, and non-violence are grouped on the side of wisdom. This clearly shows that true wisdom is endowed with these noble qualities, and that all thoughts of selfish desire, ill-will, hatred and violence are the result of a lack of wisdom—in all spheres of life whether individual, social, or political.

Right Understanding is the understanding of things as they are, and it is the Four Noble Truths that explain things as they really are. Right Understanding, therefore, is ultimately reduced to the understanding of the Four Noble Truths. This understanding is the highest wisdom which sees the Ultimate Reality. According to Buddhism there are two sorts of understanding: What we generally call understanding is knowledge, an accumulated memory, an intellectual grasping of a subject according to certain given data. This is called "knowing accordingly" (*anubodha*). It is not very deep. Real deep understanding is called "penetration" (*pativedha*), seeing a thing in its true nature, without name and label. This penetration is possible only when the mind is free from all impurities and is fully developed through meditation.

From this brief account of the Path, one may see that it is a way of life to be followed, practised and developed by each individual. It is self-discipline in body, word and mind, self-development and self-purification. It has nothing to do with belief, prayer, worship or ceremony. In that sense, it has nothing which may popularly be called "religious." It is a Path leading to the realization of Ultimate Reality, to complete freedom, happiness and peace through moral, spiritual and intellectual perfection. . . .

Confucianism

Confucius (K'ung-fu-tzu or Kongfuzi, "Master K'ung") was born in China, in the state of Lu, in 551 B.C. Like the Buddha, he was of royal or noble blood (according to tradition), and was moved, as was the Buddha, by his compassion for the poor in the political chaos of his times to develop a system within which people could live at peace. His teaching became immensely respected, even venerated; his books, known as the Confucian Classics (for the most part written by his disciples some time after his death) became the basis of the Civil Service exams in China from early in the fourteenth century to the twentieth! Because the works of Confucius formed a common educational foundation to the educated classes of Chinese, his "sayings" became the cited justifications for moral decisions, even as the Homeric writings were to the Greeks and the Bible to colonial Americans. In "The Great Learning," an essay from The Book of Rites, *the central theme is self-cultivation; note that Confucius expected that self-examination was centrally important to all efforts to improve society. The short passages from "The Doctrine of the Mean" capture the aphoristic style of the Confucian writings, and illustrate both the difficulty of constructing an extended train of "Confucian" argument and the ease of translating Confucian thought into practical applications. The writings compare usefully to the Christian Gospels—late recorded, half-remembered, disconnected lessons that still retain their moral power.*

The Great Learning

The Way of the Great Learning consists in clearly exemplifying illustrious virtue, in loving the people, and in resting in the highest good.

Only when one knows where one is to rest can one have a fixed purpose. Only with a fixed purpose can one achieve calmness of mind. Only with calmness of mind can one attain serene repose. Only in serene repose can one carry on careful deliberation. Only through careful deliberation can one have achievement. Things have their roots and branches; affairs have their beginning and end. He who knows what comes first and what comes last comes himself near the Way.

The ancients who wished clearly to exemplify illustrious virtue throughout the world would first set up good government in their states. Wishing to govern well their states, they would first regulate their families. Wishing to regulate their families, they would first cultivate their persons. Wishing to cultivate their persons, they would first rectify their minds. Wishing to rectify their minds, they would first seek sincerity in their thoughts. Wishing for sincerity in their thoughts, they would first extend their knowledge. The extension of knowledge lay in the investigation of things. For only when things are investigated is knowledge extended; only when knowledge is extended are thoughts sincere; only when thoughts are sincere are minds rectified; only when minds are rectified are our persons cultivated; only when our persons are cultivated are our families regulated; only when families are regulated are states well governed; and only when states are well governed is there peace in the world.

From the emperor down to the common people, all, without exception, must consider cultivation of the individual character as the root. If the root is in disorder, it is impossible for the branches to be in order. To treat the important as unimportant and to treat the unimportant as important—this should never be. This is called knowing the root; this is called the perfection of knowledge. . . .

What is meant by saying that "the cultivation of the person depends on the rectification of the mind" is this: When one is under the influence of anger, one's mind will not be correct; when one is under the influence of fear, it will not be correct; when one is under the influence of fond regard, it will not be correct; when one is under the influence of anxiety, it will not be correct. When the mind is not there, we gaze at things but do not see; we listen but do not hear; we eat but do not know the flavors. This is what is meant by saying that the cultivation of the person depends on the rectification of the mind. . . .

What is meant by saying that "the government of the state depends on the regulation of the family" is this: One can never teach outsiders if one cannot teach one's own family. Therefore the prince perfects the proper teaching for the whole country without going outside his family; the filial piety wherewith one serves his sovereign, the brotherly respect wherewith one treats his elders, the kindness wherewith one deals with the multitude. There is the saying in the "Announcement to K'ang" [in the *Book of History*]; "Act as if you were rearing an infant." If you set yourself to a task with heart and soul you will not go far wrong even if you do not hit the mark. No girl has ever learned to suckle an infant before she got married.

If one family [the ruler's family] exemplifies humanity, humanity will abound in the whole country. If one family exemplifies courtesy, courtesy will abound in the whole country. On the other hand, if one man [the ruler] exemplifies greed and wickedness, rebellious disorder will arise in the whole country. Therein lies the secret. Hence the proverb: One word ruins an enterprise; one man determines the fate of an empire. Yao and Shun ruled the empire with humanity, and the people followed them. Chieh and Chou ruled the empire with cruelty, and the people only submitted to them. Since these last commanded actions that they themselves would not like to take, the people refused to follow them. Thus it is that what [virtues] a prince finds in himself he may expect in others, and what [vices] he himself is free from he may condemn in others. It is impossible that a man devoid of every virtue which he might wish to have in others could be able effectively to instruct them.

Thus we see why it is that "the government of the state depends on the regulation of the family.". . .

What is meant by saying that "the establishment of peace in the world depends on the government of the state" is this: When superiors accord to the aged their due, then the common people will be inspired to practice filial piety; when superiors accord to elders their due, then the common people will be inspired to practice brotherly respect; when superiors show compassion to the orphaned, then the common people do not do otherwise. Thus the gentleman has a principle with which, as with a measuring square, he may regulate his conduct.

What a man dislikes in his superiors let him not display in his treatment of his inferiors; what he dislikes in his inferiors let him not display in his service to his superiors; what he dislikes in those before him let him not set before those who are behind him; what he dislikes in those behind him let him not therewith follow those who are before him; what he dislikes from those on his right let him not bestow upon those on his left; what he dislikes from those on his left let him not bestow upon those on his right. This is called the regulating principle of the measuring square.

The Doctrine of the Mean

Chung-ni (Confucius) said, "The superior man [exemplifies] the Mean (*chung-yung*)." The inferior man acts contrary to the Mean. The superior man [exemplifies] the Mean because, as a superior man, he can maintain the Mean at any time. The inferior man [acts contrary to] the Mean because, as an inferior man, he has no caution."

Confucius said, "Perfect is the Mean. For a long time few people have been able to follow it."

Confucius said, "I know why the Way is not pursued. The intelligent go beyond it and the stupid do not come up to it. I know why the Way is not understood. The worthy go beyond it and the unworthy do not come up to it. There is no one who does not eat and drink, but there are few who can really know flavor."

Confucius said, "Alas! How is the Way not being pursued!"

Confucius said, "Shun was indeed a man of great wisdom! He loved to question others and to examine their words, however ordinary. He concealed what was bad in them and displayed what was good. He took hold of their two extremes, took the mean between them, and applied it in his dealing with the people. This was how he became Shun (the sage-emperor)."

Confucius said, "Men all say, 'I am wise'; but when driven forward and taken in a net, a trap, or a pitfall, none knows how to escape. Men all say, 'I am wise'; but should they choose the course of the Mean, they are not able to keep it for a round month."

Confucius said, "Hui was a man who chose the course of the Mean, and when he got hold of one thing that was good, he clasped it firmly as if wearing it on his breast and never lost it."

Confucius said, "The empire, the states, and the families can be put in order. Ranks and emolument can be declined. A bare, naked weapon can be tramped upon. But the Mean cannot [easily] be attained."

Tzu-lu asked about strength. Confucius said, "Do you mean the strength of the South, the strength of the North, or the strength you should cultivate yourself? To be genial and gentle in teaching others and not to revenge unreasonable conduct—this is the strength of the people of the South. The superior man lives by it. To lie under arms and meet death without regret—this is the strength of the people of the North. The strong man lives by it. Therefore the superior man maintains harmony [in his nature and conduct] and does not waver. How unflinching is his strength! He stands in the middle position and does not lean to one side. How unflinching is his strength! When the Way prevails in the state, [if he enters public life], he does not change from what he was in private life. How unflinching is his strength! When the Way does not prevail in the state, he does not change even unto death. How unflinching is his strength!"

"There are men who seek for the abstruse, and practice wonders. Future generations may mention them. But that is what I will not do. There are superior men who act in accordance with the Way, but give up when they have gone half way. But I can never give up. There are superior men who are in accord with the Mean, retire from the world and are unknown to their age, but do not regret. It is only a sage who can do this."

"The Way of the superior man functions everywhere and yet is hidden. Men and women of simple intelligence can share its knowledge; and yet in its utmost reaches, there is something which even the sage does not know. Men and women of simple intelligence can put it into practice; and yet in its utmost reaches there is something which even the sage is not able to put into practice. Great as heaven and earth are, men still find something in them with which to be dissatisfied. Thus with [the Way of] the superior man, if one speaks of its greatness, nothing in the world can contain it, and if one speaks of its smallness, nothing in the world can split it. The *Book of Odes* says, 'The hawk flies up to heaven; the fishes leap in the deep.' This means that [the Way] is clearly seen above and below. The Way of the superior man has its simple beginnings in the relation between man and woman, but in its utmost reaches, it is clearly seen in heaven and on earth." . . .

Confucius said, "The Way is not far from man. When a man pursues the Way and yet remains away from man, his course cannot be considered the Way, The *Book of Odes* says, 'In hewing an axe handle, the pattern is not far off.' If we take an axe handle to hew another axe handle and look askance from the one to the other, we may still think the pattern is far away. Therefore the superior man governs men as men, in accordance with human nature, and as soon as they change [what is wrong], he stops. Conscientiousness (*chung*) and altruism (*shu*) are not far from the Way. What you do not wish others to do to you, do not do to them.

"There are four things in the Way of the superior man, none of which I have been able to do. To serve my father as I would expect my son to serve me: that I have not been able to do. To serve my ruler as I would expect my ministers to serve me: that I have not been able to do. To serve my elder brothers as I would expect my younger brothers to serve me: that I have not been able to do. To be the first to treat friends as I would expect them to treat me: that I have not been able to do. In practicing the ordinary virtues and in the exercise of care in ordinary conversation, when there is deficiency, the superior man never fails to make further effort, and when there is excess, never dares to go to the limit. His words correspond to his actions and his actions correspond to his words. Isn't the superior man earnest and genuine?" . . .

The superior man does what is proper to his position and does not want to go beyond this. If he is in a noble station, he does what is proper to a position of wealth and honorable station. If he is in a humble station, he does what is proper to a position of poverty and humble station. If he is in the midst of barbarian tribes, he does what is proper in the midst of barbarian tribes. In a position of difficulty and danger, he does what is proper to a position of difficulty and danger. He can find himself in no situation in which he is not at ease with himself. In a high position he does not treat his inferiors with contempt. In a low position he does not court the favor of his superiors. He rectifies himself and seeks nothing from others, hence he has no complaint to make. He does not complain against Heaven above or blame men below. Thus it is that the superior man lives peacefully and at ease and waits for his destiny (*ming*, Mandate of Heaven, fate), while the inferior man takes to dangerous courses and hopes for good luck. Confucius said, "In archery we have something resembling the Way of the superior man. When the archer misses the center of the target, he turns around and seeks for the cause of failure within himself. . . ."

Duke Ai asked about government. Confucius said, "The governmental measures of King Wen and King Wu are spread out in the records. With their kind of men, government will flourish. When their kind of men are gone, their government will come to an end. When the right principles of man operate, the growth of good government is rapid, and when the right principles of soil operate, the growth of vegetables is rapid. Indeed, government is comparable to a fast-growing plant. Therefore the conduct of government depends upon the men. The right men are obtained by the ruler's personal character. The cultivation of the person is to be done through the Way, and the cultivation of the Way is to be done through humanity. Humanity (*jen*) is [the distinguishing characteristic of] man, and the greatest application of it is in being affectionate toward relatives. Righteousness is the principle of setting things right and proper, and the greatest application of it is in honoring the worthy. The relative degree of affection we ought to feel for our relatives and the relative grades in the honoring of the worthy give rise to the rules of propriety. . .

Therefore the ruler must not fail to cultivate his personal life. Wishing to cultivate his personal life, he must not fail to serve his parents. Wishing to serve his parents, he must not fail to know man. Wishing to know man, he must not fail to know Heaven.

There are five universal ways [in human relations], and the way by which they are practiced is three. The five are those governing the relationship between ruler and minister, between father and son, between husband and wife, between elder and younger brothers, and those in the intercourse between friends. These five are universal paths in the world. Wisdom, humanity, and courage, these three are the universal virtues. The way by which they are practiced is one.

Some are born with the knowledge [of these virtues]. Some learn it through study. Some learn it through hard work. But when the knowledge is acquired, it comes to the same thing. Some practice them naturally and easily. Some practice them for their advantage. Some practice them with effort and difficulty. But when the achievement is made, it comes to the same thing.

Confucius said, "Love of learning is akin to wisdom. To practice with vigor is akin to humanity. To know to be shameful is akin to courage. He who knows these three things knows how to cultivate his personal life. Knowing how to cultivate his personal life, he knows how to govern other men. And knowing how to govern other men, he knows how to govern the empire, its states, and the families."

There are nine standards by which to administer the empire, its states, and the families. They are: cultivating the personal life, honoring the worthy, being affectionate to relatives, being respectful toward the great ministers, identifying oneself with the welfare of the whole body of officers, treating the common people as one's own children, attracting the various artisans, showing tenderness to strangers from far countries, and extending kindly and awesome influence on the feudal lords. If the ruler cultivates his personal life, the Way will be established. If he honors the worthy, he will not be perplexed. If he is affectionate to his relatives, there will be no grumbling among his uncles and brothers. If he respects the great ministers, he will not be deceived. If he identifies himself with the welfare of the whole body of officers, then the officers will repay him heavily for his courtesies. If he treats the common people as his own children, then the masses will exhort one another [to do good]. If he attracts the various artisans, there will be sufficiency of wealth and resources in the country. If he shows tenderness to strangers from far countries, people from all quarters of the world will flock to him. And if he extends kindly and awesome influence over the feudal lords, then the world will stand in awe of him.

To fast, to purify, and to be correct in dress [at the time of solemn sacrifice], and not to make any movement contrary to the rules of propriety—this is the way to cultivate the personal life. To avoid slanderers, keep away seductive beauties, regard wealth lightly, and honor virtue—this is the way to encourage the worthy. To give them honorable position, to bestow on them ample emoluments, and to share their likes and dislikes—this is the way to encourage affection for relatives. To allow them many officers to carry out their functions—this is the way to encourage the great ministers. To deal with them loyally and faithfully and to give them ample emoluments—this is the way to encourage the body of officers. To require them for service only at the proper time [without interfering with their farm work] and to tax them lightly—this is the way to encourage the common masses. To inspect them daily and examine them monthly and to reward them according to the degree of their workmanship—this is the way to encourage the various artisans. To welcome them when they come and send them off when they go and to commend the good among them and show compassion to the incompetent—this is the way to show tenderness to strangers from far countries. To restore lines of broken succession, to revive states that have been extinguished, to bring order to chaotic states, to support those states that are in danger, to have fixed times for their attendance at court, and to present them with generous gifts while expecting little when they come—this is the way to extend kindly and awesome influence on the feudal lords.

There are nine standards by which to govern the empire, its states, and the families, but the way by which they are followed is one. In all matters if there is preparation they will succeed; if there is no preparation, they will fail. If what is to be said is determined beforehand, there will be no stumbling. If the business to be done is determined beforehand, there will be no difficulty. If action to be taken is determined beforehand, there will be no trouble. And if the way to be pursued is determined beforehand, there will be no difficulties. If those in inferior positions do not have the confidence of their superiors, they will not be able to govern the people. There is a way to have the confidence of the superiors: If one is not trusted by his friends, he will not have the confidence of his superiors. There is a way to be trusted by one's friends: If one is not obedient to his parents, he will not be trusted by his friends. There is a way to obey one's parents: If one examines himself and finds himself to be insincere, he will not be obedient to his parents. There is a way to be sincere with oneself. If one does not understand what is good, he will not be sincere with himself. Sincerity is the Way of Heaven. To think how to be sincere is the way of man. He who is sincere is one who hits upon what is right without effort and apprehends without thinking. He is naturally and easily in harmony with the Way. Such a man is a sage. He who tries to be sincere is one who chooses the good and holds fast to it.

Study it (the way to be sincere) extensively, inquire into it accurately, think over it carefully, sift it clearly, and practice it earnestly. When there is anything not yet studied, or studied but not yet understood, do not give up. When there is any question not yet asked, or asked but its answer not yet known, do not give up. When there is anything not yet thought over, or thought over but not yet apprehended, do not give up. When there is anything not yet sifted, or sifted but not yet clear, do not give up. When there is anything not yet practiced, or practiced but not yet earnestly, do not give up. If another man succeed by one effort, you will use a hundred efforts. If another man succeed by ten efforts, you will use a thousand efforts. If one really follows this course, though stupid, he will surely become intelligent, and though weak, will surely become strong. . . .

Native Americans

The human race did not start out worshiping one god, let alone one male god. Wherever we have found people (in isolated tribal groups) who have not been exposed to the vigorous civilizing and evangelizing efforts of developed Western societies, we have found them worshiping a variety of local deities, most of them associated with the way the tribe supports itself economically—the sun for the crops, the sea, the land, the animals. Such religious practice assumes that all things have souls, and is generally called "animism." (If you don't like it, you'll call it "paganism," or "heathenism.") Animism is where we all started, worshiping the natural world around us and the fertility of people, animals, and land that enabled us to keep going as a species. We have little in the way of description of the ancient practices. It is hard to get accurate pictures of the religious belief and associated moral imperatives even of contemporary tribal groups, if only because they are rarely literate before we find them and the missionaries get them thoroughly confused before the anthropologists get there. Possibly our best sources are among the American Indians, or Native Americans, who maintained thriving animistic societies at least through the nineteenth century, right here where they could be observed. Although greatly reduced in number by war and especially by the European diseases we brought with us across the Atlantic, the tribes survived; and when in the latter part of the twentieth century the grandchildren of the animists sat down to describe their cultures in writing, they found memories still fresh.

Why did they start to write? Because by the latter third of the twentieth century, it had become very clear that the American's relation to the land was badly troubled, characterized by toxic emissions from factory and automobile, deforested acres of mountainside, oceans of indestructible plastic and styrofoam in shrinking "landfills." We were destroying the earth, and undermining our own existence. Hence the renewed interest in civilizations that seemed to be in touch with nature and to maintain a more sustainable relationship with the earth.

This is why we began to accumulate a body of literature on Native American approaches to the land. As early as 1887, when the (bogus) "1854 Oration of Chief Seattle" was published in the Seattle Sunday Star, *Native Americans were assigned the role of victim/judge of our national expansion and practices in the exploitation of nature. (The last selection in this text, Aldo Leopold's "The Land Ethic," puts the defense of nature in more standard Western terms.)*

From Ed McGaa ("Eagle Man"), *We Are All Related*

The plight of the non-Indian world is that it has lost respect for Mother Earth, from whom and where we all come.

We all start out in this world as tiny seeds—no different from our animal brothers and sisters, the deer, the bear, the buffalo, or the trees, the flowers, the winged people. Every particle of our bodies comes from the good things Mother Earth has put forth. Mother Earth is our real mother, because every bit of us truly comes from her, and daily she takes care of us.

The tiny seed takes on the minerals and the waters of Mother Earth. It is fueled by Wiyo, the sun, and given a spirit by *Wakan Tanka*.

This morning at breakfast we took from Mother Earth to live, as we have done every day of our lives. But did we thank her for giving us the means to live? The old Indian did. When he drove his horse in close to a buffalo running at full speed across the prairie, he drew his bowstring back and said as he did so, "Forgive me, brother, but my people must live." After he butchered the buffalo, he took the skull and faced it toward the setting sun as a thanksgiving and an acknowledgment that all things come from Mother Earth. He brought the meat back to camp and gave it first to the old, the widowed, and the weak. For thousands of years great herds thrived across the continent because the Indian never took more than he needed. Today, the buffalo is gone.

You say *ecology*. We think the words *Mother Earth* have a deeper meaning. If we wish to survive, we must respect her. It is very late, but there is still time to revive and discover the old American Indian value of respect for Mother Earth. She is very beautiful, and already she is showing us signs that she may punish us for not respecting her. Also, we must remember she has been placed in this universe by the one who is the All Powerful, the Great Spirit Above, or *Wakan Tanka*—God. But a few years ago, there lived on the North American continent people, the American Indians, who knew a respect and value system that enabled them to live on their native grounds without having to migrate, in contrast to the white brothers and sisters who migrated by the thousands from their homelands because they had developed a value system different from that of the American Indian. There is no place now to which we can migrate, which means we can no longer ignore the red man's value system.

Carbon-dating techniques say that the American Indian has lived on the North American continent for thousands upon thousands of years. If we did migrate, it was because of a natural phenomenon—a glacier. We did not migrate because of a social system, value system, and spiritual system that neglected its responsibility to the land and all living things. We Indian people say we were always here.

We, the American Indian, had a way of living that enabled us to live within the great, complete beauty that only the natural environment can provide. The Indian tribes had a common value system and a commonality of religion, without religious animosity, that preserved that great beauty that the two-leggeds definitely need. Our four commandments from the Great Spirit are: (1) respect for Mother Earth, (2) respect for the Great Spirit, (3) respect for our fellow man and woman, and (4) respect for individual freedom (provided that individual freedom does not threaten the tribe or the people or Mother Earth).

We who respect the great vision of Black Elk see the four sacred colors as red, yellow, black, and white. They stand for the four directions: red for the east, yellow for the south, black for the west, and white for the north.

From the east comes the rising sun and new knowledge from a new day.

From the south will come the warming south winds that will cause our Mother to bring forth the good foods and grasses so that we may live.

To the west where the sun goes down, the day will end, and we will sleep; and we will hold our spirit ceremonies at night, from where we will communicate with the spirit world beyond. The sacred color of the west is black; it stands for the deep intellect that we will receive from the spirit ceremonies. From the west come the life-giving rains.

From the north will come the white winter snow that will cleanse Mother Earth and put her to sleep, so that she may rest and store up energy to provide the beauty and bounty of springtime. We will prepare for aging by learning to create, through our arts and crafts, during the long winter season. Truth, honesty, strength, endurance, and courage also are represented by the white of the north. Truth and honesty in our relationships bring forth harmony.

All good things come from these sacred directions. These sacred directions, or four sacred colors, also stand for the four races of humanity: red, yellow, black, and white. We cannot be a prejudiced people, because all men and women are brothers and sisters and because we all have the same mother—Mother Earth. One who is prejudiced, who hates another because of that person's color, hates what the Great Spirit has put here. Such a one hates that which is holy and will be punished, even during this lifetime, as humanity will be punished for violating Mother Earth. Worse, one's conscience will follow into the spirit world, where it will be discovered that all beings are equal. This is what we Indian people believe.

We, the Indian people, also believe that the Great Spirit placed many people throughout this planet: red, yellow, black, and white. What about the brown people? The brown people evolved from the sacred colors coming together. Look at our Mother Earth. She, too, is brown because the four directions have come together. After the Great Spirit, *Wakan Tanka,* placed them in their respective areas, the *Wakan Tanka* appeared to each people in a different manner and taught them ways so that they might live in harmony and true beauty. Some men, some tribes, some nations have still retained the teachings of the Great Spirit. Others have not. Unfortunately, many good and peaceful religions have been assailed by narrow-minded zealots. Our religious beliefs and our traditional Indian people have suffered the stereotype that we are pagans, savages, or heathens; but we do not believe that only one religion controls the way to the spirit world that lies beyond. We believe that *Wakan Tanka* loves all of its children equally, although the Great Spirit must be disturbed at times with those children who have destroyed proven value systems that practiced sharing and generosity and kept Mother Earth viable down through time. We kept Mother Earth viable because we did not sell her or our spirituality!

Brothers and sisters, we must go back to some of the old ways if we are going to truly save our Mother Earth and bring back the natural beauty that every person seriously needs, especially in this day of vanishing species, vanishing rain forests, overpopulation, poisoned waters, acid rain, a thinning ozone layer, drought, rising temperatures, and weapons of complete annihilation.

Weapons of complete annihilation? Yes, that is how far the obsession with war has taken us. These weapons are not only hydraheaded; they are hydroheaded as well, meaning that they are the ultimate in hydrogen bomb destruction. We will have to divert our obsessions with defense and wasteful, all-life-ending weapons of war to reviving our environment. If such weapons are ever fired, we will wind up destroying ourselves. The Armageddon of war is something that we have all been very close to and exposed to daily. However, ever since that day in August when people gathered in fields and cities all across the planet to beseech for peace and harmony, it appears that we are seeing some positive steps toward solving this horror. *Maybe some day twoleggeds will read this book and missiles will no longer be pointed at them.*

The quest for peace can be more efficiently pursued through communication and knowledge than by stealth and unending superior weaponry. If the nations of the world scale back their budgets for weaponry, we will have wealth to spend to solve our serious environmental problems. Our home planet is under attack. It is not an imagined problem. This calamity is upon us now. We are in a real war with the polluting, violating blue man of Black Elk's vision.

Chief Sitting Bull advised us to take the best of the white man's ways and to take the best of the old Indian ways. He also said, "When you find something that is bad, or turns out bad, drop it and leave it alone."

The fomenting of fear and hatred is something that has turned out very badly. This can continue no longer; it is a governmental luxury maintained in order to support pork-barrel appropriations to the Department of Defense, with its admirals and generals who have substituted their patriotism for a defense contractor paycheck after retirement. War has become a business for profit. In the last two wars, we frontline warriors—mostly poor whites and minorities—were never allowed to win our wars, which were endlessly prolonged by the politicians and profiteers, who had their warrior-aged sons hidden safely away or who used their powers, bordering on treason, to keep their offspring out of danger. The wrong was that the patriotic American or the poor had to be the replacement. The way to end wars in this day and age is to do like the Indian: put the chiefs and their sons on the front lines.

Sitting Bull answered a relative, "Go ahead and follow the white man's road and do whatever the [Indian] agent tells you. But I cannot so easily give up my old ways and Indian habits; they are too deeply ingrained in me."

My friends, I will never cease to be an Indian.

I will never cease respecting the old Indian values, especially our four cardinal commandments and our values of generosity and sharing. It is true that many who came to our shores brought a great amount of good to this world. Modern medicine, transportation, communication, and food production are but a few of the great achievements that we should all appreciate. But it is also true that too many of those who migrated to North America became so greedy and excessively materialistic that great harm has been caused. We have seen good ways and bad ways. The good way of the non-Indian way I am going to keep. The very fact that we can hold peace-seeking communication and that world leaders meet and communicate for peace shows the wisdom of the brothers and sisters of this time. By all means, good technology should not be curtailed, but care must be taken lest our water, air, and earth become irreparably harmed. The good ways I will always respect and support. But, my brothers and sisters, I say we must give up this obsession with excess consumption and materialism, especially when it causes the harming of the skies surrounding our Mother and the pollution of the waters upon her. *She is beginning to warn us!*

Keep those material goods that you need to exist, but be a more sharing and generous person. You will find that you can do with less. Replace this empty lifestyle of hollow impressing of the shallow ones with active participation for your Mother Earth. At least then, when you depart into the spirit world, you can look back with pride and fulfillment. Other spirit beings will gather around you, other spirits of your own higher consciousness will gather around you and share your satisfaction with you. The eternal satisfaction of knowing you did not overuse your Mother Earth and that you were here to protect her will be a powerful satisfaction when you reach the spirit world.

Indian people do not like to say that the Great Mystery is exactly this or exactly that, but we do know there is a spirit world that lies beyond. We are allowed to know that through our ceremonies. We know that we will go into a much higher plane beyond. We know nothing of hell-fire and eternal damnation from some kind of unloving power that placed us here as little children. None of that has ever been shown to us in our powerful ceremonies, conducted by kind, considerate, proven, and very non-materialistic leaders. We do know that everything the Great Mystery makes is in the form of a circle. Our Mother Earth is a very large, powerful circle.

Therefore, we conclude that our life does not end. A part of it is within that great eternal circle. If there is a hell, then our concept of hell would be an eternal knowing that one violated or took and robbed from Mother Earth and caused this suffering that is being bestowed upon the generations unborn. This then, if it were to be imprinted upon one's eternal conscience, this would surely be a terrible, spiritual, mental hell. Worse, to have harmed and hurt one's innocent fellow beings, and be unable to alter (or conceal) the harmful actions would also be a great hell. Truth in the spirit world will not be concealed, nor will it be for sale. Lastly, we must realize that the generations unborn will also come into the spirit world. Let us be the ones that they wish to thank and congratulate, rather than eternally scorn.

While we are shedding our overabundant possessions, and linking up with those of like minds, and advancing spiritual and environmental appreciations, we should develop a respect for the aged and for family-centered traditions, even those who are single warriors, fighting for the revitalization of our Mother on a lone, solitary, but vital front. We should have more respect for an extended family, which extends beyond a son or daughter, goes beyond to grandparents and aunts and uncles, goes beyond to brothers, sisters, aunts, and uncles that we have adopted or made as relatives—and further beyond, to the animal or plant world as our brothers and sisters, to Mother Earth and Father Sky and then above to *Wakan Tanka,* the *Unci/Tankashilah,* the Grandparent of us all. When we pray directly to the Great Spirit, we say *Unci* (Grandmother) or *Tankashilah* (Grandfather) because we are so family-minded that we think of the Great Power above as a grandparent, and we are the grandchildren. Of course, this is so because every particle of our being is from Mother Earth, and our energy and life force are fueled by Father Sky. This is a vital part of the great, deep feeling and spiritual psychology that we have as Indian people. It is why we preserved and respected our ecological environment for such a long period. *Mitakuye oyasin!* We are all related!

In conclusion, our survival is dependent on the realization that Mother Earth is a truly holy being, that all things in this world are holy and must not be violated, and that we must share and be generous with one another. You may call this thought by whatever fancy words you wish—psychology, theology, sociology, or philosophy—but you must think of Mother Earth as a living being. Think of your fellow men and women as holy people who were put here by the Great Spirit. Think of being related to all things! With this philosophy in mind as we go on with our environmental ecology efforts, our search for spirituality, and our quest for peace, we will be far more successful when we truly understand the Indians' respect for Mother Earth.

THREE

The Moral Law

Of all the ancient traditions, the Greeks and the Israelites planted the seeds of Western ethics. (The other traditions simply were not available for study until relatively recently, in the modern world.) Shortly after Aristotle, the Greek tradition faced a turning point: the *polis*, or city-state, this civilization's unique political association, which had given form to the political and social assumptions of Plato and Aristotle, went into a decline from which it would not recover. With the *polis* gone, what was left of moral permanence? The path we shall explore in this section seized upon the element of law—derived from the law that governed the *polis*—as the fundamental moral structure. We shall call this the tradition of the "Moral Law," and it will be understood to combine the flowering of the "Natural Law" in the late ancient and medieval periods, the "Deontological" reasoning from formal principles advanced by Immanuel Kant, and any contemporary variants that make central the notions of law, justice, and duty.

The Stoics began the journey from the Greek ideal of excellence to the commitment to the Moral Law in about 300 B.C., when Zeno founded a school of philosophy based on the ideal of a passionless existence. Starting with their search for a life "in accordance with Nature," the Stoics' notion of necessity, reason, or natural law joined with the Judaeo-Christian notion of God's Law (originating in the Decalogue), and the fused streams gave rise to the richest source of our own political and moral traditions—the belief in a law, and individual rights, inherent in nature, evident to reason, and guaranteed by God. We shall follow the stream from its Stoic origins, through the joining of the traditions in the work of Thomas Aquinas, through the birth of "natural rights" as accepted moral teaching in Thomas Hobbes, John Locke, and Thomas Jefferson, through the reemergence of the Moral Law as the Categorical Imperative in the work of Immanuel Kant in the eighteenth century, to the work of contemporary Deontologists John Rawls and Martin Luther King, Jr.

The Stoics

The Stoics had left behind the secure aristocratic world of the polis, *and found themselves in an entirely unpredictable social universe, where oppression, slavery, and war were as likely as the recognition and respect accorded every Athenian citizen simply because he was a citizen. Of the major Stoic philosophers we know, Epictetus (ca. A.D. 55–A.D. 135) was a slave, Seneca (ca. 4 B.C.–A.D. 65) was a courtier in the Roman Imperial Court (who opened his veins on orders from Nero), and Marcus Aurelius (A.D. 180–A.D. 121) was a Roman emperor, ruler of the known world. All equally faced the question: In a turbulent world, is the Greek ideal of a serene and virtuous life possible? Their answer was that it was possible, if one were willing to accept the reversals of fortune and the world far more serenely than the ordinary Athenian citizen would have, or would have thought possible. Their model in this answer was, of course, Socrates, that most extraordinary of Athenian citizens.*

Our notion of Natural Law derives from the Stoics' insistence on the possibility of living "according to Nature," no matter what should come of Nature. The following passages are from Epictetus' Moral Discourses, a disorderly collection of his sayings as written down by his student Arrian. (Epictetus himself wrote nothing.) They show us the working of an unusually gifted mind and spirit, capable of raising itself above all the passions and hindrances of this life.

Epictetus, *Moral Discourses*

Part I

Chapter I: Of the things which are, and the things which are not, in our own power

. . . when it is in our power to take care of one thing, and to apply to one, we choose rather to take care of many, and to encumber ourselves with many; body, property, brother, friend, child and slave; and, by this multiplicity of encumbrances, we are burdened and weighed down. Thus, when the weather does not happen to be fair for sailing, we sit in distress and gaze out perpetually. Which way is the wind?— North. What do we want of that? When will the west [wind] blow? When it pleases, friend, or when Eolus pleases; for Zeus has not made you dispenser of the winds, but Eolus.

What then is to be done?

To make the best of what is in our power, and take the rest as it occurs. And how does it occur? As it pleases God.

What, then, must I be the only one to lose my head?

Why, would you have all the world, then, lose their heads for your consolation? . . . What resource have we then upon such occasions? Why what else but to distinguish between what is ours, and what not ours; what is right, and what is wrong. I must die, and must I die groaning too?—Be fettered. Must I be lamenting too?—Exiled. And what hinders me, then, but that I may go smiling, and cheerful, and serene? "Betray a secret."—I will not betray it; for this is in my own power.—"Then I will fetter you." What do you say, man? Fetter me? You will fetter my leg; but not Zeus himself can get the better of my free will.—"I will throw you into prison: I will behead that paltry body of yours." Did I ever tell you, that I alone had a head not liable to be cut off?—These things ought philosophers to study; these ought they daily to write; and in these to exercise themselves. . . .

This it is to have studied what ought to be studied; to have placed our desires and aversions above tyranny and above chance. I must die: if instantly, I will die instantly; if in a short time, I will dine first; and when the hour comes, then I will die. How? As becomes one who restores what is not his own. . . .

Chapter VI: Of Providence

From every event that happens in the world it is easy to celebrate Providence, if a person has but these two qualities in himself: a faculty of considering what happens to each individual, and a grateful temper. Without the first, he will not perceive the usefulness of things which happen; and without the other, he will not be thankful for them. If God had made colors, and had not made the faculty of seeing them, what would have been their use? None. On the other hand, if he had made the faculty of observation, without objects to observe, what would have been the use of that? None. Again; if he had formed both the faculty and the objects, but had not made light? Neither in that case would they have been of any use.

Who is it then that has fitted each of these to the other? Who is it that has fitted the sword to the scabbard, and the scabbard to the sword? Is there no such Being? From the very construction of a complete work, we are used to declare positively that it must be the operation of some artificer, and not the effect of mere chance. Does every such work, then, demonstrate an artificer; and do not visible objects, and the sense of seeing, and light, demonstrate one? . . .

What, then, do these things belong to us alone?

Many indeed; such as are peculiarly necessary for a reasonable creature; but you will find many which are common to us with mere animals.

Then, do they too understand what happens?

Not at all; for use is one affair, and understanding another. But God had need of animals, to make use of things, and of us to understand that use. It is sufficient, therefore, for them to eat, and drink, and sleep, and continue their species, and perform other such offices as belong to each of them, but to us, to whom he has given likewise a faculty of understanding, these offices are not sufficient. For if we do not proceed in a wise and systematic manner, and suitably to the nature and constitution of each thing, we shall never attain our end. For where the constitution of beings is different, their offices and ends are different likewise. Thus where the constitution is adapted only to use, there use is alone sufficient; but where understanding is added to use, unless that too be duly exercised, the end of such a being will never be attained. . . .

Chapter XXIV: How we ought to struggle with difficulties

Difficulties are things that show what men are. For the future, in case of any difficulty, remember, that God, like a gymnastic trainer, has pitted you against a rough antagonist. For what end? That you may be an Olympic conqueror; and this cannot be without toil. No man, in my opinion, has a more profitable difficulty on his hands than you have; provided you will but use it, as an athletic champion uses his antagonist. . . .

But remember the principal thing: that the door is open. Do not be more fearful than children; but as they, when the play does not please them, say, "I will play no longer," so do you, in the same case, say, "I will play no longer," and go; but if you stay, do not complain.

Chapter XXV: On the same subject

If these things are true, and if we are not stupid, or insincere, when we say that the good or ill of man lies within his own will, and that all beside is nothing to us, why are we still troubled? Why do we still fear? What truly concerns us is in no one's power: what is in the power of others concerns not us. What embarrassment have we left? . . . Apply the recognized principles. apply the demonstrations of philosophers; apply what you have often heard, and what you have said yourself, what you have read, and what you have carefully studied. . . . Do you decide between these opinions, but do not let it be with depression and anxiety, and the assumption that you are miserable; for no one compels you to that. Is there smoke in my house? If it be moderate, I will stay; if very great, I will go out. For you must always remember, and hold to this, that the door is open. "You are forbidden to live at Nicopolis." I will not live there. "Nor at Athens." Well, nor at Athens. "Nor at Rome." Nor at Rome. "But you shall live at Gyaros." I will live there. But suppose that living at Gyaros seems to me like living in a great smoke. I can then retire where no one can forbid me to live, for it is an abode open to all; and put off my last garment, this poor body of mine; beyond this, no one has any power over me.

Thus Demetrius said to Nero: "You sentence me to death; and Nature you." If I prize my body first, I have surrendered myself as a slave; if my estate, the same; for I at once betray where I am vulnerable. Just as when a reptile pulls in his head, I bid you strike at that part of him which he guards; and be you assured, that wherever you show a desire to guard yourself, there your master will attack you. Remember but this, and whom will you any longer flatter or fear? . . .

Chapter XXVI: What the rule of Life is

As someone was reading hypothetical propositions, Epictetus remarked that it was a rule in these to admit whatever was in accordance with the hypothesis; but much more a rule in life, to do what was in accordance with nature. For, if we desire in every matter and on every occasion to conform to nature, we must, on every occasion, evidently make it our aim, neither to omit anything thus conformable, nor to admit anything inconsistent. . . .

Thomas Aquinas (1225–1274)

Thomas Aquinas was a Dominican monk, son of the Count D'Aquino of Naples, who spent his working life studying, teaching, and writing at the University of Paris. His great work, the Summa Theologica, *from which the passages below were taken, unified the Natural Law tradition passed on from the Romans, the Biblical tradition through which the Law becomes identified with the mind of the living God, and the philosophical sophistication of the newly rediscovered works of Aristotle.*

Aquinas' manner of exposition takes some getting used to. He proceeds through a list of questions entirely logically, setting forth at the opening of each section the topics to be discussed and the order of discussion. Each "Question" covers one topic (in the case of the first question considered below, "the various kinds of law"); it is then subdivided into smaller questions, the "Articles." Each of these smaller questions is rigorously phrased to permit only yes-or-no answers. (Seven hundred fifty years later, the same rigor would be captured by the computer!) For example, the first of the "articles" we will consider asks, "Whether there is in us a natural law?" In each article, Aquinas first lists the "Objections," all the considerations that would lead you to answer the question one of the two possible ways. (In the case of that first article, for example, the first possible way is No, there is not, and the first "objection" is that "there can't be any natural law in us: Nature produces only things that are necessary; no law for us is necessary beyond the eternal law; therefore Nature has not produced any further law for us, including any 'natural' law.") Then he goes to the other side of the argument and lists the major considerations that would lead you to answer the other way, "On the Contrary." In the case of the first article, Aquinas quotes a traditional source to the effect that Paul was speaking of a "natural law" in Romans 2:14; whatever other authorities there may be, the Bible is always authoritative, so unless Aquinas can explain away the text, that settles

*that. Then he presents his own view ("I answer that"), a complete argument, which usu-
ally accords with "On the Contrary." Then he goes back and answers, in order, the opening considerations on the other side, in the "Replies to Objections." (The reply to the first
objection in this article, for example, is that natural law is not a law different from and
in addition to the eternal law, but is a functional part of that law, specifically, the rational creature's participation in it.) As a model of logic and clarity, Aquinas' method of
exposition has no rival. Nor is the clarity illusory: The scheme that he expounds, one ordered system of law and one great chain of being extending without break from the stone
to the Mind of God, is the most comprehensive and morally satisfying vision of reality to
which the Western tradition has given birth.*

*In Question XC, immediately preceding the opening selection below, Aquinas es-
tablishes the definition of law by identifying its four Aristotelian "causes": In its formal
cause, law is an ordinance of reason; in its final cause, law is ordained for the common
good; its efficient cause (agent) is the prince, or the legitimate ruler of the community;
and its material cause is its promulgation, or publication to all the people to whom it applies. Lacking one of these features, an ordinance is no law at all. Having established that
definition, Aquinas proceeds to consider the various kinds of law.*

From Thomas Aquinas, *Summa Theologica*

(First Part of the Second Part)

Question XCL: Of the Various Kinds of Law (in six articles)

We must now consider the various kinds of law, under which head there are six points of inquiry:
(1) Whether there is an eternal law? (2) Whether there is a natural law? (3) Whether there is a human
law? (4) Whether there is a Divine law? (5) Whether there is one Divine law, or several? (6) Whether
there is a law of sin? . . .

Article 2: Whether There Is in Us a Natural Law?

We proceed thus to the Second Article: It would seem that there is no natural law in us.

Obj. 1. Because man is governed sufficiently by the eternal law, for Augustine says *(De Lib. Arb.* 1,6)
that "the eternal law is that by which it is right that all things should be most orderly." But nature does
not abound in superfluities as neither does she fail in necessaries. Therefore no law is natural to man.

Obj. 2. Further, by the law man is ordered in his acts to the end, as stated above. . . . But the ordering of human acts to their end is not a function of nature, as is the case in irrational creatures, which
act for an end solely by their natural appetite; but man acts for an end by his reason and will. Therefore
no law is natural to man.

Obj. 3. Further, the more a man is free, the less he is under the law. But man is freer than all the animals, on account of free choice, with which he is endowed above all other animals. Since therefore
other animals are not subject to a natural law, neither is man subject to a natural law.

On the Contrary, A gloss on Romans 2:14: *When the Gentiles, who have not the law, do by nature
those things that are of the law,* comments *as follows:* "Although they have no written law, yet they have
the natural law, whereby each one knows, and is conscious of, what is good and what is evil."

I answer that, As stated above . . . law, being a rule and measure, can be in a person in two ways: in
one way as in him that rules and measures; in another way, as in that which is ruled and measured, since
a thing is ruled and measured in so far as it partakes of the rule or measure. Therefore, since all things

subject to Divine providence are ruled and measured by the eternal law . . . it is evident that all things partake somewhat of the eternal law, in so far as, namely, from its being imprinted on them, they derive their respective inclinations to their proper acts and ends. Now among all others, the rational creature is subject to Divine providence in the most excellent way, in so far as it partakes of a share of providence, by being provident both for itself and for others. Therefore it has a share of the Eternal Reason, by which it has a natural inclination to its due act and end; and this participation of the eternal law in the rational creature is called the natural law. Hence the Psalmist after saying (Ps. 4. C): *Offer up the sacrifice of justice,* as though someone asked what the works of justice are, adds: *Many say, Who showeth us good things?* in answer to which question he says: *The light of Thy countenance, O Lord, is signed upon us,* thus implying that the light of natural reason, by which we discern what is good and what is evil, which is the function of the natural law, is nothing else than an imprint on us of the Divine light. It is therefore evident that the natural law is nothing else than the rational creature's participation of the eternal law.

Repl. Obj. 1. This argument would hold if the natural law were something different from the eternal law. But it is nothing other than a participation of the eternal law, as stated above.

Repl. Obj. 2. Every operation of reason and will in us is based on that which is according to nature . . . for every act of reasoning is based on principles that are known naturally, and every act of appetite in respect of the means is derived from the natural appetite in respect of the last end. And so also the first direction of our acts to their end must be in virtue of the natural law.

Repl. Obj. 3. Even irrational animals partake in their own way of the Eternal Reason, just as the rational creature does. But because the rational creature partakes of it in an intellectual and rational manner, therefore the participation of the eternal law in the rational creature is properly called a law, since a law is something pertaining to reason. . . . Irrational creatures, however, do not partake of it in a rational manner, and so there is no participation of the eternal law in them, except by way of likeness. . . .

Question XCIV: Of the Natural Law (in six articles)

Article 2: Whether the Natural Law Contains Several Precepts, or One Only?

We proceed thus to the Second Article: It would seem that the natural law contains not several precepts, but one only.

Obj. 1. For law is a kind of precept, as stated above . . . If therefore there were many precepts of the natural law, it would follow that there are also many natural laws.

Obj. 2. Further, the natural law is consequent to human nature. But human nature, as a whole is one, though as to its parts it is manifold. Therefore, either there is but one precept of the law of nature, on account of the unity of nature as a whole, or there are many by reason of the number of parts of human nature. The result would be that even things relating to the inclination of the concupiscible faculty belong to the natural law. . . .

On the Contrary, The precepts of the natural law in man stand in relation to practical matters as the first principles to matters of demonstration. But there are several first indemonstrable principles. Therefore there are also several precepts of the natural law. *I answer that,* As stated above . . ., the precepts of the natural law are to the practical reason what the first principles of demonstration are to the speculative reason; because both are self-evident principles . . .

Since, however, good has the nature of an end, and evil, the nature of a contrary, hence it is that all those things to which man has a natural inclination are naturally apprehended by reason as being good, and consequently as objects of pursuit, and their contraries as evil, and objects of avoidance. Therefore the order of the precepts of the natural law is according to the order of natural inclinations. Because in man there is first of all an inclination to good in accordance with the nature which he has in common with all substances; that is, every substance seeks the preservation of its own being, according to its nature. And by reason of this inclination, whatever is a means of preserving human life and of warding off its obstacles belongs to the natural law. Secondly, there is in man an inclination to things that pertain to him more specially, according to that nature which he has in common with other animals. And in virtue of this inclination, those things are said to belong to the natural law "which nature has taught all animals," such as sexual intercourse, education of offspring and so forth. Thirdly, there is in man an inclination to good, according to the nature of his reason, which nature is proper to him; thus man has a natural inclination to know the truth about God, and to live in society. And in this respect, whatever pertains to this inclination belongs to the natural law; for instance, to shun ignorance, to avoid offending those among whom one has to live, and other such things regarding the above inclination.

Repl. Obj. 1. All these precepts of the law of nature have the character of one natural law because they flow from one first precept.

Repl. Obj. 2. All the inclinations of any parts whatsoever of human nature, for example, of the concupiscible and irascible parts, in so far as they are ruled by reason, belong to the natural law, and are reduced to one first precept . . . so that the precepts of the natural law are many in themselves, but are based on one common foundation.

Article 5: Whether the Natural Law Can Be Changed?

We proceed thus to the Fifth Article: It would seem that the natural law can be changed. . . .

Obj. 2. Further, the slaying of the innocent, adultery, and theft are against the natural law. But we find these things changed by God, as when God commanded Abraham to slay his innocent son . . . and when He ordered the Jews to borrow and purloin the vessels of the Egyptians . . . and when He commanded Osee to take to himself a wife of fornications . . . Therefore the natural law can be changed.

On the contrary, It is said in the Decretals: "The natural law dates from the creation of the rational creature. It does not vary according to time, but remains unchangeable."

I answer that, A change in the natural law may be understood in two ways. First by way of addition. In this sense nothing hinders the natural law from being changed, since many things for the benefit of human life have been added over and above the natural law, both by the Divine law and by human laws.

Secondly, a change in the natural law may be understood by way of subtraction, so that what previously was according to the natural law ceases to be so. In this sense, the natural law is altogether unchangeable in its first principles. But in its secondary principles, which . . . are certain detailed proximate conclusions drawn from the first principles, the natural law is not changed so that what it prescribes be not right in most cases. But it may be changed in some particular cases of rare occurrence, through some special causes hindering the observance of such precepts. . . .

Repl. Obj. 2. All men alike, both guilty and innocent, die the death of nature, which death of nature is inflicted by the power of God on account of original sin, according to I Kings 2:6: *The Lord killeth and maketh alive.* Consequently, by the command of God, death can be inflicted on any man, guilty or innocent, without any injustice whatever. In like manner adultery is intercourse with another's wife, who is allotted to him by the law emanating from God. . . .

Article 6: Whether the Law of Nature Can be Abolished from the Heart of Man?

We proceed thus to the Sixth Article: It would seem that the natural law can be abolished from the heart of man.

Obj. 1. Because in Rom. 2:14 *When the Gentiles who have not the law,* etc. a gloss says, that "the law of justice, which sin had blotted out, is graven on the heart of man when he is restored by grace." But the law of justice is the law of nature. Therefore the law of nature can be blotted out.

Obj. 2. Further, the law of grace is more efficacious than the law of nature. But the law of grace is blotted out by sin. Much more therefore can the law of nature be blotted out.

Obj. 3. Further, that which is established by law is imposed as just. But many things are enacted by men which are contrary to the law of nature. Therefore the law of nature can be abolished from the heart of man.

On the contrary, Augustine says: "Thy law is written in the hearts of men, which iniquity itself effaces not." But the law which is written in men's hearts is the natural law. Therefore the natural law cannot be blotted out.

I answer that, . . . there belong to the natural law, first, certain most common precepts, that are known to all; and secondly, certain secondary and more detailed precepts, which are, as it were, conclusions following clearly from first principles. As to those common principles, the natural law, in its universal character, can in no way be blotted out from men's hearts. But it is blotted out in the case of a particular action, in so far as reason is hindered from applying the common principle to a particular point of practice, on account of concupiscence or some other passion. . . . But as to the other, that is, the secondary precepts, the natural law can be blotted out from the human heart, either by evil persuasions, just as in speculative matters errors occur in respect of necessary conclusions; or by vicious customs and corrupt habits, as among some men, theft, and even unnatural vices, as the Apostle states (Romans 1), were not considered sinful.

Repl. Obj. 1. Sin blots out the law of nature in particular cases, not universally, except perhaps in regard to the secondary precepts of the natural law, in the way stated above.

Repl. Obj. 2. Although grace is more efficacious than nature, yet nature is more essential to man, and therefore more enduring.

Repl. Obj. 3. This argument is true of the secondary precepts of the natural law, against which some legislators have framed certain enactments which are unjust. . . .

Question XCV: Of Human Law (in four articles)

We must now consider human law; and (1) this law considered in itself, (2) its power (Q. XCVI); (3) its mutability (Q. XCVII). Under the first head there are four points of inquiry: (1) Its utility, (2) Its origin, (3) Its quality, (4) Its division.

Article 1: Whether It was Useful for Laws to Be Framed by Men?

We proceed thus to the First Article: It would seem that it was not useful for laws to be framed by men.

Obj. 1. For the purpose of every law is that man be made good thereby. . . . But men are more induced to be good willingly by means of admonitions, than against their will by means of laws. Therefore there was no need to frame laws.

Obj. 2. Further, As the Philosopher says: "men have recourse to a judge as to animate justice." But animate justice is better than inanimate justice, which is contained in laws. Therefore it would have been better for the execution of justice to be entrusted to the decision of judges than to frame laws in addition.

Obj. 3. Further, every law is framed for the direction of human actions. . . . But since human actions are about singulars, which are infinite in number, matters pertaining to the direction of human actions cannot be taken into sufficient consideration except by a wise man, who looks into each one of them. Therefore it would have been better for human acts to be directed by the judgment of wise men than by the framing of laws. Therefore there was no need of human laws.

On the contrary, Isidore says . . . "Laws were made so that in fear of them human audacity might be held in check, that innocence might be safeguarded in the midst of wickedness, and that the dread of punishment might prevent the wicked from doing harm." But these things are most necessary to mankind. Therefore it was necessary that human laws should be made.

I answer that, . . . man has a natural aptitude for virtue; but the perfection itself of virtue must be acquired by man by means of some kind of training. Thus we observe that man is helped by industry in his necessities, for instance, in food and clothing. Certain beginnings of these he has from nature, that is, his reason and his hands; but he has not the full complement, as other animals have, to whom nature has given sufficient covering and food. Now it is difficult to see how man could suffice for himself in the matter of this training; for the perfection of virtue consists chiefly in withdrawing man from undue pleasures, to which above all man is inclined, and especially the young, who are more capable of being trained. Consequently a man needs to receive this training from another, through which to arrive at the perfection of virtue. And as to those young people who are inclined to acts of virtue by their good natural disposition, or by custom, or rather by the gift of God, paternal training suffices, which is by admonitions. But since some are found to be depraved, and prone to vice, and not easily amenable to words, it was necessary for such to be restrained from evil by force and fear, in order that at least they might cease from evil-doing and leave others in peace, and that they themselves, by being accustomed in this way, might be brought to do willingly what hitherto they did from fear, and thus become virtuous. Now this kind of training, which compels through fear of punishment, is the discipline of laws. Therefore, in order that man might have peace and virtue, it was necessary for laws to be framed; for, as the Philosopher says, "as man is the most noble of animals if he be perfect in virtue, so is he the lowest of all if he be severed from law and justice," because man is armed with reason, as the other animals are not, to sate his lust and ferocity.

Repl. Obj. 1. Men who are well disposed are led willingly to virtue by being admonished better than by coercion; but men who are evilly disposed are not led to virtue unless they are compelled.

Repl. Obj. 2. the Philosopher says, "it is better that all things be regulated by law than left to be decided by judges," and this for three reasons. First, because it is easier to find a few wise men competent to frame right laws than to find the many who would be necessary to judge rightly of each single case. Secondly, because those who make laws consider long beforehand what laws to make; but judgment on each single case has to be pronounced as soon as it arises. And it is easier for man to see what is right by taking many instances into consideration, than by considering one solitary fact. Thirdly, because lawgivers judge universally and of future events, while those who sit in judgment judge of things present, towards which they are affected by love, hatred or some kind of cupidity, so that their judgment is perverted.

Since then the animated justice of the judge is not found in every man, and since it can be deflected, therefore it was necessary, whenever possible, for the law to determine how to judge, and for very few matters to be left to the decision of men.

Repl. Obj. 3. Certain individual facts which cannot be covered by the law "have necessarily to be committed to judges," as the Philosopher says in the same passage; for instance, "concerning something that has happened or not happened," and the like.

Article 2: Whether Every Human Law Is Derived from the Natural Law?

We proceed thus to the Second Article: It would seem that not every human law is derived from the natural law.

Obj. 1. For the Philosopher says that "the legal just is that which originally was a matter of indifference." But those things which arise from the natural law are not matters of indifference. Therefore the enactments of human laws are not all derived from the natural law. . . .

Obj. 3. Further, the law of nature is the same for all; since the Philosopher says that "the natural just is that which is equally valid everywhere." If therefore human laws were derived from the natural law, it would follow that they too are the same for all, which is clearly false. . . .

On the contrary, Tully says . . . . "Things which emanated from nature and were approved by custom, were sanctioned by fear and reverence for the laws."

I answer that, As Augustine says, . . . "That which is not just seems to be no law at all;" therefore the force of a law depends on the extent of its justice. Now in human affairs a thing is said to be just from being right according to the rule of reason. But the first rule of reason is the law of nature. . . . Consequently every human law has just so much of the character of law as it is derived from the law of nature. But if in any point it differs from the law of nature, it is no longer a law but a corruption of law.

But it must be noted that something may be derived from the natural law in two ways: first, as a conclusion from premises, secondly, by way of determination of certain generalities. The first way is like that by which, in the sciences, demonstrated conclusions are drawn from the principles, while the second mode is like that whereby, in the arts, common forms are determined to something particular; thus the craftsman needs to determine the common form of a house to the shape of this or that house. Some things are therefore derived from the common principles of the natural law by way of conclusions; for instance, that one must not kill may be derived as a conclusion from the principle that one should do harm to no man. But some are derived from these principles by way of determination; for instance, the law of nature has it that the evil-doer should be punished, but that he should be punished in this or that way is a determination of the law of nature.

Accordingly both modes of derivation are found in the human law. But those things which are derived in the first way are contained in human law not as emanating from it exclusively, but have some force from the natural law also. But those things which are derived in the second way have no other force than that of human law.

Repl. Obj. 1. The Philosopher is speaking of those enactments, which are by way of determination or specification of the precepts of the natural law. . . .

Repl. Obj. 3. The common principles of the natural law cannot be applied to all men in the same way on account of the great variety of human affairs, and from this arises the diversity of positive laws among various people.

Thomas Hobbes (1588–1679)

Thomas Hobbes lived in revolutionary times. For the first time in history, Puritan revolutionaries had engineered the overthrow and beheading of the English king (Charles 1, 1641). Hobbes' writing in 1651, had therefore a very recent example, as motivation for the development of his theory of government. His account of the origin of government in the social contract, later picked up by both John Locke and John Rawls as the moral basis of civil society, is for our purposes less interesting than his articulation of another notion: the "natural rights" of the citizen as the moral foundation of that government.

Older theories had discovered their moral foundation in some divine right of entitlement adhering to the king (Charles I had tried that argument, without noticeable success) or in some natural law ruling all and authorizing the few to exercise the powers of government over the many. There is a notion of natural law in Hobbes' theory; note how carefully he distinguishes it, through its Latin cognates, from the notion of natural right. The most pervasive right, or liberty, is that of self-preservation; a person may do whatever needs to be done to save his life and to procure the means to live. And, according to Hobbes, that's all the person wants to do; in common with the Utilitarians, Hobbes supposes that the only motive natural to humankind is the motive of self-interest.

But in the desire to survive and prosper, and the right to do anything necessary to survive and prosper, Hobbes has all the motivation and authority he needs to establish an autocratic State, the Leviathan. This is a beast so mighty that it can overawe all its selfish and rebellious subjects, and so keep the peace, and so protect the citizens' lives, which is all they want and all that the State is authorized to do.

And that, of course, is the point of this post-revolutionary treatise: to show that the citizen's survival, and best interest, and defense of right, depend on accepting the absolute monarch. Revolution in the name of liberty is therefore unjustified. Hobbes has introduced the notion of "natural rights" into philosophy only to show that their most reasonable exercise should be instant self-destruction. Locke and Jefferson will take the matter somewhat closer to our understanding of the concept of "rights."

From Thomas Hobbes, *Leviathan*, 1651

From Part I, "Of Man"

Chapter XIII: Of the Natural Condition of Mankind as Concerning their Felicity and Misery

Nature hath made men so equal in the faculties of body and mind as that, though there be found one man sometimes manifestly stronger in body or of quicker mind than another, yet when all is reckoned together the difference between man and man is not so considerable as that one man can there upon claim to himself any benefit to which another may not pretend as well as he. For as to the strength of the body, the weakest has strength enough to kill the strongest, either by secret machination or by confederacy with others that are in the same danger with himself.

And as to the faculties of the mind, setting aside the arts grounded upon words, and especially that skill . . . called *science. . . .* I find yet a greater equality amongst men than that of strength. For prudence is but experience, which equal time equally bestows on all men in those things they equally apply themselves unto. That which may perhaps make such equality incredible is but a vain conceit of one's own wisdom, which almost all men think they have in a greater degree than the vulgar; that is, than all men but themselves, and a few others, whom by fame, or for concurring with themselves, they approve. For such is the nature of men that howsoever they may acknowledge many others to be more witty, or more eloquent, or more learned, yet they will hardly believe there be many so wise as themselves: for they see their own wit at hand, and other men's at a distance. But this proveth rather that men are in that point equal. . . . For there is not ordinarily a greater sign of the equal distribution of anything than that every man is contented with his share.

From this equality of ability ariseth equality of hope in the attaining of our ends. And therefore if any two men desire the same thing, which nevertheless they cannot both enjoy, they become enemies; and in the way to their end (which is principally their own conservation, and sometimes their delectation only) endeavor to destroy or subdue one another. And from hence it comes to pass that where an invader hath no more to fear than another man's single power, if one plant, sow, build, or possess a convenient seat, others may probably be expected to come prepared with forces united to dispossess and deprive him, not only of the fruit of his labor, but also of his life or liberty. And the invader again is in the like danger of another.

And from this diffidence of one another, there is no way for any man to secure himself so reasonable as anticipation; that is, by force, or wiles, to master the persons of all men he can so long till he see no other power great enough to endanger him: and this is no more than his own conservation requireth, and is generally allowed. . . .

Again, men have no pleasure (but on the contrary a great deal of grief) in keeping company where there is no power able to overawe them all. For every man looketh that his companion should value him at the same rate he sets upon himself, and upon all signs of contempt or undervaluing naturally endeavors, as far as he dares (which amongst them that have no common power to keep them in quiet is far enough to make them destroy each other), to extort a greater value from his contemners, by damage; and from others, by the example.

So that in the nature of man, we find three principal causes of quarrel. First, competition; secondly, diffidence; thirdly, glory. . . .

Hereby it is manifest that during the time men live without a common power to keep them all in awe, they are in that condition which is called war, and such a war as is of every man against every man. For war consisteth not in battle only, or the act of fighting, but in a tract of time, wherein the will to contend by battle is sufficiently known; . . . the nature of war consisteth not in actual fighting, but in the known disposition thereto during all the time there is no assurance to the contrary. All other time is *peace.*

Whatsoever therefore is consequent to a time of war, where every man is enemy to every man, the same is consequent to the time wherein men live without other security than what their own strength and their own invention shall furnish them withal. In such condition there is no place for industry, because the fruit thereof is uncertain; and consequently no culture of the earth; no navigation, nor use of the commodities that may be imported by sea; no commodious building; no instruments of moving and removing such things as require much force; no knowledge of the face of the earth; no account of time; no arts; no letters; no society; and which is worst of all, continual fear, and danger of violent death; and the life of man, solitary, poor, nasty, brutish, and short.

It may seem strange to some man that has not well weighed these things that Nature should thus dissociate and render men apt to invade and destroy one another: and he may therefore, not trusting to this inference, made from the passions, desire to have the same confirmed by experience. Let him therefore consider with himself: when taking a journey, he arms himself and seeks to go well accompanied: when going to sleep, he locks his doors; when even in his house he locks his chests; and this when he knows there be laws and public officers, armed, to revenge all injuries shall be done him; what opinion he has of his fellow subjects, when he rides armed; of his fellow citizens, when he locks his doors; and of his children, and servants, when he locks his chests. Does he not there as much accuse mankind by his actions as I do by my words? But neither of us accuse man's nature in it. The desires, and other passions of man, are in themselves no sin. No more are the actions that proceed from those passions, till they know a law that forbids them; which till laws be made they cannot know, nor can any law be made till they have agreed upon the person that shall make it. . . .

To this war of every man against every man, this also is consequent; that nothing can be unjust. The notions of right and wrong, justice and injustice, have there no place. Where there is no common power, there is no law; where no law, no injustice. Force and fraud are in war the two cardinal virtues. Justice and injustice are none of the faculties neither of the body nor mind. If they were, they might be in a man that were alone in the world, as well as his senses and passions. They are qualities that relate to men in society, not in solitude. It is consequent also to the same condition that there be no propriety, no dominion, no *mine* and *thine* distinct; but only that to be every man's that he can get, and for so long as he can keep it. And thus much for the ill condition which man by mere nature is actually placed in; though with a possibility to come out of it, consisting partly in the passions, partly in his reason.

The passions that incline men to peace are: fear of death; desire of such things as are necessary to commodious living; and a hope by their industry to obtain them. And reason suggesteth convenient articles of peace upon which men may be drawn to agreement. These articles are they which otherwise are called the *laws of nature* . . .

Chapter XIV: Of the First and Second Natural Laws, and of Contracts

The *right of nature*, which writers commonly call *jus naturale*, is the liberty each man hath to use his own power as he will himself for the preservation of his own nature; that is to say, of his own life; and consequently, of doing anything which, in his own judgment and reason, he shall conceive to be the aptest means thereunto.

By *liberty* is understood, according to the proper signification of the word, the absence of external impediments; which impediments may oft take away part of a man's power to do what he would, but cannot hinder him from using the power left him according as his judgment and reason shall dictate to him.

A *law of nature, lex naturalis*, is a precept, or general rule, found out by reason, by which a man is forbidden to do that which is destructive of his life, or taketh away the means of preserving the same, and to omit that by which he thinketh it may be best preserved. For though they that speak of this subject use to confound *jus* and *lex*, *right* and *law*, yet they ought to be distinguished, because *right* consisteth in liberty to do, or to forbear; whereas *law* determineth and bindeth to one of them: so that law and right differ as much as obligation and liberty, which in one and the same matter are inconsistent.

And because the condition of man (as hath been declared in the precedent chapter) is a condition of war of every one against every one, in which case every one is governed by his own reason, and there is nothing he can make use of that may not be a help unto him in preserving his life against his enemies; it followeth that in such a condition every man has a right to every thing, even to one another's body. And therefore, as long as this natural right of every man to every thing endureth, there can be no security to any man, how strong or wise soever he be, of living out the time which nature ordinarily alloweth men to live. And consequently it is a precept, or general rule of reason: *that every man ought to endeavor peace, as far as he has hope of obtaining it, and when he cannot obtain it, that he may seek and use all helps and advantages of war.* The first branch of which rule containeth the first and fundamental law of nature, which is: to *seek peace and follow it.* The second, the sum of the right of nature, which is: *by all means we can to defend ourselves.* From this fundamental law of nature, by which men are commanded to endeavor peace, is derived this second law: *that a man be willing, when others are so too, as far forth as for peace and defense of himself he shall think it necessary, to lay down this right to all things; and be contented with so much liberty against other men as he would allow other men against himself.* For as long as every man holdeth this right, of doing anything he liketh; so long are all men in the condition of war. But if other men will not lay down their right, as well as he, then there is no reason for anyone to divest himself of his: for that were to expose himself to prey, which no man is bound to, rather than to dispose himself to peace. This is that law of the gospel: *Whatsoever you require that others should do to you, that do ye to them.* . . .

Right is laid aside, either by simply renouncing it, or by transferring it to another. . . . And when a man hath in either manner abandoned or granted away his right, then is he said to be *obliged*, or *bound*, not to hinder those to whom such right is granted, or abandoned, from the benefit of it: and that he *ought*, and it is his *duty*, not to make void that voluntary act of his own: and that such hindrance is *injustice*, and *injury*. . . . So that *injury*, or *injustice*, in the controversies of the world, is somewhat like to that which in the disputations of scholars is called *absurdity*. For as it is there called an absurdity to contradict what one maintained in the beginning; so in the world it is called *injustice*, and *injury* voluntarily to undo that which from the beginning he had voluntarily done. The way by which a man either simply renounceth or transferreth his right is a declaration, or signification, by some voluntary and sufficient sign, or signs, that he doth so renounce or transfer, or hath so renounced or transferred the same, to him that accepteth it. And those signs are either words only, or actions only; or, as it happeneth most often, both words and actions. And the same are the *bonds,* by which men are bound and obliged: bonds that have their strength, not from their own nature (for nothing is more easily broken than a man's word), but from fear of some evil consequence upon the rupture.

Whensoever a man transferreth his right, or renounceth it, it is either in consideration of some right reciprocally transferred to himself, or for some other good he hopeth for thereby. For it is a voluntary act: and of the voluntary acts of every man, the object is some good to himself. And therefore there be some rights which no man can be understood by any words, or other signs, to have abandoned or transferred. As first a man cannot lay down the right of resisting them that assault him by force to take away his life, because he cannot be understood to aim thereby at any good to himself. The same may be said of wounds, and chains, and imprisonment, both because there is no benefit consequent to such patience, as there is to the patience of suffering another to be wounded or imprisoned, as also because a man cannot tell when he seeth men proceed against him by violence whether they intend his death or not. And lastly the motive and end for which this renouncing and transferring of right is introduced is nothing else but the security of a man's person, in his life, and in the means of so preserving life as not to be weary of it. And therefore if a man by words, or other signs, seem to despoil himself of the end for which those signs were intended, he is not to be understood as if he meant it, or that it was his will, but that he was ignorant of how such words and actions were to be interpreted.

The mutual transferring of right is that which men call *contract* . . . one of the contractors may deliver the thing contracted for on his part, and leave the other to perform his part at some determinate time after, and in the meantime be trusted; and then the contract on his part is called *pact,* or *covenant* or both parts may contract now to perform hereafter, in which cases he that is to perform in time to come, being trusted, his performance is called *keeping of promise,* or *faith,* and the failing of performance, if it be voluntary, *violation of faith.* . . . He that performeth first in the case of a contract is said to *merit* that which he is to receive by the performance of the other, and he hath it as his *due.* . . .

If a covenant be made wherein neither of the parties perform presently, but trust one another, in the condition of mere nature (which is a condition of war of every man against every man) upon any reasonable suspicion, it is void: but if there be a common power set over them both, with right and force sufficient to compel performance, it is not void. For he that performeth first has no assurance the other will perform after, because the bonds of words are too weak to bridle men's ambition, avarice, anger, and other passions, without the fear of some coercive power; which in the condition of mere nature, where all men are equal, and judges of the justness of their own fears, cannot possibly be supposed. And therefore he which performeth first does but betray himself to his enemy, contrary to the right he can never abandon of defending his life and means of living.

But in a civil estate, where there is a power set up to constrain those that would otherwise violate their faith, that fear is no more reasonable; and for that cause, he which by the covenant is to perform first is obliged so to do. . . .

The matter or subject of a covenant is always something that falleth under deliberation, for to covenant is an act of the will; that is to say, an act, and the last act, of deliberation; and is therefore always understood to be something to come, and which is judged possible for him that covenanteth to perform.

And therefore, to promise that which is known to be impossible is no covenant. But if that prove impossible afterwards, which before was thought possible, the covenant is valid and bindeth, though not to the thing itself, yet to the value, or, if that also be impossible, to the unfeigned endeavor of performing as much as is possible, for to more no man can be obliged.

Men are freed of their covenants two ways; by performing, or by being forgiven. For performance is the natural end of obligation, and forgiveness the restitution of liberty, as being a retransferring of that right in which the obligation consisted.

Covenants entered into by fear, in the condition of mere nature, are obligatory. For example, if I covenant to pay a ransom, or service for my life, to an enemy, I am bound by it. For it is a contract, wherein one receiveth the benefit of life; the other is to receive money, or service for it, and consequently, where no other law (as in the condition of mere nature) forbiddeth the performance, the covenant is valid. Therefore prisoners of war, if trusted with the payment of their ransom, are obliged to pay it: and if a weaker prince make a disadvantageous peace with a stronger, for fear, he is bound to keep it; unless (as hath been said before) there ariseth some new and just cause of fear to renew the war. And even in Commonwealths, if I be forced to redeem myself from a thief by promising him money, I am bound to pay it, till the civil law discharge me. For whatsoever I may lawfully do without obligation, the same I may lawfully covenant to do through fear: and what I lawfully covenant, I cannot lawfully break.

A former covenant makes void a later. For a man that hath passed away his right to one man today hath it not to pass tomorrow to another: and therefore the later promise passeth no right, but is null.

A covenant not to defend myself from force, by force, is always void. For (as I have shown before) no man can transfer or lay down his right to save himself from death, wounds, and imprisonment, the avoiding whereof is the only end of laying down any right; and therefore the promise of not resisting force, in no covenant transferreth any right, nor is obliging. For though a man may covenant thus, *unless I do so, or so, kill me;* he cannot covenant thus, *unless I do so, or so, I will not resist you when you come to kill me.* For man by nature chooseth the lesser evil, which is danger of death in resisting, rather than the greater, which is certain and present death in not resisting. And this is granted to be true by all men, in that they lead criminals to execution, and prison, with armed men, notwithstanding that such criminals have consented to the law by which they are condemned.

A covenant to accuse oneself, without assurance of pardon, is likewise invalid. For in the condition of nature, where every man is judge, there is no place for accusation: and in the civil state the accusation is followed with punishment, which, being force, a man is not obliged not to resist. . . .

It appears also that the oath adds nothing to the obligation. For a covenant, if lawful, binds in the sight of God, without the oath, as much as with it; if unlawful, bindeth not at all, though it be confirmed with an oath.

John Locke (1632–1704)

John Locke comes from a different revolution. Shortly after Hobbes wrote, the monarchy was restored. When it threatened to become inconvenient again, the English Parliament lost patience with their king, threw him out of the country, and invited one Prince William of Orange, Prince of the Netherlands, to be their king. He was a good king. More to the point, Parliament had established that it and it alone, the representative of the people, had the right to control succession to the English throne. Despite all the flaws in the democracy of the time, England was firmly in democratic hands. Locke's writings celebrate that revolution, the Glorious Revolution of 1688.

In his political theory Locke carries on from Hobbes, with a gentler view of human nature, but with many of the same assumptions about human motivation and the consequences for human action. The primary objective of the social contract in Locke is the protection of property, in which term he includes our notions of life and liberty (for a man's body and freedom are, after all, his own), but which is most endangered, in the state of nature, in the form of physical property and its enjoyment. We need civil society primarily for the safety of lands and industry: settling boundaries, setting regulations, and establishing judges for the inevitable disputes. Here the fundamental rights of the human being—life, liberty, and property—are established, along with the role of the law in protecting those rights.

From John Locke, *Treatise of Government*

Part II
Chapter II: Of the State of Nature

4. To understand political power aright, and derive it from its original, we must consider what estate all men are naturally in, and that is, a state of perfect freedom to order their actions, and dispose of their possessions and persons as they think fit, within the bounds of the law of Nature, without asking leave or depending upon the will of any other man.

A state also of equality, wherein all the power and jurisdiction is reciprocal, no one having more than another, there being nothing more evident than that creatures of the same species and rank, promiscuously born to all the same advantages of Nature, and the use of the same faculties, should also be equal one amongst another, without subordination or subjection, unless the lord and master of them all should, by any manifest declaration of his will, set one above another, and confer on him, by an evident and clear appointment, an undoubted right to dominion and sovereignty. . . .

6. But though this be a state of liberty, yet it is not a state of licence; though man in that state have an uncontrollable liberty to dispose of his person or possessions, yet he has not liberty to destroy himself, or so much as any creature in his possession, but where some nobler use than its bare preservation calls for it. The state of Nature has a law of Nature to govern it, which obliges every one, and reason, which is that law, teaches all mankind who will but consult it, that being all equal and independent, no one ought to harm another in his life, health, liberty or possessions; for men being all the workmanship of one omnipotent and infinitely wise Maker; all the servants of one sovereign Master, sent into the world by His order and about His business; they are His property, whose workmanship they are made to last during His, not one another's pleasure. And being furnished with like faculties, sharing all in one community of Nature, there cannot be supposed any such subordination among us that may authorize us to destroy one another, as if we were made for one another's uses, as the inferior ranks of creatures are for ours. Every one as he is bound to preserve himself, and not to quit his station wilfully, so by the like reason, when his own preservation comes not in competition, ought he as much as he can to preserve the rest of mankind, and not unless it be to do justice on an offender, take away or impair the life, or what tends to the preservation of the life, the liberty, health, limb, or goods of another.

7. And that all men may be restrained from invading others' rights, and from doing hurt to one another, and the law of Nature be observed, which willeth the peace and preservation of all mankind, the execution of the law of Nature is in that state put into every man's hands, whereby every one has a right to punish the transgressors of that law to such a degree as may hinder its violation. For the law of Nature would, as all other laws that concern man in this world, be in vain if there were nobody that in the state of Nature had a power to execute that law, and thereby preserve the

innocent and restrain offenders; and if any one in the state of Nature may punish another for any evil he has done, every one may do so. For in that state of perfect equality, where naturally there is no superiority or jurisdiction of one over another, what any may do in prosecution of that law, every one must needs have a right to do.

8. And thus, in the state of Nature, one man comes by a power over another, but yet no absolute or arbitrary power to use a criminal, when he has got him in his hands, according to the passionate heats or boundless extravagancy of his own will, but only to retribute to him so far as calm reason and conscience dictate, what is proportionate to his transgression, which is so much as may serve for reparation and restraint. For these two are the only reasons why one man may lawfully do harm to another, which is that we call punishment. In transgressing the law of Nature, the offender declares himself to live by another rule than that of reason and common equity, which is that measure God has set to the actions of men for their mutual security, and so he becomes dangerous to mankind; the tie which is to secure them from injury and violence being slighted and broken by him, which being a trespass against the whole species, and the peace and safety of it, provided for by the law of Nature, every man upon this score, by the right he hath to preserve mankind in general, may restrain, or where it is necessary, destroy things noxious to them, and so may bring such evil on any one who hath transgressed that law, as may make him repent the doing of it, and thereby deter him, and, by his example, others from doing the like mischief. And in this case, and upon this ground, every man hath a right to punish the offender, and be executioner of the law of Nature.

9. I doubt not but this will seem a very strange doctrine to some men; but before they condemn it, I desire them to resolve me by what right any prince or state can put to death or punish an alien for any crime he commits in their country? It is certain their laws, by virtue of any sanction they receive from the promulgated will of the legislature, reach not a stranger. They speak not to him, nor, if they did, is he bound to hearken to them. The legislative authority by which they are in force over the subjects of that commonwealth hath no power over him. Those who have the supreme power of making laws in England, France, or Holland are, to an Indian, but like the rest of the world—men without authority. And therefore, if by the law of Nature every man hath not a power to punish offences against it, as he soberly judges the case to require, I see not how the magistrates of any community can punish an alien of another country, since, in reference to him, they can have no more power than what every man naturally may have over another.

10. Besides the crime which consists in violating the laws, and varying from the right rule of reason, whereby a man so far becomes degenerate, and declares himself to quit the principles of human nature and to be a noxious creature, there is commonly injury done, and some person or other, some other man, receives damage by his transgression; in which case, he who hath received any damage has (besides the right of punishment, common to him, with other men) a particular right to seek reparation from him that hath done it. And any other person who finds it just may also join with him that is injured, and assist him in recovering from the offender so much as may make satisfaction for the harm he hath suffered.

11. From these two distinct rights (the one of punishing the crime, for restraint and preventing the like offence, which right of punishing is in everybody, the other of taking reparation, which belongs only to the injured party) comes it to pass that the magistrate, who by being magistrate hath the common right of punishing put into his hands, can often, where the public good demands not the execution of the law, remit the punishment of criminal offences by his own authority, but yet cannot remit the satisfaction due to any private man for the damage he has received. That he who hath suffered the damage has a right to demand in his own name, and he alone can remit. The damnified person has this power of appropriating to himself the goods or service of the offender by right of self-preservation, as every man has a power to punish the crime to prevent its being committed again, by the right he has of

preserving all mankind, and doing all reasonable things he can in order to achieve that end. And thus it is that every man in the state of Nature has a power to kill a murderer, both to deter others from doing the like injury (which no reparation can compensate) by the example of the punishment that attends it from everybody, and also to secure men from the attempts of a criminal who, having renounced reason, the common rule and measure God hath given to mankind, hath, by the unjust violence and slaughter he hath committed upon one, declared war against all mankind, and therefore may be destroyed as a lion or a tiger, one of those wild savage beasts with whom men can have no society nor security. And upon this is grounded that great law of Nature, "Whoso sheddeth man's blood, by man shall his blood be shed." And Cain was so fully convinced that every one had a right to destroy such a criminal, that, after the murder of his brother, he cries out, "Every one that findeth me shall slay me," so plain was it writ in the hearts of all mankind.

12. By the same reason may a man in the state of Nature punish the lesser breaches of that law, it will, perhaps, be demanded, with death? I answer: Each transgression may be punished to that degree, and with so much severity, as will suffice to make it an ill bargain to the offender, give him cause to repent, and terrify others from doing the like. Every offence that can be committed in the state of Nature may, in the state of Nature, be also punished equally, and as far forth, as it may, in a commonwealth. For though it would be beside my present purpose to enter here into the particulars of the law of Nature, or its measures of punishment, yet it is certain there is such a law, and that too as intelligible and plain to a rational creature and a studier of that law as the positive laws of commonwealths, nay, possibly plainer; as much as reason is easier to be understood than the fancies and intricate contrivances of men, following contrary and hidden interests put into words: for truly so are a great part of the municipal laws of countries, which are only so far right as they are founded on the law of Nature, by which they are to be regulated and interpreted.

13. To this strange doctrine, viz., That in the state of Nature every one has the executive power of the law of Nature—I doubt not but it will be objected that it is unreasonable for men to be judges in their own cases, that self-love will make men partial to themselves and their friends; and, on the other side, ill-nature, passion, and revenge will carry them too far in punishing others, and hence nothing but confusion and disorder will follow, and that therefore God hath certainly appointed government to restrain the partiality and violence of men. I easily grant that civil government is the proper remedy for the inconveniences of the state of Nature, which must certainly be great where men may be judges in their own case, since it is easy to be imagined that he who was so unjust as to do his brother an injury will scarce be so just as to condemn himself for it. But I shall desire those who make this objection to remember that absolute monarchs are but men; and if government is to be the remedy of those evils which necessarily follow from men being judges in their own cases, and the state of Nature is therefore not to be endured, I desire to know what kind of government that is, and how much better it is than the state of Nature, where one man commanding a multitude has the liberty to be judge in his own case, and may do to all his subjects whatever he pleases without the least question or control of those who execute his pleasure? and in whatsoever he doth, whether led by reason, mistake, or passion, must be submitted to? which men in the state of Nature are not bound to do one to another. And if he that judges, judges amiss in his own or any other case, he is answerable for it to the rest of mankind.

14. It is often asked as a mighty objection, where are, or ever were, there any men in such a state of Nature? To which it may suffice as an answer at present, that since all princes and rulers of "independent" governments all through the world are in a state of Nature, it is plain the world never was, nor never will be, without numbers of men in that state. I have named all governors of "independent" communities, whether they are, or are not, in league with others; for it is not every compact that puts an

end to the state of Nature between men, but only this one of agreeing together mutually to enter into one community, and make one body politic; other promises and compacts men may make one with another, and yet still be in the state of Nature. . . .

Chapter V: Of Property

25. Whether we consider natural reason, which tells us that men, being once born, have a right to their preservation, and consequently to meat and drink and such other things as Nature affords for their subsistence, or "revelation," which gives us an account of those grants God made of the world to Adam, and to Noah and his sons, it is very clear that God, as King David says (Psalm cxv. 16), "has given the earth to the children of men," given it to mankind in common. . . . I shall endeavour to show how men might come to have a property in several parts of that which God gave to mankind in common, and that without any express compact of all the commoners.

26. God, who hath given the world to men in common, hath also given them reason to make use of it to the best advantage of life and convenience. The earth and all that is therein is given to men for the support and comfort of their being. And though all the fruits it naturally produces, and beasts it feeds, belong to mankind in common, as they are produced by the spontaneous hand of Nature, and nobody has originally a private dominion exclusive of the rest of mankind in any of them, as they are thus in their natural state, yet being given for the use of men, there must of necessity be a means to appropriate them some way or other before they can be of any use, or at all beneficial, to any particular men. The fruit or venison which nourishes the wild Indian, who knows no enclosure, and is still a tenant in common, must be his, and so his—i.e., a part of him, that another can no longer have any right to it before it can do him any good for the support of his life.

27. Though the earth and all inferior creatures be common to all men, yet every man has a "property" in his own "person." This nobody has any right to but himself. The "labour" of his body and the "work" of his hands, we may say, are properly his. Whatsoever, then, he removes out of the state that Nature hath provided and left it in, he hath mixed his labour with it, and joined to it something that is his own, and thereby makes it his property. It being by him removed from the common state Nature placed it in, it hath by this labour something annexed to it that excludes the common right of other men. For this "labour" being the unquestionable property of the labourer, no man but he can have a right to what that is once joined to, at least where there is enough, and as good left in common for others.

28. He that is nourished by the acorns he picked up under an oak, or the apples he gathered from the trees in the wood, has certainly appropriated them to himself. Nobody can deny but the nourishment is his. I ask, then, when did they begin to be his? when he digested? or when he ate? or when he boiled? or when he brought them home? or when he picked them up? and it is plain, if the first gathering made them not his, nothing else could. That labour put a distinction between them and common. That added something to them more than Nature, the common mother of all, had done, and so they became his private right. And will any one say he had no right to those acorns or apples he thus appropriated because he had not the consent of all mankind to make them his? Was it a robbery thus to assume to himself what belonged to all in common? If such a consent as that was necessary, man had starved, notwithstanding the plenty God had given him. We see in commons, which remain so by compact, that it is the taking any part of what is common, and removing it out of the state Nature leaves it in, which begins the property, without which the common is of no use. And the taking of this or that part does not depend on the express consent of all the commoners. Thus, the grass my horse has bit, the turfs my servant has cut, and the ore I have digged in any place, where I have a right to them in common with others, become my property without the assignation

or consent of anybody. The labour that was mine, removing them out of that common state they were in, hath fixed my property in them. . . .

30. Thus this law of reason makes the deer that Indian's who hath killed it; it is allowed to be his goods who hath bestowed his labour upon it, though, before, it was the common right of every one. And amongst those who are counted the civilised part of mankind, who have made and multiplied positive laws to determine property, this original law of Nature for the beginning of property, in what was before common, still takes place, and by virtue thereof, what fish any one catches in the ocean, that great and still remaining common of mankind; or what ambergris any one takes up here is by the labour that removes it out of that common state Nature left it in, made his property who takes that pains about it. . . .

31. It will, perhaps, be objected to this, that if gathering the acorns or other fruits of the earth, etc., makes a right to them, then any one may engross as much as he will. To which I answer, Not so. The same law of Nature that does by this means give us property, does also bound that property too. "God has given us all things richly." Is the voice of reason confirmed by inspiration? But how far has He given it us "to enjoy"? As much as any one can make use of to any advantage of life before it spoils, so much he may by his labour fix a property in. Whatever is beyond this is more than his share, and belongs to others. Nothing was made by God for man to spoil or destroy. And thus considering the plenty of natural provisions there was a long time in the world, and the few spenders, and to how small a part of that provision the industry of one man could extend itself and engross it to the prejudice of others, especially keeping within the bounds set by reason of what might serve for his use, there could be then little room for quarrels or contentions about property so established.

32. But the chief matter of property being now not the fruits of the earth and the beasts that subsist on it, but the earth itself, as that which takes in and carries with it all the rest, I think it is plain that property in that too is acquired as the former. As much land as a man tills, plants, improves, cultivates, and can use the product of, so much is his property. He by his labour does, as it were, enclose it from the common. Nor will it invalidate his right to say everybody else has an equal title to it, and therefore he cannot appropriate, he cannot enclose, without the consent of all his fellow-commoners, all mankind. God, when He gave the world in common to all mankind, commanded man also to labour, and the penury of his condition required it of him. God and his reason commanded him to subdue the earth—i.e., improve it for the benefit of life and therein lay out something upon it that was his own, his labour. He that, in obedience to this command of God, subdued, tilled, and sowed any part of it, thereby annexed to it something that was his property, which another had no title to, nor could without injury take from him.

33. Nor was this appropriation of any parcel of land, by improving it, any prejudice to any other man, since there was still enough and as good left, and more than the yet unprovided could use. So that, in effect, there was never the less left for others because of his enclosure for himself. For he that leaves as much as another can make use of does as good as take nothing at all. Nobody could think himself injured by the drinking of another man, though he took a good draught, who had a whole river of the same water left him to quench his thirst. And the case of land and water, where there is enough of both, is perfectly the same. . . .

Chapter VII: Of Political or Civil Society

77. God, having made man such a creature that, in His own judgment, it was not good for him to be alone, put him under strong obligations of necessity, convenience, and inclination, to drive him into society, as well as fitted him with understanding and language to continue and enjoy it. The first society was between man and wife, which gave beginning to that between parents and children, to which, in time, that between master and servant came to be added. And though all these might, and commonly

did, meet together, and make up but one family, wherein the master or mistress of it had some sort of rule proper to a family, each of these, or all together, came short of "political society," as we shall see if we consider the different ends, ties, and bounds of each of these. . . .

86. Let us therefore consider a master of a family with all these subordinate relations of wife, children, servants and slaves, united under the domestic rule of a family, with what resemblance soever it may have in its order, offices, and number too, with a little commonwealth, yet is very far from it both in its constitution, power, and end; or if it must be thought a monarchy, and the paterfamilias the absolute monarch in it, absolute monarchy will have but a very shattered and short power, when it is plain by what has been said before, that the master of the family has a very distinct and differently limited power both as to time and extent over those several persons that are in it. . . . But how a family, or any other society of men, differ from that which is properly a political society, we shall best see by considering wherein political society itself consists.

87. Man being born . . . with a title to perfect freedom and an uncontrolled enjoyment of all the rights and privileges of the law of Nature, equally with any other man, or number of men in the world, hath by nature a power not only to preserve his property—that is, his life, liberty and estate, against the injuries and attempts of other men, but to judge of and punish the breaches of that law in others, as he is persuaded the offence deserves, even with death itself, in crimes where the heinousness of the fact, in his opinion, requires it. But because no political society can be, nor subsist, without having in itself the power to preserve the property, and in order thereunto to punish the offences of all those of that society, there, and there only, is political society where every one of the members hath quitted this natural power, resigned it up into the hands of the community in all cases that exclude him not from appealing for protection to the law established by it. And thus all private judgment of every particular member being excluded, the community comes to be umpire, and by understanding indifferent rules and men authorized by the community for their execution, decides all the differences that may happen between any members of that society concerning any matter of right, and punishes those offences which any member hath committed against the society with such penalties as the law has established; whereby it is easy to discern who are, and are not, in political society together.

Those who are united into one body, and have a common established law and judicature to appeal to, with authority to decide controversies between them and punish offenders, are in civil society one with another; but those who have no such common appeal, I mean on earth, are still in the state of Nature, each being where there is no other, judge for himself and executioner; which is, as I have before showed it, the perfect state of Nature.

88. And thus the commonwealth comes by a power to set down what punishment shall belong to the several transgressions they think worthy of it, committed amongst the members of that society (which is the power of making laws), as well as it has the power to punish any injury done unto any of its members by any one that is not of it (which is the power of war and peace); and all this for the preservation of the property of all the members of that society, as far as is possible. But though every man entered into society has quitted his power to punish offences against the law of Nature in prosecution of his own private judgment, yet with the judgment of offences which he has given up to the legislative, in all cases where he can appeal to the magistrate, he has given up a right to the commonwealth to employ his force for the execution of the judgments of the commonwealth whenever he shall be called to it, which, indeed, are his own judgments, they being made by himself or his representative. And herein we have the original of the legislative and executive power of civil society, which is to judge by standing laws how far offences are to be punished when committed within the commonwealth; and also by occasional judgments founded on the present circumstances of the fact, how far injuries from without are to be vindicated, and in both these to employ all the force of all the members when there shall be need.

89. Wherever, therefore, any number of men so unite into one society as to quit every one his executive power of the law of Nature, and to resign it to the public, there and there only is a political or civil society. And this is done wherever any number of men, in the state of Nature, enter into society to make one people one body politic under one supreme government: or else when any one joins himself to, and incorporates with any government already made. For hereby he authorizes the society, or which is all one, the legislative thereof, to make laws for him as the public good of the society shall require, to the execution whereof his own assistance (as to his own decrees) is due. And this puts men out of a state of Nature into that of a commonwealth, by setting up a judge on earth with authority to determine all the controversies and redress the injuries that may happen to any member of the commonwealth, which judge is the legislative or magistrates appointed by it. And wherever there are any number of men, however associated, that have no such decisive power to appeal to, there they are still in the state of Nature.

90. And hence it is evident that absolute monarchy, which by some men is counted for the only government in the world, is indeed inconsistent with civil society, and so can be no form of civil government at all. For the end of civil society being to avoid and remedy those inconveniencies of the state of Nature which necessarily follow from every man's being judge in his own case, by setting up a known authority to which every one of that society may appeal upon any injury received, or controversy that may arise, and which every one of the society ought to obey. Wherever any persons are who have not such an authority to appeal to, and decide any difference between them there, those persons are still in the state of Nature. And so is every absolute prince in respect of those who are under his dominion. . . .

94. But, whatever flatterers may talk to amuse people's understandings, it never hinders men from feeling; and when they perceive that any man, in what station soever, is out of the bounds of the civil society they are of, and that they have no appeal, on earth, against any harm they may receive from him, they are apt to think themselves in the state of Nature, in respect of him whom they find to be so; and to take care, as soon as they can, to have that safety and security, in civil society, for which it was first instituted, and for which only they entered into it. . . . No man in civil society can be exempted from the laws of it. For if any man may do what he thinks fit and there be no appeal on earth for redress or security against any harm he shall do, I ask whether he be not perfectly still in the state of Nature, and so can be no part or member of that civil society, unless any one will say the state of Nature and civil society are one and the same thing, which I have never yet found any one so great a patron of anarchy as to affirm.

Chapter VIII: Of the Beginning of Political Societies

95. Men being, as has been said, by nature all free, equal, and independent, no one can be put out of this estate and subjected to the political power of another without his own consent, which is done by agreeing with other men, to join and unite into a community for their comfortable, safe, and peaceable living, one amongst another, in a secure enjoyment of their properties, and a greater security against any that are not of it. This any number of men may do, because it injures not the freedom of the rest; they are left, as they were, in the liberty of the state of Nature. When any number of men have so consented to make one community or government, they are thereby presently incorporated, and make one body politic, wherein the majority have a right to act and conclude the rest. . . .

98. For if the consent of the majority shall not in reason be received as the act of the whole, and conclude every individual, nothing but the consent of every individual can make anything to be the act of the whole, which, considering the infirmities of health and avocations of business, which in a number though much less than that of a commonwealth, will necessarily keep many away from the public assembly; and the variety of opinions and contrariety of interests which unavoidably happens

in all collections of men, it is next to impossible ever to be had. And, therefore, if coming into society be upon such terms, it will be only like Cato's coming into the theatre, *tantum ut exiret*. Such a constitution as this would make the mighty leviathan of a shorter duration than the feeblest creatures, and not let it outlast the day it was born in, which cannot be supposed till we can think that rational creatures should desire and constitute societies only to be dissolved. For where the majority cannot conclude the rest, there they cannot act as one body, and injustice. Such resistance many times makes the punishment dangerous, and frequently destructive to those who attempt it.

127. Thus mankind, notwithstanding all the privileges of the state of Nature, being but in an ill condition while they remain in it are quickly driven into society. Hence it comes to pass, that we seldom find any number of men live any time together in this state. The inconveniencies that they are therein exposed to by the irregular and uncertain exercise of the power every man has of punishing the transgressions of others, make them take sanctuary under the established laws of government, and therein seek the preservation of their property. It is this makes them so willingly give up every one his single power of punishing to be exercised by such alone as shall be appointed to it amongst them, and by such rules as the community, or those authorised by them to that purpose, shall agree on. And in this we have the original right and rise of both the legislative and executive power as well as of the governments and societies themselves.

128. For in the state of Nature to omit the liberty he has of innocent delights, a man has two powers. The first is to do whatsoever he thinks fit for the preservation of himself and others within the permission of the law of Nature; by which law, common to them all, he and all the rest of mankind are one community, make up one society distinct from all other creatures, and were it not for the corruption and viciousness of degenerate men, there would be no need of any other, no necessity that men should separate from this great and natural community, and associate into lesser combinations. The other power a man has in the state of Nature is the power to punish the crimes committed against that law. Both these he gives up when he joins in a private, if I may so call it, or particular political society, and incorporates into any commonwealth separate from the rest of mankind. . . .

131. But though men when they enter into society give up the equality, liberty, and executive power they had in the state of Nature into the hands of the society, to be so far disposed of by the legislative as the good of the society shall require, yet it being only with an intention in every one the better to preserve himself, his liberty and property (for no rational creature can be supposed to change his condition with an intention to be worse), the power of the society or legislative constituted by them can never be supposed to extend farther than the common good, but is obliged to secure every one's property by providing against those three defects above mentioned that made the state of Nature so unsafe and uneasy. And so, whoever has the legislative or supreme power of any commonwealth, is bound to govern by established standing laws, promulgated and known to the people, and not by extemporary decrees, by indifferent and upright judges, who are to decide controversies by those laws; and to employ the force of the community at home only in the execution of such laws, or abroad to prevent or redress foreign injuries and secure the community from inroads and invasion. And all this to be directed to no other end but the peace, safety, and public good of the people. . . .

142. These are the bounds which the trust that is put in them by the society and the law of God and Nature have set to the legislative power of every commonwealth, in all forms of government. First: They are to govern by promulgated established laws, not to be varied in particular cases, but to have one rule for rich and poor, for the favourite at Court, and the countryman at plough. Secondly: These laws also ought to be designed for no other end ultimately but the good of the people. Thirdly: They must not raise taxes on the property of the people without the consent of the people given by themselves or their deputies. And this properly concerns only such governments where the legislative is always in being, or at least where the people have not reserved any part of the legislative to deputies, to be from time to time

chosen by themselves. Fourthly: Legislative neither must nor can transfer the power of making laws to anybody else, or place it anywhere but where the people have. . . .

155. It may be demanded here, what if the executive power, being possessed of the force of the commonwealth, shall make use of that force to hinder the meeting and acting of the legislative, when the original constitution or the public exigencies require it? I say, using force upon the people, without authority, and contrary to the trust put in him that does so, is a state of war with the people, who have a right to reinstate their legislative in the exercise of their power. For having erected a legislative with an intent they should exercise the power of making laws, either at certain set times, or when there is need of it, when they are hindered by any force from what is so necessary to the society, and wherein the safety and preservation of the people consists, the people have a right to remove it by force. In all states and conditions the true remedy of force without authority is to oppose force to it. The use of force without authority always puts him that uses it into a state of war as the aggressor, and renders him liable to be treated accordingly. . . .

168. The old question will be asked in this matter of prerogative, "But who shall be judge when this power is made a right use of?" I answer: Between an executive power in being, with such a prerogative, and a legislative that depends upon his will for their convening, there can be no judge on earth. As there can be none between the legislative and the people, should either the executive or the legislative, when they have got the power in their hands, design, or go about to enslave or destroy them, the people have no other remedy in this, as in all other cases where they have no judge on earth, but to appeal to Heaven; for the rulers in such attempts, exercising a power the people never put into their hands, who can never be supposed to consent that anybody should rule over them for their harm, do that which they have not a right to do. And where the body of the people, or any single man, are deprived of their right, or are under the exercise of a power without right, having no appeal on earth they have a liberty to appeal to Heaven whenever they judge the cause of sufficient moment. And therefore, though the people cannot be judge, so as to have, by the constitution of that society, any superior power to determine and give effective sentence in the case, yet they have reserved that ultimate determination to themselves which belongs to all mankind, where there lies no appeal on earth, by a law antecedent and paramount to all positive laws of men, whether they have just cause to make their appeal to Heaven. And this judgment they cannot part with, it being out of a man's power so to submit himself to another as to give him a liberty to destroy him; God and Nature never allowing a man so to abandon himself as to neglect his own preservation. And since he cannot take away his own life, neither can he give another power to take it. Nor let any one think this lays a perpetual foundation for disorder; for this operates not till the inconvenience is so great that the majority feel it, and are weary of it, and find a necessity to have it amended. And this the executive power, or wise princes, never need come in danger of, and it is the thing of all others they have most need to avoid, as, of all others, the most perilous.

Jean-Jacques Rousseau (1712–1778)

Jean-Jacques Rousseau attempts to thread the path between Hobbes and Locke, for the two of them have left us with a very severe problem of legitimacy in organized human society. Let us review. For Aristotle, the "legitimacy" of the state did not need to be proved to humans any more than the legitimacy of hive-living had to be proved to bees. The state arose by nature, and by its nature it permitted human nature to be fulfilled. No more argument was needed. But now we live in the age of individualism, and each person regards herself as a sovereign state, self-sufficient, able and determined to decide by self-interested calculation whether or not any group should be joined, any "compact" entered into.

Hobbes has given her an argument from survival: submit to the leader or die, either at the leader's hands or the hands of your neighbor. As you value your life, sign the Social Contract that establishes the Leviathan, and obey it until that life is threatened by it. But that Contract abolishes all other rights, and somehow that doesn't make sense. So Locke preserves the rights, and gives us a very limited government that operates by majority vote, limiting the Ruler. Fine, but majorities can be spectacularly wrong. Is every majority vote legitimate? Locke has to say yes, allowing only for a written constitution (also terminable by the majority) to protect us from the mob.

Rousseau sees that while either of these schemas can work (both have), both are legitimate only by chance. Rousseau insists that Society, the product of the first, unanimous Contract, carries the true will of the people, the General Will, and is distinct from the State, product of a majority vote, which can only give us the Will of All. Locke therefore is wrong in his insistence that (whichever it is) the majority is always right, or at least, that there is no conceivable power to place against the majority. And Hobbes is certainly wrong in his cheerful abandonment of liberty in the name of security.

Rousseau holds that a person who does what is in his own highest interest is doing what he wants, that a person who does what he wants is free, and that therefore a society geared to do what is surely best will retain everyone's freedom (in slightly different form) enjoyed so perfectly in the state of Nature. The General Will, which cannot err, and however it is exercised, is nothing other than the repository of everyone's free choice, so if forced to conform to it, a person is only forced to be free.

Does this solution work in establishing the legitimacy of a government? Rousseau's claims have been controversial for two centuries now. Join the debate!

From Jean-Jacques Rousseau, *Of the Social Contract*

I. Subject of This First Book

Man is born free, and everywhere he is in chains. One believes himself the master of others, and yet he is a greater slave than they. How has this change come about? I do not know. What can render it legitimate? I believe that I can settle this question.

If I considered only force and the results that proceed from it, I should say that so long as a People is compelled to obey and does obey, it does well; but that, so soon as it can shake off the yoke and does shake it off, it does better; for, recovering its liberty by the same right by which it was taken away, either it is justified in resuming it, or there was no justification for depriving them of it. But the social order, is a sacred right which serves as a basis for all others. Yet this right does not come from nature; it is therefore based on conventions. The question is to know what these conventions are. Before coming to that, I must establish what I have just laid down.

II. Of the First Societies

The most ancient of all societies, and the only natural one, is the family. Nevertheless children remain bound to their father only as long as they have need of him for their own preservation. As soon as this need ceases, the natural bond is dissolved. The children freed from the obedience which they owe to their father, and the father from the cares which he owes to his children, become equally independent. If they remain united, it is no longer naturally but voluntarily, and the family itself is kept together only by convention.

This common liberty is a consequence of man's nature. His first law is to attend to his own preservation, his first cares are those which he owes to himself, and as soon as he comes to years of discretion, being sole judge of the means adapted for his own preservation, he becomes thereby his own master.

III. Of the Right of the Strongest

The strongest man is never strong enough to be always master, unless he transforms his force into right, and obedience into duty. Hence the right of the strongest—a right assumed ironically in appearance, and really established in principle. But will this word never be explained to us? Force is a physical power; I do not see what morality can result from its effects. To yield to force is an act of necessity, not of will; it is at most an act of prudence. In what sense could it be a duty?

Let us suppose for a moment this pretended right. I say that nothing results from it but an inexplicable muddle. For as soon as force constitutes right, the effect changes with the cause; every force which overcomes the first succeeds to its right (privilege). As soon as one can disobey with impunity, he may do so legitimately; and since the strongest is always in the right, it remains merely to act in such a way that one may be the strongest. But what sort of a right perishes when force ceases? If it is necessary to obey by compulsion, there is no need to obey by duty; and if men are no longer forced to obey, obligation is at an end. Obviously, then, this word "right" adds nothing to force; it means nothing here at all.

Obey the powers that be. If that means yield to force, the precept is good but superfluous; I warrant that it will never be violated. All power comes from God, I admit; but every disease does also. Does it follow that we are prohibited from calling in a physician? If a brigand should surprise me in the recesses of a wood: not only am I bound to give up my purse when forced, but am I also in conscience bound to do so when I might conceal it? For after all, the pistol which he holds is also a power.

Let us agree, then, that might does not make right, and that we are obligated to obey only legitimate powers. Thus my original questions ever recur.

IV. Of Slavery

Since no man has a natural authority over his fellow men, and since force is not the source of right, conventions remain as the basis of all legitimate authority among men.

If an individual, says Grotius, can alienate his liberty and become the slave of a master, why should a whole people not be able to alienate theirs, and subject themselves to a king? In this there are a good many equivocal words that require explanation; but let us confine ourselves to the word *alienate.* To alienate is to give or sell. Now a man who becomes another's slave does not give himself; he sells himself at the very least for his subsistence; but why does a people sell itself? Far from a king supplying to his subjects their subsistence, he draws his from them; and according to Rabelais, a king does not live on little. Do subjects, then, give up their persons on condition that their goods also shall be taken? I do not see what is left for them to keep.

It will be said that the despot secures to his subjects civil peace. Just so; but what do they gain by that, if the wars which his ambition brings upon them, together with his insatiable greed and the vexations of his administration, dishearten them more than their own dissensions would? What do they gain if this peace itself is one of their miseries? One lives peacefully also in dungeons; is this enough to find them good? The Greeks confined in the cave of the Cyclops lived peacefully until their turn came to be devoured.

To say that a man gives himself for nothing is to say something absurd and inconceivable; such an act is illegitimate and worthless, for the simple reason that he who performs it is not in his right mind. To say the same thing of a whole people is to suppose a people of madmen; and madness does not make right.

Even if each person could alienate himself, he could not alienate his children; they are born men and free; their liberty belongs to them, and no one has a right to dispose of it except themselves. Before they have come to an age of discretion, the father can, in their name, stipulate conditions for their preservation and welfare, but not surrender them irrevocably and unconditionally; for such a bequest is contrary to the ends of nature, and exceeds the rights of paternity. It would be necessary, therefore, to ensure that an arbitrary government might be legitimate, that with each generation the people have the option of accepting it or rejecting it; but in that case this government would no longer be arbitrary.

To renounce one's liberty is to renounce one's quality as a man, the rights of humanity and even its duties. For whoever renounces everything there is no possible compensation. Such renunciation is incompatible with man's nature; and to deprive his actions of all morality is tantamount to depriving his will of all freedom. Finally, a convention which stipulates absolute authority on the one side and unlimited obedience on the other is vain and contradictory. Is it not clear that one is under no obligations whatsoever toward a man from whom one has a right to demand everything? And does not this single condition, without equivalent, without exchange, entail the nullity of the act? For what right would my slave have against me, since all that he has belongs to me? His right being mine, this right of me against myself is a meaningless phrase.

V. That It Is Always Necessary to Go Back to a First Convention

Even if I were in accord with all that I have so far refuted, those who favor despotism would be no farther advanced. There will always be a great difference between subduing a multitude and ruling a society. If scattered men, however numerous they may be, are subjected successively to a single person, this seems to me only a case of master and slaves, not of a people and its chief: they form, if you will, an aggregation, but not an association, for they have neither public property nor a body politic. Such a man, had he enslaved half the world, is always only one individual; his interest, separated from that of the rest, is always only a private interest. If he dies, his empire after him is left scattered and disunited, as an oak dissolves and becomes a heap of ashes after the fire has consumed it.

A people, says Grotius, can give itself to a king. According to Grotius, a people, then, is a people before it gives itself to a king. This gift itself is a civil act, and presupposes a public deliberation. Hence, before examining the act by which a people elects a king, it would be good to examine the act by which a people is a people. For this act being necessarily anterior to the other, is the real foundation of the society.

In fact, if there were no anterior convention, where, unless the election were unanimous, would be the obligation upon the minority to submit to the decision of the majority? And whence do the hundred who desire a master derive the right to vote on behalf of ten who do not desire one? The law of the plurality of votes is itself established by convention, and presupposes unanimity at least once.

VI. Of the Social Pact

I suppose that men have reached a point at which the obstacles that endanger their preservation in the state of nature prevail by their resistance over the forces which each individual can exert in order to maintain himself in that state. Then this primitive condition can no longer subsist, and the human race would perish unless it changed its manner of being.

Now as men cannot create any new forces, but only unite and direct those that exist, they have no other means of self-preservation than to form by aggregation a sum of forces which may overcome the resistance, to put them in action by a single motive power, and to make them work in concert.

This sum of forces can be produced only by the combination of many; but the strength and freedom of each man being the primary instruments of his preservation, how can he pledge them without injuring himself, and without neglecting the care which he owes to himself? This difficulty, applied to my subject, may be stated in these terms:

"To find a form of association which defends and protects with the whole force of the community the person and goods of every associate, and by means of which each, uniting with all, nevertheless obeys only himself, and remains as free as before." Such is the fundamental problem to which the social contract gives the solution.

The clauses of this contract are so determined by the nature of the act that the slightest modification would render them vain and ineffectual; so that, although perhaps they have never been formally enunciated, they are everywhere the same, everywhere tacitly admitted and recognized; until, the social pact being violated, each man regains his initial rights and recovers his natural liberty, while losing the conventional liberty for which he renounced it.

These clauses, rightly understood, are all reducible to one only, namely the total alienation of each associate, with all of his rights, to the whole community: For, in the first place, as each gives himself up entirely, the condition is equal for all, and, the condition being equal for all, no one has any interest in making it burdensome to others.

Further, the alienation being made without reserve, the union is as perfect as it can be, and no associate has anything more to claim. For if some rights were left to individuals, since there would be no common superior who could judge between them and the public, each, being on some point his own judge, would soon claim to be so on all; the state of nature would still subsist, and the association would necessarily become tyrannical or useless.

Finally, each, in giving himself to all, gives himself to nobody; and as there is not one associate over whom we do not acquire the same rights which we concede to him over ourselves, we gain the equivalent of all that we lose, and more power to preserve what we have.

If, then, everything which is not of the essence of the social pact is set aside, one finds that it reduces itself to the following terms: *Each of us puts in common his person and his whole power under the supreme direction of the general will, and in return we receive in a body every member as an indivisible part of the whole.*

Forthwith, instead of the particular person of each contracting part, this act of association produces a moral and collective body, which is composed of as many members as the assembly has voices, and which receives from this same act its *unity*, its common *self*, its *life*, and its *will*. This public person, which is thus formed by the union of all the individual members, formerly took the name of *City [polis]* and now takes that of *Republic* or *body politic*, which is called by its members *State* when it is passive, *Sovereign* when it is active, *Power* when it is compared to similar bodies. With regard to the associates, they take collectively the name of *people,* and are called individually *Citizens,* as participating in the sovereign authority, and *Subjects,* as subjected to the laws of the State. But these terms are often confused and are mistaken one for another; it is sufficient to know how to distinguish them when they are used with complete precision.

VII. Of the Sovereign

One sees by this formula that the act of association includes a reciprocal engagement between the public and the individual, and that each individual, contracting so to speak with himself, is engaged in a double relation: namely, as a member of the Sovereign toward individuals, and as a member of the State toward the Sovereign. But we cannot apply here the maxim of civil right that no one is bound by engagements made with himself; for there is a great difference between being obligated to oneself and to a whole of which one forms a part.

It is necessary to note further that the public deliberation which can obligate all subjects to the Sovereign in consequence of the two different relations under which each of them is regarded cannot, for a contrary reason, bind the Sovereign to itself; and that accordingly it is contrary to the nature of the body politic for the Sovereign to impose on itself a law which it cannot transgress. As it can only be considered under one and the same relation, it is in the position of an individual contracting with himself; thus we see that there is not, nor can there be, any kind of fundamental law obligatory for the body of the people, not even the social contract. This does not imply that such a body cannot perfectly well enter into engagements with others in what does not derogate from this contract; for, with regard to foreigners, it becomes a simple being, an individual.

But the body politic or Sovereign, deriving its existence only from the sanctity of the contract, can never bind itself, even to others, in anything that derogates from the original act, such as to alienate some portion of itself, or submission to another Sovereign. To violate the act by which it exists would be to annihilate itself; and what is nothing produces nothing.

As soon as this multitude is thus united into one body, it is impossible to injure one of the members without attacking the body; still less to injure the body without the members feeling the effects. Thus duty and interest equally obligate the two contracting parties to give mutual assistance; and the same men should seek to combine in this twofold relationship all the advantages which are attendant on it.

Now the Sovereign, being formed only of the individuals who compose it, neither has nor can have any interest contrary to theirs; consequently the Sovereign power needs no guarantee toward its subjects, because it is impossible that the body should wish to injure all its members; and we shall see hereafter that it can injure no one in particular. The Sovereign, for the simple reason that it is, is always everything that it ought to be.

But this is not the case with respect to the relation of subjects to the Sovereign, which, notwithstanding the common interest, would have no security for the performance of their engagements, unless it found means to ensure their fidelity.

Indeed, each individual may, as a man, have a particular will contrary to, or divergent from, the general will which he has as a Citizen. His private interest may speak to him quite differently from the common interest; his absolute and naturally independent existence may make him regard what he owes to the common cause as a gratuitous contribution, the loss of which will be less harmful to others than will the payment of it be onerous to him; and viewing the moral person that constitutes the State as a being of reason because it is not a man, he would be willing to enjoy the rights of a citizen without being willing to fulfill the duties of a subject: an injustice, the progress of which would bring about the ruin of the body politic.

In order, then, that the social pact may not be a vain formula, it tacitly includes this engagement, which can alone give force to the others—that whoever refuses to obey the general will shall be constrained to do so by the whole body; which means nothing else than that he shall be forced to be free; for such is the condition which, giving each Citizen to his Fatherland, guarantees him from all personal dependence, a condition that makes up the spark and interplay of the political mechanism, and alone renders legitimate civil engagements, which, without it, would be absurd and tyrannical, and subject to the most enormous abuse.

VIII. Of the Civil State

This passage from the state of nature to the civil state produces in man a very remarkable change, by substituting in his conduct injustice for instinct, and by giving his actions the morality that they previously lacked. It is only when the voice of duty succeeds physical impulsion, and right succeeds appetite, that man, who till then had only looked after himself, sees that he is forced to act on other principles, and to consult his reason before listening to his inclinations. Although, in this state, he is deprived of many advantages he holds from nature, he gains such great ones in return, that his faculties are exercised and developed; his ideas are expanded; his feelings are ennobled; his whole soul is exalted to such a degree that, if the abuses of this new condition did not often degrade him below that from which he has emerged, he should ceaselessly bless the happy moment that removed him from it forever, and transformed him from a stupid and ignorant animal into an intelligent being and a man.

Let us reduce this whole balance to terms easy to compare. What man loses by the social contract is his natural liberty and an unlimited right to anything which tempts him and which he is able to attain; what he gains is civil liberty and the ownership of all that he possesses. In order not to be mistaken about these compensations, we must clearly distinguish natural liberty, which is limited only by the force of the individual, from civil liberty, which is limited by the general will; and possession, which is only the result of force or the right of the first occupant, from ownership, which can only be based on a positive title.

Besides the preceding, one can add to the acquisitions of the civil state the moral freedom which alone renders man truly master of himself; for the impulsion of mere appetite is slavery, and obedience to the law one prescribes to oneself is freedom. . . .

IX. Of Real Property

Each member of the community gives himself up to it at the moment of its formation, just as he actually is, himself and all his force, of which the goods he possesses form a part. It is not that by this act possession changes its nature in changing hands and becomes property in those of the Sovereign; but, as the powers of the City are incomparably greater than those of an individual, public possession is also, in fact, more secure and more irrevocable, without being more legitimate, at least for foreigners. For the State, with regard to its members, is master of all their property by the social contract, which in the State serves as the basis of all rights; but with regard to other powers it is master only by right of first occupant which it holds from private individuals.

The right of first occupant, although more real than that of the strongest, becomes a true right only after the establishment of property [ownership]. Every man has by nature a right to all that is necessary to him; but the positive act which makes him owner of certain goods excludes him from the rest. His portion having been allotted, he ought to confine himself to it, and he has no further right against the community. That is why the right of first occupant, so weak in the state of nature, is respected by every member of a civil society. In this right one respects not so much what belongs to others as what does not belong to oneself.

Generally, in order to authorize the right of first occupant over any land whatsoever, the following conditions are needed. First, the land must not yet be inhabited by anyone; second, a man must occupy only the area required for his subsistence; third, he must take possession of it not by an empty ceremony but by labor and cultivation, the only mark of ownership which, in the absence of legal title, ought to be respected by others.

Indeed, to grant the right of first occupant according to necessity and labor, is it not to extend this right as far as it can go? Can one assign limits to this right? Will the mere setting foot on common ground be sufficient to presume an immediate claim to the ownership of it? Will the power of driving away other men from it for a moment suffice to deprive them of the right of ever returning to it? How can a man or a people take possession of an immense territory and rob the whole human race of it except by a punishable usurpation, since henceforth other men are deprived of the place of residence and sustenance which nature gives to them in common? When Nunez de Balboa on the seashore took possession of the Pacific Ocean and of the whole of South America in the name of the crown of Castile, was this sufficient to dispossess all the inhabitants, and exclude from it all the Princes in the world? On this stand, such ceremonies might have been multiplied vainly enough; and the Catholic King in his cabinet might, by a single stroke, have taken possession of the whole universe; only cutting off afterward from his empire what was previously occupied by other Princes.

It can be understood how the lands of individuals, united and contiguous, become public territory, and how the right of sovereignty, extending itself from the subjects to the land which they occupy, becomes at once real and personal; this places the possessors in greater dependence, and makes their own powers a guarantee for their fidelity. An advantage which ancient monarchs do not appear to have clearly sensed, for, calling themselves only Kings of the Persians or Scythians or Macedonians, they seem to have viewed themselves as chiefs of men rather than as owners of countries. Those of today call themselves more cleverly Kings of France, Spain, England, etc. In thus holding the land they are quite sure of holding its inhabitants.

What is remarkable about this alienation is that the community, in receiving the property of individuals, far from robbing them of it, only assures them lawful possession, and changes usurpation into true right, enjoyment into ownership. Then the possesors, being considered as depositaries of the public property, and their rights being respected by all members of the State, and maintained with all its power against the foreign intruder, have, as it were, by a transfer advantageous to the public and still more to themselves, acquired all that they have given up. This is a paradox which is easily explained by distinguishing between the rights which the Sovereign and the owner have over the same property, as shall be seen later.

It may also happen that men begin to unite before they possess anything, and that afterward taking over territory sufficient for all, they enjoy it in common, or share it among themselves, either equally or in proportions fixed by the Sovereign. In whatever manner this acquisition is made, the right which every individual has over his own property is always subordinate to the right which the community has over all; otherwise there would be neither solidity in the social union, nor real force in the exercise of Sovereignty.

I shall close this chapter and this book with a remark which ought to serve as a basis for the whole social system; it is that instead of destroying natural equality, the fundamental pact, on the contrary, substitutes a moral and legitimate equality for the physical inequality which nature imposed upon men, so that, although unequal in strength or talent, they all become equal by convention and legal right.

Book Two

I say, then, that sovereignty, being only the exercise of the general will, can never be alienated, and that the Sovereign, which is only a collective being, can be represented only by itself; power can well be transmitted, but will cannot.

In fact, if it is not impossible that a private will agree on some point with the general will, it is at least impossible that this agreement should be lasting and constant, for the private will naturally tends to preferences, and the general will to equality. It is still more impossible to have a guarantee for this agreement; even though it should always exist, it would be an effect not of art but of chance. The Sovereign may indeed say: I now will what a certain man wills, or at least what he says that he wills; but it cannot say: what that man wills tomorrow, I shall also will; since it is absurd that the will should bind itself for the future and since it is not incumbent on any will to consent to anything contrary to the good of the being that wills. If, then, the people promises simply to obey, it dissolves itself by that act, it loses its quality as a people; at the instant that there is a master, there is no longer a Sovereign, and forthwith the body politic is destroyed.

This is not to say that the orders of the chiefs cannot pass for expressions of the general will, so long as the Sovereign, free to oppose them, does not do so. In such case, from the universal silence one should presume the consent of the people. This will be explained at greater length.

I. That Sovereignty Is Inalienable

The first and most important consequence of the principles established above is that the general will can only direct the forces of the State in keeping with the end for which it was instituted, which is the common good; for if the opposition of private interests has made the establishment of societies necessary, the harmony of these same interests has made it possible. That which is common to these different interests forms the social bond; and if there were not some point in which all interests agree, no society could exist. Now it is only on this common interest that the society should be governed. . . .

II. That Sovereignty Is Indivisible

For the same reason that sovereignty is inalienable, it is indivisible. For either the will is general or it is not; it is the will either of the body of the people, or only of a part. In the first case, this declared will is an act of sovereignty and constitutes law. In the second case, it is only a private will, or an act of magistracy; it is at most a decree.

But our political men, not being able to divide sovereignty in its principles, divide it in its object: they divide it into force and will, into legislative power and executive power; into rights of taxation, of justice, and of war; into internal administration and power of treating with foreigners: sometimes they confound all these parts and sometimes separate them. They make the Sovereign to be a fantastic being formed of borrowed pieces; it is as if they composed a man from several bodies, one having eyes, another having arms, another having feet, and nothing more. Charlatans of Japan, it is said, cut up a child before the eyes of the spectators; then, throwing all its limbs, one after another, into the air, they make the child come back down alive and whole. Such almost are the juggler's tricks of our politicians; after dismembering the social body by a deception worthy of a carnival, they recombine the parts, one knows not how.

This error comes from not having formed exact notions of sovereign authority, and from having taken as parts of this authority what are only emanations from it. Thus, for example, the act of declaring war and that of making peace have been looked at as acts of sovereignty; but this is not the case, since each of these acts is not a law, but only an application of the law, a particular act which determines the case of the law, as will be clearly seen when the idea attached to the word law will be fixed.

In following out the other divisions in the same way, one would find that whenever sovereignty appears divided, a mistake has been made; that the rights which are taken as parts of that sovereignty are all subordinate to it, and always suppose supreme wills of which these rights are merely the execution.

III. Whether the General Will Can Err

It follows from what precedes that the general will is always upright and always tends toward the public utility; but it does not follow that the deliberations of the people always have the same rectitude. One wishes always his own good, but does not always discern it. The people is never corrupted, though often deceived, and then only does it seem to will that which is bad.

There is frequently a difference between the *will of all* and the *general will*; the latter regards only the common interest, the other regards private interests and is only the sum of particular wills: but remove from these wills the pluses and minuses which cancel each other out and the general will remains as the sum of the differences.

If, when an adequately informed people deliberates, the Citizens having no communication among themselves, from the large number of small differences the general will would always result, and the deliberation would always be good. But when factions are formed, partial associations at the expense of the whole, the will of each of these associations becomes general with regard to its members, and in particular with regard to the State: one is then able to say that there are no longer as many voters as there are men, but only as many as there are associations. The differences become less numerous and yield a less general result. Finally, when one of these associations is so large that it overcomes the rest, you no longer have a sum of small differences as the result, but a unique difference; then there no longer is a general will, and the opinion which dominates is only a private opinion.

It matters, then, in order to have the general will expressed well, that there be no partial societies in the State, and that each Citizen speak only his own opinions. Such was the unique and sublime institution of the great Lycurgus. But if there are partial associations, it is necessary to multiply their number and so prevent inequality, as was done by Solon, Numa, and Servius. These precautions are the only valid ones, in order that the general will always be enlightened and that the people are not deceived. . . .

Thomas Jefferson (1743–1826)

In the passages cited from John Locke and Jean-Jacques Rousseau, we have seen the emergence, in virtually final form, of the pattern of assumptions about human nature and rights that inform our political, legal, and ethical discourse to this day. In Locke and Rousseau, we find the culmination of the political form of the Moral Law tradition: in the law, specifically in the legal life of the civil society, we find the most elementary and necessary exercise of human reason and the highest protection of human nature. Aristotle told us, briefly and elliptically, that man was a "political animal," the sort of animal that realizes its potential best in the polis, or political association. In Locke and Rousseau, the polis is given modern form and a language to describe it. The language is that of law.

In the legal protection for the rights of the individual, we find the recognition of the right of the individual to moral agency, liberty, autonomy—the society will protect the rights of individuals to live their own lives and make their own decisions. Since this law, and those liberties, are equally extended to all (what we call "the rule of law"), the notion of justice is written into the very fabric of the society; we are ruled by laws, not men. And in Locke's and Rousseau's insistence, following Thomas Aquinas, that all legislation must be for the common good, we find concern for welfare, or happiness, perfectly instituted in the society. In Locke and Rousseau, all three of the basic ethical principles are institutionalized in the form of presuppositions of the legal system; in theory at least, law and morals are one. The influence of Locke especially, on our legal and moral thought cannot be overestimated; indeed, the total interpenetration of the ethical and the legal in the political theory of Locke makes it noticeably difficult for us to think only of morality without constant reference to the law.

Revolution, which had terrified Hobbes and inspired Locke, swept through the European world in the century after Locke's writing; the powerful political-philosophical synthesis forged in his writings left a deep imprint on the affairs of the times. In France, the overthrow of the French monarchy, and with it a world-system a millennium long, was achieved on such theory. In America, a Revolution of much less world consequence was born of the same ideas. Thomas Jefferson, a young revolutionary aristocrat in America, summarized the consequences of Locke's theory for the political affairs of America in the second paragraph of the Declaration of Independence (1776).

From Thomas Jefferson, *The Declaration of Independence*

When, in the course of human events, it becomes necessary for one people to dissolve the political bands which have connected them with another, and to assume, among the powers of the earth, the separate and equal station to which the laws of nature and of nature's God entitle them, a decent respect to the opinions of mankind requires that they should declare the causes which impel them to the separation.

We hold these truths to be self-evident, that all men are created equal, that they are endowed by their Creator with certain unalienable rights, that among these are life, liberty, and the pursuit of happiness—That, to secure these rights, governments are instituted among men, deriving their just powers from the consent of the governed—that, whenever any form of government becomes destructive of these ends, it is the right of the people to alter or to abolish it, and to institute a new government, laying its foundation on such principles, and organizing its powers in such form, as to them shall seem most likely to effect their safety and happiness. Prudence, indeed, will dictate that governments long established should not be changed for light and transient causes; and, accordingly, all experience hath shown, that mankind are more disposed to suffer, while evils are sufferable, than to right themselves by abolishing the forms to which they are accustomed. But, when a long train of abuses and usurpations, pursuing invariably the same object, evinces a design to reduce them under absolute despotism, it is their right, it is their duty, to throw off such government, and to provide new guards for their future security. Such has been the patient sufferance of these colonies, and such is now the necessity which constrains them to alter their former systems of government....

The thorough integration of moral principle and civil law renders unnecessary the former custom of protecting and subsidizing a Church to keep people moral. When law can protect individual rights universally, rationally, and in an orderly manner, it becomes unreasonable to expect an irrational cult to improve on the enterprise. With this new republican thought comes the disestablishment of religion. The reasoning behind the move is well stated in Jefferson's "Act for Establishing Religious Freedom," written in 1779 and passed in the Assembly of Virginia in the beginning of the year 1786:

From Thomas Jefferson, *An Act Establishing Religious Freedom*

Well aware that Almighty God hath created the mind free; that all attempts to influence it by temporal punishments or burdens, or by civil incapacitations, tend only to beget habits of hypocrisy and meanness, and are a departure from the plan of the Holy Author of our religion, who being Lord both of body and mind, yet chose not to propagate it by coercions on either, as was in his Almighty power to do; that the impious presumption of legislators and rulers, civil as well as ecclesiastical, who, being themselves but fallible and uninspired men have assumed dominion over the faith of others, setting up their own opinions and modes of thinking as the only true and infallible, and as such endeavoring to impose them on others, hath established and maintained false religions over the greatest part of the world, and through all time; that to compel a man to furnish contributions of money for the propagation of opinions which he disbelieves, is sinful and tyrannical; that even the forcing him to support this or that teacher of his own religious persuasion, is depriving him of the comfortable liberty of giving his contributions to the particular pastor whose morals he would make his pattern, and whose powers he feels most persuasive to righteousness, and is withdrawing from the ministry those temporal rewards, which proceeding from an approbation of their personal conduct, are an additional incitement to earnest and unremitting labors for the instruction of mankind; that our civil rights have no dependence on our religious opinions, more than our opinions in physics or geometry; that, therefore, the proscribing any citizen as unworthy of the public confidence by laying upon him an incapacity of being called to the offices of trust and emolument, unless he profess or renounce this or that religious opinion, is depriving him injuriously of those privileges and advantages to which in common with his fellow citizens he has a natural right;

that it tends also to corrupt the principles of that very religion it is meant to encourage, by bribing, with a monopoly of worldly honors and emoluments, those who will externally profess and conform to it; that though indeed those are criminal who do not withstand such temptation, yet neither are those innocent who lay the bait in their way; that to suffer the civil magistrate to intrude his powers into the field of opinion and to restrain the profession or propagation of principles, on the supposition of their ill tendency, is a dangerous fallacy, which at once destroys all religious liberty, because he being of course judge of that tendency, will make his opinions the rule of judgment, and approve or condemn the sentiments of others only as they shall square with or differ from his own; that it is time enough for the rightful purposes of civil government, for its offices to interfere when principles break out into overt acts against peace and good order; and finally, that truth is great and will prevail if left to herself, that she is the proper and sufficient antagonist to error, and has nothing to fear from the conflict, unless by human interposition disarmed of her natural weapons, free argument and debate, errors ceasing to be dangerous when it is permitted freely to contradict them.

Be it therefore enacted by the General Assembly, That no man shall be compelled to frequent or support any religious worship, place or ministry whatsoever, nor shall be enforced, restrained, molested, or burthened in his body or goods, nor shall otherwise suffer on account of his religious opinions or belief; but that all men shall be free to profess, and by argument to maintain, their opinions in matters of religion, and that the same shall in nowise diminish, enlarge, or affect their civil capacities. . . .

Letter to Edward Carrington

(Paris, January 16, 1787)

Dear Sir, . . . The tumults in America [viz. Shays' Rebellion, a revolt of the Massachusetts farmers in 1786] I expected would have produced in Europe an unfavorable opinion of our political state. But it has not. On the contrary, the small effect of these tumults seems to have given more confidence in the firmness of our governments. The interposition of the people themselves on the side of government has had a great effect on the opinion here. I am persuaded myself that the good sense of the people will always be found to be the best army. They may be led astray for a moment, but will soon correct themselves. The people are the only censors of their governors: and even their errors will tend to keep these to the true principles of their institution. To punish these errors too severely would be to suppress the only safeguard of the public liberty. The way to prevent these irregular interpositions of the people is to give them full information of their affairs thro' the channel of the public papers, and to contrive that those papers should penetrate the whole mass of the people. The basis of our governments being the opinion of the people, the very first object should be to keep that right; and were it left to me to decide whether we should have a government without newspapers or newspapers without a government, I should not hesitate a moment to prefer the latter. But I should mean that every man should receive those papers and be capable of reading them. I am convinced that those societies (as the Indians) which live without government enjoy in their general mass an infinitely greater degree of happiness than those who live under the European governments. Among the former, public opinion is in the place of law, and restrains morals as powerfully as laws ever did anywhere. Among the latter, under pretence of governing they have divided their nations into two classes, wolves and sheep. I do not exaggerate. This is a true picture of Europe. Cherish therefore the spirit of our people, and keep alive their attention. Do not be too severe upon their errors, but reclaim them by enlightening them. If once they become inattentive to the public affairs, you and I, and Congress and Assemblies, judges and governors shall all become wolves. It seems to be the law of our general nature, in spite of individual exceptions; and experience declares that man is the only animal which devours his own kind, for I can apply no milder term to the governments of Europe, and to the general prey of the rich on the poor. . . .

Immanuel Kant (1724–1804)

In Kant a new tendency appears, not just new for this chapter or tradition, but new in the history of philosophy. In the works that are central to his ethical theory, he does not address the great problems of policy and the life of the state, nor even, save indirectly, the universal law by which God governs the universe. He pays attention, instead, to the notion of "the moral" itself. By virtue of what characteristic, he asks, are the acts of human beings called right or wrong, when those words are used purely in their moral sense? The questions go back to Socrates, but the answers are new. In his careful elucidation of these meanings, and attempts to illustrate by example the exact extent and limits of the notion of morality, Kant gives birth to "conceptual analysis," an altogether new approach to ethics, which has dominated the field in the two centuries since his writing.

The answer to the central question Kant finds in the peculiarly human characteristic of rationality, and from that point, in the possibility of rational moral agency. Unlike other animals, the human does not just act in response to impulse, instinct, or (as in the case of domesticated animals) the rules worked out by others for us to obey. We can conceive of choice, and laws, and judge the laws good or bad; we can hold the laws in our mind even as we choose to act, and compare the act to the law, and choose to obey or disobey. When we act, we know what we are doing, and we know the moral nature of the act, whether it be right or wrong—and if those two conditions do not apply in a particular case, we judge that individual to be "insane." (Those two criteria, as a matter of fact, do define the original legal definition of insanity, "McNaughton's Rule": An accused criminal is not guilty by reason of insanity if, when he committed the act in question, "he did not know what he was doing, or if he did, he did not know that it was wrong.") When such a one is discovered, he is treated "inhumanly," not as a human, in two ways: he is forgiven every sin, and he is deprived of every liberty, confined for his own safety and ours. Moral agency, the ability to make and to take responsibility for moral decisions, is the precondition for ordinary human existence and human society. What kind of reason provides moral justification for action? The first characteristic for such a reason (or "maxim," as it is ordinarily translated in the writings of Kant) is that it must be universal in nature and apply equally to all cases; it must be the kind of reasoning you would be willing to see used for all actions, by yourself or by others directed to you. That is the requirement of the first formulation of Kant's famous "Categorical Imperative": "Act so that you can simultaneously will that the maxim of your action should become universal law." The second characteristic of such reasoning is that it honors the fundamental value of humanity. Like the other animals, we are creatures capable of suffering, and should, as Jeremy Bentham had insisted (See Chapter 4, "Utilitarianism"), be treated with kindness and spared pain if possible. But, and much more important, we are also moral agents; we have dignity, inherent worth, and must be treated with respect. We must not be treated as means to the ends of others, as the other animals ultimately are; we are, and must be respected as, ends in ourselves. A third characteristic of such reasoning is that it presupposes autonomy—the ability to be both legislator and subject in a society of simultaneous sovereigns and subjects of the moral law—and recognizes all who are subject to the law as autonomous beings. We get the concept of autonomy, the most basic concept of the Western ethical traditions, from Immanuel Kant.

From Immanuel Kant, *Foundations of the Metaphysics of Morals*

(From the "Introduction")

Since my purpose here is directed to moral philosophy, I narrow the proposed question to this: Is it not of the utmost necessity to construct a pure moral philosophy which is completely freed from everything which may be only empirical and thus belong to anthropology? That there must be such a philosophy is self-evident from the common idea of duty and moral laws. Everyone must admit that a law, if it is to hold morally, i.e., as a ground of obligation, must imply absolute necessity; he must admit that the command, "Thou shalt not lie," does not apply to men only, as if other rational beings had no need to observe it. The same is true for all other moral laws properly so called. He must concede that the ground of obligation here must not be sought in the nature of man or in the circumstances in which he is placed, but sought *a priori* solely in the concepts of pure reason, and that every other precept which rests on principles of mere experience, even a precept which is in certain respects universal, so far as it leans in the least on empirical grounds (perhaps only in regard to the motive involved), may be called a practical rule but never a moral law.

Thus not only are moral laws together with their principles essentially different from all practical knowledge in which there is anything empirical, but all moral philosophy rests solely on its pure part. Applied to man, it borrows nothing from knowledge of him (anthropology) but gives him, as a rational being, *a priori* laws. No doubt these laws require a power of judgment sharpened by experience, partly in order to decide in what cases they apply and partly to procure for them an access to man's will and an impetus to their practice. For man is affected by so many inclinations that, though he is capable of the idea of a practical pure reason, he is not so easily able to make it concretely effective in the conduct of his life.

A metaphysics of morals is therefore indispensable, not merely because of motives to speculate on the source of the *a priori* practical principles which lie in our reason, but also because morals themselves remain subject to all kinds of corruption so long as the guide and supreme norm for their correct estimation is lacking. For it is not sufficient to that which should be morally good that it conform to the law; it must be done for the sake of the law. Otherwise the conformity is merely contingent and spurious, because, though the unmoral ground may indeed now and then produce lawful actions, more often it brings forth unlawful ones. But the moral law can be found in its purity and genuineness (which is the central concern in the practical) nowhere else than in a pure philosophy; therefore, this (i.e., metaphysics) must lead the way, and without it there can be no moral philosophy. Philosophy which mixes pure principles with empirical ones does not deserve the name, for what distinguishes philosophy from common rational knowledge is its treatment in separate sciences of what is confusedly comprehended in such knowledge. Much less does it deserve the name of moral philosophy, since by this confusion it spoils the purity of morals themselves and works contrary to its own end.

From Immanuel Kant, *Foundations of the Metaphysics of Morals*

First Section: Transition from the common rational knowledge of morals to the philosophical.

Nothing in the world—indeed nothing even beyond the world—can possibly be conceived which could be called good without qualification except a good will. Intelligence, wit, judgment, and the other talents of the mind, however they may be named, or courage, resoluteness, and perseverance as qualities of temperament, are doubtless in many respects good and desirable. But they can become extremely bad and harmful if the will, which is to make use of these gifts of nature and which in its special constitution is called character, is not good. It is the same with the gifts of fortune. Power, riches, honor, even health, general well-being, and the contentment with one's condition which is called happiness, make for pride and even arrogance if there is not a good will to correct their influence on the mind and on its principles of action so as to make it universally conformable to its end. It need hardly be mentioned that the sight of a being adorned with no feature of a pure and good will, yet enjoying uninterrupted prosperity, can never give pleasure to a rational impartial observer. Thus the good will seems to constitute the indispensable condition even of worthiness to be happy. . . .

The good will is not good because of what it effects or accomplishes or because of its adequacy to achieve some proposed end; it is good only because of its willing, i.e., it is good of itself. And, regarded for itself, it is to be esteemed incomparably higher than anything which could be brought about by it in favor of any inclination or even of the sum total of all inclinations. Even if it should happen that, by a particularly unfortunate fate or by the niggardly provision of a stepmotherly nature, this will should be wholly lacking in power to accomplish its purpose, and if even the greatest effort should not avail it to achieve anything of its end, and if there remained only the good will (not as a mere wish but as the summoning of all the means in our power), it would sparkle like a jewel in its own right, as something that had its full worth in itself. Usefulness or fruitlessness can neither diminish nor augment this worth. Its usefulness would be only its setting, as it were, so as to enable us to handle it more conveniently in commerce or to attract the attention of those who are not yet connoisseurs, but not to recommend it to those who are experts or to determine its worth. . . .

. . . Reason is given to us as a practical faculty, i.e., one which is meant to have an influence on the will. As nature has elsewhere distributed capacities suitable to the functions they are to perform, reason's proper function must be to produce a will good in itself and not only good merely as a means, for to the former reason is absolutely essential. This will must indeed not be the sole and complete good but the highest good and the condition of all others, even of the desire for happiness. In this case it is entirely compatible with the wisdom of nature that the cultivation of reason, which is required for the former unconditional purpose, at least in this life restricts in many ways—indeed can reduce to less than nothing—the achievement of the latter conditional purpose, happiness. For one perceives that nature here does not proceed unsuitably to its purpose, because reason, which recognizes its highest practical vocation in the establishment of a good will, is capable only of a contentment of its own kind, i.e., one that springs from the attainment of a purpose which is determined by reason, even though this injures the ends of inclination. . . .

To be kind where one can is duty, and there are, moreover, many persons so sympathetically constituted that without any motive of vanity or selfishness they find an inner satisfaction in spreading joy, and rejoice in the contentment of others which they have made possible. But I say that, however dutiful and amiable it may be, that kind of action has no true moral worth. It is on a level with [actions arising from] other inclinations, such as the inclination to honor, which, if fortunately directed to what in fact accords with duty and is generally useful and thus honorable, deserve praise and encouragement but no esteem. For the maxim lacks the moral import of an action done not from inclination but from duty. But assume that the mind of that friend to mankind was clouded by a sorrow of his own which extinguished all sympathy with the lot of others and that he still had the power to benefit others in distress, but that their need left him untouched because he was preoccupied with his own need. And now suppose him to tear himself, unsolicited by inclination, out of this dead insensibility and to perform this action only from duty and without any inclination—then for the first time his action has genuine moral worth. . . .

[Thus the first proposition of morality is that to have moral worth an action must be done from duty.] The second proposition is: An action performed from duty does not have its moral worth in the purpose which is to be achieved through it but in the maxim by which it is determined. Its moral value, therefore, does not depend on the realization of the object of the action but merely on the principle or volition by which the action is done without any regard to the objects of the faculty of desire. From the preceding discussion it is clear that the purposes we may have for our actions and their effects as ends and incentives of the will cannot give the actions any unconditional and moral worth. Wherein, then, can this worth lie, if it is not in the will in relation to its hoped-for effect? It can lie nowhere else than in the principle of the will, irrespective of the ends which can be realized by such action. For the will stands, as it were, at the crossroads halfway between its *a priori* principle which is formal and its *a posteriori* incentive which is material. Since it must be determined by something, if it is done from duty it must be determined by the formal principle of volition as such since every material principle has been withdrawn from it.

The third principle, as a consequence of the two preceding, I would express as follows: Duty is the necessity of an action executed from respect for law. I can certainly have an inclination to the object as an effect of the proposed action, but I can never have respect for it precisely because it is a mere effect and not an activity of a will. Similarly, I can have no respect for any inclination whatsoever, whether my own or that of another; in the former case I can at most approve of it and in the latter I can even love it, i.e., see it as favorable to my own advantage. But that which is connected with my will merely as ground and not as consequence, that which does not serve my inclination but overpowers it or at least excludes it from being considered in making a choice—in a word, law itself can be an object of respect and thus a command. Now as an act from duty wholly excludes the influence of inclination and therewith every object of the will, nothing remains which can determine the will objectively except the law, and nothing subjectively except pure respect for this practical law. This subjective element is the maxim that I ought to follow such a law even if it thwarts all my inclinations. . . .

But what kind of a law can that be, the conception of which must determine the will without reference to the expected result? Under this condition alone the will can be called absolutely good without qualification. Since I have robbed the will of all impulses which could come to it from obedience to any law, nothing remains to serve as a principle of the will except universal conformity of its action to law as such. That is, I should never act in such a way that I could not also will that my maxim should be a universal law. Mere conformity to law as such (without assuming any particular law applicable to certain actions) serves as the principle of the will, and it must serve as such a principle if duty is not to be a vain delusion and chimerical concept.

> *Central to Kant's understanding of the Moral Law is the distinction between hypothetical and categorical imperatives. From that distinction he develops the notion of one Categorical Imperative that governs all of morality.*

Everything in nature works according to laws. Only a rational being has the capacity of acting according to the conception of laws, i.e., according to principles. This capacity is will. Since reason is required for the derivation of actions from laws, will is nothing else than practical reason. If reason infallibly determines the will, the actions which such a being recognizes as objectively necessary are also subjectively necessary.

That is, the will is a faculty of choosing only that which reason, independently of inclination, recognizes as practically necessary, i.e., as good. But if reason of itself does not sufficiently determine the will, and if the will is subjugated to subjective conditions (certain incentives) which do not always agree with objective conditions; in a word, if the will is not of itself in complete accord with reason (the actual case of men), then the actions which are recognized as objectively necessary are subjectively contingent, and the determination of such a will according to objective laws is constraint. That is, the relation of objective laws to a will which is not completely good is conceived as the determination of the will of a rational being by principles of reason to which this will is not by nature necessarily obedient.

The conception of an objective principle so far as it constrains a will, is a command (of reason), and the formula of this command is called an imperative.

All imperatives are expressed by an "ought" and thereby indicate the relation of an objective law of reason to a will which is not in its subjective constitution necessarily determined by this law. This relation is that of constraint. Imperatives say that it would be good to do or to refrain from doing something, but they say it to a will which does not always do something simply because it is presented as a good thing to do. Practical good is what determines the will by means of the conception of reason and hence not by subjective causes but, rather, objectively, i.e., on grounds which are valid for every rational being as such. It is distinguished from the pleasant as that which has an influence on the will only by means of a sensation from merely subjective causes, which hold only for the senses of this or that person and not as a principle of reason which holds for everyone.

A perfectly good will, therefore, would be equally subject to objective laws (of the good), but it could not be conceived as constrained by them to act in accord with them, because, according to its own subjective constitution, it can be determined to act only through the conception of the good. Thus no imperatives hold for the divine will or, more generally, for a holy will. The "ought" is here out of place, for the volition of itself is necessarily in unison with the law. Therefore imperatives are only formulas expressing the relation of objective laws of volition in general to the subjective imperfection of the will of this or that rational being, e.g., the human will.

All imperatives command either hypothetically or categorically. The former present the practical necessity of a possible action as a means to achieving something else which one desires (or which one may possibly desire). The categorical imperative would be one which presented an action as of itself objectively necessary, without regard to any other end.

Since every practical law presents a possible action as good and thus as necessary for a subject practically determinable by reason, all imperatives are formulas of the determination of action which is necessary by the principle of a will which is in any way good. If the action is good only as a means to something else, the imperative is hypothetical; but if it is thought of as good in itself, and hence as necessary in a will which of itself conforms to reason as the principle of this will, the imperative is categorical.

The imperative thus says what action possible to me would be good, and it presents the practical rule in relation to a will which does not forthwith perform an action simply because it is good, in part because the subject does not always know that the action is good and in part (when he does know it) because his maxims can still be opposed to the objective principles of practical reason.

The hypothetical imperative, therefore, says only that the action is good to some purpose, possible or actual . . . The categorical imperative, which declares the action to be of itself objectively necessary without making any reference to a purpose, i.e., without having any other end, holds as an apodictical (practical) principle. . . .

There is one end, however, which we may presuppose as actual in all rational beings so far as imperatives apply to them, i.e., so far as they are dependent beings; there is one purpose not only which they can have but which we can presuppose that they all do have by a necessity of nature. This purpose is happiness. The hypothetical imperative which represents the practical necessity of action as means to the promotion of happiness is an assertorical imperative. We may not expound it as merely necessary to an uncertain and merely possible purpose, but as necessary to a purpose which we can *a priori* and with assurance assume for everyone because it belongs to his essence. Skill in the choice of means to one's own highest welfare can be called prudence in the narrowest sense. Thus the imperative which refers to the choice of means to one's own happiness, i.e. the precept of prudence, is still only hypothetical; the action is not absolutely commanded but commanded only as a means to another end.

Finally, there is one imperative which directly commands a certain conduct without making its condition some purpose to be reached by it. This imperative is categorical. It concerns not the material of the action and its intended result but the form and the principle from which it results. What is essentially good in it consists in the intention, the result being what it may. This imperative may be called the imperative of morality.

Volition according to these three principles is plainly distinguished by dissimilarity in the constraint to which they subject the will. In order to clarify this dissimilarity, I believe that they are most suitably named if one says that they are either rules of skill, counsels of prudence, or commands (laws) of morality, respectively. For law alone implies the concept of an unconditional and objective and hence universally valid necessity, and commands are laws which must be obeyed, even against inclination. Counsels do indeed involve necessity, but a necessity that can hold only under a subjectively contingent condition, i.e., whether this or that man counts this or that as part of his happiness; but the categorical imperative, on the other hand, is restricted by no condition. As absolutely, though practically, necessary it can be called a command in the strict sense. We could also call the first imperative technical (belonging to art), the second pragmatic (belonging to welfare), and the third moral (belonging to free conduct as such, i.e., to morals). . . .

These distinctions—carefully removing all consequential thinking, all pursuit of happiness, from the field of morality *per se*—lead us finally to the ground of morals, the Categorical Imperative.

If I think of a hypothetical imperative as such, I do not know what it will contain until the condition is stated [under which it is an imperative]. But if I think of a categorical imperative, I know immediately what it contains. For since the imperative contains besides the law only the necessity that the maxim should accord with this law, while the law contains no condition to which it is restricted, there is nothing remaining in it except the universality of law as such to which the maxim of the action should conform; and in effect this conformity alone is represented as necessary by the imperative.

There is, therefore, only one categorical imperative. It is: *Act only according to that maxim by which you can at the same time will that it should become a universal law.*

Now if all imperatives of duty can be derived from this one imperative as a principle, we can at least show what we understand by the concept of duty and what it means, even though it remain undecided whether that which is called duty is an empty concept or not.

The universality of law according to which effects are produced constitutes what is properly called nature in the most general sense (as to form), i.e. the existence of things so far as it is determined by universal laws. [By analogy], then, the universal imperative of duty can be expressed as follows: Act as though the maxim of your action were by your will to become a universal law of nature. . . .

> *Kant proceeds, in the discussion, to what amounts to a "second formulation" of the Categorical Imperative, a "practical imperative," which gives content to the purely formal rule stated above.*

The will is thought of as a faculty of determining itself to action in accordance with the conception of certain laws. Such a faculty can be found only in rational beings. That which serves the will as the objective ground of its self-determination is an end, and, if it is given by reason alone, it must hold alike for all rational beings. On the other hand, that which contains the ground of the possibility of the action, whose result is an end, is called the means. The subjective ground of desire is the incentive, while the objective ground of volition is the motive. Thus arises the distinction between subjective ends, which rest on incentives, and objective ends, which depend on motives valid for every rational being. Practical principles are formal when they disregard all subjective ends; they are material when they have subjective ends, and thus certain incentives, as their basis. The ends which a rational being arbitrarily proposes to himself as consequences of his action are material ends and are without exception only relative, for only their relation to a particularly constituted faculty of desire in the subject gives them their worth. And this worth cannot, therefore, afford any universal principles for all rational beings or valid and necessary principles for every volition. That is, they cannot give rise to any practical laws. All these relative ends, therefore, are grounds for hypothetical imperatives only.

But suppose that there were something the existence of which in itself had absolute worth, something which, as an end in itself, could be a ground of definite laws. In it and only in it could lie the ground of a possible categorical imperative, i.e. of a practical law.

Now, I say, man and, in general, every rational being exists as an end in himself and not merely as a means to be arbitrarily used by this or that will. In all his actions, whether they are directed to himself or to other rational beings, he must always be regarded at the same time as an end. All objects of inclinations have only a conditional worth, for if the inclinations and the needs founded on them did not exist, their object would be without worth. The inclinations themselves as the sources of needs, however, are so lacking in absolute worth that the universal wish of every rational being must be indeed to free himself completely from them. Therefore, the worth of any objects to be obtained by our actions is at all times conditional. Beings whose existence does not depend on our will but on nature, if they are not rational beings, have only a relative worth as means and are therefore called "things"; on the other hand, rational beings are designated "persons" because their nature indicates that they are ends in themselves, i.e., things which may not be used merely as means. Such a being is thus an object of respect and, so far, restricts all [arbitrary] choice. Such beings are not merely subjective ends whose existence as a result of our action has a worth for us, but are objective ends, i.e., beings whose existence in itself is an end. Such an end is one for which no other end can be substituted, to which these beings should serve merely as means. For, without them, nothing of absolute worth could be found, and if all worth is conditional and thus contingent, no supreme practical principle for reason could be found anywhere.

Thus if there is to be a supreme practical principle and a categorical imperative for the human will, it must be one that forms an objective principle of the will from the conception of that which is necessarily an end for everyone because it is an end in itself. Hence this objective principle can serve as a universal practical law. The ground of this principle is: rational nature exists as an end in itself. Man necessarily thinks of his own existence in this way; thus far it is a subjective principle of human actions. Also every other rational being thinks of his existence by means of the same rational ground which holds also for myself; thus it is at the same time an objective principle from which, as a supreme practical ground, it must be possible to derive all laws of the will. The practical imperative, therefore, is the following: Act so that you treat humanity, whether in your own person or in that of another, always as an end and never as a means only. Let us now see whether this can be achieved. . . .

> *A third formulation of this imperative ties it in with the theory of community: given (first formulation) the necessary universality of any law, given (second formulation) that the only beings to which law applies are ends in themselves, Kant simply goes on to require that, in conceiving rules, we conceive rules that might be legislation in a kingdom of autonomous (free) people, who are ends in themselves and conscious of the moral responsibility this places upon them.*

This principle of humanity and of every rational creature as an end in itself is the supreme limiting condition on freedom of the actions of each man. It is not borrowed from experience, first, because of its universality, since it applies to all rational beings generally and experience does not suffice to determine anything about them; and, secondly, because in experience humanity is not thought of (subjectively) as the end of men, i.e., as an object which we of ourselves really make our end. Rather it is thought of as the objective end which should constitute the supreme limiting condition of all subjective ends, whatever they may be. Thus this principle must arise from pure reason. Objectively the ground of all practical legislation lies (according to the first principle) in the rule and in the form of universality, which makes it capable of being a law (at most a natural law); subjectively, it lies in the end. But the subject of all ends is every rational being as an end in itself (by the second principle); from this there follows the third practical principle of the will as the supreme condition of its harmony with universal practical reason, viz. the idea of the will of every rational being as making universal law.

By this principle all maxims are rejected which are not consistent with the universal lawgiving of will. The will is thus not only subject to the law but subject in such a way that it must be regarded also as self-legislative and only for this reason as being subject to the law (of which it can regard itself as the author).

And this is what it all means:

If we now look back upon all previous attempts which have ever been undertaken to discover the principle of morality, it is not to be wondered at that they all had to fail. Man was seen to be bound to laws by his duty, but it was not seen that he is subject only to his own, yet universal, legislation, and that he is only bound to act in accordance with his own will, which is, however, designed by nature to be a will giving universal laws. For if one thought of him as subject only to a law (whatever it may be), this necessarily implied some interest as a stimulus or compulsion to obedience because the law did not arise from his will. Rather, his will was constrained by something else according to a law to act in a certain way. By this strictly necessary consequence, however, all the labor of finding a supreme ground for duty was irrevocably lost, and one never arrived at duty but only at the necessity of action from a certain interest. This might be his own interest or that of another, but in either case the imperative always had to be conditional and could not at all serve as a moral command. This principle I will call the principle of *autonomy* of the will in contrast to all other principles which I accordingly count under *heteronomy*.

The concept of each rational being as a being that must regard itself as giving universal law through all the maxims of its will, so that it may judge itself and its actions from this standpoint, leads to a very fruitful concept, namely, that of a *realm of ends*.

By "realm" I understand the systematic union of different rational beings through common laws. Because laws determine ends with regard to their universal validity, if we abstract from the personal difference of rational beings and thus from all content of their private ends, we can think of a whole of all ends in systematic connection, a whole of rational beings as ends in themselves as well as of the particular ends which each may set for himself. This is a realm of ends, which is possible on the aforesaid principles. For all rational beings stand under the law that each of them should treat himself and all others never merely as means but in every case also as an end in himself. Thus there arises a systematic union of rational beings through common objective laws. This is a realm which may be called a realm of ends (certainly only an ideal), because what these laws have in view is just the relation of these beings to each other as ends and means.

A rational being belongs to the realm of ends as a member when he gives universal laws in it while also himself subject to these laws. He belongs to it as sovereign when he, as legislating, is subject to the will of no other. The rational being must regard himself always as legislative in a realm of ends possible through the freedom of the will, whether he belongs to it as member or as sovereign. He cannot maintain the latter position merely through the maxims of his will but only when he is a completely independent being without need and with power adequate to his will.

Morality, therefore, consists in the relation of every action to that legislation through which alone a realm of ends is possible. This legislation, however, must be found in every rational being. It must be able to arise from his will, whose principle then is to take no action according to any maxim which would be inconsistent with its being a universal law and thus to act only so that the will through its maxims could regard itself at the same time as universally lawgiving. If now the maxims do not by their nature already necessarily conform to this objective principle of rational beings as universally lawgiving, the necessity of acting according to that principle is called practical constraint, i.e., duty. Duty pertains not to the sovereign in the realm of ends, but rather to each member, and to each in the same degree.

The practical necessity of acting according to this principle, i.e., duty, does not rest at all on feelings, impulses, and inclinations; it rests merely on the relation of rational beings to one another, in which the will of a rational being must always be regarded as legislative, for otherwise it could not be thought of as an end in itself. Reason, therefore, relates every maxim of the will as giving universal laws to every other will and also to every action toward itself, it does so not for the sake of any other practical motive or future advantage but rather from the idea of the dignity of a rational being who obeys no law except that which he himself also gives.

In the realm of ends everything has either a *price* or a *dignity*. Whatever has a price can be replaced by something else as its equivalent; on the other hand, whatever is above all price, and therefore admits of no equivalent, has a dignity.

That which is related to general human inclinations and needs has a *market price*. That which, without presupposing any need, accords with a certain taste, i.e., with pleasure in the mere purposeless play of our faculties, has an *affective price*. But that which constitutes the condition under which alone something can be an end in itself does not have mere relative worth, i.e., a price, but an intrinsic worth, i.e., *dignity*.

Now morality is the condition under which alone a rational being can be an end in itself, because only through it is it possible to be a legislative member in the realm of ends. Thus morality and humanity, so far as it is capable of morality, alone have dignity. Skill and diligence in work have a market value; wit, lively imagination, and humor have an affective price; but fidelity in promises and benevolence on principle (not from instinct) have intrinsic worth. Nature and likewise art contain nothing which could replace their lack, for their worth consists not in effects which flow from them, nor in advantage and utility which they procure, it consists only in intentions, i.e., maxims of the will which are ready to reveal themselves in this manner through actions even though success does not favor them. These actions need no recommendation from any subjective disposition or taste in order that they may be looked upon with immediate favor and satisfaction, nor do they have need for any immediate propensity or feeling directed to them. They exhibit the will which performs them as the object of an immediate respect, since nothing but reason is required in order to impose them on the will. The will is not to be cajoled into them, for this, in the case of duties, would be a contradiction. This esteem lets the worth of such a turn of mind be recognized as dignity and puts it infinitely beyond any price, with which it cannot in the least be brought into competition or comparison without, as it were, violating its holiness.

And what is it that justifies the morally good disposition or virtue in making such lofty claims? It is nothing less than the participation it affords the rational being in giving universal laws. He is thus fitted to be a member in a possible realm of ends to which his own nature already destined him. For, as an end in himself, he is destined to be legislative in the realm of ends, free from all laws of nature and obedient only to those which he himself gives. Accordingly, his maxims can belong to a universal legislation to which he is at the same time also subject. A thing has no worth other than that determined for it by the law. The legislation which determines all worth must therefore have a dignity, i.e., unconditional and incomparable worth. For the esteem which a rational being must have for it, only the word "respect" is a suitable expression. Autonomy is thus the basis of the dignity of both human nature and every rational nature.

The three aforementioned ways of presenting the principle of morality are fundamentally only so many formulas of the very same law, and each of them unites the others in itself. There is, nevertheless, a difference in them, but the difference is more subjectively than objectively practical, for it is intended to bring an idea of reason closer to intuition (by means of a certain analogy) and thus nearer to feeling. All maxims have:

1. A form, which consists in universality; and in this respect the formula of the moral imperative requires that the maxims be chosen as though they should hold as universal laws of nature.
2. A material, i.e., an end; in this respect the formula says that the rational being, as by its nature an end and thus as an end in itself, must serve in every maxim as the condition restricting all merely relative and arbitrary ends.
3. A complete determination of all maxims by the formula that all maxims which stem from autonomous legislation ought to harmonize with a possible realm of ends as with a realm of nature.

A Note on Fiduciary Duty

Our next selection is by Josiah Royce, philosopher of "loyalty." He was, to the best of our ability to determine, the only philosopher to take that notion as central, in his time or until today. He was never popular, or even well-respected in the fields of philosophy; as a thesis in moral philosophy, his work has had few followers.

Yet a species of loyalty, or fidelity, dominates professional fields today as it has for 2500 years—the duty a professional has to his or her client, known as a "fiduciary duty." The panelists refer to it obliquely throughout the Ethics in America *tapes: The fiduciary obligation binds the lawyer to his client, to maintain confidentiality come what may; it binds the physician to the patient, the corporate officer to the Board of Trustees (and through them to the investors), and the public servant to the public. Curiously, there is little philosophical work on this centrally important obligation, primarily because (as we pointed out in the introduction to the Locke passages above) Americans do a fair amount of their moral philosophizing in the law. To explain Fiduciary Duty, then, we turn to the Law; specifically, to an online legal advice service known as The 'Lectric Law Library, from their Legal Lexicon.*

The 'Lectric Law Library's Legal Lexicon on Fiduciary/Fiduciary Duty

FIDUCIARY: This term is borrowed from the civil law. The Roman laws called a fiduciary heir, the person who was instituted heir and who was charged to deliver the succession to a person designated by the testament. But some say that it properly signifies the person to whom a testator has sold his inheritance, under the condition that he should sell it to another. Fiduciary may be defined to be in trust, in confidence.

A fiduciary contract is defined to be an agreement by which a person delivers a thing to another on the condition that he will restore it to him.

FIDUCIARY DUTY: An obligation to act in the best interest of another party. For instance, a corporation's board member has a fiduciary duty to the shareholders, a trustee has a fiduciary duty to the trust's beneficiaries, and an attorney has a fiduciary duty to a client.

A fiduciary obligation exists whenever one person, the client, places special trust and confidence in another person and relies upon that person, the fiduciary, to exercise his discretion or expertise in acting for the client; and the fiduciary knowingly accepts that trust and confidence and thereafter undertakes to act in behalf of the client by exercising his, the fiduciary's, own discretion and expertise.

Of course, the mere fact that a business relationship comes into being between two persons does not mean that either owes a fiduciary obligation to the other. If one person engages or employs another and thereafter directs or supervises or approves his actions, the person so employed is not a fiduciary. Rather, as previously stated, it is only when one party reposes, and the other accepts, a special trust and confidence involving the exercise of professional expertise and discretion that a fiduciary relationship comes into being.

When one person does undertake to act for another in a fiduciary relationship, the law forbids the fiduciary from acting in any manner adverse or contrary to the interests of the client, or from acting for his own benefit in relation to the subject matter. The client is entitled to the best efforts of the fiduciary on his behalf and the fiduciary must exercise all of the skill, care and diligence at his disposal when acting on behalf of the client.

A person acting in a fiduciary capacity is required to make truthful and complete disclosures to those placing trust in him, and he is forbidden to obtain an unreasonable advantage at the latter's expense.

Josiah Royce (1855–1916)

Josiah Royce was an American philosopher, part of the flowering of American philosophy in the early twentieth century. The major teacher of that period, John Dewey, was a consequentialist, who believed that all ethical principles could be tested by their results and established by the ordinary methods of science. Royce's method, by contrast, is deontological: He selects a principle which he takes to represent the highest duty and origin of other duties, and judges action on whether or not it conforms to that duty. For him, that duty is loyalty, which in Kantian manner he takes to be commitment first and in general to the idea of duty itself, second and in particular to the duties, perspectives, and ideals chosen by you and peculiar to your station or situation. Notice how the basic moral principles elaborated at the outset of this course—autonomy, justice, beneficence—are reproduced, in Royce's system, as aspects of loyalty.

In the first two chapters of his summary work on the subject, The Philosophy of Loyalty *(1924), Royce associates loyalty with its most conspicuous manifestations in the zeal of the patriot and the obsession with honor of the medieval knight and Japanese samurai. But loyalty has as its major function the carrying out of duties to people who need your protection and expect your devotion—parents, children, and above all the professional's clients. The best forerunner for Royce is actually Confucius, who understood the particular duties to kin and to supplicant, deriving their force not from any contract but from need and the ability to address that need. In the tradition of the giant Immanuel Kant, Royce tries valiantly to generalize loyalty into some absolute principle, independent of the actual people to whom you must be loyal. It doesn't really work.*

But here's his attempt. As a first pass at understanding this virtue, he presents the case of a humble bureaucrat:

From Josiah Royce, *Philosophy of Loyalty*

Chapter III

Now, I myself have for years used in my own classes, as an illustration of the personal worth and beauty of loyalty, an incident of English history, which has often been cited as a precedent in discussions of the constitutional privileges of the House of Commons, but which, as I think, has not been sufficiently noticed by moralists. Let me set that incident now before your imagination. Thus, I say, do the loyal bear themselves: In January, 1642, just before the outbreak of hostilities between King Charles I and the Commons, the King resolved to arrest certain leaders of the opposition party in Parliament. He accordingly sent his herald to the House to demand the surrender of these members into his custody. The Speaker of the House in reply solemnly appealed to the ancient privileges of the House, which gave to that body jurisdiction over its own members, and which forbade their arrest without its consent. The conflict between the privileges of the House and the royal prerogative was herewith definitely initiated. The King resolved by a show of force to assert at once his authority; and, on the day following that upon which the demand sent through his herald had been refused, he went in person, accompanied by soldiers, to the House. Then, having placed his guards at the doors, he entered, went up to the Speaker, and, naming the members whom he desired to arrest, demanded, "Mr. Speaker, do you espy these persons in the House?"

You will observe that the moment was an unique one in English history. Custom, precedent, convention, obviously were inadequate to define the Speaker's duty in this most critical instance. How, then, could he most admirably express himself? How best preserve his genuine personal dignity? What response would secure to the Speaker his own highest good? Think of the matter merely as one of the Speaker's individual worth and reputation. By what act could he do himself most honor?

In fact, as the well-known report, entered in the Journal of the House, states, the Speaker at once fell on his knee before the King and said: "Your Majesty, I am the Speaker of this House, and, being such, I have neither eyes to see nor tongue to speak save as this House shall command; and I humbly beg your Majesty's pardon if this is the only answer that I can give to your Majesty."

Now, I ask you not, at this point, to consider the Speaker's reply to the King as a deed having historical importance, or in fact as having value for anybody but himself. I want you to view the act merely as an instance of a supremely worthy personal attitude. The beautiful union of formal humility (when the Speaker fell on his knee before the King) with unconquerable self-assertion (when the reply rang with so clear a note of lawful defiance); the willing and complete identification of his whole self with his cause (when the Speaker declared that he had no eye or tongue except as his office gave them to him)—these are characteristics typical of a loyal attitude. . . . The King might be offended at the refusal; but he could not fail to note that, for the moment, he had met with a personal dignity greater than kingship,—the dignity that any loyal man, great or humble, possesses whenever he speaks and acts in the service of his cause. . . .

[But when we proceed] to consider what the causes are to which men ought to be loyal . . . [we encounter these] apparent difficulties. . . . Loyalty is a good for the loyal man; but it may be mischievous for those whom his cause assails. Conflicting loyalties may mean general social disturbances; and the fact that loyalty is good for the loyal does not of itself decide whose cause is right when various causes stand opposed to one another. And if, in accordance with our own argument . . . we declare that the best form of loyalty, for the loyal individual, is the one that he freely chooses for himself, so much the greater seems to be the complication of the moral world, and so much the more numerous become the chances that the loyalties of various people will conflict with one another. . . .

In order to overcome such difficulties, now that they have arisen in our way, and in order to discover a principle whereby one may be guided in choosing a right object for his loyalty, we must steadfastly bear in mind that, when we declared loyalty to be a supreme good for the loyal man himself, we were not speaking of a good that can come to a few men only—to heroes or to saints of an especially exalted mental type. As we expressly said, the mightiest and the humblest members of any social order can be morally equal in the exemplification of loyalty. . . .

This being true, let us next note that all the complications which we just reported are obviously due, in the main, to the fact that, as loyal men at present are, their various causes, and so their various loyalties, are viewed by them as standing in mutual, sometimes in deadly conflict. In general, as is plain if somebody's loyalty to a given cause, as for instance to a family, or to a state, so expresses itself as to involve a feud with a neighbor's family, or a warlike assault upon a foreign state, the result is obviously an evil; and at least part of the reason why it is an evil is that, by reason of the feud or the war, a certain good, namely, the enemy's loyalty, together with the enemy's opportunity to be loyal, is assailed, is thwarted, is endangered, is, perhaps, altogether destroyed. . . .

If loyalty is a supreme good, the mutually destructive conflict of loyalties is in general a supreme evil. If loyalty is a good for all sorts and conditions of men, the war of man against man has been especially mischievous, not so much because it has hurt, maimed, impoverished, or slain men, as because it has so often robbed the defeated of their causes, of their opportunities to be loyal, and sometimes of their very spirit of loyalty.

If, then, we look over the field of human life to see where good and evil have most clustered, we see that the best in human life is its loyalty; while the worst is whatever has tended to make loyalty impossible, or to destroy it when present, or to rob it of its own while it still survives. And of all things that thus have warred with loyalty, the bitterest woe of humanity has been that so often it is the loyal themselves who have thus blindly and eagerly gone about to wound and to slay the loyalty of their brethren. . . . Where such a conflict occurs, the best, namely, loyalty, is used as an instrument in order to compass the worst, namely, the destruction of loyalty.

It is true, then, that some causes are good, while some are evil. But the test of good and evil in the causes to which men are loyal is now definable in terms which we can greatly simplify in view of the foregoing considerations. . . .

. . . Loyalty, as we have defined it, is the willing devotion of a self to a cause. In answering the ethical individualists, we have insisted that all of the higher types of loyalty involve autonomous choice. The cause that is to appeal to me at all must indeed have some elemental fascination for me. It must stir me, arouse me, please me, and in the end possess me. Moreover, it must, indeed, be set before me by my social order as a possible, a practically significant, a living cause, which binds many selves in the unity of one life. But, nevertheless, if I am really awake to the significance of my own moral choices, I must be in the position of accepting this cause, as the Speaker of the House . . . had freely accepted his Speakership. My cause cannot be merely forced upon me. It is I who make it my own. It is I who willingly say: "I have no eyes to see nor tongue to speak save as this cause shall command." However much the cause may seem to be assigned to me by my social station, I must cooperate in the choice of the cause, before the act of loyalty is complete.

Since this is the case, since my loyalty never is my mere fate, but is always also my choice, I can of course determine my loyalty, at least to some extent, by the consideration of the actual good and ill which my proposed cause does to mankind. And since I now have the main criterion of the good and ill of causes before me, I can define a principle of choice which may so guide me that my loyalty shall become a good, not merely to myself, but to mankind.

This principle is now obvious. I may state it thus: In so far as it lies in your power, so choose your cause and so serve it, that, by reason of your choice and of your service, there shall be more loyalty in the world rather than less. And, in fact, so choose and so serve your individual cause as to secure thereby the greatest possible increase of loyalty amongst men. More briefly: *In choosing and in serving the cause to which you are to be loyal, be, in any case, loyal to loyalty. . . .*

Now this divided being of ours demands reconciliation with itself; it is one long struggle for unity. Its inner and outer realms are naturally at war. Yet it wills both realms. It wants them to become one. Such unity, however, only loyalty furnishes to us—loyalty, which finds the inner self intensified and exalted even by the very act of outward looking and of upward looking, of service and obedience—loyalty, which knows its eyes and its tongue to be never so much and so proudly its own as when it earnestly insists that it can neither see nor speak except as the cause demands—loyalty, which is most full of life at the instant when it is most ready to become weary, or even to perish in the act of devotion to its own. Such loyalty unites private passion and outward conformity in one life. . . .

Loyalty, then, is a good for all men. And it is in any man just as much a true good as my loyalty could be in me. And so, then, if indeed I seek a cause, a worthy cause, what cause could be more worthy than the cause of loyalty to loyalty; that is, the cause of making loyalty prosper amongst men? If I could serve that cause in a sustained and effective life, if some practical work for the furtherance of universal human loyalty could become to me what the House was to the Speaker, then indeed my own life-task would be found; and I could then be assured at every instant of the worth of my cause by virtue of the very good that I personally found in its service.

Here would be for me not only an unity of inner and outer, but an unity with the unity of all human life. What I sought for myself I should then be explicitly seeking for my whole world. All men would be my fellow-servants of my cause. In principle I should be opposed to no man's loyalty. I should be opposed only to men's blindness in their loyalty, I should contend only against that tragic disloyalty to loyalty which the feuds of humanity now exemplify. I should preach to all others, I should strive to practise myself, that active mutual furtherance of universal loyalty which is what humanity obviously most needs, if indeed loyalty, just as the willing devotion of a self to a cause, is a supreme good. . . .

Yet I fear that as you have listened to this sketch of a possible and reasonable cause, such as could be a proper object of our loyalty, you will all the while have objected: This may be a definition of a possible cause, but it is an unpractical definition. For what is there that one can do to further the loyalty of mankind in general? Humanitarian efforts are an old story. They constantly are limited in their effectiveness both by the narrowness of our powers, and by the complexity of the human nature which we try to improve. And if any lesson of philanthropy is well known, it is this, that whoever tries simply to help mankind as a whole, loses his labor, so long as he does not first undertake to help those nearest to him. Loyalty to the cause of universal loyalty—how, then, shall it constitute any practical working scheme of life?

I answer at once that the individual man, with his limited powers, can indeed serve the cause of universal loyalty only by limiting his undertakings to some decidedly definite personal range. He must have his own special and personal cause. But this cause of his can indeed be chosen and determined so as to constitute a deliberate effort to further universal loyalty. . . . My thesis is *that all the commonplace virtues, in so far as they are indeed defensible and effective, are special forms of loyalty to loyalty,* and are to be justified, centralized, inspired, by the one supreme effort to do good, namely, the effort to make loyalty triumphant in the lives of all men.

The first consideration which I shall here insist upon is this: Loyalty, as we have all along seen, depends upon a very characteristic and subtle union of natural interest, and of free choice. Nobody who merely follows his natural impulses as they come is loyal. Yet nobody can be loyal without depending upon and using his natural impulses. If I am to be loyal, my cause must from moment to moment fascinate me, awaken my muscular vigor, stir me with some eagerness for work, even if this be painful work. I cannot be loyal to barren abstractions. I can only be loyal to what my life can interpret in bodily deeds. Loyalty has its elemental appeal to my whole organism. My cause must become one with my human life. Yet all this must occur not without my willing choice. I must control my devotion. It will possess me, but not without my voluntary complicity; for I shall accept the possession. It is, then, with the cause to which you personally are loyal, as it was with divine grace in an older theology. The cause must control you, as divine grace took saving control of the sinner; but only your own will can accept this control, and a grace that merely compels can never save. . . .

. . . Loyalty to loyalty is then no unpractical cause. And you serve it not by becoming a mere citizen of the world, but by serving your own personal cause. We set before you, then, no unpractical rule when we repeat our moral formula in this form: Find your own cause, your interesting, fascinating, personally engrossing cause; serve it with all your might and soul and strength; but so choose your cause, and so serve it, that thereby you show forth your loyalty to loyalty, so that because of your choice and service of your cause, there is a maximum of increase of loyalty amongst your fellow-men. . . .

. . . Loyalty to loyalty is not a novel undertaking. It began to be effective from the time when first people could make and keep a temporary truce during a war, and when first strangers were regarded as protected by the gods, and when first the duties of hospitality were recognized. The way to be loyal to loyalty is therefore laid down in precisely the rational portion of the conventional morality which human experience has worked out. . . . In other words, all the recognized virtues can be defined in terms of our concept of loyalty. And this is why I assert that, when rightly interpreted, loyalty is the whole duty of man.

For consider the best-known facts as to the indirect influence of certain forms of loyal conduct. When I speak the truth, my act is directly an act of loyalty to the personal tie which then and there binds me to the man to whom I consent to speak. My special cause is, in such a case, constituted by this tie. My fellow and I are linked in a certain unity—the unity of some transaction which involves our speech one to another. To be ready to speak the truth to my fellow is to have, just then, no eye to see and no tongue to speak save as this willingly accepted tie demands. In so far, then, speaking the truth is a special instance of loyalty. But whoever speaks the truth, thereby does what he then can do to help everybody to speak the truth. For he acts so as to further the general confidence of man in man. How far such indirect influence may extend, no man can predict.

Precisely so, in the commercial world, honesty in business is a service, not merely and not mainly to the others who are parties to the single transaction in which at any one time this faithfulness is shown. The single act of business fidelity is an act of loyalty to that general confidence of man in man upon which the whole fabric of business rests. On the contrary, the unfaithful financier whose disloyalty is the final deed that lets loose the avalanche of a panic, has done far more harm to general public confidence than he could possibly do to those whom his act directly assails. Honesty, then, is owed not merely and not even mainly to those with whom we directly deal when we do honest acts; it is owed to mankind at large, and it benefits the community and the general cause of commercial loyalty.

Such a remark is in itself a commonplace; but it serves to make concrete my general thesis that every form of dutiful action is a case of loyalty to loyalty. For what holds thus of truthfulness and of commercial honesty holds, I assert, of every form of dutiful action. Each such form is a special means for being, by a concrete deed, loyal to loyalty.

We have sought for the worthy cause; and we have found it. This simplest possible of considerations serves to turn the chaotic mass of separate precepts of which our ordinary conventional moral code consists into a system unified by the one spirit of universal loyalty. By your individual deed you indeed cannot save the world, but you can at any moment do what in you lies to further the cause which both for you and for the human world constitutes the supreme good, namely, the cause of universal loyalty. . . . Have I private and personal rights, which I ought to assert? Yes, precisely in so far as my private powers and possessions are held in trust for the cause, and are, upon occasion, to be defended for the sake of the cause. My rights are morally the outcome of my loyalty. It is my right to protect my service, to maintain my office, and to keep my own merely in order that I may use my own as the cause commands. But rights which are not determined by my loyalty are vain pretence.

As to my duties to my neighbors, these are defined by a well-known tradition in terms of two principles, justice and benevolence. These two principles are mere aspects of our one principle. Justice means, in general, fidelity to human ties in so far as they are ties. Justice thus concerns itself with what may be called the mere forms in which loyalty expresses itself. Justice, therefore, is simply one aspect of loyalty—the more formal and abstract side of loyal life. If you are just, you are decisive in your choice of your personal cause, you are faithful to the loyal decision once made, you keep your promise, you speak the truth, you respect the loyal ties of all other men, and you contend with other men only in so far as the defence of your own cause, in the interest of loyalty to the universal cause of loyalty, makes such contest against aggression unavoidable. All these types of activity, within the limits that loyalty determines, are demanded if you are to be loyal to loyalty. Our principle thus at once requires them, and enables us to define their range of application. But justice, without loyalty, is a vicious formalism.

Benevolence, on the other hand, is that aspect of loyalty which directly concerns itself with your influence upon the inner life of human beings who enjoy, who suffer, and whose private good is to be affected by your deeds. Since no personal good that your fellow can possess is superior to his own loyalty, your own loyalty to loyalty is itself a supremely benevolent type of activity. And since your fellow-man is an instrument for the furtherance of the cause of universal loyalty, his welfare also concerns you, in so far as, if you help him to a more efficient life, you make him better able to be loyal. Thus benevolence is an inevitable attendant of loyalty. And the spirit of loyalty to loyalty enables us to define wherein consists a wise benevolence. Benevolence without loyalty is a dangerous sentimentalism. Thus viewed, then, loyalty to universal loyalty is indeed the fulfillment of the whole law.

John Rawls (1921–2002)

The impetus behind John Rawls' great work, A Theory of Justice *(1971), is the recognition of a problem in the ordinary explanation of the principle of justice. In the Utilitarian arguments that are usually advanced to explain social institutions, it is entirely possible to endorse arrangements that totally ignore the "underclass," the least advantaged members of society. For the underclass is a small minority of the whole, and the resources that are required to bring them up to the level of those in the middle of the socioeconomic scale are enormous, and well beyond the kinds of resources needed by others. Nor is the expenditure of the resources likely to yield a proportionate return in the form of higher productivity. The advantage of the majority, then—the greatest good of the greatest number in the long run—will be served by permanently abandoning such people. But how can that be just?*

In the social contract tradition, especially as represented by John Locke, Rawls found a philosophical setting for justice that permitted conclusions more compatible with our intuitions on the subject. We can see how an established society, including very rich, very poor, and a broad middle class, might decide to allow its very poor to languish in their poverty for the benefit of everyone else. But if we were all going to be assigned to live in such a society, and had no idea at the time of the assignment what position we would hold in it—top, bottom, or somewhere in the middle—we might not be so casual about the existence of misery and destitution. No society of equals, planning a set of institutions by which they will all be bound, without knowing just what position they will hold in those institutions, would agree to provisions that would allow some of them to suffer poverty all their lives and for generations to come. They would make certain that the very poor would be taken care of by the society—after all, they might turn out to be among those poor. That original planning session, called by Rawls the "original position," where all institutional practices are determined, is precisely the situation conceived by the social contract theorists, in which the state of nature is rejected and the civil society is formed. The "original contract," seen only as a useful fiction in the earlier contractarians, revives as a model for a just society: given intelligent people bargaining for the best possible society for themselves, not knowing whether they will be the most or the least advantaged members of that society, under no pressure and at no disadvantage relative to each other—any set of rules they can agree on will have to be fair to all, and can serve admirably as the fundamental rules of justice.

The passages that follow set forth Rawls' theory of justice.

From John Rawls, *A Theory of Justice*

---

3. The Main Idea of the Theory of Justice

My aim is to present a conception of justice which generalizes and carries to a higher level of abstraction the familiar theory of the social contract as found, say, in Locke, Rousseau and Kant. In order to do this we are not to think of the original contract as one to enter a particular society or to set up a particular form of government. Rather, the guiding idea is that the principles of justice for the basic structure of society are the object of the original agreement. They are the principles that free and rational persons concerned to further their own interests would accept in an initial position of equality as defining the fundamental terms of their association. These principles are to regulate all further agreements; they specify the kinds of social cooperation that can be entered into and the forms of government that can be established. This way of regarding the principles of justice I shall call justice as fairness.

Thus we are to imagine that those who engage in social cooperation choose together, in one joint act, the principles which are to assign basic rights and duties and to determine the division of social benefits. Men are to decide in advance how they are to regulate their claims against one another and what is to be the foundation charter of their society. Just as each person must decide by rational reflection what constitutes his good, that is, the system of ends which it is rational for him to pursue, so a group of persons must decide once and for all what is to count among them as just and unjust. The choice which rational men would make in this hypothetical situation of equal liberty, assuming for the present that this choice problem has a solution, determines the principles of justice.

In justice as fairness the original position of equality corresponds to the state of nature in the traditional theory of the social contract. This original position is not, of course, thought of as an actual historical state of affairs, much less as a primitive condition of culture. It is understood as a purely hypothetical situation characterized so as to lead to a certain conception of justice. Among the essential features of this situation is that no one knows his place in society, his class position or social status, nor does any one know his fortune in the distribution of natural assets and abilities, his intelligence, strength, and the like. I shall even assume that the parties do not know their conceptions of the good or their special psychological propensities. The principles of justice are chosen behind a veil of ignorance. This ensures that no one is advantaged or disadvantaged in the choice of principles by the outcome of natural chance or the contingency of social circumstances. Since all are similarly situated and no one is able to design principles to favor his particular condition, the principles of justice are the result of a fair agreement or bargain. For given the circumstances of the original position, the symmetry of everyone's relations to each other, this initial situation is fair between individuals as moral persons, that is, as rational beings with their own ends and capable, I shall assume, of a sense of justice. The original position is, one might say, the appropriate initial status quo, and thus the fundamental agreements reached in it are fair. This explains the propriety of the name "justice as fairness", it conveys the idea that the principles of justice are agreed to in an initial situation that is fair. . . .

Justice as fairness begins, as I have said, with one of the most general of all choices which persons might make together, namely, with the choice of the first principles of a conception of justice which is to regulate all subsequent criticism and reform of institutions. Then, having chosen a conception of justice, we can suppose that they are to choose a constitution and a legislature to enact laws, and so on, all in accordance with the principles of justice initially agreed upon. Our social situation is just if it is such that by this sequence of hypothetical agreements we would have contracted into the general system of rules which defines it. Moreover, assuming that the original position does determine a set of principles (that is, that a particular conception of justice would be chosen), it will then be true that whenever social institutions satisfy these principles those engaged in them can say to one another that they are cooperating on terms to which they would agree if they were free and equal persons whose relations with respect to one another were fair. They could all view their arrangements as meeting the stipulations which they would acknowledge in an initial situation that embodies widely accepted and reasonable constraints on the choice of principles. The general recognition of this fact would provide the basis for a public acceptance of the corresponding principles of justice. No society can, of course, be a scheme of cooperation which men enter voluntarily in a literal sense; each person finds himself placed at birth in some particular position in some particular society, and the nature of this position materially affects his life prospects. Yet a society satisfying the principles of justice as fairness comes as close as a society can to being a voluntary scheme, for it meets the principles which free and equal persons would assent to under circumstances that are fair. In this sense its members are autonomous and the obligations they recognize self-imposed. . . .

In working out the conception of justice as fairness one main task clearly is to determine which principles of justice would be chosen in the original position. To do this we must describe this situation in some detail and formulate with care the problem of choice which it presents. These matters I shall take up in the immediately succeeding chapters. It may be observed, however, that once the principles of justice are thought of as arising from an original agreement in a situation of equality, it is an open question whether the principle of utility would be acknowledged. Offhand it hardly seems likely that persons who view themselves as equals, entitled to press their claims upon one another, would agree to a principle which may require lesser life prospects for some simply for the sake of a greater sum of advantages enjoyed by others. Since each desires to protect his interests, his capacity to advance his conception of the good, no one has a reason to acquiesce in an enduring loss for himself in order to bring about a greater net balance of satisfaction. In the absence of strong and lasting benevolent impulses, a rational man would not accept a basic structure merely because it maximized the algebraic sum of advantages irrespective of its permanent effects on his own basic rights and interests. Thus it seems that the principle of utility is incompatible with the conception of social cooperation among equals for mutual advantage. It appears to be inconsistent with the idea of reciprocity implicit in the notion of a well-ordered society. . . .

I shall maintain instead that the persons in the initial situation would choose two rather different principles: the first requires equality in the assignment of basic rights and duties, while the second holds that social and economic inequalities, for example inequalities of wealth and authority, are just only if they result in compensating benefits for everyone, and in particular for the least advantaged members of society. These principles rule out justifying institutions on the grounds that the hardships of some are offset by a greater good in the aggregate. It may be expedient but it is not just that some should have less in order that others may prosper. But there is no injustice in the greater benefits earned by a few provided that the situation of persons not so fortunate is thereby improved. The intuitive idea is that since everyone's well-being depends upon a scheme of cooperation without which no one could have a satisfactory life, the division of advantages should be such as to draw forth the willing cooperation of everyone taking part in it, including those less well situated. Yet this can be expected only if reasonable terms are proposed. The two principles mentioned seem to be a fair agreement on the basis of which those better endowed, or more fortunate in their social position, neither of which we can be said to deserve, could expect the willing cooperation of others when some workable scheme is a necessary condition of the welfare of all. Once we decide to look for a conception of justice that nullifies the accidents of natural endowment and the contingencies of social circumstance as counters in quest for political and economic advantage, we are led to these principles. They express the result of leaving aside those aspects of the social world that seem arbitrary from a moral point of view. . . .

Rawls describes, in somewhat more detail, the "initial situation," or "original position" introduced above, and concludes:

It seems reasonable to suppose that the parties in the original position are equal. That is, all have the same rights in the procedure for choosing principles: each can make proposals, submit reasons for their acceptance, and so on. Obviously the purpose of these conditions is to represent equality between human beings as moral persons, as creatures having a conception of their good and capable of a sense of justice. The basis of equality is taken to be similarity in these two respects. Systems of ends are not ranked in value; and each man is presumed to have the requisite ability to understand and to act upon whatever principles are adopted. Together with the veil of ignorance, these conditions define the principles of justice as those which rational persons concerned to advance their interests would consent to as equals when none are known to be advantaged or disadvantaged by social and natural contingencies. . . .

11. Two Principles of Justice

I shall now state in a provisional form the two principles of justice that I believe would be chosen in the original position. . . .

The first statement of the two principles reads as follows:

First: each person is to have an equal right to the most extensive basic liberty compatible with a similar liberty for others.

Second: social and economic inequalities are to be arranged so that they are both (a) reasonably expected to be to everyone's advantage, and (b) attached to positions and offices open to all. . . .

By way of general comment, these principles primarily apply, as I have said, to the basic structure of society. They are to govern the assignment of rights and duties and to regulate the distribution of social and economic advantages. As their formulation suggests, these principles presuppose that the social structure can be divided into two more or less distinct parts, the first principle applying to the one, the second to the other. They distinguish between those aspects of the social system that define and secure the equal liberties of citizenship and those that specify and establish social and economic inequalities. The basic liberties of citizens are, roughly speaking, political liberty (the right to vote and to be eligible for public office) together with freedom of speech and assembly; liberty of conscience and freedom of thought; freedom of the person along with the right to hold (personal) property; and freedom from arbitrary arrest and seizure as defined by the concept of the rule of law. These liberties are all required to be equal by the first principle, since citizens of a just society are to have the same basic rights.

The second principle applies, in the first approximation, to the distribution of income and wealth and to the design or organizations that make use of differences in authority and responsibility, or chains of command. While the distribution of wealth and income need not be equal, it must be to everyone's advantage, and at the same time, positions of authority and offices of command must be accessible to all. One applies the second principle by holding positions open, and then, subject to this constraint, arranges social and economic inequalities so that everyone benefits.

These principles are to be arranged in a serial order with the first principle prior to the second. This ordering means that a departure from the institutions of equal liberty required by the first principle cannot be justified by, or compensated for, by greater social and economic advantages. The distribution of wealth and income, and the hierarchies of authority, must be consistent with both the liberties of equal citizenship and equality of opportunity.

As a first step, suppose that the basic structure of society distributes certain primary goods, that is, things that every rational man is presumed to want. These goods normally have a use whatever a person's rational plan of life. For simplicity, assume that the chief primary goods at the disposition of society are rights and liberties, powers and opportunities, income and wealth. . . . These are the social primary goods. Other primary goods such as health and vigor, intelligence and imagination, are natural goods; although their possession is influenced by the basic structure, they are not so directly under its control. Imagine, then, a hypothetical initial arrangement in which all the social primary goods are equally distributed: everyone has similar rights and duties, and income and wealth are evenly shared. This state of affairs provides a benchmark for judging improvements. If certain inequalities of wealth and organizational powers would make everyone better off than in this hypothetical starting situation, then they accord with the general conception.

Now it is possible, at least theoretically, that by giving up some of their fundamental liberties men are sufficiently compensated by the resulting social and economic gains. The general conception of justice imposes no restrictions on what sort of inequalities are permissible; it only requires that everyone's position be improved. We need not suppose anything so drastic as consenting to a condition of slavery. Imagine instead that men forego certain political rights when the economic returns are significant and their capacity to influence the course of policy by the exercise of these rights would be marginal in any case. It is this kind of exchange which the two principles as stated rule out; being arranged in serial order they do not permit exchanges between basic liberties and economic and social gains. The serial ordering of principles expresses an underlying preference among primary social goods. When this preference is rational so likewise is the choice of these principles in this order.

The fact that the two principles apply to institutions has certain consequences. Several points illustrate this. First of all, the rights and liberties referred to by these principles are those which are defined by the public rules of the basic structure. Whether men are free is determined by the rights and duties established by the major institutions of society. Liberty is a certain pattern of social forms. The first principle simply requires that certain sorts of rules, those defining basic liberties, apply to everyone equally and that they allow the most extensive liberty compatible with a like liberty for all. The only reason for circumscribing the rights defining liberty and making men's freedom less extensive than it might otherwise be is that these equal rights as institutionally defined would interfere with one another. . . .

Now the second principle insists that each person benefit from permissible inequalities in the basic structure. This means that it must be reasonable for each relevant representative man defined by this structure, when he views it as a going concern, to prefer his prospects with the inequality to his prospects without it. One is not allowed to justify differences in income or organizational powers on the ground that the disadvantages of those in one position are outweighed by the greater advantages of those in another. Much less can infringements of liberty be counterbalanced in this way. Applied to the basic structure, the principle of utility would have us maximize the expectations of representative men (weighted by the number of persons they represent, on the classical view); and this would permit us to compensate for the losses of some by the gains of others. Instead, the two principles require that everyone benefit from economic and social inequalities. . . .

These considerations suggest the idea of treating the question of distributive shares as a matter of pure procedural justice. . . . A number of men are to divide a cake: assuming that the fair division is an equal one, which procedure, if any, will give this outcome? Technicalities aside, the obvious solution is to have one man divide the cake and get the last piece, the others being allowed their pick before him. He will divide the cake equally, since in this way he assures for himself the largest share possible. This example illustrates the two characteristic features of perfect procedural justice. First, there is an independent criterion for what is a fair division, a criterion defined separately from and prior to the procedure which is to be followed. And second, it is possible to devise a procedure that is sure to give the desired outcome.

Martin Luther King, Jr. (1939–1968)

It is appropriate to end this selection of readings from the tradition of the Moral Law with one of its more recent martyrs, a man who gave his life to the cause of justice. In King we find the themes that have been with us since Epictetus: From the Stoics, the disdain for the punishments, including fetters and prisons, that the unjust world visits upon the just man in the attempt to silence him. From Aquinas, citing Augustine (as does King), the certainty that the unjust law is no law at all, and should in no way be obeyed. From Hobbes, Locke, and Jefferson, the willingness not only to assert constitutional rights, but to insist that they be incorporated into the law of the land—of all the lands of the United States, in this case. We may add, from Jefferson, the acceptance of a certain quota of violence as the cost of liberty. From Kant, the centrality of the notion of human dignity. From Royce, the fierce devotion to that cause which fulfilled and consumed his life. And with Rawls, his contemporary, the recognition that peace and plenty are worthless without justice.

You might wish to refer back, at this point, to the Biblical Tradition section of this book, and trace the self-same theme of justice from Amos through Jesus through Aquinas to King. King simply makes explicit what is implicit in them all: The obligation to do justice overrides the timid utilitarian considerations of possible violence and unpleasant threats to prosperity and "order." When justice is done, then we shall have peace, a peace worth keeping.

The excerpts that follow are from "A Letter from a Birmingham Jail," which was just that. In the spring of 1963, King and his Southern Christian Leadership Council initiated a boycott of white stores in Birmingham, Alabama, accompanied by demonstrations in which several of the leaders were arrested. Eight of Alabama's top white religious leaders issued a formal statement calling the boycott "unwise and untimely." From his cell in the Birmingham Jail, the Reverend King answered the Roman Catholic, Protestant, and Jewish religious leaders in a personal letter, which was eventually published in Ebony *and in King's book,* Why We Can't Wait.

From Martin Luther King, Jr., *A Letter from a Birmingham Jail*

My Dear Fellow Clergymen,

While confined here in the Birmingham city jail, I came across your recent statement calling our present activities "unwise and untimely. . . ." Since I feel that you are men of genuine good will and that your criticisms are sincerely set forth, I want to try to answer your statement in what I hope will be patient and reasonable terms.

I think I should indicate why I am here in Birmingham, since you have been influenced by the view which argues against "outsiders coming in. . . ." I, along with several members of my staff, am here because I was invited here. I am here because I have organizational ties here.

But more basically, I am in Birmingham because injustice is here. Just as the prophets of the eighth century B.C. left their villages and carried their "thus saith the Lord" far beyond the boundaries of their home towns, and just as the Apostle Paul left his village of Tarsus and carried the gospel of Jesus Christ to the far corners of the GrecoRoman world, so am I compelled to carry the gospel of freedom beyond my own home town. Like Paul, I must constantly respond to the Macedonian call for aid. . . .

You express a great deal of anxiety over our willingness to break laws. This is certainly a legitimate concern. Since we so diligently urge people to obey the Supreme Court's decision of 1954 outlawing segregation in the public schools, at first glance it may seem rather paradoxical for us consciously to break laws. One may well ask: "How can you advocate breaking some laws and obeying others?" The answer lies in the fact that there are two types of laws: just and unjust. . . . I would agree with St. Augustine that "an unjust law is no law at all."

Now, what is the difference between the two? How does one determine whether a law is just or unjust? A just law is a man-made code that squares with the moral law or the law of God. An unjust law is a code that is out of harmony with the moral law. To put it in the terms of St. Thomas Aquinas: An unjust law is a human law that is not rooted in eternal law and natural law. Any law that uplifts human personality is just. Any law that degrades human personality is unjust. All segregation statutes are unjust because segregation distorts the soul and damages the personality. It gives the segregator a false sense of superiority and the segregated a false sense of inferiority. Segregation, to use the terminology of the Jewish philosopher Martin Buber, substitutes an "I-it" relationship for an "I-thou" relationship and ends up relegating persons to the status of things. Hence segregation is not only politically, economically and sociologically unsound, it is morally wrong and sinful. Paul Tillich has said that sin is separation. Is not segregation an existential expression of man's tragic separation, his awful estrangement, his terrible sinfulness? Thus it is that I urge men to obey the 1954 decision of the Supreme Court, for it is morally right; and I can urge them to disobey segregation ordinances, for they are morally wrong. . . .

I hope you are able to see the distinction I am trying to point out. In no sense do I advocate evading or defying the law, as would the rabid segregationist. That would lead to anarchy. One who breaks an unjust law must do so openly, lovingly, and with a willingness to accept the penalty. I submit that an individual who breaks a law that conscience tells him is unjust, and who willingly accepts the penalty of imprisonment in order to arouse the conscience of the community over its injustice, is in reality expressing the highest respect for law. . . .

I must make two honest confessions to you, my Christian and Jewish brothers. First, I must confess that over the past few years I have been gravely disappointed with the white moderate. I have almost reached the regrettable conclusion that the Negro's great stumbling block is not the White Citizen's Councilor or the Ku Klux Klanner, but the white moderate, who is more devoted to "order" than to justice; who prefers a negative peace which is the absence of tension, to a positive peace which is the presence of justice; who constantly says: "I agree with you in the goal you seek, but I cannot agree with your methods of direct action"; who paternalistically believes he can set the timetable for another man's freedom; who lives by a mythical concept of time and who constantly advises the Negro to wait for a "more convenient season." Shallow understanding from people of good will is more frustrating than absolute misunderstanding from people of ill will. . . .

In your statement you asserted that our actions, even though peaceful, must be condemned because they precipitate violence. But is this a logical assertion? Isn't this like condemning a robbed man because his possession of money precipitated the evil act of robbery? Isn't this like condemning Socrates because his unswerving commitment to truth and his philosophical inquiries precipitated the act by the misguided populace in which they made him drink the hemlock? Isn't this like condemning Jesus because his unique God-Consciousness and never-ceasing devotion to God's will precipitated the evil act of crucifixion? We must come to see that, as the federal courts have consistently affirmed, it is wrong to urge an individual to cease his efforts to gain his basic constitutional rights because the quest may precipitate violence. Society must protect the robbed and punish the robber. . . .

FOUR

Utilitarianism

Philosophies of pleasure and pain are universal. As long as we human beings live in mortal bodies, wired with the type of nervous system that we happen to have, we must classify states and situations of life as enjoyable or as painful. When all else fails, when all other grounds of judgment seem confused and obscure, pleasure and pain provide us with moral constants. At least we know that some good will come of the production of pleasure; at least we can be sure that it is wrong to produce pain, even if we do it for the sake of a greater good.

Epicurus

Epicurus (341 B.C.–270 B.C.) was a contemporary of Zeno the Stoic. His philosophy, like that of the Stoics, can best be understood as the response of the moral philosopher to post-political conditions. The polis *no longer provides the moral structure of the good human life. Then where shall we find it? For the Stoics the answer was to be found in eternal necessity, a law beyond all human associations or sensations. For Epicurus, no such necessity appeared; he was more impressed by the ability of philosophers to find a serene and enjoyable life by careful management of the appetites.*

The Utilitarians, inheritors of Epicurus' approach, can best be understood as the moral philosophers' response to the scientific revolution. Physics had proved that the way to understand the universe was through observation, and simple laws that subsumed the observations and accurately predicted observations to come. Very well then, ethics could be elucidated according to the same methods. The Utilitarians set out to organize a simple and repeatable set of observations by simple laws, and to find quantifiable and measurable states of being that could be evaluated mathematically to show what was right and what was wrong. That was the enterprise of the first of the great Utilitarian philosophers, Jeremy Bentham. But such quantification has to be qualified, as the next generation of Utilitarians realized, for the moral life will not be held within the bounds of any calculus, "felicific" or otherwise. In the work of the heir of Utility, John

Stuart Mill, we find a humane and sophisticated culmination of this welfare-driven orientation. The Utilitarians may have been the best philosophers of legislation who ever wrote, and their insights guide our public thinking to this day.

Hedonists Ancient and Modern

Here we track them from their ancient roots, as we did the philosophers of the Moral Law. These passages from Epicurus offer a sampling from the very few writings extant.

From Epicurus, *The Extant Remains*

Become accustomed to the belief that death is nothing to us. For all good and evil consists in sensation, but death is deprivation of sensation. And therefore a right understanding that death is nothing to us makes the mortality of life enjoyable, not because it adds to it an infinite span of time, but because it takes away the craving for immortality. For there is nothing terrible in life for the man who has truly comprehended that there is nothing terrible in not living. So that the man speaks but idly who says that he fears death not because it will be painful when it comes, but because it is painful in anticipation. For that which gives no trouble when it comes, is but an empty pain in anticipation. So death, the most terrifying of ills, is nothing to us, since so long as we exist death is not with us; but when death comes, then we do not exist. It does not then concern either the living or the dead, since for the former it is not, and the latter are no more.

But the many at one moment shun death as the greatest of evils, at another yearn for it as a respite from the evils in life. But the wise man neither seeks to escape life nor fears the cessation of life, for neither does life offend him nor does the absence of life seem to be any evil. And just as with food he does not seek simply the larger share and nothing else, but rather the most pleasant, so he seeks to enjoy not the longest period of time, but the most pleasant. . . .

We must consider that of desires some are natural, others vain, and of the natural some are necessary and others merely natural; and of the necessary some are necessary for happiness, others for the repose of the body, and others for very life. The right understanding of these facts enables us to refer all choice and avoidance to the health of the body and the soul's freedom from disturbance, since this is the aim of the life of blessedness. For it is to obtain this end that we always act, namely, to avoid pain and fear. And when this is once secured for us, all the tempest of the soul is dispersed, since the living creature has not to wander as though in search of something that is missing, and to look for some other thing by which he can fulfil the good of the soul and the good of the body. For it is then that we have need of pleasure, when we feel pain owing to the absence of pleasure; but when we do not feel pain, we no longer need pleasure. And for this cause we call pleasure the beginning and end of the blessed life. For we recognize pleasure as the first good innate in us, and from pleasure we begin every act of choice and avoidance, and to pleasure we return again, using the feeling as the standard by which we judge every good. . . .

And since pleasure is the first good and natural to us, for this very reason we do not choose every pleasure, but sometimes we pass over many pleasures, when greater discomfort accrues to us as the result of them; and similarly we think many pains better than pleasures, since a greater pleasure comes to us when we have endured pains for a long time. Every pleasure then because of its natural kinship to us is good, yet not every pleasure is to be chosen; even as every pain also is an evil, yet not all are always of a nature to be avoided. . . .

When, therefore, we maintain that pleasure is the end, we do not mean the pleasures of profligates and those that consist in sensuality, as is supposed by some who are either ignorant or disagree with us or do not understand, but freedom from pain in the body and from trouble in the mind. For it is not continuous drinkings and revellings, nor the satisfaction of lusts, nor the enjoyment of fish and other luxuries of the wealthy table, which produce a pleasant life, but sober reasoning, searching out the motives for all choice and avoidance, and banishing mere opinions, to which are due the greatest disturbance of the spirit. . . .

Of all this the beginning and the greatest good is prudence. Wherefore prudence is a more precious thing even than philosophy: for from prudence are sprung all the other virtues, and it teaches us that it is not possible to live pleasantly without living prudently and honorably and justly, nor, again to live a life of prudence, honour and justice without living pleasantly. For the virtues are by nature bound up with the pleasant life, and the pleasant life is inseparable from them. . . .

Jeremy Bentham (1748–1832)

Epicurus combines the Greek orientation to the serene and virtuous life with the hedonism of his pre-Socratic heritage to produce this gentle philosophy. While the style of Jeremy Bentham is very different from that of his Greek predecessor, the structure of the ethical reasoning is very similar.

From Jeremy Bentham, *Principles of Morals and Legislation*

Chapter I. Of the Principle of Utility

1. Nature has placed mankind under the governance of two sovereign masters, *pain* and *pleasure*. It is for them alone to point out what we ought to do, as well as to determine what we shall do. On the one hand the standard of right and wrong, on the other the chain of causes and effects, are fastened to their throne. They govern us in all we do, in all we say, in all we think: every effort we can make to throw off our subjection, will serve but to demonstrate and confirm it. In words a man may pretend to abjure their empire: but in reality he will remain subject to it all the while. The *principle of utility* recognizes this subjection, and assumes it for the foundation of that system, the object of which is to rear the fabric of felicity by the hands of reason and of law. Systems which attempt to question it, deal in sounds instead of senses, in caprice instead of reason, in darkness instead of light.

But enough of metaphor and declamation: it is not by such means that moral science is to be improved.

2. The principle of utility is the foundation of the present work: it will be proper therefore at the outset to give an explicit and determinate account of what is meant by it. By the principle of utility is meant that principle which approves or disapproves of every action whatsoever, according to the tendency which it appears to have to augment or diminish the happiness of the party whose interest is in question: or, what is the same thing in other words, to promote or to oppose that happiness. I say of every action whatsoever; and therefore not only of every action of a private individual, but of every measure of government.

3. By utility is meant that property in any object, whereby it tends to produce benefit, advantage, pleasure, good, or happiness, (all this in the present case comes to the same thing) or (what comes again to the same thing) to prevent the happening of mischief, pain, evil, or unhappiness to the party whose interest is considered: if that party be the community in general, then the happiness of the community: if a particular individual, then the happiness of that individual.

4. The interest of the community is one of the most general expressions that can occur in the phraseology of morals: no wonder that the meaning of it is often lost. When it has a meaning, it is this. The community is a fictitious *body,* composed of the individual persons who are considered as constituting as it were its *members.* The interest of the community then is, what?—the sum of the interests of the several members who compose it.

5. It is in vain to talk of the interest of the community, without understanding what is the interest of the individual. A thing is said to promote the interest, or to be for the interest, of an individual, when it tends to add to the sum total of his pleasures: or, what comes to the same thing, to diminish the sum total of his pains.

6. An action then may be said to be conformable to the principle of utility, or, for shortness sake, to utility, (meaning with respect to the community at large) when the tendency it has to augment the happiness of the community is greater than any it has to diminish it.

7. A measure of government (which is but a particular kind of action, performed by a particular person or persons) may be said to be conformable to or dictated by the principle of utility, when in like manner the tendency which it has to augment the happiness of the community is greater than any which it has to diminish it.

8. When an action, or in particular a measure of government, is supposed by a man to be conformable to the principle of utility, it may be convenient, for the purposes of discourse, to imagine a kind of law or dictate, called a law or dictate of utility; and to speak of the action in question, as being conformable to such law or dictate.

9. A man may be said to be a partisan of the principle of utility, when the approbation or disapprobation he annexes to any action, or to any measure, is determined by and proportioned to the tendency which he conceives it to have to augment or to diminish the happiness of the community: or in other words, to its conformity or unconformity to the laws or dictates of utility.

10. Of an action that is conformable to the principle of utility one may always say either that it is one that ought to be done, or at least that it is not one that ought not to be done. One may say also, that it is right it should be done; at least that it is not wrong it should be done: that it is a right action; at least that it is not a wrong action. When thus interpreted, the words *ought,* and *right* and *wrong,* and others of that stamp, have a meaning: when otherwise, they have none.

11. Has the rectitude of this principle been ever formally contested? It should seem that it had, by those who have not known what they have been meaning. Is it susceptible of any direct proof? it should seem not: for that which is used to prove every thing else, cannot itself be proved: a chain of proofs must have their commencement somewhere. To give such proof is as impossible as it is needless.

12. Not that there is or ever has been that human creature breathing, however stupid or perverse, who has not on many, perhaps on most occasions of his life, deferred to it. By the natural constitution of the human frame, on most occasions of their lives men in general embrace this principle without thinking of it: if not for the ordering of their own actions, yet for the trying of their own actions, as well as of those of other men. There have been, at the same time, not many, perhaps, even of the most intelligent, who have been disposed to embrace it purely and without reserve. There are even few who have not taken some occasion or other to quarrel with it, either on account of their not understanding always how to apply it, or on account of some prejudice or other which they were afraid to examine into, or could not bear to part with. For such is the stuff that man is made of, in principle and in practice, in a right track and in a wrong one, the rarest of all human qualities is consistency.

13. When a man attempts to combat the principle of utility, it is with reasons drawn, without his being aware of it, from that very principle itself. His arguments, if they prove any thing, prove not that the principle *is wrong,* but that, according to the applications he supposes to be made of it, it is

misapplied. Is it possible for a man to move the earth? Yes; but he must first find out another earth to stand upon.

14. To disprove the propriety of it by arguments is impossible; but, from the causes that have been mentioned, or from some confused or partial view of it, a man may happen to be disposed not to relish it. Where this is the case, if he thinks the settling of his opinions on such a subject worth the trouble, let him take the following steps and at length, perhaps, he may come to reconcile himself to it.

1. Let him settle with himself, whether he would wish to discard this principle altogether; if so, let him consider what it is that all his reasonings (in matters of politics especially) can amount to?

2. If he would, let him settle with himself, whether he would judge and act without any principle, or whether there is any other he would judge and act by?

3. If there be, let him examine and satisfy himself whether the principle he thinks he has found is really any separate intelligible principle; or whether it be not a mere principle in words, a kind of phrase, which at bottom expresses neither more nor less than the mere averment of his own unfounded sentiments; that is, what in another person he might be apt to call caprice?

4. If he is inclined to think that his own approbation or disapprobation, annexed to the idea of an act, without any regard to its consequences, is a sufficient foundation for him to judge and act upon, let him ask himself whether his sentiment is to be a standard of right and wrong, with respect to every other man, or whether every man's sentiment has the same privilege of being a standard to itself.

5. In the first case, let him ask himself whether his principle is not despotical, and hostile to all the rest of human race?

6. In the second case, whether it is not anarchical, and whether at this rate there are not as many different standards of right and wrong as there are men? and whether even to the same man, the same thing, which is right to-day, may not (without the least change in its nature) be wrong to-morrow? and whether the same thing is not right and wrong in the same place at the same time? and in either case, whether all argument is not at an end? and whether, when two men have said, "I like this," and "I don't like it," they can (upon such a principle) have any thing more to say?

7. If he should have said to himself, No: for that the sentiment which he proposes as a standard must be grounded on reflection, let him say on what particulars the reflection is to turn? if on particulars having relation to the utility of the act, then let him say whether this is not deserting his own principle, and borrowing assistance from that very one in opposition to which he sets it up: or if not on those particulars, on what other particulars?

8. If he should be for compounding the matter, and adopting his own principle in part, and the principle of utility in part, let him say how far he will adopt it?

9. When he has settled with himself where he will stop, then let him ask himself how he justifies to himself the adopting it so far? and why he will not adopt it any farther?

10. Admitting any other principle than the principle of utility to be a right principle, a principle that it is right for a man to pursue; admitting (what is not true) that the word *right* can have a meaning without reference to utility, let him say whether there is any such thing as a motive that a man can have to pursue the dictates of it: if there is, let him say what that motive is, and how it is to be distinguished from those which enforce the dictates of utility: if not, then lastly let him say what it is this other principle can be good for? . . .

> *In Bentham's hands, the principle of utility is perfectly clear, easy to understand and to validate. Yet utility is not always easy to apply, if only because it demands that you stop and think before acting, and imagine how your action will seem to others, and*

*how its consequences will affect their lives and the community as a whole. Enforced con-
sideration of others is not always enjoyable. Most people, Bentham points out, would
prefer to leave morality to their own interest of the moment, or their own impulse, rather
than consult the general good of the community to decide the rights and wrongs of a
proposed action. In a memorable footnote to Chapter II of the* Introduction, *he mentions some of the "moral systems" of his acquaintance which embody this preference in
high language:*

From Chapter II, Note

It is curious enough to observe the variety of inventions men have hit upon, and the variety of phrases
they have brought forward, in order to conceal from the world, and, if possible, from themselves, this
very general and therefore very pardonable self-sufficiency.

1. One man says, he has a thing made on purpose to tell him what is right and what is wrong; and
that it is called a *moral sense*: and then he goes to work at his ease, and says, such a thing is right, and
such a thing is wrong—why? "because my moral sense tells me it is."

2. Another man comes and alters the phrase: leaving out *moral*, and putting in *common*, in the room
of it. He then tells you, that his common sense teaches him what is right and wrong, as surely as the
other's moral sense did: meaning by common sense, a sense of some kind or other, which, he says, is possessed by all mankind: the sense of those, whose sense is not the same as the author's, being struck out of
the account as not worth taking. This contrivance does better than the other, for a moral sense, being a
new thing, a man may feel about him a good while without being able to find it out: but common sense
is as old as the creation; and there is no man but would be ashamed to be thought not to have as much
of it as his neighbours. It has another great advantage: by appearing to share power, it lessens envy. . . .

3. Another man comes, and says, that as to a moral sense indeed, he cannot find that he has any
such thing: that however he has an *understanding*, which will do quite as well. This understanding, he
says, is the standard of right and wrong: it tells him so and so. All good and wise men understand as he
does: if other men's understanding differ in any point from his, so much the worse for them: it is a sure
sign they are either defective or corrupt.

4. Another man says, that there is an eternal and immutable Rule of Right: that the rule of right
dictates so and so: and then he begins giving you his sentiments upon any thing that comes uppermost:
and these sentiments (you are to take for granted) are so many branches of the eternal rule of right.

5. Another man, or perhaps the same man (it's no matter) says, that there are certain practices conformable, and others repugnant, to the Fitness of Things; and then he tells you, at his leisure, what
practices are conformable and what repugnant: just as he happens to like a practice or dislike it.

6. A great multitude of people are continually talking of the Law of Nature; and then they go on
giving you their sentiments about what is right and what is wrong: and these sentiments, you are to
understand, are so many chapters and sections of the Law of Nature. . . .

9. The fairest and openest of them all is that sort of man who speaks out, and says, I am of the
number of the Elect: now God himself takes care to inform the Elect what is right: and that with so
good effect, and let them strive ever so, they cannot help not only knowing it but practising it. If therefore a man wants to know what is right and what is wrong, he has nothing to do but to come to me.

It is upon the principle of antipathy that such and such acts are often reprobated on the score of
their being unnatural: the practice of exposing children, established among the Greeks and Romans,
was an unnatural practice. Unnatural, when it means anything, means unfrequent: and there it means
something; although nothing to the present purpose. But here it means no such thing: for the frequen-
cy of such acts is perhaps the great complaint. It therefore means nothing; nothing, I mean, which there

is in the act itself. All it can serve to express is, the disposition of the person who is talking of it: the disposition he is in to be angry at the thoughts of it. Does it merit his anger? Very likely it may: but whether it does or no is a question, which, to be answered rightly, can only be answered upon the principle of utility.

Unnatural is as good a word as moral sense, or common sense; and would be as good a foundation for a system. Such an act is unnatural; that is repugnant to nature: for I do not like to practise it: and consequently, do not practise it. It is therefore repugnant to what ought to be the nature of everybody else.

The mischief common to all these ways of thinking and arguing (which, in truth, as we have seen, are but one and the same method, couched in different forms of words) is their serving as a cloke and pretence, and aliment, to despotism: if not a despotism in practice, a despotism however in disposition: which is but too apt, when pretence and power offer, to show itself in practice. The consequence is, that with intentions very commonly of the purest kind, a man becomes a torment either to himself or his fellow-creatures. If he be of the melancholy cast, he sits in silent grief, bewailing their blindness and depravity: if of the irascible, he declaims with fury and virulence against all who differ from him; blowing up the coals of fanaticism, and branding with the charge of corruption and insincerity, every man who does not think, or profess to think, as he does.

If such a man happens to possess the advantages of style, his book may do a considerable deal of mischief before the nothingness of it is understood.

These principles, if such they can be called, it is more frequent to see applied to morals than to politics: but their influence extends itself to both. In politics, as well as morals, a man will be at least equally glad of a pretence for deciding any question in the manner that best pleases him, without the trouble of inquiry. If a man is an infallible judge of what is right and wrong in the actions of private individuals, why not in the measures to be observed by public men in the direction of those actions? accordingly (not to mention other chimeras) I have more than once known the pretended law of nature set up in legislative debates, in opposition to arguments derived from the principle of utility.

"But is it never, then, from any other considerations than those of utility, that we derive our notions of right and wrong?" I do not know: I do not care. Whether a moral sentiment can be originally conceived from any other source than a view of utility, is one question: whether upon examination and reflection it can, in point of fact, be actually persisted in and justified on any other ground, by a person reflecting within himself, is another: whether in point of right it can properly be justified on any other ground, by a person addressing himself to the community, is a third. The two first are questions of speculation: it matters not, comparatively speaking, how they are decided. The last is a question of practice: the decision of it is of as much importance as that of any can be.

"I feel in myself," (say you) "a disposition to approve of such or such an action in a moral view: but this is not owing to any notions I have of its being a useful one to the community. I do not pretend to know whether it be an useful one or not: it may be, for aught I know, a mischievous one." "But is it then," (say I) "a mischievous one? examine; and if you can make yourself sensible that it is so, then if duty means any thing, that is, moral duty, it is your *duty* at least to abstain from it: and more than that, if it is what lies in your power, and can be done without too great a sacrifice, to endeavour to prevent it. It is not your cherishing the notion of it in your bosom, and giving it the name of virtue, that will excuse you."

"I feel in myself," (say you again) "a disposition to detest such or such an action in a moral view; but this is not owing to any notions I have of its being a mischievous one to the community. I do not pretend to know whether it be a mischievous one or not: it may be not a mischievous one: it may be, for aught I know, an useful one." "May it indeed," (say I) "an useful one? but let me tell you then, that unless duty, and right and wrong, be just what you please to make them, if it really be not a mischievous one, and any body has a mind to do it, it is no duty of yours, but, on the contrary, it would be very wrong in you, to take upon you to prevent him: detest it within yourself as much as you please; for your not doing it yourself, but if you go about, by word or deed, to do any thing to hinder him, or make him suffer for it, it is you, and not he, that have done wrong: it is not your setting yourself to blame his conduct, or branding it with the name of vice, that will make him culpable or you blameless. Therefore if you can make yourself content that he shall be of one mind, and you of another, about this matter, and so continue, it is well: But if nothing will serve you, but that you and he must needs be of the same mind, I'll tell you what you have to do: it is for you to get the better of your antipathy, not for him to truckle to it."

From Chapter IV

Value of a Lot of Pleasure or Pain. How to be Measured:

1. Pleasures, then, and the avoidance of pains, are the *ends* which the legislator has in view: it behoves him therefore to understand their *value*. Pleasures and pains are the *instruments* he has to work with: it behoves him therefore to understand their force, which is again, in other words, their value.

2. To a person considered *by himself,* the value of a pleasure or pain considered *by itself,* will be greater or less, according to the four following circumstances:

1. Its *intensity.*
2. Its *duration.*
3. Its *certainty* or *uncertainty.*
4. Its *propinquity* or *remoteness.*

3. These are the circumstances which are to be considered in estimating a pleasure or a pain considered each of them by itself. But when the value of any pleasure or pain is considered for the purpose of estimating the tendency of any *act* by which it is produced, there are two other circumstances to be taken into account; these are,

5. Its *fecundity,* or the chance it has of being followed by sensations of the *same* kind: that is, pleasures, if it be a pleasure: pains, if it be a pain.
6. Its *purity,* or the chance it has of not being followed by sensations of the *opposite* kind: that is, pains, if it be a pleasure: pleasures, if it be a pain.

These two last, however are in strictness scarcely to be deemed properties of the pleasure or the pain itself, they are not, therefore, in strictness to be taken into the account of the value of that pleasure or that pain. They are in strictness to be deemed properties only of the act, or other event, by which such pleasure or pain has been produced; and accordingly are only to be taken into the account of the tendency of such act or such event.

4. To a *number* of persons, with reference to each of whom the value of a pleasure or a pain is considered, it will be greater or less, according to seven circumstances: to wit, the six preceding ones; *viz.*

1. Its *intensity.*
2. Its *duration.*
3. Its *certainty* or *uncertainty.*
4. Its *propinquity* or *remoteness.*
5. Its *fecundity.*
6. Its *purity.*

And one other; to wit:

7. Its *extent*; that is, the number of persons to whom it *extends*; or (in other words) who are affected by it.

5. To take an exact account then of the general tendency of any act, by which the interests of a community are affected, proceed as follows. Begin with any one person of those whose interests seem most immediately to be affected by it: and take an account,

1. Of the value of each distinguishable *pleasure* which appears to be produced by it in the *first* instance.
2. Of the value of each *pain* which appears to be produced by it in the *first* instance.
3. Of the value of each pleasure which appears to be produced by it *after* the first. This constitutes the *fecundity* of the first *pleasure* and the *impurity* of the first *pain*.
4. Of the value of each *pain* which appears to be produced by it after the first. This constitutes the *fecundity* of the first *pain*, and the *impurity* of the first *pleasure*.
5. Sum up all the values of all the *pleasures* on the one side, and those of all the *pains* on the other. The balance, if it be on the side of pleasure, will give the *good* tendency of the act upon the whole, with respect to the interests of that *individual* person; if on the side of pain, the *bad* tendency of it upon the whole.
6. Take an account of the *number* of persons whose interests appear to be concerned; and repeat the above process with respect to each. *Sum up* the numbers expressive of the degrees of *good* tendency, which the act has, with respect to each individual, in regard to whom the tendency of it is *good* upon the whole: do this again with respect to each individual, in regard to whom the tendency of it is *bad* upon the whole. Take the *balance;* which, if on the side of *pleasure*, will give the general *good tendency* of the act, with respect to the total number of the community of individuals concerned; if on the side of pain, the general *evil tendency*, with respect to the same community.

6. It is not to be expected that this process should be strictly pursued previously to every moral judgment, or to every legislative or judicial operation. It may, however, be always kept in view: and as near as the process actually pursued on these occasions approaches to it, so near will such process approach to the character of an exact one.

7. The same process is alike applicable to pleasure and pain, in whatever shape they appear: and by whatever denomination they are distinguished: to pleasure, whether it be called *good* (which is properly the cause or instrument of pleasure,) or *profit* (which is distant pleasure, or the cause or instrument of distant pleasure,) or *convenience,* or *advantage, benefit, emolument, happiness,* and so forth: to pain, whether it be called *evil,* (which corresponds to *good*) or *mischief,* or *inconvenience,* or *disadvantage,* or *loss,* or *unhappiness,* and so forth.

Adam Smith (1723–1790)

Adam Smith's Wealth of Nations, *as it is generally known, was published in 1776, the same year as Bentham's* Fragment on Government *and the* Declaration of Independence. *Revolution was in the air—against the dead prescriptions of Church and Crown, protecting ancient rules against any investigation of what harm or good they might be up to, against colonial structures that impoverished the imperial nations (Smith was also the author of* The Costs of Empire*) even as they stripped subjects of their liberties, and against all rotting doctrines of national pride and enrichment based on the prevailing mercantilism. Smith is doing for the economy what Bentham did for community life—subjecting it to careful analysis of cause and consequence to find out what arrangements will most work to human benefit. He introduces to the language of economic calculation the interplay of supply and demand, the notion of productivity, the*

*centrality of efficiency (the ratio between effort and product, cost and benefit), and
above all the concept of the Invisible Hand—that unfelt economic force that leads the
most selfish of us, left at liberty to satisfy our own interests only, to support the general
welfare.*

From Adam Smith, *An Inquiry into the Nature and Causes of the Wealth of Nations*

Of the Division of Labour

The greatest improvement in the productive powers of labour, and the greater part of the skill, dexterity, and judgment with which it is anywhere directed or applied, seem to have been the effect of the division of labour.

The effects of the division of labour, in the general business of society, will be more easily understood by considering in what manner it operates in some particular manufactures. It is commonly supposed to be carried furthest in some very trifling ones; not perhaps that it really is carried further in them than in others of more importance: but in those trifling manufactures which are destined to supply the small wants of but a small number of people, the whole number of workmen must necessarily be small; and those employed in every different branch of the work can often be collected into the same workhouse, and placed at once under the view of the spectator. In those great manufactures, on the contrary, which are destined to supply the great wants of the great body of the people, every different branch of the work employs so great a number of workmen, that it is impossible to collect them all into the same workhouse. We can seldom see more, at one time, than those employed in one single branch. Though in such manufactures, therefore, the work may really be divided into a much greater number of parts than in those of a more trifling nature, the division is not near so obvious, and has accordingly been much less observed.

To take an example, therefore, from a very trifling manufacture, but one in which the division of labour has been very often taken notice of, the trade of the pin-maker; a workman not educated to this business (which the division of labour has rendered a distinct trade), nor acquainted with the use of the machinery employed in it (to the invention of which the same division of labour has probably given occasion), could scarce, perhaps, with his utmost industry, make one pin in a day, and certainly could not make twenty. But in the way in which this business is now carried on, not only the whole work is a peculiar trade, but it is divided into a number of branches, of which the greater part are likewise peculiar trades. One man draws out the wire, another straights it, a third cuts it, a fourth points it, a fifth grinds it at the top for receiving the head; to make the head requires two or three distinct operations; to put it on is a peculiar business, to whiten the pins is another; it is even a trade by itself to put them into the paper; and the important business of making a pin is, in this manner, divided into about eighteen distinct operations, which in some manufactories are all performed by distinct hands, though in others the same man will sometimes perform two or three of them. I have seen a small manufactory of this kind where ten men only were employed, and where some of them consequently performed two or three distinct operations. But though they were very poor, and therefore but indifferently accommodated with the necessary machinery, they could, when they exerted themselves, make among them about twelve pounds of pins in a day. There are in a pound upwards of four thousand pins of a middling size. Those ten persons, therefore, could make among them upwards of forty-eight thousand pins in a day. Each person, therefore, making a tenth part of forty-eight thousand pins, might be considered as making four thousand eight hundred pins in a day. But if they had all wrought separately and independently, and without any of them having been educated to this peculiar business, they certainly could not each of them have made twenty, perhaps not one pin in a day; that is, certainly, not the two hundred and fortieth, perhaps not the four thousand eight hundredth part of what they are at present capable of performing, in consequence of a proper division and combination of their different operations. . . .

This great increase of the quantity of work, which, in consequence of the division of labour, the same number of people are capable of performing, is owning to three different circumstances: first, to the increase of dexterity in every particular workman; secondly, to the saving of the time which is commonly lost in passing from one species of work to another; and lastly, to the invention of a great number of machines which facilitate and abridge labour, and enable one man to do the work of many. . . .

It is the great multiplication of the productions of all the different arts, in consequence of the division of labour, which occasions, in a well-governed society, that universal opulence which extends itself to the lowest ranks of the people. Every workman has a great quantity of his own work to dispose of beyond what he himself has occasion for: and every other workman being exactly in the same situation, he is enabled to exchange a great quantity of his own goods for a great quantity, or, what comes to the same thing, for the price of a great quantity of theirs. He supplies them abundantly with what they have occasion for, and they accommodate him as amply with what he has occasion for, and a general plenty diffuses itself through all the different ranks of the society.

Observe the accommodation of the most common artificer or daylabourer in a civilised and thriving country, and you will perceive that the number of people of whose industry a part, though but a small part, has been employed in procuring him this accommodation exceeds all computation. The woollen coat, for example, which covers the day-labourer, as coarse and rough as it may appear, is the produce of the joint labour of a great multitude of workmen. The shepherd, the sorter of the wool, the wool-comber or carder, the dyer, the scribbler, the spinner, the weaver, the fuller, the dresser, with many others, must all join their different arts in order to complete even this homely production. How many merchants and carriers, besides, must have been employed in transporting the materials from some of those workmen to others who often live in a very distant part of the country! How much commerce and navigation in particular, how many ship-builders, sailors, sail-makers, ropemakers, must have been employed in order to bring together the different drugs made use of by the dyer, which often come from the remotest corners of the world! What a variety of labour too is necessary in order to produce the tools of the meanest of those workmen! To say nothing of such complicated machines as the ship of the sailor, the mill of the fuller, or even the loom of the weaver, let us consider only what a variety of labour is requisite in order to form that very simple machine, the shears with which the shepherd clips the wool. The miner, the builder of the furnace for smelting the ore, the fetter of the timber, the burner of the charcoal to be made use of in the smelting-house, the brickmaker, the bricklayer, the workmen who attend the furnace, the millwright, the forger, the smith, must all of them join their different arts in order to produce them. Were we to examine, in the same manner, all the different parts of his dress and household furniture, the coarse linen shirt which he wears next his skin, the shoes which cover his feet, the bed which he lies on, and all the different parts which compose it, the kitchen-grate at which he prepares his victuals, the coals which he makes use of for that purpose, dug from the bowels of the earth, and brought to him perhaps by a long sea and a long land carriage, all the other utensils of his kitchen, all the furniture of his table, the knives and forks, the earthen or pewter plates upon which he serves up and divides his victuals, the different hands employed in preparing his bread and his beer, the glass window which lets in the heat and the light and keeps out the wind and the rain, with all the knowledge and art requisite for preparing that beautiful and happy invention, without which these northern parts of the world could scarce have afforded a very comfortable habitation, together with the tools of all the different workmen employed in producing those different conveniences; if we examine, I say, all these things, and consider what a variety of labour is employed about each of them, we shall be sensible that without the assistance and co-operation of many thousands, the very meanest person in a civilised country could not be provided, even according to, what we very falsely imagine, the easy and simple manner in which he is commonly accommodated. Compared, indeed, with the more extravagant luxury of the great, his accommodation must no doubt appear extremely simple and easy; and yet it may be true, perhaps, that the accommodation of an European prince does not always so much exceed that of an industrious and frugal peasant, as the accommodation of the latter exceeds that of many an African king, the absolute master of the lives and liberties of ten thousand naked savages.

Of the Principle Which Gives Occasion to the Division of Labour

This division of labour, from which so many advantages are derived, is not originally the effect of any human wisdom, which foresees and intends that general opulence to which it gives occasion. It is the necessary, though very slow and gradual consequence of a certain propensity in human nature which has in view no such extensive utility; the propensity to truck, barter, and exchange one thing for another.

Whether this propensity be one of those original principles in human nature, of which no further account can be given; or whether, as seems more probable, it be the necessary consequence of the faculties of reason and speech, it belongs not to our present subject to inquire. It is common to all men, and to be found in no other race of animals, which seem to know neither this nor any other species of contracts. . . . But man has almost constant occasion for the help of his brethren, and it is in vain for him to expect it from their benevolence only. He will be more likely to prevail if he can interest their self-love in his favour, and show them that it is for their own advantage to do for him what he requires of them. Whoever offers to another a bargain of any kind, proposes to do this. Give me that which I want, and you shall have this which you want, is the meaning of every such offer; and it is in this manner that we obtain from one another the far greater part of those good offices which we stand in need of. It is not from the benevolence of the butcher, the brewer, or the baker, that we expect our dinner, but from their regard to their own interest. We address ourselves, not to their humanity but to their self-love, and never talk to them of our own necessities but of their advantages. Nobody but a beggar chooses to depend chiefly upon the benevolence of his fellow-citizens. Even a beggar does not depend upon it entirely. The charity of well-disposed people, indeed, supplies him with the whole fund of his subsistence. But though this principle ultimately provides him with all the necessaries of life which he has occasion for, it neither does nor can provide him with them as he has occasion for them. The greater part of his occasional wants are supplied in the same manner as those of other people, by treaty, by barter, and by purchase. With the money which one man gives him he purchases food. The old clothes which another bestows upon him he exchanges for other old clothes which suit him better, or for lodging, or for food, or for money, with which he can buy either food, clothes, or lodging, as he has occasion.

. . . Each animal is still obliged to support and defend itself, separately and independently, and derives no sort of advantage from that variety of talents with which nature has distinguished its fellows. Among men, on the contrary, the most dissimilar geniuses are of use to one another; the different produces of their respective talents, by the general disposition to truck, barter, and exchange, being brought, as it were, into a common stock, where every man may purchase whatever part of the produce of other men's talents he has occasion for. . . .

Of Restraints Upon the Importation From Foreign Countries of Such Goods as Can Be Produced at Home

. . . The general industry of the society never can exceed what the capital of the society can employ. As the number of workmen that can be kept in employment by any particular person must bear a certain proportion to his capital, so the number of those that can be continually employed by all the members of a great society, must bear a certain proportion to the whole capital of that society, and never can exceed that proportion. No regulation of commerce can increase the quantity of industry in any society beyond what its capital can maintain. It can only divert a part of it into a direction into which it might not otherwise have gone; and it is by no means certain that this artificial direction is likely to be more advantageous to the society than that into which it would have gone of its own accord. Every individual is continually exerting himself to find out the most advantageous employment for whatever capital he can demand. It is his own advantage, indeed, and not that of the society, which he has in view. But the study of his own advantage naturally, or rather necessarily, leads him to prefer that employment which is most advantageous to the society.

First, every individual endeavours to employ his capital as near home as he can, and consequently as much as he can in the support of domestic industry; provided always that he can thereby obtain the ordinary, or not a great deal less than the ordinary, profits of stock. Thus, upon equal or nearly equal profits, every wholesale merchant naturally prefers the home trade to the foreign trade of consumption, and the foreign trade of consumption to the carrying trade. In the home trade his capital is never so long out of his sight as it frequently is in the foreign trade of consumption. He can know better the character and situation of the persons whom he trusts, and, if he should happen to be deceived, he knows better the laws of the country from which he must seek redress. In the carrying trade, the capital of the merchant is, as it were, divided between two foreign countries, and no part of it is ever necessarily brought home, or placed under his own immediate view and command. The capital which an Amsterdam merchant employs in carrying corn from Konigsberg to Lisbon, and fruit and wine from Lisbon to Konigsberg, must generally be the one half of it at Konigsberg and the other half at Lisbon. No part of it need ever come to Amsterdam. The natural residence of such a merchant should either be at Konigsberg or Lisbon, and it can only be some very particular circumstance which can make him prefer the residence of Amsterdam. The uneasiness, however, which he feels at being separated so far from his capital, generally determines him to bring part both of the Konigsberg goods which he destines for the market of Lisbon, and of the Lisbon goods which he destines for that of Konigsberg, to Amsterdam; and though this necessarily subjects him to a double charge of loading and unloading, as well as to the payment of some duties and customs, yet for the sake of having some part of his capital always under his own view and command, he willingly submits to this extraordinary charge; and it is in this manner that every country which has any considerable share of the carrying trade, becomes always the emporium, or general market, for the goods of all the different countries whose trade it carries on. The merchant, in order to save a second loading and unloading, endeavours always to sell in the home market as much of the goods of all those different countries as he can, and thus, so far as he can, to convert his carrying trade into a foreign trade of consumption. A merchant, in the same manner, who is engaged in the foreign trade of consumption, when he collects goods for foreign markets, will always be glad, upon equal or nearly equal profits, to sell as great a part of them at home as he can. He saves himself the risk and trouble of exportation, when, so far as he can, he thus converts his foreign trade of consumption into a home trade. Home is in this manner the centre, if I may say so, round which the capitals of the inhabitants of every country are continually circulating, and towards which they are always tending, though by particular causes they may sometimes be driven off and repelled from it towards more distant employments. But a capital employed in the home trade, it has already been shown, necessarily puts into motion a greater quantity of domestic industry, and gives revenue and employment to a greater number of the inhabitants of the country, than an equal capital employed in the foreign trade of consumption; and one employed in the foreign trade of consumption has the same advantage over an equal capital employed in the carrying trade. Upon equal, or only nearly equal profits, therefore, every individual naturally inclines to employ his capital in the manner in which it is likely to afford the greatest support to domestic industry, and to give revenue and employment to the greatest number of people of his own country. Secondly, every individual who employs his capital in the support of domestic industry, necessarily endeavours so to direct that industry, that its produce may be of the greatest possible value.

The produce of industry is what it adds to the subject or materials upon which it is employed. In proportion as the value of this produce is great or small, so will likewise be the profits of the employer. But it is only for the sake of profit that any man employs a capital in the support of industry; and he will always, therefore, endeavour to employ it in the support of that industry of which the produce is likely to be of the greatest value, or to exchange for the greatest quantity either of money or of other goods.

But the annual revenue of every society is always precisely equal to the exchangeable value of the whole annual produce of its industry, or rather is precisely the same thing with that exchangeable value. As every individual, therefore, endeavours as much as he can both to employ his capital in the support of domestic industry, and so to direct that industry that its produce may be of the greatest value, every individual necessarily labours to render the annual revenue of the society as great as he can. He generally, indeed, neither intends to promote the public interest, nor knows how much he is promoting it. By preferring the support of domestic to that of foreign industry, he intends only his own security; and by directing that industry in such a manner as its produce may be of the greatest value, he intends only his own gain, and he is in this, as in many other cases, led by an invisible hand to promote an end which was no part of his intention. Nor is it always the worse for the society that it was no part of it. By pursuing his own interest he frequently promotes that of the society more effectually than when he really intends to promote it. I have never known much good done by those who affected to trade for the public good. It is an affectation, indeed, not very common among merchants, and very few words need be employed in dissuading them from it.

What is the species of domestic industry which his capital can employ, and of which the produce is likely to be of the greatest value, every individual, it is evident, can, in his local situation, judge much better than any statesman or lawgiver can do for him. The statesman, who should attempt to direct private people in what manner they ought to employ their capitals, would not only load himself with a most unnecessary attention, but assume an authority which could safely be trusted, not only to no single person, but to no council or senate whatever, and which would nowhere be so dangerous as in the hands of a man who had folly and presumption enough to fancy himself fit to exercise it.

To give the monopoly of the home market to the produce of domestic industry, in any particular art or manufacture, is in some measure to direct private people in what manner they ought to employ their capitals, and must, in almost all cases, be either a useless or a hurtful regulation. If the produce of domestic can be brought there as cheap as that of foreign industry, the regulation is evidently useless. If it cannot, it must generally be hurtful. It is the maxim of every prudent master of a family, never to attempt to make at home what it will cost him more to make than to buy. The tailor does not attempt to make his own shoes, but buys them of the shoemaker. The shoemaker does not attempt to make his own clothes, but employs a tailor. The farmer attempts to make neither the one nor the other, but employs those different artificers. All of them find it for their interest to employ their whole industry in a way in which they have some advantage over their neighbours, and to purchase with a part of its produce, or, what is the same thing, with the price of a part of it, whatever else they have occasion for.

What is prudence in the conduct of every private family, can scarce be folly in that of a great kingdom. If a foreign country can supply us with a commodity cheaper than we ourselves can make it, better buy it of them with some part of the produce of our own industry, employed in a way in which we have some advantage. The general industry of the country, being always in proportion to the capital which employs it, will not thereby be diminished, no more than that of the above-mentioned artificers, but only left to find out the way in which it can be employed with the greatest advantage. It is certainly not employed to the greatest advantage, when it is thus directed towards an object which it can buy cheaper than it can make. The value of its annual produce is certainly more or less diminished, when it is thus turned away from producing commodities evidently of more value than the commodity which it is directed to produce. According to the supposition, that commodity could be purchased from foreign countries cheaper than it can be made at home. It could, therefore, have been purchased with a part only of the commodities, or, what is the same thing, with a part only of the price of the commodities, which the industry employed by an equal capital would have produced at home, had it been left to follow its natural course. The industry of the country, therefore, is thus turned away from a more to a less advantageous employment, and the exchangeable value of its annual produce, instead of being increased, according to the intention of the lawgiver, must necessarily be diminished by every such regulation.

By means of such regulations, indeed, a particular manufacture may sometimes be acquired sooner than it could have been otherwise, and after a certain time may be made at home as cheap or cheaper than in the foreign country. But though the industry of the society may be thus carried with advantage into a particular channel sooner than it could have been otherwise, it will by no means follow that the sum total, either of its industry or of its revenue, can ever be augmented by any such regulation. The industry of the society can augment only in proportion as its capital augments, and its capital can augment only in proportion to what can be gradually saved out of its revenue. But the immediate effect of every such regulation is to diminish its revenue, and what diminishes its revenue is certainly not very likely to augment its capital faster than it would have augmented of its own accord, had both capital and industry been left to find out their natural employments.

Though for want of such regulations the society should never acquire the proposed manufacture, it would not, upon that account, necessarily be the poorer in any one period of its duration. In every period of its duration its whole capital and industry might still have been employed, though upon different objects, in the manner that was most advantageous at the time. In every period its revenue might have been the greatest which its capital could afford, and both capital and revenue might have been augmented with the greatest possible rapidity.

The natural advantages which one country has over another in producing particular commodities are sometimes so great, that it is acknowledged by all the world to be in vain to struggle with them. By means of glasses, hot-beds, and hot-walls, very good grapes can be raised in Scotland, and very good wine too can be made of them, at about thirty times the expense for which at least equally good can be brought from foreign countries. Would it be a reasonable law to prohibit the importation of all foreign wines, merely to encourage the making of claret and burgundy in Scotland? But if there would be a manifest absurdity in turning towards any employment thirty times more of the capital and industry of the country than would be necessary to purchase from foreign countries an equal quantity of the commodities wanted, there must be an absurdity, though not altogether so glaring, yet exactly of the same kind, in turning towards any such employment a thirtieth or even a three-hundredth part more of either. Whether the advantages which one country has over another be natural or acquired, is in this respect of no consequence. As long as the one country has those advantages and the other wants them, it will always be more advantageous for the latter rather to buy of the former than to make. It is an acquired advantage only which one artificer has over his neighbour who exercises another trade; and yet they both find it more advantageous to buy of one another than to make what does not belong to their particular trades.

John Stuart Mill (1806–1873)

It fell to John Stuart Mill, son of Jeremy Bentham's best friend James Mill, to qualify and expand the very limited doctrine set out by Bentham earlier in this chapter to account for our certainty that pleasure is not all of a piece, but varies by quality as well as quantity. Beyond that modification, he made very little change in Bentham's teachings. But by the time Mill wrote, the learned community had had time to examine Bentham's work and raise objections to it, both as to its consequences and its ground for justification. In the passages that follow, Mill expounds the doctrine of Utilitarianism, and defends it against the criticism of the time.

From John Stuart Mill, *Utilitarianism*

Chapter V

The creed which accepts as the foundation of morals, Utility, or the Greatest Happiness Principle, holds that actions are right in proportion as they tend to promote happiness, wrong as they tend to produce the reverse of happiness. By happiness is intended pleasure, and the absence of pain; by unhappiness, pain, and the privation of pleasure. To give a clear view of the moral standard set up by the theory, much more requires to be said, in particular, what things it includes in the ideas of pain and pleasure; and to what extent this is left an open question. But these supplementary explanations do not affect the theory of life on which this theory of morality is grounded—namely, that pleasure, and freedom from pain, are the only things desirable as ends; and that all desirable things (which are as numerous in the utilitarian as in any other scheme) are desirable either for the pleasure inherent in themselves, or as means to the promotion of pleasure and the prevention of pain.

Now, such a theory of life excites in many minds, and among them in some of the most estimable in feeling and purpose, inveterate dislike. To suppose that life has (as they express it) no higher end than pleasure—no better and nobler object of desire and pursuit—they designate as utterly mean and grovelling; as a doctrine worthy only of swine, to whom the followers of Epicurus were, at a very early period, contemptuously likened; and modern holders of the doctrine are occasionally made the subject of equally polite comparisons by its German, French, and English assailants.

When thus attacked, the Epicureans have always answered, that it is not they, but their accusers, who represent human nature in a degrading light; since the accusation supposes human beings to be capable of no pleasures except those of which swine are capable. If this supposition were true, the charge could not be gainsaid, but would then be no longer an imputation; for if the sources of pleasure were precisely the same to human beings and to swine, the rule of life which is good enough for the one would be good enough for the other. The comparison of the Epicurean life to that of beasts is felt as degrading, precisely because a beast's pleasures do not satisfy a human being's conceptions of happiness. Human beings have faculties more elevated than the animal appetites, and when once made conscious of them, do not regard anything as happiness which does not include their gratification. I do not, indeed, consider the Epicureans to have been by any means faultless in drawing out their scheme of consequences from the utilitarian principle. To do this in any sufficient manner, many Stoic, as well as Christian elements require to be included. But there is no known Epicurean theory of life which does not assign to the pleasures of the intellect, of the feelings and imagination, and of the moral sentiments, a much higher value as pleasures than to those of mere sensation. It must be admitted, however, that utilitarian writers in general have placed the superiority of mental over bodily pleasures chiefly in the greater permanency, safety, uncostliness, &c., of the former—that is, in their circumstantial advantages rather than in their intrinsic nature. And on all these points utilitarians have fully proved their case; but they might have taken the other, and, as it may be called, higher ground, with entire consistency. It is quite compatible with the principle of utility to recognise the fact, that some *kinds* of pleasure are more desirable and more valuable than others. It would be absurd that while, in estimating all other things, quality is considered as well as quantity, the estimation of pleasures should be supposed to depend on quantity alone.

If I am asked, what I mean by difference of quality in pleasures, or what makes one pleasure more valuable than another, merely as a pleasure, except its being greater in amount, there is but one possible answer. Of two pleasures, if there be one to which all or almost all who have experience of both give a decided preference, irrespective of any feeling of moral obligation to prefer it, that is the more desirable pleasure. If one of the two is, by those who are competently acquainted with both, placed so far above the other that they prefer it, even though knowing it to be attended with a greater amount of discontent, and would not resign it for any quantity of the other pleasure which their nature is capable of, we are justified in ascribing to the preferred enjoyment a superiority in quality, so far outweighing quantity as to render it, in comparison, of small account.

Now it is an unquestionable fact that those who are equally acquainted with, and equally capable of appreciating and enjoying, both, do give a most marked preference to the manner of existence which employs their higher faculties. Few human creatures would consent to be changed into any of the lower animals, for a promise of the fullest allowance of a beast's pleasures; no intelligent human being would consent to be a fool, no instructed person would be an ignoramus, no person of feeling and conscience would be selfish and base, even though they should be persuaded that the fool, the dunce, or the rascal is better satisfied with his lot than they are with theirs. They would not resign what they possess more than he, for the most complete satisfaction of all the desires which they have in common with him. If they ever fancy they would, it is only in cases of unhappiness so extreme, that to escape from it they would exchange their lot for almost any other, however undesirable in their own eyes. A being of higher faculties requires more to make him happy, is capable probably of more acute suffering, and is certainly accessible to it at more points, than one of an inferior type; but in spite of these liabilities, he can never really wish to sink into what he feels to be a lower grade of existence. We may give what explanation we please of this unwillingness; we may attribute it to pride, a name which is given indiscriminately to some of the most and to some of the least estimable feelings of which mankind are capable; we may refer it to the love of liberty and personal independence, an appeal to which was with the Stoics one of the most effective means for the inculcation of it, to the love of power, or to the love of excitement, both of which do really enter into and contribute to it: but its most appropriate appellation is a sense of dignity, which all human beings possess in one form or another, and in some, though by no means in exact, proportion to their higher faculties, and which is so essential a part of the happiness of those in whom it is strong, that nothing which conflicts with it could be, otherwise than momentarily, an object of desire to them. Whoever supposes that this preference takes place at a sacrifice of happiness that the superior being, in anything like equal circumstances, is not happier than the inferior—confounds the two very different ideas, of happiness, and content. It is indisputable that the being whose capacities of enjoyment are low, has the greatest chance of having them fully satisfied; and a highly-endowed being will always feel that any happiness which he can look for, as the world is constituted, is imperfect. But he can learn to bear its imperfections, if they are at all bearable; and they will not make him envy the being who is indeed unconscious of the imperfections, but only because he feels not at all the good which those imperfections qualify. It is better to be a human being dissatisfied than a pig satisfied; better to be Socrates dissatisfied than a fool satisfied. And if the fool, or the pig, is of a different opinion, it is because they only know their own side of the question. The other party to the comparison knows both sides. It may be objected, that many who are capable of the higher pleasures, occasionally, under the influence of temptation, postpone them to the lower. But this is quite compatible with a full appreciation of the intrinsic superiority of the higher. Men often, from infirmity of character, make their election for the nearer good, though they know it to be the less valuable; and this no less when the choice is between two bodily pleasures, than when it is between bodily and mental. They pursue sensual indulgences to the injury of health, though perfectly aware that health is the greater good. It may be further objected, that many who begin with youthful enthusiasm for everything noble, as they advance in years sink into indolence and selfishness. But I do not believe that those who undergo this very common change, voluntarily choose the lower description of pleasures in preference to the higher. I believe that before they devote themselves exclusively to the one, they have already become incapable of the other. Capacity for the nobler feelings is in most natures a very tender plant, easily killed, not only by hostile influences, but by mere want of sustenance; and in the majority of young persons it speedily dies away if the occupations to which their position in life has devoted them, and the society into which it has thrown them, are not favorable to keeping that higher capacity in exercise. Men lose their high aspirations as they lose their intellectual tastes, because they have not time or opportunity for indulging them; and they addict themselves to inferior pleasures, not because they deliberately prefer them, but because they are either the only ones to which they have access, or the only ones which they are any longer capable of enjoying. It may be questioned whether any one who has remained equally susceptible to both classes of pleasures, ever knowingly and calmly preferred the lower; though many, in all ages, have broken down in an ineffectual attempt to combine both.

From this verdict of the only competent judges, I apprehend there can be no appeal. On a question which is the best worth having of two pleasures, or which of two modes of existence is the most grateful to the feelings, apart from its moral attributes and from its consequences, the judgment of those who are qualified by knowledge of both, or, if they differ, that of the majority among them, must be admitted as final. And there needs be the less hesitation to accept this judgment respecting the quality of pleasures, since there is no other tribunal to be referred to even on the question of quantity. What means are there of determining which is the acutest of two pains, or the intensest of two pleasurable sensations, except the general suffrage of those who are familiar with both? Neither pains nor pleasures are homogeneous, and pain is always heterogeneous with pleasure. What is there to decide whether a particular pleasure is worth purchasing at the cost of a particular pain, except the feelings and judgment of the experienced? When, therefore, those feelings and judgment declare the pleasures derived from the higher faculties to be preferable *in kind,* apart from the question of intensity, to those of which the animal nature, disjoined from the higher faculties, is susceptible, they are entitled on this subject to the same regard.

I have dwelt on this point, as being a necessary part of a perfectly just conception of Utility or Happiness, considered as the directive rule of human conduct. But it is by no means an indispensable condition to the acceptance of the utilitarian standard; for that standard is not the agent's own greatest happiness, but the greatest amount of happiness altogether; and if it may possibly be doubted whether a noble character is always the happier for its nobleness, there can be no doubt that it makes other people happier, and that the world in general is immensely a gainer by it. Utilitarianism, therefore, could only attain its end by the general cultivation of nobleness of character, even if each individual were only benefited by the nobleness of others, and his own, so far as happiness is concerned, were a sheer deduction from the benefit. But the bare enunciation of such an absurdity as this last, renders refutation superfluous. . . .

According to the Greatest Happiness Principle, as above explained, the ultimate end, with reference to and for the sake of which all other things are desirable (whether we are considering our own good or that of other people), is an existence exempt as far as possible from pain, and as rich as possible in enjoyments, both in point of quantity and quality; the test of quality, and the rule for measuring it against quantity, being the preference felt by those who, in their opportunities of experience, to which must be added their habits of self-consciousness and self-observation, are best furnished with the means of comparison. This, being, according to the utilitarian opinion, the end of human action, is necessarily also the standard of morality; which may accordingly be defined, the rules and precepts for human conduct, by the observance of which an existence such as has been described might be, to the greatest extent possible, secured to all mankind; and not to them only, but, so far as the nature of things admits, to the whole sentient creation. . . .

Unquestionably it is possible to do without happiness; it is done involuntarily by nineteen-twentieths of mankind, even in those parts of our present world which are least deep in barbarism; and it often has to be done voluntarily by the hero or the martyr, for the sake of something which he prizes more than his individual happiness. But this something, what is it, unless the happiness of others, or some of the requisites of happiness? It is noble to be capable of resigning entirely one's own portion of happiness, or chances of it: but, after all, this self-sacrifice must be for some end; it is not its own end; and if we are told that its end is not happiness, but virtue, which is better than happiness, I ask, would the sacrifice be made if the hero or martyr did not believe that it would earn for others immunity from similar sacrifices? Would it be made, if he thought that his renunciation of happiness for himself would produce no fruit for any of his fellow creatures, but to make their lot like his, and place them also in the condition of persons who have renounced happiness? All honour to those who can abnegate for themselves the personal enjoyment of life, when by such renunciation they contribute worthily to increase the amount of happiness in the world; but he who does it, or professes to do it, for any other purpose, is no more deserving of admiration than the ascetic mounted on his pillar. He may be an inspiriting proof of what men *can* do, but assuredly not an example of what they *should*.

Though it is only in a very imperfect state of the world's arrangements that any one can best serve the happiness of others by the absolute sacrifice of his own, yet so long as the world is in that imperfect state, I fully acknowledge that the readiness to make such a sacrifice is the highest virtue which can be found in man. I will add, that in this condition of the world, paradoxical as the assertion may be, the conscious ability to do without happiness gives the best prospect of realizing such happiness as is attainable. For nothing except that consciousness can raise a person above the chances of life, by making him feel that, let fate and fortune do their worst, they have not power to subdue him: which, once felt, frees him from excess of anxiety concerning the evils of life, and enables him, like many a Stoic in the worst times of the Roman Empire, to cultivate in tranquility the sources of satisfaction accessible to him, without concerning himself about the uncertainty of their duration, any more than about their inevitable end.

Meanwhile, let utilitarians never cease to claim the morality of self-devotion as a possession which belongs by as good a right to them, as either to the Stoic or to the Transcendentalist. The utilitarian morality does recognize in human beings the power of sacrificing their own greatest good for the good of others. It only refuses to admit that the sacrifice is itself a good. A sacrifice which does not increase, or tend to increase, the sum total of happiness, it considers as wasted. The only self-renunciation which it applauds, is devotion to the happiness, or to some of the means of happiness, of others; either of mankind collectively, or of individuals within the limits imposed by the collective interests of mankind.

I must again repeat, what the assailants of utilitarianism seldom have the justice to acknowledge, that the happiness which forms the utilitarian standard of what is right in conduct, is not the agent's own happiness, but that of all concerned. As between his own happiness and that of others, utilitarianism requires him to be as strictly impartial as a disinterested and benevolent spectator. In the golden rule of Jesus of Nazareth, we read the complete spirit of the ethics of utility. To do as one would be done by, and to love one's neighbour as oneself, constitute the ideal perfection of utilitarian morality. As the means of making the nearest approach to this ideal, utility would enjoin, first, that laws and social arrangements should place the happiness, or (as speaking practically it may be called) the interest, of every individual, as nearly as possible in harmony with the interest of the whole; and secondly, that education and opinion, which have so vast a power over human character, should so use that power as to establish in the mind of every individual an indissoluble association between his own happiness and the good of the whole; especially between his own happiness and the practice of such modes of conduct, negative and positive, as regard for the universal happiness prescribes: so that not only may he be unable to conceive the possibility of happiness to himself, consistently with conduct opposed to the general good, but also that a direct impulse to promote the general good may be in every individual one of the habitual motives of action, and the sentiments connected therewith may fill a large and prominent place in every human being's sentient existence. If the impugners of the utilitarian morality represented it to their own minds in this its true character, I know not what recommendation possessed by any other morality they could possibly affirm to be wanting to it: what more beautiful or more exalted developments of human nature any other ethical system can be supposed to foster, or what springs of action, not accessible to the utilitarian, such systems rely on for giving effect to their mandates.

The objectors to utilitarianism cannot always be charged with representing it in a discreditable light. On the contrary, those among them who entertain anything like a just idea of its disinterested character, sometimes find fault with its standard as being too high for humanity. They say it is exacting too much to require that people shall always act from the inducement of promoting the general interests of society. But this is to mistake the very meaning of a standard of morals, and to confound the rule of action with the motive of it. It is the business of ethics to tell us what are our duties, or by what test we may know them: but no system of ethics requires that the sole motive of all we do shall be a feeling of duty; on the contrary, ninety-nine hundredths of all our actions are done from other motives, and rightly so done, if the rule of duty does not condemn them. It is the more unjust to utilitarianism that this particular misapprehension should be made a ground of objection to it, inasmuch as utilitarian moralists have gone beyond almost all others in affirming that the motive has nothing to do with the morality of the action, though much with the worth of the agent. He who saves a fellow creature from drowning does what is morally right, whether his motive be duty, or the hope of being paid for his trouble: he who betrays the friend that trusts him, is guilty of a crime, even if his object be to serve another friend to whom he is under greater obligations.

> *We interrupt this passage for a footnote, inserted at this point by J. S. Mill himself, in the second edition of this work. I include it (1) for the validity of its argument—it's a good objection; and (2) for the evidence it provides of Mill's generosity and fair-mindedness, qualities that are admirable in any profession and remarkable in professional philosophy.*

An opponent, whose intellectual and moral fairness it is a pleasure to acknowledge (the Rev. J. Llewellyn Davies), has objected to this passage, saying, "Surely the rightness or wrongness of saving a man from drowning does depend very much upon the motive with which it is done. Suppose that a tyrant, when his enemy jumped into the sea to escape from him, saved him from drowning simply in order that he might inflict upon him more exquisite tortures, would it tend to clearness to speak of that rescue as a morally right action? Or suppose again, according to one of the stock illustrations of ethical inquiries, that a man betrayed a trust received from a friend, because the discharge of it would fatally injure that friend himself or some one belonging to him, would utilitarianism compel one to call the betrayal 'a crime' as much as if it had been done from the meanest motive?"...

> *[Editor's note: the "stock illustration" is of course the dilemma over whether to return a borrowed weapon to a friend who has gone mad, found in the opening passages of Plato's* The Republic *(Chapter 1, "The Greek Tradition").]*
> *The passage continues:*

But to speak only of actions done from the motive of duty, and in direct obedience to principle: it is a misapprehension of the utilitarian mode of thought, to conceive it as implying that people would fix their minds upon so wide a generality as the world, or society at large. The great majority of good actions are intended, not for the benefit of the world, but for that of individuals, of which the good of the world is made up; and the thoughts of the most virtuous man need not on these occasions travel beyond the particular persons concerned, except so far as is necessary to assure himself that in benefiting them he is not violating the rights—that is, the legitimate and authorized expectation—of any one else. The multiplication of happiness is, according to the utilitarian ethics, the object of virtue: the occasions on which any person (except one in a thousand) has it in his power to do this on an extended scale, in other words, to be a public benefactor, are but exceptional; and on these occasions alone is he called on to consider public utility; in every other case, private utility, the interest or happiness of some few persons, is all he has to attend to. Those alone the influence of whose actions extends to society in general, need concern themselves habitually about so large an object. In the case of abstinences indeed—of things which people forbear to do, from moral considerations, though the consequences in the particular case might be beneficial—it would be unworthy of an intelligent agent not to be consciously aware that the action is of a class which, if practised generally, would be generally injurious, and that this is the ground of the obligation to abstain from it. The amount of regard for the public interest implied in this recognition, is no greater than is demanded by every system of morals; for they all enjoin to abstain from whatever is manifestly pernicious to society....

Again, Utility is often summarily stigmatized as an immoral doctrine by giving it the name of Expediency, and taking advantage of the popular use of that term to contrast it with Principle. But the Expedient, in the sense in which it is opposed to the Right, generally means that which is expedient for the particular interest of the agent himself; as when a minister sacrifices the interest of his country to keep himself in place. When it means anything better than this, it means that which is expedient for some immediate object, some temporary purpose, but which violates a rule whose observance is expedient in a much higher degree. The Expedient, in this sense, instead of being the same thing with the useful, is a branch of the hurtful. Thus, it would often be expedient, for the purpose of getting over some momentary embarrassment, or attaining some object immediately useful to ourselves or others, to tell a lie. But inasmuch as the cultivation in ourselves of a sensitive feeling on the subject of veracity, is one of the most useful, and the enfeeblement of that feeling one of the most hurtful, things to which our conduct can be instrumental; and inasmuch as any, even unintentional, deviation from truth, does that much towards weakening the trustworthiness of human assertion, which is not only the principal support of all present social well-being, but the Insufficiency of which does more than any one thing that can be named to keep back civilization, virtue, everything on which human happiness on the largest scale depends; we feel that the violation, for a present advantage, of a rule of such transcendent expediency, is not expedient, and that he who, for the sake of a convenience to himself or to some other individual, does what depends on him to deprive mankind of the good, and inflict upon them the evil, involved in the greater or less reliance which they can place in each other's word, acts the part of one of their worst enemies. Yet that even this rule, sacred as it is, admits of possible exceptions, is acknowledged by all moralists; the chief of which is when the withholding of some fact (as of information from a malefactor, or of bad news from a person dangerously ill) would preserve some one (especially a person other than oneself) from great and unmerited evil, and when the withholding can only be effected by denial. But in order that the exception may not extend itself beyond the need, and may have the least possible effect in weakening reliance on veracity, it ought to be recognised, and, if possible, its limits defined; and if the principle of utility is good for anything, it must be good for weighing these conflicting utilities against one another, and marking out the region within which one or the other preponderates. . . .

Again, defenders of utility often find themselves called upon to reply to such objections as this—that there is not time, previous to action, for calculating and weighing the effects of any line of conduct on the general happiness. This is exactly as if any one were to say that it is impossible to guide our conduct by Christianity, because there is not time on every occasion on which anything has to be done, to read through the Old and New Testaments. The answer to the objection is, that there has been ample time, namely, the whole past duration of the human species. During all that time mankind have been learning by experience the tendencies of actions; on which experience all the prudence, as well as all the morality of life, is dependent. People talk as if the commencement of this course of experience had hitherto been put off, and as if, at the moment when some man feels tempted to meddle with the property or life of another, he had to begin considering for the first time whether murder and theft are injurious to human happiness. Even then I do not think that he would find the question very puzzling, but, at all events, the matter is now done to his hand. It is truly a whimsical supposition that if mankind were agreed in considering utility to be the test of morality, they would remain without any agreement as to what is useful, and would take no measures for having their notions on the subject taught to the young, and enforced by law and opinion. There is no difficulty in proving any ethical standard whatever to work ill, if we suppose universal idiocy to be conjoined with it; but on any hypothesis short of that, mankind must by this time have acquired positive beliefs as to the effects of some actions on their happiness; and the beliefs which have thus come down are the rules of morality for the multitude, and for the philosopher until he has succeeded in finding better. That philosophers might easily do this, even now, on many subjects; that the received code of ethics is by no means of divine right; and that mankind have still much to learn as to the effects of actions on the general happiness, I admit, or rather, earnestly maintain. The corollaries from the principle of utility, like the precepts of every practical art, admit of indefinite improvement, and, in a progressive state of the human mind, their improvement is perpetually going on. But to consider the rules of morality as improvable, is one thing; to pass over the intermediate generalizations entirely, and endeavour to test each individual action directly by the first principle, is another. It is a strange notion that the acknowledgement of a first principle is inconsistent with the admission of secondary ones. To inform a traveler respecting the place of his ultimate destination, is not to forbid the use of landmarks and direction-posts on the way. The proposition that happiness is the end and aim of morality, does not mean that no road ought to be laid down to that goal, or that persons going thither should not be advised to take one direction rather than another. Men really ought to leave off talking a kind of nonsense on this subject, which they would neither talk nor listen to on other matters of practical concernment. Nobody argues that the art of navigation is not founded on astronomy, because sailors cannot wait to calculate the Nautical Almanack. Being rational creatures, they go to sea with it ready calculated; and all rational creatures go out upon the sea of life with their minds made up on the common questions of right and wrong, as well as on many of the far more difficult questions of wise and foolish. And this, as long as foresight is a human quality, it is to be presumed they will continue to do. Whatever we adopt as the fundamental principle of morality, we require subordinate principles to apply it by: the impossibility of doing without them, being common to all systems, can afford no argument against any one in particular: but gravely to argue as if no such secondary principles could be had, and as if mankind had remained till now, and always must remain, without drawing any general conclusions from the experience of human life, is as high a pitch, I think, as absurdity has ever reached in philosophical controversy.

The remainder of the stock arguments against utilitarianism mostly consist in laying to its charge the common infirmities of human nature, and the general difficulties which embarrass conscientious persons in shaping their course through life. We are told that a utilitarian will be apt to make his own particular case an exception to moral rules, and, when under temptation, will see an utility in the breach of a rule, greater than he will see in its observance. But is utility the only creed which is able to furnish us with excuses for evil doing, and means of cheating our own conscience? They are afforded in abundance by all doctrines which recognize as a fact in morals the existence of conflicting considerations; which all doctrines do, that have been believed by sane persons. It is not the fault of any creed, but of the complicated nature of human affairs, that rules of conduct cannot be so framed as to require no exceptions, and that hardly any kind of action can safely be laid down as either always obligatory or always condemnable. There is no ethical creed which does not temper the rigidity of its laws, by giving a certain latitude, under the moral responsibility of the agent, for accommodation to peculiarities of circumstances; and under every creed, at the opening thus made, self-deception and dishonest casuistry get in. There exists no moral system under which there do not arise unequivocal cases of conflicting obligation. These are the real difficulties, the knotty points both in the theory of ethics, and in the conscientious guidance of personal conduct. They are overcome practically with greater or with less success according to the intellect and virtue of the individual, but it can hardly be pretended that any one will be the less qualified for dealing with them, from possessing an ultimate standard to which conflicting rights and duties can be referred. . . .

Chapter III. Of the Ultimate Sanction of the Principle of Utility

The question is often asked, and properly so, in regard to any supposed moral standard—What is its sanction? what are the motives to obey it? or more specifically, what is the source of its obligation? whence does it derive its binding force? It is a necessary part of moral philosophy to provide the answer to this question; which, though frequently assuming the shape of an objection to the utilitarian morality, as if it had some special applicability to that above others, really arises in regard to all standards. It arises, in fact, whenever a person is called on to *adopt* a standard, or refer morality to any basis on which he has not been accustomed to rest it. For the customary morality, that which education and opinion have consecrated, is the only one which presents itself to the mind with the feeling of being in *itself* obligatory; and when a person is asked to believe that this morality *derives* its obligation from some general principle round which custom has not thrown the same halo, the assertion is to him a paradox; the supposed corollaries seem to have a more binding force than the original theorem; the superstructure seems to stand better without, than with, what is represented as its foundation. He says to himself, I feel that I am bound not to rob or murder, betray or deceive; but why am I bound to promote the general happiness? If my own happiness lies in something else, why may I not give that the preference?

If the view adopted by the utilitarian philosophy of the nature of the moral sense be correct, this difficulty will always present itself, until the influences which form moral character have taken the same hold of the principle which they have taken of some of the consequences—until, by the improvement of education the feeling of unity with our fellow creatures shall be (what it cannot be doubted that Christ intended it to be) as deeply rooted in our character, and to our own consciousness as completely a part of our nature, as the horror of crime is in an ordinarily well-brought up young person. In the mean time, however, the difficulty has no peculiar application to the doctrine of utility, but is inherent in every attempt to analyse morality and reduce it to principles; which, unless the principle is already in men's minds invested with as much sacredness as any of its applications, always seems to divest them of a part of their sanctity.

The principle of utility either has, or there is no reason why it might not have, all the sanctions which belong to any other system of morals. Those sanctions are either external or internal. Of the external sanctions it is not necessary to speak at any length. They are, the hope of favour and the fear of displeasure from our fellow creatures or from the Ruler of the Universe, along with whatever we may have of sympathy or affection for them, or of love and awe of Him, inclining us to do his will independently of selfish consequences. There is evidently no reason why all these motives for observance should not attach themselves to the utilitarian morality, as completely and as powerfully as to any other. Indeed, those of them which refer to our fellow creatures are sure to do so, in proportion to the amount of general intelligence; for whether there be any other ground of moral obligation than the general happiness or not, men do desire happiness; and however imperfect may be their own practice, they desire and commend all conduct in others towards themselves, by which they think their happiness is promoted. With regard to the religious motive, if men believe, as most profess to do, in the goodness of God, those who think that conduciveness to the general happiness is the essence, or even only the criterion, of good, must necessarily believe that it is also that which God approves. The whole force therefore of external reward and punishment, whether physical or moral, and whether proceeding from God or from our fellow men, together with all that the capacities of human nature admit, of disinterested devotion to either, become available to enforce the utilitarian morality, in proportion as that morality is recognized; and the more powerfully, the more the appliances of education and general cultivation are bent to the purpose.

So far as to external sanctions. The internal sanction of duty, whatever our standard of duty may be, is one and the same—a feeling in our own mind; a pain, more or less intense, attendant on violation of duty, which in properly-cultivated moral natures rises, in the more serious cases, into shrinking from it as an impossibility. This feeling, when disinterested, and connecting itself with the pure idea of duty, and not with some particular form of it, or with any of the merely accessory circumstances, is the essence of Conscience; though in that complex phenomenon as it actually exists, the simple fact is in general all encrusted over with collateral associations, derived from sympathy, from love, and still more from fear; from all the forms of religious feeling; from the recollections of childhood and of all our past life; from self-esteem, desire of the esteem of others, and occasionally even self-abasement. This extreme complication is, I apprehend, the origin of the sort of mystical character which, by a tendency of the human mind of which there are many other examples, is apt to be attributed to the idea of moral obligation, and which leads people to believe that the idea cannot possibly attach itself to any other objects than those which, by a supposed mysterious law, are found in our present experience to excite it. Its binding force, however, consists in the existence in man of a feeling which must be broken through in order to do what violates our standard of right, and which, if we do nevertheless violate that standard, will probably have to be encountered afterwards in the form of remorse. Whatever theory we have of the nature or origin of conscience, this is what essentially constitutes it.

The ultimate sanction, therefore, of all morality (external motives apart) being a subjective feeling in our own minds, I see nothing embarrassing to those whose standard is utility, in the question, what is the sanction of that particular standard? We may answer, the same as of all other moral standards—the conscientious feelings of mankind. Undoubtedly this sanction has no binding efficacy on those who do not possess the feelings it appeals to; but neither will these persons be more obedient to any other moral principle than to the utilitarian one. On them morality of any kind has no hold but through the external sanctions. Meanwhile the feelings exist, a fact in human nature, the reality of which, and the great power with which they are capable of acting on those in whom they have been duly cultivated, are proved by experience. No reason has ever been shown why they may not be cultivated to as great intensity in connexion with the utilitarian, as with any other rule of morals.

There is, I am aware, a disposition to believe that a person who sees in moral obligation a transcendental fact, an objective reality belonging to the province of "Things in themselves," is likely to be more obedient to it than one who believes it to be entirely subjective, having its seat in human consciousness only. But whatever a person's opinion may be on this point of Ontology, the force he is really urged by is his own subjective feeling, and is exactly measured by its strength. No one's belief that Duty is an objective reality is stronger than the belief that God is so; yet the belief in God, apart from the expectation of actual reward and punishment, only operates on conduct through, and in proportion to, the subjective religious feeling. The sanction, so far as it is disinterested, is always in the mind itself; and the notion therefore of the transcendental moralists must be, that this sanction will not exist to the mind unless it is believed to have its root out of the mind; and that if a person is able to say to himself, This which is restraining me, and which is called my conscience, is only a feeling in my own mind, he may possibly draw the conclusion that when the feeling ceases the obligation ceases, and that if he find the feeling inconvenient, he may disregard it, and endeavour to get rid of it. But is this danger confined to the utilitarian morality? Does the belief that moral obligation has its seat outside the mind make the feeling of it too strong to be got rid of? The fact is so far otherwise, that all moralists admit and lament the ease with which, in the generality of minds, conscience can be silenced or stifled. The question, Need I obey my conscience? is quite as often put to themselves by persons who never heard of the principle of utility, as by its adherents. Those whose conscientious feelings are so weak as to allow of their asking this question, if they answer it affirmatively, will not do so because they believe in the transcendental theory, but because of the external sanctions.

It is not necessary, for the present purpose, to decide whether the feeling of duty is innate or implanted. Assuming it to be innate, it is an open question to what objects it naturally attaches itself, for the philosophic supporters of that theory are now agreed that the intuitive perception is of principles or morality, and not of the details. If there be anything innate in the matter, I see no reason why the feeling which is innate should not be that of regard to the pleasures and pains of others. If there is any principle of morals which is intuitively obligatory, I should say it must be that. If so, the intuitive ethics would coincide with the utilitarian, and there would be no further quarrel between them. Even as it is, the intuitive moralists, though they believe that there are other intuitive moral obligations, do already believe this to be one; for they unanimously hold that a large portion of morality turns upon the consideration due to the interests of our fellow creatures. Therefore, if the belief in the transcendental origin of moral obligation gives any additional efficacy to the internal sanction, it appears to me that the utilitarian principle has already the benefit of it.

On the other hand, if, as is my own belief, the moral feelings are not innate, but acquired, they are not for that reason the less natural. It is natural to man to speak, to reason, to build cities, to cultivate the ground, though these are acquired faculties. The moral feelings are not indeed a part of our nature, in the sense of being in any perceptible degree present in all of us; but this, unhappily, is a fact admitted by those who believe the most strenuously in their transcendental origin. Like the other acquired capacities above referred to, the moral faculty, if not a part of our nature, is a natural outgrowth from it; capable, like them, in a certain small degree, of springing up spontaneously; and susceptible of being brought by cultivation to a high degree of development. Unhappily it is also susceptible, by a sufficient use of the external sanctions and of the force of early impressions, of being cultivated in almost any direction: so that there is hardly anything so absurd or so mischievous that it may not, by means of these influences, be made to act on the human mind with all the authority of conscience. To doubt that the same potency might be given by the same means to the principle of utility, even if it had no foundation in human nature, would be flying in the face of all experience.

But moral associations which are wholly of artificial creation, when intellectual culture goes on, yield by degrees to the dissolving force of analysis: and if the feeling of duty, when associated with utility, would appear equally arbitrary; if there were no leading department of our nature, no powerful class of sentiments, with which that association would harmonize, which would make us feel it congenial, and incline us not only to foster it in others (for which we have abundant interested motives), but also to cherish it in ourselves; if there were not, in short, a natural basis of sentiment for utilitarian morality, it might well happen that this association also, even after it had been implanted by education, might be analysed away.

But there is this basis of powerful natural sentiment; and this it is which, when once the general happiness is recognized as the ethical standard, will constitute the strength of the utilitarian morality. This firm foundation is that of the social feelings of mankind; the desire to be in unity with our fellow creatures, which is already a powerful principle in human nature, and happily one of those which tend to become stronger, even without express inculcation, from the influences of advancing civilization. The social state is at once so natural, so necessary, and so habitual to man, that, except in some unusual circumstances or by an effort of voluntary abstraction, he never conceives himself otherwise than as a member of a body; and this association is riveted more and more, as mankind are further removed from the state of savage independence. Any condition, therefore, which is essential to a state of society, becomes more and more an inseparable part of every person's conception of the state of things which he is born into, and which is the destiny of a human being. Now, society between human beings, except in the relation of master and slave, is manifestly impossible on any other footing than that the interests of all are to be consulted. Society between equals can only exist on the understanding that the interests of all are to be regarded equally. And since in all states of civilization, every person, except an absolute monarch, has equals, every one is obliged to live on these terms with somebody; and in every age some advance is made towards a state in which it will be impossible to live permanently on other terms with anybody. In this way people grow up unable to conceive as possible to them a state of total disregard of other people's interests. They are under a necessity of conceiving themselves as at least abstaining from all the grosser injuries, and (if only for their own protection) living in a state of constant protest against them. They are also familiar with the fact of co-operating with others, and proposing to themselves a collective, not an individual, interest, as the aim (at least for the time being) of their actions. So long as they are co-operating, their ends are identified with those of others; there is at least a temporary feeling that the interests of others are their own interests. Not only does all strengthening of social ties, and all healthy growth of society, give to each individual a stronger personal interest in practically consulting the welfare of others; it also leads him to identify his *feelings* more and more with their good, or at least with an ever greater degree of practical consideration for it. He comes, as though instinctively, to be conscious of himself as a being who *of course* pays regard to others. The good of others becomes to him a thing naturally and necessarily to be attended to, like any of the physical conditions of our existence. Now, whatever amount of this feeling a person has, he is urged by the strongest motives both of interest and of sympathy to demonstrate it, and to the utmost of his power encourage it in others; and even if he has none of it himself, he is as greatly interested as any one else that others should have it. Consequently, the smallest germs of the feeling are laid hold of and nourished by the contagion of sympathy and the influences of education; and a complete web of corroborative association is woven round it, by the powerful agency of the external sanctions. This mode of conceiving of ourselves and human life, as civilization goes on, is felt to be more and more natural. Every step in political improvement renders it more so, by removing the sources of opposition of interest, and leveling those inequalities of legal privilege between individuals or classes, owing to which there are large portions of mankind whose happiness it is still practicable to disregard. In an improving state of the human mind, the influences are constantly on the increase, which tend to generate in each individual a feeling of unity with all the rest; which feeling, if perfect, would make him never think of, or desire, any beneficial condition for himself, in the benefits of which they are not included. If we now suppose this feeling of unity to be taught as a religion, and the whole force of education, of institutions, and of opinion, directed, as it once was in the case of religion, to make every person grow up from infancy surrounded on all sides both by the profession and by the practice of it, I think that no one, who can realize this conception, will feel any misgiving about the sufficiency of the ultimate sanction for the Happiness morality. . . .

Neither is it necessary to the feeling which constitutes the binding force of the utilitarian morality on those who recognise it, to wait for those social influences which would make its obligation felt by mankind at large. In the comparatively early state of human advancement in which we now live, a person cannot indeed feel that entireness of sympathy with all others, which would make any real discordance in the general direction of their conduct in life impossible; but already a person in whom the social feeling is at all developed, cannot bring himself to think of the rest of his fellow creatures as struggling rivals with him for the means of happiness, whom he must desire to see defeated in their object in order that he may succeed in his. The deeply-rooted conception which every individual even now has of himself as a social being, tends to make him feel it one of his natural wants that there should be harmony between his feelings and aims and those of his fellow creatures. If differences of opinion and of mental culture make it impossible for him to share many of their actual feelings—perhaps make him denounce and defy those feelings—he still needs to be conscious that his real aim and theirs do not conflict; that he is not opposing himself to what they really wish for, namely, their own good, but is, on the contrary, promoting it. This feeling in most individuals is much inferior in strength to their selfish feelings, and is often wanting altogether. But to those who have it, it possesses all the characters of a natural feeling. It does not present itself to their minds as a superstition of education, or a law despotically imposed by the power of society, but as an attribute which it would not be well for them to be without. This conviction is the ultimate sanction of the greatest-happiness morality. This it is which makes any mind, of well-developed feelings, work with, and not against, the outward motives to care for others, afforded by what I have called the external sanctions; and when those sanctions are wanting, or act in an opposite direction, constitutes in itself a powerful internal binding force, in proportion to the sensitiveness and thoughtfulness of the character; since few but those whose mind is a moral blank, could bear to lay out their course of life on the plan of paying no regard to others except so far as their own private interest compels.

> *In the course of the discussion about the "ultimate sanction" of the greatest happiness principle, Mill has also successfully defended Utilitarianism against the charge that it is a heartless, profit-and-loss, businessman's morality with no appeal to the heart or the higher things of life. He has not addressed, in this chapter, the place of human rights in the Utilitarian scheme of things. He addresses the Utilitarian justification of justice later in the work, and treats of rights at that point. To liberty, however, he devotes an entire volume, on the conviction, well supported in that volume, that we need appeal to no natural and eternal rights to defend individual liberty. A simple appeal to utility, to general happiness, will do the job. The Utilitarian grounding of what we know as civil*

rights, and the presumption of liberty in civil society, are found in the most widely quoted chapter of On Liberty: *Chapter 4, "Of the Limits to the Authority of Society over the Individual." In the excerpt from that chapter which follows, Mill presents an argument for individual freedom that parallels Adam Smith's arguments, above, for "free enterprise," or economic liberty.*

From John Stuart Mill, *On Liberty*

What, then, is the rightful limit to the sovereignty of the individual over himself? Where does the authority of society begin? How much of human life should be assigned to individuality, and how much to society?

Each will receive its proper share, if each has that which more particularly concerns it. To individuality should belong the part of life in which it is chiefly the individual that is interested; to society, the part which chiefly interests society.

Though society is not founded on a contract, and though no good purpose is answered by inventing a contract in order to deduce social obligations from it, every one who receives the protection of society owes a return for the benefit, and the fact of living in society renders it indispensable that each should be bound to observe a certain line of conduct towards the rest. This conduct consists first, in not injuring the interests of one another; or rather certain interests, which, either by express legal provision or by tacit understanding, ought to be considered as rights; and secondly, in each person's bearing his share (to be fixed on some equitable principle) of the labours and sacrifices incurred for defending the society or its members from injury and molestation. These conditions society is justified in enforcing at all costs to those who endeavour to withhold fulfilment. Nor is this all that society may do. The acts of an individual may be hurtful to others, or wanting in due consideration for their welfare, without going the length of violating any of their constituted rights. The offender may then be justly punished by opinion, though not by law. As soon as any part of a person's conduct affects prejudicially the interests of others, society has jurisdiction over it, and the question whether the general welfare will or will not be promoted by interfering with it, becomes open to discussion. But there is no room for entertaining any such question when a person's conduct affects the interests of no persons besides himself, or needs not affect them unless they like (all the persons concerned being of full age, and the ordinary amount of understanding). In all such cases there should be perfect freedom, legal and social, to do the action and stand the consequences.

It would be a great misunderstanding of this doctrine to suppose that it is one of selfish indifference, which pretends that human beings have no business with each other's conduct in life, and that they should not concern themselves about the well-doing or well-being of one another, unless their own interest is involved. Instead of any diminution, there is need of a great increase of disinterested exertion to promote the good of others. But disinterested benevolence can find other instruments to persuade people to their good, than whips and scourges, either of the literal or the metaphorical sort. I am the last person to undervalue the self-regarding virtues; they are only second in importance, if even second, to the social. It is equally the business of education to cultivate both. But even education works by conviction and persuasion as well as by compulsion, and it is by the former only that, when the period of education is past, the self-regarding virtues should be inculcated. Human beings owe to each other help to distinguish the better from the worse, and encouragement to choose the former and avoid the latter. They should be for ever stimulating each other to increased exercise of their higher faculties, and increased direction of their feelings and aims towards wise instead of foolish, elevating instead of degrading, objects and contemplations. But neither one person, nor any number of persons, is warranted in saying to another human creature of ripe years, that he shall not do with his life for his own benefit what he chooses to do with it.

He is the person most interested in his own well-being: the interest which any other person, except in cases of strong personal attachment, can have in it, is trifling, compared with that which he himself has; the interest which society has in him individually (except as to his conduct to others) is fractional, and altogether indirect: while, with respect to his own feelings and circumstances, the most ordinary man or woman has means of knowledge immeasurably surpassing those that can be possessed by any one else. The interference of society to overrule his judgment and purposes in what only regards himself, must be grounded on general presumptions; which may be altogether wrong, and even if right, are as likely as not to be misapplied to individual cases, by persons no better acquainted with the circumstances of such cases than those are who look at them merely from without. In this department, therefore, of human affairs, Individuality has its proper field of action. In the conduct of human beings towards one another, it is necessary that general rules should for the most part be observed, in order that people may know what they have to expect; but in each person's own concerns, his individual spontaneity is entitled to free exercise. Considerations to aid his judgment, exhortations to strengthen his will, may be offered to him, even obtruded on him, by others; but he himself is the final judge. All errors which he is likely to commit against advice and warning, are far outweighed by the evil of allowing others to constrain him to what they deem his good.

I do not mean that the feelings with which a person is regarded by others, ought not to be in any way affected by his self-regarding qualities or deficiencies. This is neither possible nor desirable. If he is eminent in any of the qualities which conduce to his own good, he is, so far, a proper object of admiration. He is so much the nearer to the ideal perfection of human nature. If he is grossly deficient in those qualities, a sentiment the opposite of admiration will follow. There is a degree of folly, and a degree of what may be called (though the phrase is not unobjectionable) lowness or depravation of taste, which, though it cannot justify doing harm to the person who manifests it, renders him necessarily and properly a subject of distaste, or, in extreme cases, even of contempt: a person could not have the opposite qualities in due strength without entertaining these feelings. Though doing no wrong to any one, a person may so act as to compel us to judge him, and feel to him, as a fool, or as a being of an inferior order: and since this judgment and feeling are a fact which he would prefer to avoid, it is doing him a service to warn him of it beforehand, as of any other disagreeable consequence to which he exposes himself. It would be well, indeed, if this good office were much more freely rendered than the common notions of politeness at present permit, and if one person could honestly point out to another that he thinks him in fault, without being considered unmannerly or presuming. We have a right, also, in various ways, to act upon our unfavourable opinion of any one, not to the oppression of his individuality, but in the exercise of ours. We are not bound, for example, to seek his society; we have a right to avoid it (though not to parade the avoidance), for we have a right to choose the society most acceptable to us. We have a right, and it may be our duty, to caution others against him, if we think his example or conversation likely to have a pernicious effect on those with whom he associates. We may give others a preference over him in optional good offices, except those which tend to his improvement. In these various modes a person may suffer very severe penalties at the hands of others, for faults which directly concern only himself, but he suffers these penalties only in so far as they are the natural, and, as it were, the spontaneous consequences of the faults themselves, not because they are purposely inflicted on him for the sake of punishment. . . .

What I contend for is, that the inconveniences which are strictly inseparable from the unfavourable judgment of others, are the only ones to which a person should ever be subjected for that portion of his conduct and character which concerns his own good, but which does not affect the interests of others in their relations with him. Acts injurious to others require a totally different treatment. Encroachment on their rights; infliction on them of any loss or damage not justified by his own rights; falsehood or duplicity in dealing with them; unfair or ungenerous use of advantages over them; even selfish abstinence from defending them against injury—these are fit objects of moral reprobation, and, in grave cases, of moral retribution and punishment. And not only these acts, but the dispositions which lead to them, are properly immoral, and fit subjects of disapprobation which may rise to abhorrence. Cruelty of disposition; malice and ill-nature; that most anti-social and odious of all passions, envy; dissimulation and insincerity; irascibility on insufficient cause, and resentment disproportioned to the provocation, the love of domineering over others: the desire to engross more than one's share of advantages...; the pride which derives gratification from the abasement of others; the egotism which thinks self and its concerns more important than everything else, and decides all doubtful questions in its own favour;—these are moral vices, and constitute a bad and odious moral character: unlike the self-regarding faults previously mentioned, which are not properly immoralities, and to whatever pitch they may be carried, do not constitute wickedness. They may be proofs of any amount of folly, or want of personal dignity and self-respect; but they are only a subject of moral reprobation when they involve a breach of duty to others, for whose sake the individual is bound to have care for himself. What are called duties to ourselves are not socially obligatory, unless circumstances render them at the same time duties to others. The term duty to oneself, when it means anything more than prudence, means self-respect or self-development; and for none of these is any one accountable to his fellow creatures, because for none of them is it for the good of mankind that he be held accountable to them.

The distinction between the loss of consideration which a person may rightly incur by defect of prudence or of personal dignity, and the reprobation which is due to him for an offence against the rights of others, is not a merely nominal distinction. It makes a vast difference both in our feelings and in our conduct towards him, whether he displeases us in things in which we think we have a right to control him, or in things in which we know that we have not. If he displeases us, we may express our distaste, and we may stand aloof from a person as well as from a thing that displeases us; but we shall not therefore feel called on to make his life uncomfortable. We shall reflect that he already bears, or will bear, the whole penalty of his error; if he spoils his life by mismanagement, we shall not, for that reason, desire to spoil it still further: instead of wishing to punish him, we shall rather endeavour to alleviate his punishment, by showing him how he may avoid or cure the evils his conduct tends to bring upon him. He may be to us an object of pity, perhaps of dislike, but not of anger or resentment; we shall not treat him like an enemy of society: the worst we shall think ourselves justified in doing is leaving him to himself, if we do not interfere benevolently by showing interest or concern for him. It is far otherwise if he has infringed the rules necessary for the protection of his fellow-creatures, individually or collectively. The evil consequences of his acts do not then fall on himself, but on others; and society, as the protector of all its members, must retaliate on him; must inflict pain on him for the express purpose of punishment, and must take care that it be sufficiently severe. In the one case, he is an offender at our bar, and we are called on not only to sit in judgment on him, but, in one shape or another, to execute our own sentence: in the other case, it is not our part to inflict any suffering on him, except what may incidentally follow from our using the same liberty in the regulation of our own affairs, which we allow to him in his.

The distinction here pointed out between the part of a person's life which concerns only himself, and that which concerns others, many persons will refuse to admit. How (it may be asked) can any part of the conduct of a member of society be a matter of indifference to the other members? No person is an entirely isolated being; it is impossible for a person to do anything seriously or permanently hurtful to himself, without mischief reaching at least to his near connexions, and often far beyond them. If he injures his property, he does harm to those who directly or indirectly derived support from it, and usually diminishes, by a greater or less amount, the general resources of the community. If he deteriorates his bodily or mental faculties, he not only brings evil upon all who depended on him for any portion of their happiness, but disqualifies himself for rendering the services which he owes to his fellow creatures generally; perhaps becomes a burthen on their affection or benevolence; and if such conduct were very frequent, hardly any offence that is committed would detract more from the general sum of good. Finally, if by his vices or follies a person does no direct harm to others, he is nevertheless (it may be said) injurious by his example; and ought to be compelled to control himself, for the sake of those whom the sight or knowledge of his conduct might corrupt or mislead.

And even (it will be added) if the consequences of misconduct could be confined to the vicious or thoughtless individual, ought society to abandon to their own guidance those who are manifestly unfit for it? If protection against themselves is confessedly due to children and persons under age, is not society equally bound to afford it to persons of mature years who are equally incapable of self-government? If gambling, or drunkenness, or incontinence, or idleness, or uncleanliness, are as injurious to happiness, and as great a hindrance to improvement, as many or most of the acts prohibited by law, why (it may be asked) should not law, so far as is consistent with practicability and social convenience, endeavour to repress these also? And as a supplement to the unavoidable imperfections of law, ought not opinion at least to organize a powerful police against these vices, and visit rigidly with social penalties those who are known to practise them? There is no question here (it may be said) about restricting individuality, or impeding the trial of new and original experiments in living. The only things it is sought to prevent are things which have been tried and condemned from the beginning of the world until now; things which experience has shown not to be useful or suitable to any person's individuality. There must be some length of time and amount of experience, after which a moral or prudential truth may be regarded as established: and it is merely desired to prevent generation after generation from falling over the same precipice which has been fatal to their predecessors.

I fully admit that the mischief which a person does to himself may seriously affect, both through their sympathies and their interests, those nearly connected with him, and in a minor degree, society at large. When, by conduct of this sort, a person is led to violate a distinct and assignable obligation to any other person or persons, the case is taken out of the self-regarding class, and becomes amenable to moral disapprobation in the proper sense of the term. If, for example, a man, through intemperance or extravagance, becomes unable to pay his debts, or, having undertaken the moral responsibility of a family, becomes from the same cause incapable of supporting or educating them, he is deservedly reprobated, and might be justly punished; but it is for the breach of duty to his family or creditors, not for the extravagance. If the resources which ought to have been devoted to them, had been diverted from them for the most prudent investment, the moral culpability would have been the same. . . . Again, in the frequent case of a man who causes grief to his family by addiction to bad habits, he deserves reproach for his unkindness or ingratitude; but so he may for cultivating habits not in themselves vicious, if they are painful to those with whom he passes his life, or who from personal ties are dependent on him for their comfort. Whoever fails in the consideration generally due to the interests and feelings of others, not being compelled by some more imperative duty, or justified by allowable self-preference, is a subject of moral disapprobation for that failure, but not for the cause of it, nor for the errors, merely personal to himself, which may have remotely led to it. In like manner, when a person disables himself, by conduct purely self-regarding, from the performance of some definite duty incumbent on him to the public, he is guilty of a social offence. No person ought to be punished simply for being drunk; but a soldier or a policeman should be punished for being drunk on duty. Whenever, in short, there is a definite damage, or a definite risk of damage, either to an individual or to the public, the case is taken out of the province of liberty, and placed in that of morality or law.

But with regard to the merely contingent, or, as it may be called, constructive injury which a person causes to society, by conduct which neither violates any specific duty to the public, nor occasions perceptible hurt to any assignable individual except himself, the inconvenience is one which society can afford to bear, for the sake of the greater good of human freedom. If grown persons are to be punished for not taking proper care of themselves, I would rather it were for their own sake, than under pretence of preventing them from impairing their capacity of rendering to society benefits which society does not pretend it has a right to exact. But I cannot consent to argue the point as if society had no means of bringing its weaker members up to its ordinary standard of rational conduct, except waiting till they do something irrational, and then punishing them, legally or morally, for it. Society has had absolute power over them during all the early portion of their existence; it has had the period of childhood and nonage in which to try whether it could make them capable of rational conduct in life. The existing generation is master both of the training and the entire circumstances of the generation to come; it cannot indeed make them perfectly wise and good, because it is itself so lamentably deficient in goodness and wisdom; and its best efforts are not always, in individual cases, its most successful ones; but it is perfectly well able to make the rising generation, as a whole, as good as, and a little better than, itself. If society lets any considerable number of its members grow up mere children, incapable of being acted on by rational consideration of distant motives, society has itself to blame for the consequences.

. . . With respect to what is said of the necessity of protecting society from the bad example set to others by the vicious or the self-indulgent; it is true that bad example may have a pernicious effect, especially the example of doing wrong to others with impunity to the wrong-doer. But we are now speaking of conduct which, while it does no wrong to others, is supposed to do great harm to the agent himself. and I do not see how those who believe this, can think otherwise than that the example, on the whole, must be more salutary than hurtful, since, if it displays the misconduct, it displays also the painful or degrading consequences which, if the conduct is justly censured, must be supposed to be in all or most cases attendant on it.

But the strongest of all the arguments against the interference of the public with purely personal conduct, is that when it does interfere, the odds are that it interferes wrongly, and in the wrong place. On questions of social morality, of duty to others, the opinion of the public, that is, of an overruling majority, though often wrong, is likely to be still oftener right; because on such questions they are only required to judge of their own interests; of the manner in which some mode of conduct, if allowed to be practised, would affect themselves. But the opinion of a similar majority, imposed as a law on the minority, on questions of self-regarding conduct, is quite as likely to be wrong as right; for in these cases public opinion means, at the best, some people's opinion of what is good or bad for other people; while very often it does not even mean that; the public, with the most perfect indifference, passing over the pleasure or convenience of those whose conduct they censure, and considering only their own preference. There are many who consider as an injury to themselves any conduct which they have a distaste for, and resent it as an outrage to their feelings; as a religious bigot, when charged with disregarding the religious feelings of others, has been known to retort that they disregard his feelings, by persisting in their abominable worship or creed. But there is no parity between the feeling of a person for his own opinion, and the feeling of another who is offended at his holding it; no more than between the desire of a thief to take a purse, and the desire of the right owner to keep it. And a person's taste is as much his own peculiar concern as his opinion or his purse. It is easy for any one to imagine an ideal public, which leaves the freedom and choice of individuals in all uncertain matters undisturbed, and only requires them to abstain from modes of conduct which universal experience has condemned. But where has there been seen a public which set any such limit to its censorship? or when does the public trouble itself about universal experience? In its interferences with personal conduct it is seldom thinking of anything but the enormity of acting or feeling differently from itself; and this standard of judgment, thinly disguised, is held up to mankind as the dictate of religion and philosophy, by nine-tenths of all moralists and speculative writers. These teach that things are right because they are right; because we feel them to be so. They tell us to search in our own minds and hearts for laws of conduct binding on ourselves and on all others. What can the poor public do but apply these instructions, and make their own personal feelings of good and evil, if they are tolerably unanimous in them, obligatory on all the world?

Conclusion, of a Sort

This excursion through modern philosophy—especially through the works of Immanuel Kant, J. S. Mill, and John Rawls—while maddeningly hurried and inevitably superficial, still presents us with the major systems we use in practical decision making. You will have noticed that they conflict. Kant's emphasis on the motive of the individual moral agent as crucial to moral evaluation of the act conflicts with Rawls' orientation to constitution and the social context of moral acts; both Kant and Rawls dismiss Mill as talking about something other than morality or, on occasion, sanctioning flatly immoral results. We are left with strong imperatives to respect the autonomy and moral agency of the individual (Kant), and to presume the sanctity of his liberty (Mill); yet by Rawls we are also enjoined to restrain the exercise of individual liberty insofar as it damages the poor or least advantaged (and in this society, it usually does), or when in general the greatest happiness is not furthered by such exercise (Bentham and Mill). The natural human impulse is to assign priority to one of the imperatives and try to derive the others from it—that's what Mill did with utilitarianism, for instance. But a more helpful course might be to acknowledge that human nature is complex, and that the imperatives sometimes conflict because they address the conditions for flourishing of three different (sometimes conflicting) aspects of human nature. [Editor's note: the topic is covered in detail in the Introduction to the Ethics in America Study Guide.*] The document that first advanced the trio of modern ethical imperatives was a U.S. Government document, the "Belmont Report," up next.*

FIVE

The Belmont Report

AGENCY: Department of Health, Education, and Welfare.

ACTION: Notice of Report for Public Comment.

SUMMARY: On July 12, 1974, the National Research Act (Pub. L. 93-348) was signed into law, thereby creating the National Commission for the Protection of Human Subjects of Biomedical and Behavioral Research. One of the charges to the Commission was to identify the basic ethical principles that should underlie the conduct of biomedical and behavioral research involving human subjects and to develop guidelines which should be followed to assure that such research is conducted in accordance with those principles. In carrying out the above, the Commission was directed to consider: (i) the boundaries between biomedical and behavioral research and the accepted and routine practice of medicine, (ii) the role of assessment of risk-benefit criteria in the determination of the appropriateness of research involving human subjects, (iii) appropriate guidelines for the selection of human subjects for participation in such research and (iv) the nature and definition of informed consent in various research settings.

The Belmont Report attempts to summarize the basic ethical principles identified by the Commission in the course of its deliberations. It is the outgrowth of an intensive four-day period of discussions that were held in February 1976 at the Smithsonian Institution's Belmont Conference Center supplemented by the monthly deliberations of the Commission that were held over a period of nearly four years. It is a statement of basic ethical principles and guidelines that should assist in resolving the ethical problems that surround the conduct of research with human subjects. By publishing the Report in the Federal Register, and providing reprints upon request, the Secretary intends that it may be made readily available to scientists, members of Institutional Review Boards, and Federal employees. The two-volume Appendix, containing the lengthy reports of experts and specialists who assisted the Commission in fulfilling this part of its charge, is available as DHEW Publication No. (OS) 78-0013 and No. (OS) 78-0014, for sale by the Superintendent of Documents, U.S. Government Printing Office, Washington, D.C. 20402.

Unlike most other reports of the Commission, the Belmont Report does not make specific recommendations for administrative action by the Secretary of Health, Education, and Welfare. Rather, the

Commission recommended that the Belmont Report be adopted in its entirety, as a statement of the Department's policy. The Department requests public comment on this recommendation.

National Commission for the Protection of Human Subjects of Biomedical and Behavioral Research

Members of the Commission

Kenneth John Ryan, MD., Chairman, Chief of Staff, Boston Hospital for Women.
Joseph V. Brady, Ph.D., Professor of Behavioral Biology, Johns Hopkins University.
Robert E. Cooke, MD., President, Medical College of Pennsylvania.
Dorothy I. Height, President, National Council of Negro Women, Inc.
Albert R. Jonsen, Ph.D., Associate Professor of Bioethics, University of California at San Francisco.
Patricia King, JD., Associate Professor of Law, Georgetown University Law Center.
Karen Lebacqz, Ph.D., Associate Professor of Christian Ethics, Pacific School of Religion.

* * * David W. Louisell, JD., Professor of Law, University of California at Berkeley.

Donald W. Seldin, MD., Professor and Chairman, Department of Internal Medicine, University of Texas at Dallas.
Eliot Stellar, Ph.D., Provost of the University and Professor of Physiological Psychology, University of Pennsylvania.

* * * Robert H. Turtle, LL. B., Attorney, VomBaur, Coburn, Simmons & Turtle, Washington, D.C.

* * * Deceased.

Table of Contents

A. Boundaries Between Practice and Research
B. Basic Ethical Principles

1. Respect for Persons
2. Beneficence
3. Justice

C. Applications

1. Informed Consent
2. Assessment of Risk and Benefits
3. Selection of Subjects

Ethical Principles & Guidelines for Research Involving Human Subjects

Scientific research has produced substantial social benefits. It has also posed some troubling ethical questions. Public attention was drawn to these questions by reported abuses of human subjects in biomedical experiments, especially during the Second World War. During the Nuremberg War Crime Trials, the Nuremberg code was drafted as a set of standards for judging physicians and scientists who had conducted biomedical experiments on concentration camp prisoners. This code became the prototype of many later codes, intended to assure that research involving human subjects would be carried out in an ethical manner.

The codes consist of rules, some general, others specific, that guide the investigators or the reviewers of research in their work. Such rules often are inadequate to cover complex situations; at times they come into conflict, and they are frequently difficult to interpret or apply. Broader ethical principles will provide a basis on which specific rules may be formulated, criticized and interpreted.

Three principles, or general prescriptive judgments, that are relevant to research involving human subjects are identified in this statement. Other principles may also be relevant. These three are comprehensive, however, and are stated at a level of generalization that should assist scientists, subjects, reviewers and interested citizens to understand the ethical issues inherent in research involving human subjects. These principles cannot always be applied so as to resolve beyond dispute particular ethical problems. The objective is to provide an analytical framework that will guide the resolution of ethical problems arising from research involving human subjects.

This statement consists of a distinction between research and practice, a discussion of the three basic ethical principles, and remarks about the application of these principles.

Part A: Boundaries Between Practice & Research

It is important to distinguish between biomedical and behavioral research, on the one hand, and the practice of accepted therapy on the other, in order to know what activities ought to undergo review for the protection of human subjects of research. The distinction between research and practice is blurred partly because both often occur together (as in research designed to evaluate a therapy) and partly because notable departures from standard practice are often called "experimental" when the terms "experimental" and "research" are not carefully defined.

For the most part, the term "practice" refers to interventions that are designed solely to enhance the well-being of an individual patient or client and that have a reasonable expectation of success. The purpose of medical or behavioral practice is to provide diagnosis, preventive treatment or therapy to particular individuals. By contrast, the term "research" designates an activity designed to test an hypothesis, permit conclusions to be drawn, and thereby to develop or contribute to generalizable knowledge (expressed, for example, in theories, principles, and statements of relationships). Research is usually described in a formal protocol that sets forth an objective and a set of procedures designed to reach that objective.

When a clinician departs in a significant way from standard or accepted practice, the innovation does not, in and of itself, constitute research. The fact that a procedure is "experimental," in the sense of new, untested or different, does not automatically place it in the category of research. Radically new procedures of this description should, however, be made the object of formal research at an early stage in order to determine whether they are safe and effective. Thus, it is the responsibility of medical practice committees, for example, to insist that a major innovation be incorporated into a formal research project.

Research and practice may be carried on together when research is designed to evaluate the safety and efficacy of a therapy. This need not cause any confusion regarding whether or not the activity requires review; the general rule is that if there is any element of research in an activity, that activity should undergo review for the protection of human subjects.

Part B: Basic Ethical Principles

The expression "basic ethical principles" refers to those general judgments that serve as a basic justification for the many particular ethical prescriptions and evaluations of human actions. Three basic principles, among those generally accepted in our cultural tradition, are particularly relevant to the ethics of research involving human subjects: the principles of respect of persons, beneficence and justice.

1. **Respect for Persons**—Respect for persons incorporates at least two ethical convictions: first, that individuals should be treated as autonomous agents, and second, that persons with diminished

autonomy are entitled to protection. The principle of respect for persons thus divides into two separate moral requirements: the requirement to acknowledge autonomy and the requirement to protect those with diminished autonomy.

An autonomous person is an individual capable of deliberation about personal goals and of acting under the direction of such deliberation. To respect autonomy is to give weight to autonomous persons' considered opinions and choices while refraining from obstructing their actions unless they are clearly detrimental to others. To show lack of respect for an autonomous agent is to repudiate that person's considered judgments, to deny an individual the freedom to act on those considered judgments, or to withhold information necessary to make a considered judgment, when there are no compelling reasons to do so.

However, not every human being is capable of self-determination. The capacity for self-determination matures during an individual's life, and some individuals lose this capacity wholly or in part because of illness, mental disability, or circumstances that severely restrict liberty.

Respect for the immature and the incapacitated may require protecting them as they mature or while they are incapacitated.

Some persons are in need of extensive protection, even to the point of excluding them from activities which may harm them; other persons require little protection beyond making sure they undertake activities freely and with awareness of possible adverse consequence. The extent of protection afforded should depend upon the risk of harm and the likelihood of benefit. The judgment that any individual lacks autonomy should be periodically reevaluated and will vary in different situations.

In most cases of research involving human subjects, respect for persons demands that subjects enter into the research voluntarily and with adequate information. In some situations, however, application of the principle is not obvious. The involvement of prisoners as subjects of research provides an instructive example. On the one hand, it would seem that the principle of respect for persons requires that prisoners not be deprived of the opportunity to volunteer for research. On the other hand, under prison conditions they may be subtly coerced or unduly influenced to engage in research activities for which they would not otherwise volunteer. Respect for persons would then dictate that prisoners be protected. Whether to allow prisoners to "volunteer" or to "protect" them presents a dilemma. Respecting persons, in most hard cases, is often a matter of balancing competing claims urged by the principle of respect itself.

2. **Beneficence**—Persons are treated in an ethical manner not only by respecting their decisions and protecting them from harm, but also by making efforts to secure their well-being. Such treatment falls under the principle of beneficence. The term "beneficence" is often understood to cover acts of kindness or charity that go beyond strict obligation. In this document, beneficence is understood in a stronger sense, as an obligation. Two general rules have been formulated as complementary expressions of beneficent actions in this sense: (1) do not harm and (2) maximize possible benefits and minimize possible harms.

The Hippocratic maxim "do no harm" has long been a fundamental principle of medical ethics. Claude Bernard extended it to the realm of research, saying that one should not injure one person regardless of the benefits that might come to others. However, even avoiding harm requires learning what is harmful; and, in the process of obtaining this information, persons may be exposed to risk of harm. Further, the Hippocratic Oath requires physicians to benefit their patients "according to their best judgment." Learning what will in fact benefit may require exposing persons to risk. The problem posed by these imperatives is to decide when it is justifiable to seek certain benefits despite the risks involved, and when the benefits should be foregone because of the risks.

The obligations of beneficence affect both individual investigators and society at large, because they extend both to particular research projects and to the entire enterprise of research. In the case of particular projects, investigators and members of their institutions are obliged to give forethought to the maximization of benefits and the reduction of risk that might occur from the research investigation. In the case of scientific research in general, members of the larger society are obliged to recognize the longer term benefits and risks that may result from the improvement of knowledge and from the development of novel medical, psychotherapeutic, and social procedures.

The principle of beneficence often occupies a well-defined justifying role in many areas of research involving human subjects. An example is found in research involving children. Effective ways of treating childhood diseases and fostering healthy development are benefits that serve to justify research involving children—even when individual research subjects are not direct beneficiaries. Research also makes it possible to avoid the harm that may result from the application of previously accepted routine practices that on closer investigation turn out to be dangerous. But the role of the principle of beneficence is not always so unambiguous. A difficult ethical problem remains, for example, about research that presents more than minimal risk without immediate prospect of direct benefit to the children involved. Some have argued that such research is inadmissible, while others have pointed out that this limit would rule out much research promising great benefit to children in the future. Here again, as with all hard cases, the different claims covered by the principle of beneficence may come into conflict and force difficult choices.

3. **Justice**—Who ought to receive the benefits of research and bear its burdens? This is a question of justice, in the sense of "fairness in distribution" or "what is deserved." An injustice occurs when some benefit to which a person is entitled is denied without good reason or when some burden is imposed unduly. Another way of conceiving the principle of justice is that equals ought to be treated equally. However, this statement requires explication. Who is equal and who is unequal? What considerations justify departure from equal distribution? Almost all commentators allow that distinctions based on experience, age, deprivation, competence, merit and position do sometimes constitute criteria justifying differential treatment for certain purposes. It is necessary, then, to explain in what respects people should be treated equally. There are several widely accepted formulations of just ways to distribute burdens and benefits. Each formulation mentions some relevant property on the basis of which burdens and benefits should be distributed. These formulations are (1) to each person an equal share, (2) to each person according to individual need, (3) to each person according to individual effort, (4) to each person according to societal contribution, and (5) to each person according to merit.

Questions of justice have long been associated with social practices such as punishment, taxation and political representation. Until recently these questions have not generally been associated with scientific research. However, they are foreshadowed even in the earliest reflections on the ethics of research involving human subjects. For example, during the 19th and early 20th centuries the burdens of serving as research subjects fell largely upon poor ward patients, while the benefits of improved medical care flowed primarily to private patients. Subsequently, the exploitation of unwilling prisoners as research subjects in Nazi concentration camps was condemned as a particularly flagrant injustice. In this country, in the 1940's, the Tuskegee syphilis study used disadvantaged, rural black men to study the untreated course of a disease that is by no means confined to that population. These subjects were deprived of demonstrably effective treatment in order not to interrupt the project, long after such treatment became generally available.

Against this historical background, it can be seen how conceptions of justice are relevant to research involving human subjects. For example, the selection of research subjects needs to be scrutinized in order to determine whether some classes (e.g., welfare patients, particular racial and ethnic minorities, or persons confined to institutions) are being systematically selected simply because of their easy availability, their compromised position, or their manipulability, rather than for reasons directly related to the problem being studied. Finally, whenever research supported by public funds leads to the development of therapeutic devices and procedures, justice demands both that these not provide advantages only to those who can afford them and that such research should not unduly involve persons from groups unlikely to be among the beneficiaries of subsequent applications of the research.

Part C: Applications

Applications of the general principles to the conduct of research leads to consideration of the following requirements: informed consent, risk/benefit assessment, and the selection of subjects of research.

1. **Informed Consent**—Respect for persons requires that subjects, to the degree that they are capable, be given the opportunity to choose what shall or shall not happen to them. This opportunity is provided when adequate standards for informed consent are satisfied. While the importance of informed consent is unquestioned, controversy prevails over the nature and possibility of an informed consent. Nonetheless, there is widespread agreement that the consent process can be analyzed as containing three elements: information, comprehension and voluntariness.

Information • Most codes of research establish specific items for disclosure intended to assure that subjects are given sufficient information. These items generally include: the research procedure, their purposes, risks and anticipated benefits, alternative procedures (where therapy is involved), and a statement offering the subject the opportunity to ask questions and to withdraw at any time from the research. Additional items have been proposed, including how subjects are selected, the person responsible for the research, etc.

However, a simple listing of items does not answer the question of what the standard should be for judging how much and what sort of information should be provided. One standard frequently invoked in medical practice, namely the information commonly provided by practitioners in the field or in the locale, is inadequate since research takes place precisely when a common understanding does not exist. Another standard, currently popular in malpractice law, requires the practitioner to reveal the information that reasonable persons would wish to know in order to make a decision regarding their care. This, too, seems insufficient since the research subject, being in essence a volunteer, may wish to know considerably more about risks gratuitously undertaken than do patients who deliver themselves into the hand of a clinician for needed care. It may be that a standard of "the reasonable volunteer" should be proposed: the extent and nature of information should be such that persons, knowing that the procedure is neither necessary for their care nor perhaps fully understood, can decide whether they wish to participate in the furthering of knowledge. Even when some direct benefit to them is anticipated, the subjects should understand clearly the range of risk and the voluntary nature of participation.

A special problem of consent arises where informing subjects of some pertinent aspect of the research is likely to impair the validity of the research. In many cases, it is sufficient to indicate to subjects that they are being invited to participate in research of which some features will not be revealed until the research is concluded. In all cases of research involving incomplete disclosure, such research is justified only if it is clear that (1) incomplete disclosure is truly necessary to accomplish the goals of the research, (2) there are no undisclosed risks to subjects that are more than minimal, and (3) there is an adequate plan for debriefing subjects, when appropriate, and for dissemination of research results to them. Information about risks should never be withheld for the purpose of eliciting the cooperation of subjects, and truthful answers should always be given to direct questions about the research. Care should be taken to distinguish cases in which disclosure would destroy or invalidate the research from cases in which disclosure would simply inconvenience the investigator.

Comprehension • The manner and context in which information is conveyed is as important as the information itself. For example, presenting information in a disorganized and rapid fashion, allowing too little time for consideration or curtailing opportunities for questioning, all may adversely affect a subject's ability to make an informed choice.

Because the subject's ability to understand is a function of intelligence, rationality, maturity and language, it is necessary to adapt the presentation of the information to the subject's capacities. Investigators are responsible for ascertaining that the subject has comprehended the information. While there is always an obligation to ascertain that the information about risk to subjects is complete and adequately comprehended, when the risks are more serious, that obligation increases. On occasion, it may be suitable to give some oral or written tests of comprehension.

Special provision may need to be made when comprehension is severely limited—for example, by conditions of immaturity or mental disability. Each class of subjects that one might consider as incompetent (e.g., infants and young children, mentally disabled patients, the terminally ill and the comatose) should be considered on its own terms. Even for these persons, however, respect requires giving them the opportunity to choose to the extent that they are able, whether or not to participate in research. The objections of these subjects to involvement should be honored, unless the research entails providing them a therapy unavailable elsewhere. Respect for persons also requires seeking the permission of other parties in order to protect the subjects from harm.

The third parties chosen should be those who are most likely to understand the incompetent subject's situation and to act in that person's best interest. The person authorized to act on behalf of the subject should be given an opportunity to observe the research as it proceeds in order to be able to withdraw the subject from the research, if such action appears in the subject's best interest.

Voluntariness • An agreement to participate in research constitutes a valid consent only if voluntarily given. This element of informed consent requires conditions free of coercion and undue influence. Coercion occurs when an overt threat of harm is intentionally presented by one person to another in order to obtain compliance. Undue influence, by contrast, occurs through an offer of an excessive, unwarranted, inappropriate or improper reward or other overture in order to obtain compliance. Also, inducements that would ordinarily be acceptable may become undue influences if the subject is especially vulnerable.

Unjustifiable pressures usually occur when persons in positions of authority or commanding influence—especially where possible sanctions are involved—urge a course of action for a subject. A continuum of such influencing factors exists, however, and it is impossible to state precisely where justifiable persuasion ends and undue influence begins. But undue influence would include actions such as manipulating a person's choice through the controlling influence of a close relative and threatening to withdraw health services to which an individual would otherwise be entitled.

2. **Assessment of risks and benefits**—The assessment of risks and benefits requires a careful arrayal of relevant data, including, in some cases, alternative ways of obtaining the benefits sought in the research. Thus, the assessment presents both an opportunity and a responsibility to gather systematic and comprehensive information about proposed research. For the investigator, it is a means to examine whether the proposed research is properly designed. For a review committee, it is a method for determining whether the risks that will be presented to subjects are justified. For prospective subjects, the assessment will assist the determination whether or not to participate.

The Nature and Scope of Risks and Benefits • The requirement that research be justified on the basis of a favorable risk/benefit assessment bears a close relation to the principle of beneficence, just as the moral requirement that informed consent be obtained is derived primarily from the principle of respect for persons. The term "risk" refers to a possibility that harm may occur. However, when expressions such as "small risk," or "high risk", are used, they usually refer (often ambiguously) both to the chance (probability) of experiencing a harm and the severity (magnitude) of the envisioned harm.

The term "benefit" is used in the research context to refer to something of positive value related to health or welfare. Unlike "risk," "benefit" is not a term that expresses probabilities. Risk is properly contrasted to probability of benefits, and benefits are properly contrasted with harms rather than risks of harm. Accordingly, so-called risk/benefit assessments are concerned with the probabilities and magnitudes of possible harm and anticipated benefits. Many kinds of possible harms and benefits need to be taken into account. There are, for example, risks of psychological harm, physical harm, legal harm, social harm and economic harm and the corresponding benefits. While the most likely types of harms to research subjects are those of psychological or physical pain or injury, other possible kinds should not be overlooked.

Risks and benefits of research may affect the individual subjects, the families of the individual subjects, and society at large (or special groups of subjects in society). Previous codes and Federal regulations have required that risks to subjects be outweighed by the sum of both the anticipated benefit to the subject, if any, and the anticipated benefit to society in the form of knowledge to be gained from the research. In balancing these different elements, the risks and benefits affecting the immediate research subject will normally carry special weight. On the other hand, interests other than those of the subject may on some occasions be sufficient by themselves to justify the risks involved in the research, so long as the subjects' rights have been protected. Beneficence thus requires that we protect against risk of harm to subjects and also that we be concerned about the loss of the substantial benefits that might be gained from research.

The Systematic Assessment of Risks and Benefits • It is commonly said that benefits and risks must be "balanced" and shown to be "in a favorable ratio." The metaphorical character of these terms draws attention to the difficulty of making precise judgments. Only on rare occasions will quantitative techniques be available for the scrutiny of research protocols. However, the idea of systematic, nonarbitrary analysis of risks and benefits should be emulated insofar as possible. This ideal requires those making decisions about the justifiability of research to be thorough in the accumulation and assessment of information about all aspects of the research, and to consider alternatives systematically. This procedure renders the assessment of research more rigorous and precise, while making communication between review board members and investigators less subject to misinterpretation, misinformation and conflicting judgments. Thus, there should first be a determination of the validity of the presuppositions of the research; then the nature, probability and magnitude of risk should be distinguished with as much clarity as possible. The method of ascertaining risks should be explicit, especially where there is no alternative to the use of such vague categories as small or slight risk. It should also be determined whether an investigator's estimates of the probability of harm or benefits are reasonable, as judged by known facts or other available studies.

Finally, assessment of the justifiability of research should reflect at least the following considerations: (i) Brutal or inhumane treatment of human subjects is never morally justified. (ii) Risks should be reduced to those necessary to achieve the research objective. It should be determined whether it is in fact necessary to use human subjects at all. Risk can perhaps never be entirely eliminated, but it can often be reduced by careful attention to alternative procedures. (iii) When research involves significant risk of serious impairment, review committees should be extraordinarily insistent on the justification of the risk (looking usually to the likelihood of benefit to the subject—or, in some rare cases, to the manifest voluntariness of the participation). (iv) When vulnerable populations are involved in research, the appropriateness of involving them should itself be demonstrated. A number of variables go into such judgments, including the nature and degree of risk, the condition of the particular population involved, and the nature and level of the anticipated benefits. (v) Relevant risks and benefits must be thoroughly arrayed in documents and procedures used in the informed consent process.

3. **Selection of Subjects**—Just as the principle of respect for persons finds expression in the requirements for consent, and the principle of beneficence in risk/benefit assessment, the principle of justice gives rise to moral requirements that there be fair procedures and outcomes in the selection of research subjects.

Justice is relevant to the selection of subjects of research at two levels: the social and the individual. Individual justice in the selection of subjects would require that researchers exhibit fairness: thus, they should not offer potentially beneficial research only to some patients who are in their favor or select only "undesirable" persons for risky research. Social justice requires that distinction be drawn between classes of subjects that ought, and ought not, to participate in any particular kind of research, based on the ability of members of that class to bear burdens and on the appropriateness of placing further burdens on already burdened persons. Thus, it can be considered a matter of social justice that there is an order of preference in the selection of classes of subjects (e.g., adults before children) and that some classes of potential subjects (e.g., the institutionalized mentally infirm or prisoners) may be involved as research subjects, if at all, only on certain conditions.

Injustice may appear in the selection of subjects, even if individual subjects are selected fairly by investigators and treated fairly in the course of research. Thus injustice arises from social, racial, sexual and cultural biases institutionalized in society. Thus, even if individual researchers are treating their research subjects fairly, and even if the Institutional Review Boards (IRBs) are taking care to assure that subjects are selected fairly within a particular institution, unjust social patterns may nevertheless appear in the overall distribution of the burdens and benefits of research. Although individual institutions or investigators may not be able to resolve a problem that is pervasive in their social setting, they can consider distributive justice in selecting research subjects.

Some populations, especially institutionalized ones, are already burdened in many ways by their infirmities and environments. When research is proposed that involves risks and does not include a therapeutic component, other less burdened classes of persons should be called upon first to accept these risks of research, except where the research is directly related to the specific conditions of the class involved. Also, even though public funds for research may often flow in the same directions as public funds for health care, it seems unfair that populations dependent on public health care constitute a pool of preferred research subjects if more advantaged populations are likely to be the recipients of the benefits.

One special instance of injustice results from the involvement of vulnerable subjects. Certain groups, such as racial minorities, the economically disadvantaged, the very sick, and the institutionalized may continually be sought as research subjects, owing to their ready availability in settings where research is conducted. Given their dependent status and their frequently compromised capacity for free consent, they should be protected against the danger of being involved in research solely for administrative convenience, or because they are easy to manipulate as a result of their illness or socioeconomic condition.

Notes

(1) Since 1945, various codes for the proper and responsible conduct of human experimentation in medical research have been adopted by different organizations. The best known of these codes are the Nuremberg Code of 1947, the Helsinki Declaration of 1964 (revised in 1975), and the 1971 Guidelines (codified into Federal Regulations in 1974) issued by the U.S. Department of Health, Education, and Welfare Codes for the conduct of social and behavioral research have also been adopted, the best known being that of the American Psychological Association, published in 1973.

(2) Although practice usually involves interventions designed solely to enhance the well-being of a particular individual, interventions are sometimes applied to one individual for the enhancement of the well-being of another (e.g., blood donation, skin grafts, organ transplants) or an intervention may have the dual purpose of enhancing the well-being of a particular individual, and, at the same time, providing some benefit to others (e.g., vaccination, which protects both the person who is vaccinated and society generally). The fact that some forms of practice have elements other than immediate benefit to the individual receiving an intervention, however, should not confuse the general distinction between research and practice. Even when a procedure applied in practice may benefit some other person, it remains an intervention designed to enhance the well-being of a particular individual or groups of individuals; thus, it is practice and need not be reviewed as research.

(3) Because the problems related to social experimentation may differ substantially from those of biomedical and behavioral research, the Commission specifically declines to make any policy determination regarding such research at this time. Rather, the Commission believes that the problem ought to be addressed by one of its successor bodies.

SIX

Doubts and Experiments

In *After Virtue,* his monumental essay on modern philosophy, Alasdair McIntyre characterized the whole effort to find clear moral directives, nurtured in reason and validated by science, as "the Enlightenment Project." Nothing to do with Buddhism, it was meant to be the collective effort of Western thought, from the exuberant optimists of the Renaissance (Pico della Mirandola and his like) to the methodical pragmatists of the early twentieth century (John Dewey rounding out the tradition), to reduce—the word is used intentionally—all moral thought and the very soul of the human to something that could be analyzed, understood, planned, evaluated, and eventually directed upon the right path, the path that would lead to the simple, rational, and satisfying life for all. The world could be filled, there were those who believed, with rational relationships, peace, prosperity, beauty, and above all education. The rational life was possible. All the philosophers we have read so far, always excepting Thucydides, subscribed to these beliefs.

Yet there were doubts. Some protests came from adherents of religious faith. Those of spiritual orientation, as opposed to legalistic (and every faith has both), felt that we sell the human experiment too cheaply if we regard it as a mere reason machine for satisfying needs and gratifying desires (or, for that matter, slogging through duties). Is there not something in us that seeks a higher end, fulfillment not in perfect hedonism but in transcendence? Others, depressed by what they saw as the mechanical sameness of life lived only according to reason, bravely affirmed the worth of Heart, Hope, and Imagination over the triumphant sway of Head, Fact, and Calculation; these we call the Romantics. Yet others, observing human action on the stage of history, in all its willful and appalling perversity, regarded the confident positivists of the Enlightenment cast as hopelessly naïve, lost on the garden path they had created for themselves. Dostoevsky, who wrote the selection immediately below in 1864, was one of these. Yet others, fuming at the injustice of the vast industrial civilization that seemed to be following from the rational utilitarians of Adam Smith's persuasions, followed Karl Marx into a completely new view of history that rendered Smith's calculations not only irrelevant and silly, but viciously and intentionally misleading. Marx is represented by the first part of *The Communist Manifesto,* written in 1848. It changed the world.

During the twentieth century, more voices joined the chorus of those convinced that rationalism, classicism, had left something out. This short concluding section of this text is designed to give you a taste, just a taste, of the many-sided critique to which the rational ethics of the modern period has been subjected in the late nineteenth and twentieth centuries. (Alasdair McIntyre himself, for instance, thought that the wholesome tradition of virtue ethics, derived from Aristotle, had been neglected and should be revived.) Dostoevsky is generally accounted one of the forerunners of the Existentialist school, represented in this text by Jean-Paul Sartre; existentialists tend to hold that the entire project of "defining" the human is misguided. Feminists and environmentalists, among many others, point out that ethics as written in the West has always assumed the voice, and role, of the European or North American white propertied male human being, ignoring women, people of color, Asia, the South, the poor of all races (except as very occasional objects of charity), non-human animals (although they, too, feel pleasure and pain), and indeed the entire natural world around us.

In previous sections of this text, we have scrupulously pointed out our inadequacies. Only a very few selections can be made from each of the eras of importance to Western ethics, we have reminded you; many strong and worthy voices have been left out of the previous sections. But in this section especially, we feel the hopelessness of providing even a fair sampling of that cacophony of sound that has replaced the ordered contrapuntal symphony of the rationalist ethics. Let us rest with this warning: there are alternatives to everything you have read, there are criticisms from a dozen angles of all the classics, there are values that only now rise to prominence, rights and goods that only recently have claimed a place in the canon, and when you have finished this part, you will have had the appetizer for a truly delightful meal. But you'll have to do the shopping and cooking for yourself.

Fyodor Mikhailovic Dostoevsky (1821–1881)

Dostoevsky's life was troubled, plagued with family deaths and financial crises, but nowhere near as disturbed as some of his writings, including the one below, might suggest. His father was a physician, he got a standard boys' education, went to military college and joined the army. He was sent to prison camp in Siberia in consequence of various forbidden political activities; served his sentence, was released, joined the army again, was arrested again, all before he started writing seriously. He is best known for his novels—Crime and Punishment, The Brothers Karamazov, The Idiot, The Possessed. (Notes from Underground *is also a novel, not autobiography!) In all his writings, Dostoevsky places himself crosswise of Rousseau, Bentham, Mill, and all the rest who taught his age that humans were born good, or could become good with proper education. Note, especially in Section VII of the following piece, what he does to Utilitarianism. This is surely the herald of a new age in ethics.*

From Fyodor Dostoevsky, *Notes from Underground*

Selections from Part I

I am a sick man . . . I am a spiteful man. I am an unattractive man. I believe my liver is diseased. However, I know nothing at all about my disease, and do not know for certain what ails me. I don't consult a doctor for it, and never have, though I have a respect for medicine and doctors. Besides, I am extremely superstitious, sufficiently so to respect medicine, anyway (I am well-educated enough not to be superstitious, but I am superstitious). No, I refuse to consult a doctor from spite. That you probably will not understand. Well, I understand it, though. Of course, I can't explain who it is precisely that I am mortifying in this case by my spite: I am perfectly well aware that I cannot "pay out" the doctors by not consulting them; I know better than any one that by all this I am only injuring myself and no one else. But still, if I don't consult a doctor it is from spite. My liver is bad, well—let it get worse!

I have been going on like that for a long time—twenty years. Now I am forty. I used to be in the government service, but am no longer. I was a spiteful official. I was rude and took pleasure in being so. I did not take bribes, you see, so I was bound to find a recompense in that, at least. (A poor jest, but I will not scratch it out. I wrote it thinking it would sound very witty; but now that I have seen myself that I only wanted to show off in a despicable way, I will not scratch it out on purpose!)

When petitioners used to come for information to the table at which I sat, I used to grind my teeth at them, and felt intense enjoyment when I succeeded in making anybody unhappy. I almost always did succeed. For the most part they were all timid people—of course, they were petitioners. But of the up-pish ones there was one officer in particular I could not endure. He simply would not be humble, and clanked his sword in a disgusting way. I carried on a feud with him for eighteen months over that sword. At last I got the better of him. He left off clanking it. That happened in my youth, though.

But do you know, gentlemen, what was the chief point about my spite? Why, the whole point, the real sting of it lay in the fact that continually, even in the moment of the acutest spleen, I was inwardly conscious with shame that I was not only not a spiteful but not even an embittered man, that I was simply scaring sparrows at random and amusing myself by it. I might foam at the mouth but bring me a doll to play with, give me a cup of tea with sugar in it, and maybe I should be appeased. I might even be genuinely touched, though probably I should grind my teeth at myself afterwards and lie awake at night with shame for months after. That was my way.

I was lying when I said just now that I was a spiteful official. I was lying from spite. I was simply amusing myself with the petitioners and with the officer, and in reality I never could become spiteful. I was conscious every moment in myself of many, very many elements absolutely opposite to that. I felt them positively swarming in me, these opposite elements. I knew that they had been swarming in me all my life and craving some outlet from me, but I would not let them, would not let them, purposely would not let them come out. They tormented me till I was ashamed—they drove me to convulsions and—sickened me, at last, how they sickened me! Now, are not you fancying, gentlemen, that I am ex-pressing remorse for something now, that I am asking your forgiveness for something? I am sure you are fancying that. . . . However, I assure you I do not care if you are. . . .

It was not only that I could not become spiteful, I did not know how to become anything: neither spiteful nor kind, neither a rascal nor an honest man, neither a hero nor an insect. Now, I am living out my life in my corner, taunting myself with the spiteful and useless consolation that an intelligent man cannot become anything seriously, and it is only the fool who becomes anything. Yes, a man in the nineteenth century must and morally ought to be pre-eminently a characterless creature; a man of character, an active man is pre-eminently a limited creature. That is my conviction of forty years. I am forty years old now, and you know forty years is a whole life-time; you know it is extreme old age. To live longer than forty years is bad manners, is vulgar, immoral. Who does live beyond forty? Answer that, sincerely and honestly. I will tell you who do: fools and worthless fellows. I tell all old men that to their face, all these venerable old men, all these silver-haired and reverend seniors! I tell the whole world that to its face! I have a right to say so, for I shall go on living to sixty myself. To seventy! To eighty! . . . Stay, let me take breath. . . .

But what can a decent man speak of with most pleasure?

Answer: Of himself.

Well, so I will talk about myself.

I want now to tell you, gentlemen, whether you care to hear it or not, why I could not even become an insect. I tell you solemnly that I have many times tried to become an insect. But I was not equal even to that. I swear, gentlemen, that to be too conscious is an illness—a real thoroughgoing illness. For man's everyday needs, it would have been quite enough to have the ordinary human consciousness, that is, half or a quarter of the amount which falls to the lot of a cultivated man of our unhappy nineteenth century, especially one who has the fatal ill-luck to inhabit Petersburg, the most theoretical and intentional town on the whole terrestrial globe. (There are intentional and unintentional towns.) It would have been quite enough, for instance, to have the consciousness by which all so-called direct persons and men of action live. I bet you think I am writing all this from affectation, to be witty at the expense of men of action; and what is more, that from ill-bred affectation, I am clanking a sword like my officer. But, gentlemen, whoever can pride himself on his diseases and even swagger over them?

Though, after all, every one does do that; people do pride themselves on their diseases, and I do, may be, more than any one. We will not dispute it; my contention was absurd. But yet I am firmly persuaded that a great deal of consciousness, every sort of consciousness, in fact, is a disease. I stick to that. Let us leave that, too, for a minute. Tell me this: why does it happen that at the very, yes, at the very moments when I am most capable of feeling every refinement of all that is "good and beautiful," as they used to say at one time, it would, as though of design, happen to me not only to feel but to do such ugly things, such that . . . Well, in short, actions that all, perhaps, commit; but which, as though purposely, occurred to me at the very time when I was most conscious that they ought not to be committed. The more conscious I was of goodness and of all that was "good and beautiful," the more deeply I sank into my mire and the more ready I was to sink in it altogether. But the chief point was that all this was, as it were, not accidental in me, but as though it were bound to be so. It was as though it were my most normal condition, and not in the least disease or depravity, so that at last all desire in me to struggle against this depravity passed. It ended by my almost believing (perhaps actually believing) that this was perhaps my normal condition. But at first, in the beginning, what agonies I endured in that struggle! I did not believe it was the same with other people, and all my life I hid this fact about myself as a secret. I was ashamed (even now, perhaps, I am ashamed): I got to the point of feeling a sort of secret, abnormal, despicable enjoyment in returning home to my corner on some disgusting Petersburg night, acutely conscious that that day I had committed a loathsome action again, that what was done could never be undone, and secretly, inwardly gnawing, gnawing at myself for it, tearing and consuming myself till at last the bitterness turned into a sort of shameful accursed sweetness, and at last—into positive real enjoyment! Yes, into enjoyment, into enjoyment! I insist upon that. I have spoken of this because I keep wanting to know for a fact whether other people feel such enjoyment? I will explain; the enjoyment was just from the too intense consciousness of one's own degradation; it was from feeling oneself that one had reached the last barrier, that it was horrible, but that it could not be otherwise; that there was no escape for you; that you never could become a different man; that even if time and faith were still left you to change into something different you would most likely not wish to change; or if you did wish to, even then you would do nothing; because perhaps in reality there was nothing for you to change into.

III

With people who know how to revenge themselves and to stand up for themselves in general, how is it done? Why, when they are possessed, let us suppose, by the feeling of revenge, then for the time there is nothing else but that feeling left in their whole being. Such a gentleman simply dashes straight for his object like an infuriated bull with its horns down, and nothing but a wall will stop him. (By the way: facing the wall, such gentlemen—that is, the "direct" persons and men of action—are genuinely nonplussed. For them, a wall is not an evasion, as for us people who think and consequently do nothing; it is not an excuse for turning aside, an excuse for which we are always very glad, though we scarcely believe in it ourselves, as a rule. No, they are nonplussed in all sincerity. The wall has for them something tranquillizing, morally soothing, final—maybe even something mysterious . . . but of the wall later.)

Well, such a direct person I regard as the real normal man, as his tender mother nature wished to see him when she graciously brought him into being on the earth. I envy such a man till I am green in the face. He is stupid. I am not disputing that, but perhaps the normal man should be stupid, how do you know? Perhaps it is very beautiful, in fact. And I am the more persuaded of that suspicion, if one can call it so, by the fact that if you take, for instance, the antithesis of the normal man, that is, the man of acute consciousness, who has come, of course, not out of the lap of nature but out of a retort (this is almost mysticism, gentlemen, but I suspect this, too), this retort-made man is sometimes so nonplussed in the presence of his antithesis that with all his exaggerated consciousness he genuinely thinks of himself as a mouse and not a man. It may be an acutely conscious mouse, yet it is a mouse, while the other is a man, and therefore, et cetera, et cetera. And the worst of it is, he himself, his very own self, looks on himself as a mouse; no one asks him to do so; and that is an important point. Now let us look at this mouse in action. Let us suppose, for instance, that it feels insulted, too (and it almost always does feel insulted), and wants to revenge itself, too. There may even be a greater accumulation of spite in it than in *l'homme de la nature et de la verité*. The base and nasty desire to vent that spite on its assailant rankles perhaps even more nastily in it than in *l'homme de la nature et de la verité*. For through his innate stupidity the latter looks upon his revenge as justice pure and simple; while in consequence of his acute consciousness the mouse does not believe in the justice of it. To come at last to the deed itself, to the very act of revenge. Apart from the one fundamental nastiness the luckless mouse succeeds in creating around it so many other nastinesses in the form of doubts and questions, adds to the one question so many unsettled questions that there inevitably works up around it a sort of fatal brew, a stinking mess, made up of its doubts, emotions, and of the contempt spat upon it by the direct men of action who stand solemnly about it as judges and arbitrators, laughing at it till their healthy sides ache. Of course the only thing left for it is to dismiss all that with a wave of its paw, and, with a smile of assumed contempt in which it does not even itself believe, creep ignominiously into its mouse-hole. There in its nasty, stinking, underground home our insulted, crushed and ridiculed mouse promptly becomes absorbed in cold, malignant and, above all, everlasting spite. For forty years together it will remember its injury down to the smallest, most ignominious details, and every time will add, of itself, details still more ignominious, spitefully teasing and tormenting itself with its own imagination. It will itself be ashamed of its imaginings, but yet it will recall it all, it will go over and over every detail, it will invent unheard of things against itself, pretending that those things might happen, and will forgive nothing. Maybe it will begin to revenge itself, too, but, as it were, piecemeal, in trivial ways, from behind the stove, incognito, without believing either in its own right to vengeance, or in the success of its revenge, knowing that from all its efforts at revenge it will suffer a hundred times more than he on whom it revenges itself, while he, I daresay, will not even scratch himself. On its deathbed it will recall it all over again, with interest accumulated over all the years. . . .

I will continue calmly concerning persons with strong nerves who do not understand a certain refinement of enjoyment. Though in certain circumstances these gentlemen bellow their loudest like bulls, though this, let us suppose, does them the greatest credit, yet, as I have said already, confronted with the impossible they subside at once. The impossible means the stone wall! What stone wall? Why of course, the laws of nature, the deductions of natural science, mathematics. As soon as they prove to you, for instance, that you are descended from a monkey, then it is no use scowling, accept it for a fact. When they prove to you that in reality one drop of your own fat must be dearer to you than a hundred thousand of your fellow-creatures, and that this conclusion is the final solution of all so-called virtues and duties and all such prejudices and fancies, then you have just to accept it, there is no help for it, for twice two is a law of mathematics. Just try refuting it.

"Upon my word," they will shout at you, "it is no use protesting: it is a case of twice two makes four! Nature does not ask your permission, she has nothing to do with your wishes, and whether you like her laws or dislike them, you are bound to accept her as she is, and consequently all her conclusions. A wall, you see, is a wall . . . and so on, and so on."

Merciful Heavens! but what do I care for the laws of nature and arithmetic, when, for some reason, I dislike those laws and the fact that twice two makes four? Of course I cannot break through the wall by battering my head against it if I really have not the strength to knock it down, but I am not going to be reconciled to it simply because it is a stone wall and I have not the strength. As though such a stone wall really were a consolation, and really did contain some word of conciliation, simply because it is as true as twice two makes four. Oh, absurdity of absurdities! How much better it is to understand it all, to recognize it all, all the impossibilities and the stone wall; not to be reconciled to one of those impossibilities and stone walls if it disgusts you to be reconciled to it; by the way of the most inevitable, logical combinations to reach the most revolting conclusions on the everlasting theme, that even for the stone wall you are yourself somehow to blame, though again it is as clear as day you are not to blame in the least, and therefore grinding your teeth in silent impotence to sink into luxurious inertia, brooding on the fact that there is no one even for you to feel vindictive against, that you have not, and perhaps never will have, an object for your spite, that it is a sleight of hand, a bit of juggling, a cardsharper's trick, that it is simply a mess, no knowing what and no knowing who, but in spite of all these uncertainties and jugglings, still there is an ache in you, and the more you do not know, the worse the ache. . . .

VII

But these are all golden dreams. Oh, tell me, who was it first announced, who was it first proclaimed, that man only does nasty things because he does not know his own interests; and that if he were enlightened, if his eyes were opened to his real normal interests, man would at once cease to do nasty things, would at once become good and noble because, being enlightened and understanding his real advantage, he would see his own advantage in the good and nothing else, and we all know that not one man can, consciously, act against his own interests, consequently, so to say, through necessity, he would begin doing good? Oh, the babe! Oh, the pure, innocent child! Why, in the first place, when in all these thousands of years has there been a time when man has acted only from his own interest? What is to be done with the millions of facts that bear witness that men, consciously, that is fully understanding their real interests, have left them in the background and have rushed headlong on another path, to meet peril and danger, compelled to this course by nobody and by nothing, but, as it were, simply disliking the beaten track, and have obstinately, willfully, struck out another difficult, absurd way, seeking it almost in the darkness. So, I suppose, this obstinacy and perversity were pleasanter to them than any advantage. . . . Advantage! What is advantage? And will you take it upon yourself to define with perfect accuracy in what the advantage of man consists? And what if it so happens that a man's advantage, *sometimes*, not only may, but even must, consist in his desiring in certain cases what is harmful to himself and not advantageous. And if so, if there can be such a case, the whole principle falls into dust. What do you think—are there such cases? You laugh; laugh away, gentlemen, but only answer me:—have man's advantages been reckoned up with perfect certainty? Are there not some which not only have not been included but cannot possibly be included under any classification? You see, you gentlemen have, to the best of my knowledge, taken your whole register of human advantages from the averages of statistical figures and politico-economical formulas. Your advantages are prosperity, wealth, freedom, peace—and so on, and so on. So that the man who should, for instance, go openly and knowingly in opposition to all that list would, to your thinking, and indeed mine, too, of course, be an obscurantist or an absolute madman: would not he? But, you know, this is what is surprising: why does it so happen that all these statisticians, sages and lovers of humanity, when they reckon up human advantages invariably leave out one? They don't even take it into their reckoning in the form in which it should be taken, and the whole reckoning depends upon that. It would be no great matter, they would simply have to take it, this advantage, and add it to the list. But the trouble is, that this strange advantage does not fall under any classification and is not in place in any list. I have a friend for instance . . . Ech! gentlemen, but of course he is your friend, too; and indeed there is no one, no one, to whom he is not a friend! When he prepares for any undertaking this gentleman immediately explains to you, elegantly and clearly, exactly how he must act in accordance with the laws of reason and truth. What is more, he will talk to you with excitement and passion of the true normal interests of man; with irony he will upbraid the shortsighted fools who do not understand their own interests, nor the true significance of virtue; and, within a quarter of an hour, without any sudden outside provocation, but simply—through something inside him which is stronger than all his interests, he will go off on quite a different tack—that is, act in direct opposition to what he has just been saying about himself, in opposition to the laws of reason, in opposition to his own advantage, in fact in opposition to everything . . . I warn you that my friend is a compound personality, and therefore it is difficult to blame him as an individual. The fact is, gentlemen, it seems there must really exist something that is dearer to almost every man than his greatest advantages, or (not to be illogical) there is a most advantageous advantage (the very one omitted of which we spoke just now) which is more important and more advantageous than all other advantages, for the sake of which a man if necessary is ready to act in opposition to all laws; that is, in opposition to reason, honour, peace, prosperity—in fact, in opposition to all those excellent and useful things if only he can attain that fundamental, most advantageous advantage which is dearer to him than all. "Yes, but it's advantage all the same" you will retort. But excuse me, I'll make the point clear, and it is not a case of playing upon words. What matters is, that this advantage is remarkable from the very fact that it breaks down all our classifications, and continually shatters every system constructed by lovers of mankind for the benefit of mankind. In fact, it upsets everything. But before I mention this advantage to you, I want to compromise myself personally, and therefore I boldly declare that all these fine systems, all these theories for explaining to mankind their real normal interests, in order that inevitably striving to pursue these interests they may at once become good and noble—are, in my opinion, so far, mere logical exercises! Yes, logical exercises. Why, to maintain this theory of the regeneration of mankind by means of the pursuit of his own advantage is to my mind almost the same thing as . . . as to affirm, for instance, following Buckle, that through civilization mankind becomes softer, and consequently less bloodthirsty and less fitted for warfare. Logically it does seem to follow from his arguments. But man has such a predilection for systems and abstract deductions that he is ready to distort the truth intentionally, he is ready to deny the evidence of his senses only to justify his logic. I take this example because it is the most glaring instance of it. Only look about you: blood is being spilt in streams, and in the merriest way, as though it were champagne. Take the whole of the nineteenth century in which Buckle lived. Take Napoleon—the Great and also the present one. Take North America—the eternal union. Take the farce of Schleswig-Holstein. . . . And what is it that civilization softens in us? The only gain of civilization for mankind is the greater capacity for variety of sensations— and absolutely nothing more. And through the development of this many-sidedness man may come to find enjoyment in bloodshed. In fact, this has already happened to him. Have you noticed that it is the most civilized gentlemen who have been the subtlest slaughterers, to whom the Attilas and Stenka Razins could not hold a candle, and if they are not so conspicuous as the Attilas and Stenka Razins it is simply because they are so often met with, are so ordinary and have become so familiar to us. In any case civilization has made mankind if not more bloodthirsty, at least more vilely, more loathsomely bloodthirsty. In old days he saw justice in bloodshed and with his conscience at peace exterminated those he thought proper. Now we do think bloodshed abominable and yet we engage in this abomination, and with more energy than ever. Which is worse? Decide that for yourselves. They say that Cleopatra (excuse an instance from Roman history) was fond of sticking gold pins into her slave-girls' breasts and derived gratification from their screams and writhings. You will say that that was in the comparatively barbarous times; that these are barbarous times too, because also, comparatively speaking, pins are stuck in even now; that though man has now learned to see more clearly than in barbarous ages, he is still far from having learnt to act as reason and science would dictate. But yet you are fully convinced that he will be sure to learn when he gets rid of certain old bad habits, and when common sense and science have completely re-educated human nature and turned it in a normal direction. You are confident that then man will cease from intentional error and will, so to say, be compelled not to want to set his will against his normal interests. That is not all; then, you say, science itself will teach man (though to my mind it's a superfluous luxury) that he never has really had any caprice or will of his own, and that he himself is something of the nature of a piano-key or the stop of an organ, and that there are, besides, things called the laws of nature; so that everything he does is not done by his willing it, but is done of itself, by the laws of nature. Consequently we have only to discover these laws of nature, and man will no longer have to answer for his actions and life will become exceedingly easy for him. All human actions will then, of course, be tabulated according to these laws, mathematically, like tables of logarithms up to 108,000, and entered in an index; or, better still, there would be published certain edifying works of the nature of encyclopaedic lexicons, in which everything will be so clearly calculated and explained that there will be no more incidents or adventures in the world.

Then—this is all what you say—new economic relations will be established, all ready-made and worked out with mathematical exactitude, so that every possible question will vanish in the twinkling of an eye, simply because every possible answer to it will be provided. Then the "Palace of Crystal" will be built. Then . . . In fact, those will be halcyon days. Of course, there is no guaranteeing (this is my comment) that it will not be, for instance, frightfully dull then (for what will one have to do when everything will be calculated and tabulated), but on the other hand everything will be extraordinarily rational. Of course boredom may lead you to anything. It is boredom sets one sticking golden pins into people, but all that would not matter. What is bad (this is my comment again) is that I dare say people will be thankful for the golden pins then. Man is stupid, you know, phenomenally stupid; or rather he is not at all stupid, but he is so ungrateful that you could not find another like him in all creation. I, for instance, would not be in the least surprised if all of a sudden, a propos of nothing, in the midst of general prosperity a gentleman with an ignoble, or rather with a reactionary and ironical, countenance were to arise and, putting his arms akimbo, say to us all: "I say, gentlemen, hadn't we better kick over the whole show and scatter rationalism to the winds, simply to send these logarithms to the devil, and to enable us to live once more at our own sweet foolish will!" That again would not matter, but what is annoying is that he would be sure to find followers—such is the nature of man. And all that for the most foolish reason, which, one would think, was hardly worth mentioning: that is, that man everywhere and at all times, whoever he may be, has preferred to act as he chose and not in the least as his reason and advantage dictated. And one may choose what is contrary to one's own interests, and sometimes one positively ought (that is my idea). One's own free unfettered choice, one's own caprice, however wild it may be, one's own fancy worked up at times to frenzy—is that very "most advantageous advantage" which we have overlooked, which comes under no classification and against which all systems and theories are continually being shattered to atoms. And how do these wiseacres know that man wants a normal, a virtuous choice? What has made them conceive that man must want a rationally advantageous choice? What man wants is simply *independent* choice, whatever that independence may cost and wherever it may lead. And choice, of course, the devil only knows what choice.

VIII

"Ha! ha! ha! But you know there is no such thing as choice in reality, say what you like," you will interpose with a chuckle. "Science has succeeded in so far analyzing man that we know already that choice and what is called freedom of will is nothing else than . . ."

Stay, gentlemen, I meant to begin with that myself. I confess, I was rather frightened. I was just going to say that the devil only knows what choice depends on, and that perhaps that was a very good thing, but I remembered the teaching of science . . . and pulled myself up. And here you have begun upon it. Indeed, if there really is some day discovered a formula for all our desires and caprices—that is, an explanation of what they depend upon, by what laws they arise, how they develop, what they are aiming at it one case and in another and so on, that is a real mathematical formula—then, most likely, man will at once cease to feel desire, indeed, he will be certain to. For who would want to choose by rule? Besides, he will at once be transformed from a human being into an organ-stop or something of the sort; for what is a man without desires, without freewill and without choice, if not a stop in an organ? What do you think? Let us reckon the chances—can such a thing happen or not?

"H'm!" you decide. "Our choice is usually mistaken from a false view of our advantage. We sometimes choose absolute nonsense because in our foolishness we see in that nonsense the easiest means for attaining a supposed advantage. But when all that is explained and worked out on paper (which is perfectly possible, for it is contemptible and senseless to suppose that some laws of nature man will never understand), then certainly so-called desires will no longer exist. For if a desire should come into conflict with reason we shall then reason and not desire, because it will be impossible retaining our reason to be *senseless* in our desires, and in that way knowingly act against reason and desire to injure ourselves. And as all choice and reasoning can be really calculated—because there will some day be discovered the laws of our so-called freewill—so, joking apart, there may one day be something like a table constructed of them, so that we really shall choose in accordance with it. If, for instance, some day they calculate and prove to me that I made a long nose at some one because I could not help making a long nose at him and that I had to do it in that particular way, what *freedom is* left me, especially if I am a learned man and have taken my degree somewhere? Then I should be able to calculate my whole life for thirty years beforehand. In short, if this could be arranged there would be nothing left for us to do; anyway, we should have to understand that. And, in fact, we ought unwearyingly to repeat to ourselves that at such and such a time and in such and such circumstances nature does not ask our leave; that we have got to take her as she is and not fashion her to suit our fancy, and if we really aspire to formulas and tables of rules, and well, even . . . to the chemical retort, there's no help for it, we must accept the retort too, or else it will be accepted without our consent. . . ."

Yes, but here I come to a stop! Gentlemen, you must excuse me for being over-philosophical: it's the result of forty years underground! Allow me to indulge my fancy. You see, gentlemen, reason is an excellent thing, there's no disputing that, but reason is nothing but reason and satisfies only the rational side of man's nature, while will is a manifestation of the whole life, that is, of the whole human life including reason and all the impulses. And although our life, in this manifestation of it, is often worthless, yet it is life and not simply extracting square roots. Here I, for instance, quite naturally want to live, in order to satisfy all my capacities for life, and not simply my capacity for reasoning, that is, not simply one twentieth of my capacity for life. What does reason know? Reason only knows what it has succeeded in learning (some things, perhaps, it will never learn; this is a poor comfort, but why not say so frankly?) and human nature acts as a whole, with everything that is in it, consciously or unconsciously, and, even if it goes wrong, it lives. I suspect, gentlemen, that you are looking at me with compassion; you tell me again that an enlightened and developed man, such, in short, as the future man will be, cannot consciously desire anything disadvantageous to himself, that that can be proved mathematically. I thoroughly agree, it can—by mathematics. But I repeat for the hundredth time, there is one case, one only, when man may consciously, purposely, desire what is injurious to himself, what is stupid, very stupid—simply in order to have the right to desire for himself even what is very stupid and not to be bound by an obligation to desire only what is sensible. Of course, this very stupid thing, this caprice of ours, may be in reality, gentlemen, more advantageous for us than anything else on earth, especially in certain cases. And in particular it may be more advantageous than any advantage even when it does us obvious harm, and contradicts the soundest conclusions of our reason concerning our advantage—for in any circumstances it preserves for us what is most precious and most important—that is, our personality, our individuality. Some, you see, maintain that this really is the most precious thing for mankind; choice can, of course, if it chooses, be in agreement with reason; and especially if this be not abused but kept within bounds. It is profitable and sometimes even praiseworthy. But very often, and even most often, choice is utterly and stubbornly opposed to reason . . . and . . . and . . . do you know that that, too, is profitable, sometimes even praiseworthy? Gentlemen, let us suppose that man is not stupid. (Indeed one cannot refuse to suppose that, if only from the one consideration, that, if man is stupid, then who is wise?) But if he is not stupid, he is monstrously ungrateful! Phenomenally ungrateful. In fact, I believe that the best definition of man is the ungrateful biped. But that is not all, that is not his worst defect; his worst defect is his perpetual moral obliquity, perpetual—from the days of the Flood to the Schleswig-Holstein period. Moral obliquity and consequently lack of good sense; for it has long been accepted that lack of good sense is due to no other cause than moral obliquity. Put it to the test and cast your eyes upon the history of mankind. What will you see? Is it a grand spectacle? Grand, if you like. Take the Colossus of Rhodes, for instance, that's worth something. With good reason Mr. Anaevsky testifies of it that some say that it is the work of man's hands, while others maintain that it has been created by nature herself. Is it many-coloured? May be it is many-coloured, too: if one takes the dress uniforms, military and civilian, of all peoples in all ages—that alone is worth something, and if you take the undress uniforms you will never get to the end of it; no historian would be equal to the job. Is it monotonous? Maybe it's monotonous too: it's fighting and fighting; they are fighting now, they fought first and they fought last—you will admit, that it is almost too monotonous. In short, one may say anything about the history of the world—anything that might enter the most disordered imagination. The only thing one can't say is that it's rational. The very word sticks in one's throat. And, indeed, this is the odd thing that is continually happening: there are continually turning up in life moral and rational persons, sages and lovers of humanity who make it their object to live all their lives as morally and rationally as possible, to be, so to speak, a light to their neighbours simply in order to show them that it is possible to live morally and rationally in this world. And yet we all know that those very people sooner or later have been false to themselves, playing some queer trick, often a most unseemly one. Now I ask you: what can be expected of man since he is a being endowed with such strange qualities? Shower upon him every earthly blessing, drown him in a sea of happiness, so that nothing but bubbles of bliss can be seen on the surface; give him economic prosperity, such that he should have nothing else to do but sleep, eat cakes and busy himself with the continuation of his species, and even then out of sheer ingratitude, sheer spite, man would play you some nasty trick. He would even risk his cakes and would deliberately desire the most fatal rubbish, the most uneconomical absurdity, simply to introduce into all this positive good sense his fatal fantastic element. It is just his fantastic dreams, his vulgar folly that he will desire to retain, simply in order to prove to himself—as though that were so necessary—that men still are men and not the keys of a piano, which the laws of nature threaten to control so completely that soon one will be able to desire nothing but by the calendar. And that is not all: even if man really were nothing but a piano-key, even if this were proved to him by natural science and mathematics, even then he would not become reasonable, but would purposely do something perverse out of simple ingratitude, simply to gain his point. And if he does not find means he will contrive destruction and chaos, will contrive sufferings of all sorts, only to gain his point! He will launch a curse upon the world, and as only man can curse (it is his privilege, the primary distinction between him and other animals), may be by his curse alone he will attain his object—that is, convince himself that he is a man and not a piano-key! If you say that all this, too, can be calculated and tabulated—chaos and darkness and curses, so that the mere possibility of calculating it all beforehand would stop it all, and reason would reassert itself, then man would purposely go mad in order to be rid of reason and gain his point! I believe in it, I answer for it, for the whole work of man really seems to consist in nothing but proving to himself every minute that he is a man and not a piano-key! It may be at the cost of his skin, it may be by cannibalism! And this being so, can one help being tempted to rejoice that it has not yet come off, and that desire still depends on something we don't know?

You will scream at me (that is, if you condescend to do so) that no one is touching my free will, that all they are concerned with is that my will should of itself, of its own free will, coincide with my own normal interests, with the laws of nature and arithmetic.

Good Heavens, gentlemen, what sort of free will is left when we come to tabulation and arithmetic, when it will all be a case of twice two makes four? Twice two makes four without my will. As if free will meant that!

IX

Gentlemen, I am joking, and I know myself that my jokes are not brilliant, but you know one can't take everything as a joke. I am, perhaps, jesting against the grain. Gentlemen, I am tormented by questions; answer them for me. You, for instance, want to cure men of their old habits and reform their will in accordance with science and good sense. But how do you know, not only that it is possible, but also that it *is desirable,* to reform man in that way? And what leads you to the conclusion that man's inclinations *need* reforming? In short, how do you know that such a reformation will be a benefit to man? And to go to the root of the matter, why are you so positively convinced that not to act against his real normal interests guaranteed by the conclusions of reason and arithmetic is certainly always advantageous for man and must always be a law for mankind? So far, you know, this is only your supposition. It may be the law of logic, but not the law of humanity. You think, gentlemen, perhaps that I am mad? Allow me to defend myself. I agree that man is pre-eminently a creative animal, predestined to strive consciously for an object and to engage in engineering—that is, incessantly and eternally to make new roads, *wherever they may lead.* But the reason why he wants sometimes to go off at a tangent may just be that he *is predestined to* make the road, and perhaps, too, that however stupid the "direct" practical man may be, the thought sometimes will occur to him that the road almost always does lead *somewhere,* and that the destination it leads to is less important than the process of making it, and that the chief thing is to save the well-conducted child from despising engineering, and so giving way to the fatal idleness, which, as we all know, is the mother of all the vices. Man likes to make roads and to create, that is a fact beyond dispute. But why has he such a passionate love for destruction and chaos also? Tell me that! But on that point I want to say a couple of words myself. May it not be that he loves chaos and destruction (there can be no disputing that he does sometimes love it) because he is instinctively afraid of attaining his object and completing the edifice he is constructing? Who knows, perhaps he only loves that edifice from a distance, and is by no means in love with it at close quarters; perhaps he only loves building it and does not want to live in it, but will leave it, when completed, for the use of *les animaux domestiques* such as the ants, the sheep, and so on. Now the ants have quite a different taste. They have a marvelous edifice of that pattern which endures for ever—the ant-heap.

With the ant-heap the respectable race of ants began and with the ant-heap they will probably end, which does the greatest credit to their perseverance and good sense. But man is a frivolous and incongruous creature, and perhaps, like a chess player, loves the process of the game, not the end of it. And who knows (there is no saying with certainty), perhaps the only goal on earth to which mankind is striving lies in this incessant process of attaining, in other words, in life itself, and not in the thing to be attained, which must always be expressed as a formula, as positive as twice two makes four, and such positiveness is not life, gentlemen, but is the beginning of death. Anyway, man has always been afraid of this mathematical certainty, and I am afraid of it now. Granted that man does nothing but seek that mathematical certainty, he traverses oceans, sacrifices his life in the quest, but to succeed, really to find it, he dreads, I assure you. He feels that when he has found it there will be nothing for him to look for. When workmen have finished their work they do at least receive their pay, they go to the tavern, then they are taken to the police-station—and there is occupation for a week. But where can man go? Anyway, one can observe a certain awkwardness about him when he has attained such objects. He loves the process of attaining, but does not quite like to have attained, and that, of course, is very absurd. In fact, man is a comical creature; there seems to be a kind of jest in it all. But yet mathematical certainty is, after all, something insufferable. Twice two makes four seems to me simply a piece of insolence. Twice two makes four is a pert coxcomb who stands with arms akimbo barring your path and spitting. I admit that twice two makes four is an excellent thing, but if we are to give everything its due, twice two makes five is sometimes a very charming thing too.

And why are you so firmly, so triumphantly, convinced that only the normal and the positive—in other words, only what is conducive to welfare—is for the advantage of man? Is not reason in error as regards advantage? Does not man, perhaps, love something besides well-being? Perhaps he is just as fond of suffering? Perhaps suffering is just as great a benefit to him as well-being? Man is sometimes extraordinarily, passionately, in love with suffering, and that is a fact. There is no need to appeal to universal history to prove that; only ask yourself, if you are a man and have lived at all. As far as my personal opinion is concerned, to care only for well-being seems to me positively ill-bred. Whether it's good or bad, it is sometimes very pleasant, too, to smash things. I hold no brief for suffering nor for well-being either. I am standing for . . . my caprice, and for its being guaranteed to me when necessary. Suffering would be out of place in vaudevilles, for instance; I know that. In the "Palace of Crystal" it is unthinkable; suffering means doubt, negation, and what would be the good of a "palace of crystal" if there could be any doubt about it? And yet I think man will never renounce real suffering, that is, destruction and chaos. Why, suffering is the sole origin of consciousness. Though I did lay it down at the beginning that consciousness is the greatest misfortune for man, yet I know man prizes it and would not give it up for any satisfaction. Consciousness, for instance, is infinitely superior to twice two makes four. Once you have mathematical certainty there is nothing left to do or to understand. There will be nothing left but to bottle up your five senses and plunge into contemplation. While if you stick to consciousness, even though the same result is attained, you can at least flog yourself at times, and that will, at any rate, liven you up. Reactionary as it is, corporal punishment is better than nothing. . . .

Marxism

"Marxism" has been at the center of controversy for the last century—essentially, 1870 to 1990. Claiming adherents worldwide, it became the equivalent of a popular religion, economic theory, form of government and all-purpose left-wing threat to the West, all at once. It may be understood (to oversimplify a century and a half of scholarship) as three separate claims upon the intellectual tradition.

First, it is a theory of history. Hegel, Karl Marx's teacher, was famously the first philosopher to see history as a progression determined by its own laws. He had posited a dialectical process of the ideas that made up the historical phases of the West. One age's dominant idea (its "thesis") would be confronted, as an "antithesis," by its contradiction; as the age rolled on, the antithesis would absorb the thesis, but be transformed in the process, becoming a "synthesis" of the two. Marx contemptuously pointed out that the conditions that determined the way people made a living, and the economic constraints on them, had a lot more to do with what happened in history than "ideas"; for Hegel's dialectical idealism, Marx substituted "dialectical materialism," explaining the progress of history as a series of transformations in ownership of the means of production. The upshot was that the bourgeois capitalist society in which we lived was inevitably to be overcome by the new proletarian society, after the revolution of the masses that would destroy the bourgeoisie, that is, us. You see why Marx was unpopular in the U.S.

Second, Marxism is an economic and political theory, a careful analysis of capitalism in terms of its mode of operation, its capacity for constructing the means of production that produced the proletariat to begin with, and the human relationships that it establishes. Not the least in his analysis of bourgeois society is his reading of our famed Liberty and Democracy: we have the liberty to do anything we can finance, so the poor have no liberty at all; we can choose, by our vote, among several wealthy and well-financed candidates who owe the election to the rich no matter how the poor vote, so there is no democracy; should the poor complain of their lot, we have freedom of religion, and every religion teaches that we should be humble in this life and enjoy the benefits of our good behavior in the Hereafter. Any attempts to better the lot of the poor, should such a notion come to the Congress, will instantly be rejected by the ruling class of the rich as an unconstitutional attack on "freedom." So all the liberties cherished by Thomas Jefferson (the slave-owner) are so many masks for the unbridled dominance of the rich, their license to enrich themselves beyond reason and without limit. He concluded calmly, on almost Platonic grounds, that capitalism would destroy itself, drowning in its own greed. His economic theory was no more popular on our shores than his theory of history, but it turned out to have a good deal more staying power. Observers of the contemporary scene in the securities and money markets, not to mention campaign finance, have been heard to draw similar conclusions.

Third, Marx was a prophet, in the tradition of Amos. He saw injustice and he hated it. His critique of bourgeois society, sketched above, echoed Amos and Jesus of Nazareth: the rich prosper without regard to the poor, enjoying their rich dainties while the children of the poor die from hunger; the rich corrupt the judges and the legislators, buying laws and judgments favorable to themselves while the poor are turned away and ignored; the rich own the churches, the access to God, and turn even religion (Marx called it "the opiate of the people") to their selfish purposes. Woe unto you, Scribes, Pharisees, Wall Street brokers, fat CEOs, and all your lackeys! You will be swept away in the coming conflagration!

The "Marxist" governments that dominated so much of the world during the twentieth century had little to do with Karl Marx. The Soviet Union after Lenin—from the moment, to be exact, when Stalin ran Trotsky out of the country—was an updated nuclear-powered Czarist dictatorship; China was an empire in the old style, only with a new emphasis on public service (now in rapid decline). Marx was preaching to Western Europe, the only area sufficiently industrialized for his Proletarian Revolution to work. When it didn't happen there, it couldn't happen anywhere. Yet Marx remains the most effective teacher in the modern world, with an intellectual reach to be compared with the great religious leaders of the ancient world. We will wait a long time for another thinker of his power and influence.

Karl Marx and Frederick Engels, *The Communist Manifesto*

Chapter 1

A spectre is haunting Europe—the spectre of communism. All the powers of old Europe have entered into a holy alliance to exorcise this spectre: Pope and Tsar, Metternich and Guizot, French Radicals and German police-spies.

Where is the party in opposition that has not been decried as communistic by its opponents in power? Where is the opposition that has not hurled back the branding reproach of communism, against the more advanced opposition parties, as well as against its reactionary adversaries?

Two things result from this fact:

1. Communism is already acknowledged by all European powers to be itself a power.
2. It is high time that Communists should openly, in the face of the whole world, publish their views, their aims, their tendencies, and meet this nursery tale of the spectre of communism with a manifesto of the party itself.

To this end, Communists of various nationalities have assembled in London and sketched the following manifesto . . .

Bourgeois and Proletarians

The history of all hitherto existing society is the history of class struggles. Freeman and slave, patrician and plebeian, lord and serf, guildmaster and journeyman, in a word, oppressor and oppressed, stood in constant opposition to one another, carried on an uninterrupted, now hidden, now open fight, a fight that each time ended, either in a revolutionary reconstitution of society at large, or in the common ruin of the contending classes. In the earlier epochs of history, we find almost everywhere a complicated arrangement of society into various orders, a manifold gradation of social rank. In ancient Rome we have patricians, knights, plebeians, slaves; in the Middle Ages, feudal lords, vassals, guild-masters, journeymen, apprentices, serfs; in almost all of these classes, again, subordinate gradations.

The modern bourgeois society that has sprouted from the ruins of feudal society has not done away with class antagonisms. It has but established new classes, new conditions of oppression, new forms of struggle in place of the old ones. Our epoch, the epoch of the bourgeoisie, possesses, however, this distinct feature: it has simplified class antagonisms. Society as a whole is more and more splitting up into two great hostile camps, into two great classes directly facing each other—bourgeoisie and proletariat. From the serfs of the Middle Ages sprang the chartered burghers of the earliest towns. From these burgesses the first elements of the bourgeoisie were developed.

The discovery of America, the rounding of the Cape, opened up fresh ground for the rising bourgeoisie. The East-Indian and Chinese markets, the colonisation of America, trade with the colonies, the increase in the means of exchange and in commodities generally, gave to commerce, to navigation, to industry, an impulse never before known, and thereby, to the revolutionary element in the tottering feudal society, a rapid development.

The feudal system of industry, in which industrial production was monopolized by closed guilds, now no longer suffices for the growing wants of the new markets. The manufacturing system took its place. The guild-masters were pushed aside by the manufacturing middle class; division of labor between the different corporate guilds vanished in the face of division of labor in each single workshop.

Meantime, the markets kept ever growing, the demand ever rising. Even manufacturers no longer sufficed. Thereupon, steam and machinery revolutionized industrial production. The place of manufacture was taken by the giant, Modern Industry; the place of the industrial middle class by industrial millionaires, the leaders of the whole industrial armies, the modern bourgeois.

Modern industry has established the world market, for which the discovery of America paved the way. This market has given an immense development to commerce, to navigation, to communication by land. This development has, in turn, reacted on the extension of industry; and in proportion as industry, commerce, navigation, railways extended, in the same proportion the bourgeoisie developed, increased its capital, and pushed into the background every class handed down from the Middle Ages.

We see, therefore, how the modern bourgeoisie is itself the product of a long course of development, of a series of revolutions in the modes of production and of exchange. Each step in the development of the bourgeoisie was accompanied by a corresponding political advance in that class. An oppressed class under the sway of the feudal nobility, an armed and self-governing association of medieval commune; here independent urban republic (as in Italy and Germany); there taxable "third estate" of the monarchy (as in France); afterward, in the period of manufacturing proper, serving either the semi-feudal or the absolute monarchy as a counterpoise against the nobility, and, in fact, cornerstone of the great monarchies in general—the bourgeoisie has at last, since the establishment of Modern Industry and of the world market, conquered for itself, in the modern representative state, exclusive political sway. The executive of the modern state is but a committee for managing the common affairs of the whole bourgeoisie.

The bourgeoisie, historically, has played a most revolutionary part. The bourgeoisie, wherever it has got the upper hand, has put an end to all feudal, patriarchal, idyllic relations. It has pitilessly torn asunder the motley feudal ties that bound man to his "natural superiors", and has left no other nexus between man and man than naked self-interest, than callous "cash payment". It has drowned out the most heavenly ecstasies of religious fervor, of chivalrous enthusiasm, of philistine sentimentalism, in the icy water of egotistical calculation. It has resolved personal worth into exchange value, and in place of the numberless indefeasible chartered freedoms, has set up that single, unconscionable freedom—Free Trade. In one word, for exploitation, veiled by religious and political illusions, it has substituted naked, shameless, direct, brutal exploitation.

The bourgeoisie has stripped of its halo every occupation hitherto honored and looked up to with reverent awe. It has converted the physician, the lawyer, the priest, the poet, the man of science, into its paid wage laborers.

The bourgeoisie has torn away from the family its sentimental veil, and has reduced the family relation into a mere money relation.

The bourgeoisie has disclosed how it came to pass that the brutal display of vigor in the Middle Ages, which reactionaries so much admire, found its fitting complement in the most slothful indolence. It has been the first to show what man's activity can bring about. It has accomplished wonders far surpassing Egyptian pyramids, Roman aqueducts, and Gothic cathedrals; it has conducted expeditions that put in the shade all former exoduses of nations and crusades.

The bourgeoisie cannot exist without constantly revolutionizing the instruments of production, and thereby the relations of production, and with them the whole relations of society. Conservation of the old modes of production in unaltered form, was, on the contrary, the first condition of existence for all earlier industrial classes. Constant revolutionizing of production, uninterrupted disturbance of all social conditions, everlasting uncertainty and agitation distinguish the bourgeois epoch from all earlier ones. All fixed, fast, frozen relations, with their train of ancient and venerable prejudices and opinions, are swept away, all new-formed ones become antiquated before they can ossify. All that is solid melts into air, all that is holy is profaned, and man is at last compelled to face with sober senses his real condition of life and his relations with his kind.

The need of a constantly expanding market for its products chases the bourgeoisie over the entire surface of the globe. It must nestle everywhere, settle everywhere, establish connections everywhere.

The bourgeoisie has, through its exploitation of the world market, given a cosmopolitan character to production and consumption in every country. To the great chagrin of reactionaries, it has drawn from under the feet of industry the national ground on which it stood. All old-established national industries have been destroyed or are daily being destroyed. They are dislodged by new industries, whose introduction becomes a life and death question for all civilized nations, by industries that no longer work up indigenous raw material, but raw material drawn from the remotest zones; industries whose products are consumed, not only at home, but in every quarter of the globe. In place of the old wants, satisfied by the production of the country, we find new wants, requiring for their satisfaction the products of distant lands and climes. In place of the old local and national seclusion and self-sufficiency, we have intercourse in every direction, universal inter-dependence of nations. And as in material, so also in intellectual production. The intellectual creations of individual nations become common property. National one-sidedness and narrow-mindedness become more and more impossible, and from the numerous national and local literatures, there arises a world literature.

The bourgeoisie, by the rapid improvement of all instruments of production, by the immensely facilitated means of communication, draws all, even the most barbarian, nations into civilization. The cheap prices of commodities are the heavy artillery with which it forces the barbarians' intensely obstinate hatred of foreigners to capitulate. It compels all nations, on pain of extinction, to adopt the bourgeois mode of production; it compels them to introduce what it calls civilization into their midst, i.e., to become bourgeois themselves. In one word, it creates a world after its own image.

The bourgeoisie has subjected the country to the rule of the towns. It has created enormous cities, has greatly increased the urban population as compared with the rural, and has thus rescued a considerable part of the population from the idiocy of rural life. Just as it has made the country dependent on the towns, so it has made barbarian and semi-barbarian countries dependent on the civilized ones, nations of peasants on nations of bourgeois, the East on the West.

The bourgeoisie keeps more and more doing away with the scattered state of the population, of the means of production, and of property. It has agglomerated population, centralized the means of production, and has concentrated property in a few hands. The necessary consequence of this was political centralization. Independent, or but loosely connected provinces, with separate interests, laws, governments, and systems of taxation, became lumped together into one nation, with one government, one code of laws, one national class interest, one frontier, and one customs tariff.

The bourgeoisie, during its rule of scarce one hundred years, has created more massive and more colossal productive forces than have all preceding generations together. Subjection of nature's forces to man, machinery, application of chemistry to industry and agriculture, steam navigation, railways, electric telegraphs, clearing of whole continents for cultivation, canalization or rivers, whole populations conjured out of the ground—what earlier century had even a presentiment that such productive forces slumbered in the lap of social labor?

We see then: the means of production and of exchange, on whose foundation the bourgeoisie built itself up, were generated in feudal society. At a certain stage in the development of these means of production and of exchange, the conditions under which feudal society produced and exchanged, the feudal organization of agriculture and manufacturing industry, in one word, the feudal relations of property became no longer compatible with the already developed productive forces; they became so many fetters. They had to be burst asunder; they were burst asunder.

Into their place stepped free competition, accompanied by a social and political constitution adapted in it, and the economic and political sway of the bourgeois class.

A similar movement is going on before our own eyes. Modern bourgeois society, with its relations of production, of exchange and of property, a society that has conjured up such gigantic means of production and of exchange, is like the sorcerer who is no longer able to control the powers of the nether world whom he has called up by his spells. For many a decade past, the history of industry and commerce is but the history of the revolt of modern productive forces against modern conditions of production, against the property relations that are the conditions for the existence of the bourgeois and of its rule. It is enough to mention the commercial crises that, by their periodical return, put the existence of the entire bourgeois society on its trial, each time more threateningly. In these crises, a great part not only of the existing products, but also of the previously created productive forces, are periodically destroyed. In these crises, there breaks out an epidemic that, in all earlier epochs, would have seemed an absurdity—the epidemic of overproduction. Society suddenly finds itself put back into a state of momentary barbarism; it appears as if a famine, a universal war of devastation, had cut off the supply of every means of subsistence; industry and commerce seem to be destroyed. And why? Because there is too much civilization, too much means of subsistence, too much industry, too much commerce. The productive forces at the disposal of society no longer tend to further the development of the conditions of bourgeois property; on the contrary, they have become too powerful for these conditions, by which they are fettered, and so soon as they overcome these fetters, they bring disorder into the whole of bourgeois society, endanger the existence of bourgeois property. The conditions of bourgeois society are too narrow to comprise the wealth created by them. And how does the bourgeoisie get over these crises? On the one hand, by enforced destruction of a mass of productive forces; on the other, by the conquest of new markets, and by the more thorough exploitation of the old ones. That is to say, by paving the way for more extensive and more destructive crises, and by diminishing the means whereby crises are prevented.

The weapons with which the bourgeoisie felled feudalism to the ground are now turned against the bourgeoisie itself. But not only has the bourgeoisie forged the weapons that bring death to itself, it has also called into existence the men who are to wield those weapons—the modern working class—the proletarians.

In proportion as the bourgeoisie, i.e., capital, is developed, in the same proportion is the proletariat, the modern working class, developed—a class of laborers, who live only so long as they find work, and who find work only so long as their labor increases capital. These laborers, who must sell themselves piecemeal, are a commodity, like every other article of commerce, and are consequently exposed to all the vicissitudes of competition, to all the fluctuations of the market.

Owing to the extensive use of machinery, and to the division of labor, the work of the proletarians has lost all individual character, and, consequently, all charm for the workman. He becomes an appendage of the machine, and it is only the most simple, most monotonous, and most easily acquired knack, that is required of him. Hence, the cost of production of a workman is restricted, almost entirely, to the means of subsistence that he requires for maintenance, and for the propagation of his race. But the price of a commodity, and therefore also of labor, is equal to its cost of production. In proportion, therefore, as the repulsiveness of the work increases, the wage decreases. What is more, in proportion as the use of machinery and division of labor increases, in the same proportion the burden of toil also increases, whether by prolongation of the working hours, by the increase of the work exacted in a given time, or by increased speed of machinery, etc.

Modern Industry has converted the little workshop of the patriarchal master into the great factory of the industrial capitalist. Masses of laborers, crowded into the factory, are organized like soldiers. As privates of the industrial army, they are placed under the command of a perfect hierarchy of officers and sergeants. Not only are they slaves of the bourgeois class, and of the bourgeois state; they are daily and hourly enslaved by the machine, by the overseer, and, above all, in the individual bourgeois manufacturer himself. The more openly this despotism proclaims gain to be its end and aim, the more petty, the more hateful and the more embittering it is.

The less the skill and exertion of strength implied in manual labor, in other words, the more modern industry becomes developed, the more is the labor of men superseded by that of women. Differences of age and sex have no longer any distinctive social validity for the working class. All are instruments of labor, more or less expensive to use, according to their age and sex.

No sooner is the exploitation of the laborer by the manufacturer, so far at an end, that he receives his wages in cash, than he is set upon by the other portion of the bourgeoisie, the landlord, the shopkeeper, the pawnbroker, etc.

The lower strata of the middle class—the small trades people, shopkeepers, and retired tradesmen generally, the handicraftsmen and peasants—all these sink gradually into the proletariat, partly because their diminutive capital does not suffice for the scale on which Modern Industry is carried on, and is swamped in the competition with the large capitalists, partly because their specialized skill is rendered worthless by new methods of production. Thus, the proletariat is recruited from all classes of the population.

The proletariat goes through various stages of development. With its birth begins its struggle with the bourgeoisie. At first, the contest is carried on by individual laborers, then by the work of people of a factory, then by the operative of one trade, in one locality, against the individual bourgeois who directly exploits them. They direct their attacks not against the bourgeois condition of production, but against the instruments of production themselves; they destroy imported wares that compete with their labor, they smash to pieces machinery, they set factories ablaze, they seek to restore by force the vanished status of the workman of the Middle Ages.

At this stage, the laborers still form an incoherent mass scattered over the whole country, and broken up by their mutual competition. If anywhere they unite to form more compact bodies, this is not yet the consequence of their own active union, but of the union of the bourgeoisie, which class, in order to attain its own political ends, is compelled to set the whole proletariat in motion, and is moreover yet, for a time, able to do so. At this stage, therefore, the proletarians do not fight their enemies, but the enemies of their enemies, the remnants of absolute monarchy, the landowners, the non-industrial bourgeois, the petty bourgeois. Thus, the whole historical movement is concentrated in the hands of the bourgeoisie; every victory so obtained is a victory for the bourgeoisie.

But with the development of industry, the proletariat not only increases in number; it becomes concentrated in greater masses, its strength grows, and it feels that strength more. The various interests and conditions of life within the ranks of the proletariat are more and more equalized, in proportion as machinery obliterates all distinctions of labor, and nearly everywhere reduces wages to the same low level. The growing competition among the bourgeois, and the resulting commercial crises, make the wages of the workers ever more fluctuating. The increasing improvement of machinery, ever more rapidly developing, makes their livelihood more and more precarious; the collisions between individual workmen and individual bourgeois take more and more the character of collisions between two classes. Thereupon, the workers begin to form combinations (trade unions) against the bourgeois; they club together in order to keep up the rate of wages; they found permanent associations in order to make provision beforehand for these occasional revolts. Here and there, the contest breaks out into riots.

Now and then the workers are victorious, but only for a time. The real fruit of their battles lie not in the immediate result, but in the ever expanding union of the workers. This union is helped on by the improved means of communication that are created by Modern Industry, and that place the workers of different localities in contact with one another. It was just this contact that was needed to centralize the numerous local struggles, all of the same character, into one national struggle between classes. But every class struggle is a political struggle. And that union, to attain which the burghers of the Middle Ages, with their miserable highways, required centuries, the modern proletarian, thanks to railways, achieve in a few years.

This organization of the proletarians into a class, and, consequently, into a political party, is continually being upset again by the competition between the workers themselves. But it ever rises up again, stronger, firmer, mightier. It compels legislative recognition of particular interests of the workers, by taking advantage of the divisions among the bourgeoisie itself. Thus, the Ten-Hours Bill in England was carried.

Altogether, collisions between the classes of the old society further in many ways the course of development of the proletariat. The bourgeoisie finds itself involved in a constant battle. At first with the aristocracy; later on, with those portions of the bourgeoisie itself, whose interests have become antagonistic to the progress of industry; at all time with the bourgeoisie of foreign countries. In all these battles, it sees itself compelled to appeal to the proletariat, to ask for help, and thus to drag it into the political arena. The bourgeoisie itself, therefore, supplies the proletariat with its own elements of political and general education, in other words, it furnishes the proletariat with weapons for fighting the bourgeoisie.

Further, as we have already seen, entire sections of the ruling class are, by the advance of industry, precipitated into the proletariat, or are at least threatened in their conditions of existence. These also supply the proletariat with fresh elements of enlightenment and progress.

Finally, in times when the class struggle nears the decisive hour, the progress of dissolution going on within the ruling class, in fact within the whole range of old society, assumes such a violent, glaring character, that a small section of the ruling class cuts itself adrift, and joins the revolutionary class, the class that holds the future in its hands. Just as, therefore, at an earlier period, a section of the nobility went over to the bourgeoisie, so now a portion of the bourgeoisie goes over to the proletariat, and in particular, a portion of the bourgeois ideologists, who have raised themselves to the level of comprehending theoretically the historical movement as a whole.

Of all the classes that stand face to face with the bourgeoisie today, the proletariat alone is a genuinely revolutionary class. The other classes decay and finally disappear in the face of Modern Industry; the proletariat is its special and essential product.

The lower middle class, the small manufacturer, the shopkeeper, the artisan, the peasant, all these fight against the bourgeoisie, to save from extinction their existence as fractions of the middle class. They are therefore not revolutionary, but conservative. Nay, more, they are reactionary, for they try to roll back the wheel of history. If, by chance, they are revolutionary, they are only so in view of their impending transfer into the proletariat; they thus defend not their present, but their future interests; they desert their own standpoint to place themselves at that of the proletariat.

The "dangerous class," the social scum, that passively rotting mass thrown off by the lowest layers of the old society, may, here and there, be swept into the movement by a proletarian revolution; its conditions of life, however, prepare it far more for the part of a bribed tool of reactionary intrigue.

In the condition of the proletariat, those of old society at large are already virtually swamped. The proletarian is without property; his relation to his wife and children has no longer anything in common with the bourgeois family relations; modern industry labor, modern subjection to capital, the same in England as in France, in America as in Germany, has stripped him of every trace of national character. Law, morality, religion, are to him so many bourgeois prejudices, behind which lurk in ambush just as many bourgeois interests.

All the preceding classes that got the upper hand sought to fortify their already acquired status by subjecting society at large to their conditions of appropriation. The proletarians cannot become masters of the productive forces of society, except by abolishing their own previous mode of appropriation, and thereby also every other previous mode of appropriation. They have nothing of their own to secure and to fortify; their mission is to destroy all previous securities for, and insurances of, individual property.

All previous historical movements were movements of minorities, or in the interest of minorities. The proletarian movement is the self-conscious, independent movement of the immense majority, in the interest of the immense majority. The proletariat, the lowest stratum of our present society, cannot stir, cannot raise itself up, without the whole super incumbent strata of official society being sprung into the air.

Though not in substance, yet in form, the struggle of the proletariat with the bourgeoisie is at first a national struggle. The proletariat of each country must, of course, first of all settle matters with its own bourgeoisie.

In depicting the most general phases of the development of the proletariat, we traced the more or less veiled civil war, raging within existing society, up to the point where that war breaks out into open revolution, and where the violent overthrow of the bourgeoisie lays the foundation for the sway of the proletariat.

Hitherto, every form of society has been based, as we have already seen, on the antagonism of oppressing and oppressed classes. But in order to oppress a class, certain conditions must be assured to it under which it can, at least, continue its slavish existence. The serf, in the period of serfdom, raised himself to membership in the commune, just as the petty bourgeois, under the yoke of the feudal absolutism, managed to develop into a bourgeois. The modern laborer, on the contrary, instead of rising with the process of industry, sinks deeper and deeper below the conditions of existence of his own class. He becomes a pauper, and pauperism develops more rapidly than population and wealth. And here it becomes evident that the bourgeoisie is unfit any longer to be the ruling class in society, and to impose its conditions of existence upon society as an overriding law. It is unfit to rule because it is incompetent to assure an existence to its slave within his slavery, because it cannot help letting him sink into such a state, that it has to feed him, instead of being fed by him. Society can no longer live under this bourgeoisie, in other words, its existence is no longer compatible with society.

The essential conditions for the existence and for the sway of the bourgeois class is the formation and augmentation of capital; the condition for capital is wage labor. Wage labor rests exclusively on competition between the laborers. The advance of industry, whose involuntary promoter is the bourgeoisie, replaces the isolation of the laborers, due to competition, by the revolutionary combination, due to association. The development of Modern Industry, therefore, cuts from under its feet the very foundation on which the bourgeoisie produces and appropriates products. What the bourgeoisie therefore produces, above all, are its own gravediggers. Its fall and the victory of the proletariat are equally inevitable. . . .

The Communists everywhere support every revolutionary movement against the existing social and political order of things.

In all these movements, they bring to the front, as the leading question in each, the property question, no matter what its degree of development at the time.

Finally, they labor everywhere for the union and agreement of the democratic parties of all countries.

The Communists disdain to conceal their views and aims. They openly declare that their ends can be attained only by the forcible overthrow of all existing social conditions. Let the ruling classes tremble at a communist revolution. The proletarians have nothing to lose but their chains. They have a world to win.

WORKERS OF THE WORLD, UNITE!

Jean-Paul Sartre (1905–1980)

Jean-Paul Sartre, one of the most respected intellectuals in the twentieth century, wrote prolifically; in the course of his writings he critiqued an era (the middle of the century, in all its military struggles and crises of identity) and defined, as clearly as it would ever be defined, that movement called "existentialism," characterized primarily by the thesis that "human nature" is not formed, has no constants, cannot be discussed except as realized in individual human beings. The following selections show him in two of those roles. In "Portrait of an Anti-Semite," Sartre describes the personality that makes racial hatred possible. It had not seemed possible when the first edition of this text came out in 1989, but the kind of hatred he describes—directed, again, at Jews—still haunts our world, spreading its horror not with gas chambers but with terror bombings of civilians. In preparation for dealing with it, we thought it might be useful to include Jean-Paul Sartre's very useful analysis of it, which turns out still to be relevant. In "Existentialism is a Humanism," Sartre gives us a good picture of existentialist belief and tries to put it in the context of Western thought.

Portrait of an Anti-Semite

If a man attributes all or part of his own or the country's misfortunes to the presence of Jewish elements in the French community, if he proposes remedying this state of affairs by depriving the Jews of some of their rights or by expelling or exterminating them, he is then said to hold antisemitic *opinions*.

This word *opinion* gives us food for thought. It is the word which the mistress of the house uses to end a discussion that is becoming too embittered. It suggests that all judgments are of equal value, thus reassuming and giving an inoffensive cast to thoughts by assimilating them to tastes. There are all kinds of tastes in nature, all opinions are permissible; tastes, ideas, opinions must not be discussed. In the name of democratic institutions, in the name of freedom of opinion, the antisemite claims the right to preach his anti-Jewish crusade everywhere. At the same time, used as we are since the Revolution to seeing each object in an analytical spirit, that is as if it were a whole which can be divided into its component parts, we look at people and characters as if they were mosaics, every stone of which coexists with the others without this coexistence affecting its inherent nature. Thus an antisemitic opinion appears like a molecule which can combine with any other set of molecules without changing itself. A man can be a good father and a good husband, a zealous citizen, cultured, philanthropic and an antisemite at the same time. He may like to go fishing and he may like the pleasures of love, he may be tolerant about religion, full of generous ideas about the condition of the natives of Central Africa—and still despise the Jews. If he does not like them, people say, it is because his experience has taught him that they are bad, because statistics have taught him that they are dangerous, because certain historical factors have influenced his judgment. Thus this opinion seems to be the result of external causes and those who want to study it will neglect the antisemite himself and make much of the percentage of Jews mobilized in 1914, of the percentage of Jews who are bankers, industrialists, doctors, lawyers, of the history of the Jews in France. They will succeed in laying before us a strictly objective situation determining a certain current of likewise objective opinion which they will call antisemitism, a chart of which they can draw up or the variations of which they can establish from 1870 to 1944. In this way, antisemitism seems to be both a subjective taste which combines with other tastes to form the person, and an impersonal and social phenomenon which can be expressed by means of statistics and averages, conditioned by economic, historical and political constants.

I do not say that these two concepts are necessarily contradictory. I say that they are dangerous and false. I might, strictly speaking, admit that one might have an "opinion" about the government's wine-growing policy, that is, that one might decide for this or that reason to approve or condemn the free importation of wines from Algeria. But I refuse to call an opinion a doctrine which is expressly directed toward particular persons and which tends to suppress their rights or to exterminate them. The Jew whom the antisemite wants to reach is not a schematic being defined only by his function as in administrative law, or by his position or his acts as in the legal code. He is a Jew, son of a Jew, recognizable by his physical traits, by the color of his hair, by his clothing perhaps, and they say by his character. Antisemitism is not in the category of thoughts protected by the right to freedom of opinion.

Moreover, it is much more than an idea. It is first and foremost a passion. Doubtless it can present itself in the form of a theoretical proposition. The "moderate" antisemite is a polite person who gently remarks: "I don't detest Jews. I simply prefer for such and such a reason that they play a lesser part in the activity of the nation." But a moment later—if you have won his confidence—he will add the following with more abandon: "You see there must be 'something' about the Jews: physically they are irritating to me." This argument, which I have heard a hundred times, is worth examining. First of all it is the result of using logic dictated by passion. For can you imagine someone saying seriously: "There must be something about tomatoes because I can't bear them." . . .

This involvement is not provoked by experience. I have questioned a hundred people about the reasons for their antisemitism. Most of them limit themselves to enumerating the faults which are traditionally attributed to the Jew. "I hate them because they are selfish, intriguing, hard to get rid of, oily, tactless, etc."—"But at least you do go with [know] some Jews?"—"Indeed not!" A painter said to me: "I'm hostile to Jews because, with their critical habit of mind, they encourage our servants to become undisciplined." Here are some more precise experiences. A young actor without talent asserted that the Jews kept him from having a career in the theater by always giving him servile jobs. A young woman said to me: "I've had terrible rows with furriers, they've robbed me, they've burned the furs I entrusted to them. Well, they were all Jews." But why did she choose to hate Jews rather than furriers? Why Jews or furriers rather than such and such a Jew or such and such a furrier? Because she had a predisposition to antisemitism. A classmate of mine at the lycee told me that Jews "irritated" him because of the thousand injustices which "bejewed" social organizations committed in their favor. "A Jew got a scholarship the year I missed it and you're not going to try to make me believe that that fellow whose father came from Krakow or Lemberg understood one of Ronsard's poems or one of Virgil's eclogues better than I." But he admitted the next moment that he disdained the scholarship, that it was all a muddle and that he hadn't prepared for the competition. Thus he had two systems of interpretation to explain his failure, like an insane man who in his delirium pretends to be the King of Hungary but when suddenly put to the test admits that he is a shoemaker. His thinking moves on two planes without the least difficulty. Better still, he will succeed in justifying his past laziness by saying that it would have been too silly to prepare for an examination in which Jews are passed in preference to good Frenchmen. Moreover he was 27th on the final list. There were 26 before him, 12 of whom were accepted and 14 were not. Would he have gotten any further if Jews had been excluded altogether? And even if he had been the first of those who were not accepted, even if by eliminating one of the successful candidates he could have had his chance to be accepted, my classmate had to adopt in advance a certain idea of the Jew, of his nature, of his social role. And in order to be able to decide that among 26 more fortunate contestants it was the

Jew who stole his place, he would apriori have to be the kind of person who runs his life on the basis of emotional reasoning.

It becomes obvious that no external factor can induce antisemitism in the antisemite. It is an attitude totally and freely self-chosen, a global attitude which is adopted not only in regard to Jews but in regard to men in general, to history and society; it is a passion and at the same time a concept of the world. No doubt certain characteristics are more pronounced in such and such an antisemite than in another. But they are always present together and they govern one another. It is this syncretic totality which we must now try to describe.

I stated a few minutes ago that antisemitism presents itself as a passion. Everyone has understood that it is a question of hate or anger. But ordinarily hate and anger are provoked: I hate the person who has made me suffer, the person who scorns or insults me. We have just seen that the antisemitic passion is not of such a nature: it precedes the facts which should arouse it, it seeks them out to feed upon, it must even interpret them in its own way in order to render them really offensive. And yet if you speak of the Jew to an antisemite, he evinces signs of lively irritation. If we remember, moreover, that we must *consent* to anger before it can manifest itself, and that we grow angry, to use the correct expression, we must admit that antisemitism has chosen to exist on the passionate level. It is not unusual to choose an emotional way of life rather than a reasonable one. But ordinarily one loves the *objects* of passion: women, glory, power, money. Since the antisemite has chosen hatred, we are forced to conclude that it is the emotional *state* that he loves. Ordinarily this kind of feeling is not pleasing: he who passionately desires a woman is passionate because of the woman and in spite of passion: one distrusts emotional reasoning which by every means aims at pointing out opinions dictated by love or jealousy or hate; one mistrusts passionate aberrations and that which has been termed monoideism. And this is what the antisemite chooses first of all. But how can one choose to reason falsely? Because one feels the nostalgia of impermeability. The rational man seeks the truth gropingly, he knows that his reasoning is only probable, that other considerations will arise to make it doubtful; he never knows too well where he's going, he is "open," he may even appear hesitant. But there are people who are attracted by the durability of stone. They want to be massive and impenetrable, they do not want to change: where would change lead them? This is an original fear of oneself and a fear of truth. And what frightens them is not the content of truth which they do not even suspect, but the very form of the true—that thing of indefinite approximation. It is as if their very existence were perpetually in suspension. They want to exist all at once and right away. They do not want acquired opinions, they want them to be innate; since they are afraid of reasoning, they want to adopt a mode of life in which reasoning and research play but a subordinate role, in which one never seeks but that which one has already found, in which one never becomes other than what one already was. Only passion can produce this. Nothing but a strong emotional bias can give instant certitude, it alone can hold reasoning within limits, it alone can remain impervious to experience and last an entire lifetime. The antisemite has chosen hate because hate is a religion: he has originally chosen to devaluate words and reasons. Since he then feels at ease, since discussions about the right of the Jew appear futile and empty to him, he has at the outset placed himself on another level. If out of courtesy he consents momentarily to defend his point of view, he lends himself without giving himself; he simply tries to project his intuitive certainty onto the field of speech. . . .

Existentialism is a Humanism

At bottom, what is alarming in the doctrine that I am about to try to explain to you is—is it not? that it confronts man with a possibility of choice. To verify this, let us review the whole question upon the strictly philosophic level. What, then, is this that we call existentialism?

Most of those who are making use of this word would be highly confused if required to explain its meaning. For since it has become fashionable, people cheerfully declare that this musician or that painter is "existentialist." A columnist in Clartes signs himself "The Existentialist," and, indeed, the word is now so loosely applied to so many things that it no longer means anything at all. It would appear that, for the lack of any novel doctrine such as that of surrealism, all those who are eager to join in the latest scandal or movement now seize upon this philosophy in which, however, they can find nothing to their purpose. For in truth this is of all teachings the least scandalous and the most austere: it is intended strictly for technicians and philosophers. All the same, it can easily be defined.

The question is only complicated because there are two kinds of existentialists. There are, on the one hand, the Christians, amongst whom I shall name Jaspers and Gabriel Marcel, both professed Catholics; and on the other the existential atheists, amongst whom we must place Heidegger as well as the French existentialists and myself. What they have in common is simply the fact that they believe that *existence* comes before *essence*—or, if you will, that we must begin from the subjective. What exactly do we mean by that?

If one considers an article of manufacture—as, for example, a book or a paper-knife—one sees that it has been made by an artisan who had a conception of it; and he has paid attention, equally, to the conception of a paper-knife and to the pre-existent technique of production which is a part of that conception and is, at bottom, a formula. Thus the paper-knife is at the same time an article producible in a certain manner and one which, on the other hand, serves a definite purpose, for one cannot suppose that a man would produce a paper-knife without knowing what it was for. Let us say, then, of the paper-knife that its essence—that is to say, the sum of the formulae and the qualities which made its production and its definition possible—precedes its existence. The presence of such-and-such a paper-knife or book is thus determined before my eyes. Here, then, we are viewing the world from a technical standpoint, and we can say that production precedes existence.

When we think of God as the creator, we are thinking of him, most of the time, as a supernal artisan. Whatever doctrine we may be considering, whether it be a doctrine like that of Descartes, or of Leibnitz himself, we always imply that the will follows, more or less, from the understanding or at least accompanies it, so that when God creates he knows precisely what he is creating. Thus, the conception of man in the mind of God is comparable to that of the paper-knife in the mind of the artisan: God makes man according to a procedure and a conception, exactly as the artisan manufactures a paper-knife, following a definition and a formula. Thus each individual man is the realization of a certain conception which dwells in the divine understanding. In the philosophic atheism of the eighteenth century, the notion of God is suppressed, but not, for all that, the idea that essence is prior to existence; something of that idea we still find everywhere, in Diderot, in Voltaire and even in Kant. Man possesses a human nature; that "human nature," which is the conception of human being, is found in every man; which means that each man is a particular example of a universal conception, the conception of Man. In Kant, this universality goes so far that the wild man of the woods, man in the state of nature and the bourgeois are all contained in the same definition and have the same fundamental qualities. Here again, the essence of man precedes that historic existence which we confront in experience.

Atheistic existentialism, of which I am a representative, declares with greater consistency that if God does not exist there is at least one being whose existence comes before its essence, a being which exists before it can be defined by any conception of it. That being is man or, as Heidegger has it, the human reality. What do we mean by saying that existence precedes essence? We mean that man first of all exists, encounters himself, surges up in the world—and defines himself afterwards. If man as the existentialist sees him is not definable, it is because to begin with he is nothing. He will not be anything until later, and then he will be what he makes of himself. Thus, there is no human nature, because there is no God to have a conception of it. Man simply is. Not that he is simply what he conceives himself to be, but he is what he wills, and as he conceives himself after already existing—as he wills to be after that leap towards existence. Man is nothing else but that which he makes of himself. That is the first principle of existentialism. And this is what people call its "subjectivity," using the word as a reproach against us. But what do we mean to say by this, but that man is of a greater dignity than a stone or a table? For we mean to say that man primarily exists—that man is, before all else, something which propels itself towards a future and is aware that it is doing so. Man is, indeed, a project which possesses a subjective life, instead of being a kind of moss, or a fungus or a cauliflower. Before that projection of the self nothing exists; not even in the heaven of intelligence: man will only attain existence when he is what he purposes to be. Not, however, what he may wish to be. For what we usually understand by wishing or willing is a conscious decision taken—much more often than not—after we have made ourselves what we are. I may wish to join a party, to write a book or to marry—but in such a case what is usually called my will is probably a manifestation of a prior and more spontaneous decision. If, however, it is true that existence is prior to essence; man is responsible for what he is. Thus, the first effect of existentialism is that it puts every man in possession of himself as he is, and places the entire responsibility for his existence squarely upon his own shoulders. And, when we say that man is responsible for himself, we do not mean that he is responsible only for his own individuality, but that he is responsible for all men. The word "subjectivism" is to be understood in two senses, and our adversaries play upon only one of them. Subjectivism means, on the one hand, the freedom of the individual subject and, on the other, that man cannot pass beyond human subjectivity. It is the latter which is the deeper meaning of existentialism. When we say that man chooses himself, we do mean that every one of us must choose himself; but by that we also mean that in choosing for himself he chooses for all men. For in effect, of all the actions a man may take in order to create himself as he wills to be, there is not one which is not creative, at the same time, of an image of man such as *he* believes he ought to be. To choose between this or that is at the same time to affirm the value of that which is chosen; for we are unable ever to choose the worse. What we choose is always the better; and nothing can be better for us unless it is better for all. If, moreover, existence precedes essence and we will to exist at the same time as we fashion our image, that image is valid for all and for the entire epoch in which we find ourselves. Our responsibility is thus much greater than we had supposed, for it concerns mankind as a whole. If I am a worker, for instance, I may choose to join a Christian rather than a Communist trade union. And if, by that membership, I choose to signify that resignation is, after all, the attitude that best becomes a man, that man's kingdom is not upon this earth, I do not commit myself alone to that view. Resignation is my will for everyone, and my action is, in consequence, a commitment on behalf of all mankind. Or if, to take a more personal case, I decide to marry and to have children, even though this decision proceeds simply from my situation, from my passion or my desire, I am thereby committing not only myself, but humanity as a whole, to the practice of monogamy. I am thus responsible for myself and for all men, and I am creating a certain image of man as I would have him to be. In fashioning myself I fashion man.

This may enable us to understand what is meant by such terms—perhaps a little grandiloquent—as anguish, abandonment and despair. As you will soon see, it is very simple. First, what do we mean by anguish? The existentialist frankly states that man is in anguish. His meaning is as follows: When a man commits himself to anything, fully realizing that he is not only choosing what he will be, but is thereby at the same time a legislator deciding for the whole of mankind—in such a moment a man cannot escape from the sense of complete and profound responsibility. There are many, indeed, who show no such anxiety. But we affirm that they are merely disguising their anguish or are in flight from it. Certainly, many people think that in what they are doing they commit no one but themselves to anything: and if you ask them, "What would happen if everyone did so?" they shrug their shoulders and reply, "Everyone does not do so." But in truth, one ought always to ask oneself what would happen if everyone did as one is doing; nor can one escape from that disturbing thought except by a kind of self-deception. The man who lies in self-excuse, by saying "Everyone will not do it" must be ill at ease in his conscience, for the act of lying implies the universal value which it denies. By its very disguise his anguish reveals itself. This is the anguish that Kierkegaard called "the anguish of Abraham." You know the story: An angel commanded Abraham to sacrifice his son: and obedience was obligatory, if it really was an angel who had appeared and said, "Thou, Abraham, shalt sacrifice thy son." But anyone in such a case would wonder, first, whether it was indeed an angel and secondly, whether I am really Abraham. Where are the proofs? A certain mad woman who suffered from hallucinations said that people were telephoning to her, and giving her orders. The doctor asked, "But who is it that speaks to you?" She replied: "He says it is God." And what, indeed, could prove to her that it was God? If an angel appears to me, what is the proof that it is an angel; or, if I hear voices, who can prove that they proceed from heaven and not from hell, or from my own subconscious or some pathological condition? Who can prove that they are really addressed to me?

Who, then, can prove that I am the proper person to impose, by my own choice, my conception of man upon mankind? I shall never find any proof whatever; there will be no sign to convince me of it. If a voice speaks to me, it is still I myself who must decide whether the voice is or is not that of an angel. If I regard a certain course of action as good, it is only I who choose to say that it is good and not bad. There is nothing to show that I am Abraham: nevertheless I also am obliged at every instant to perform actions which are examples. Everything happens to every man as though the whole human race had its eyes fixed upon what he is doing and regulated its conduct accordingly. So every man ought to say, "Am I really a man who has the right to act in such a manner that humanity regulates itself by what I do?" If a man does not say that, he is dissembling his anguish. Clearly, the anguish with which we are concerned here is not one that could lead to quietism or inaction. It is anguish pure and simple, of the kind well known to all those who have borne responsibilities. When, for instance, a military leader takes upon himself the responsibility for an attack and sends a number of men to their death, he chooses to do it and at bottom he alone chooses. No doubt he acts under a higher command, but its orders, which are more general, require interpretation by him and upon that interpretation depends the life of ten, fourteen or twenty men. In making the decision, he cannot but feel a certain anguish. All leaders know that anguish. It does not prevent their acting, on the contrary it is the very condition of their action, for the action presupposes that there is a plurality of possibilities, and in choosing one of these, they realize that it has value only because it is chosen. Now it is anguish of that kind which existentialism describes, and moreover, as we shall see, makes explicit through direct responsibility towards other men who are concerned. Far from being a screen which could separate us from action, it is a condition of action itself.

And when we speak of "abandonment"—a favorite word of Heidegger—we only mean to say that God does not exist, and that it is necessary to draw the consequences of his absence right to the end. The existentialist is strongly opposed to a certain type of secular moralism which seeks to suppress God at the least possible expense. Towards 1880, when the French professors endeavored to formulate a secular morality, they said something like this:—God is a useless and costly hypothesis, so we will do without it. However, if we are to have morality, a society and a law-abiding world, it is essential that certain values should be taken seriously; they must have an *a priori* existence ascribed to them. It must be considered obligatory *a priori* to be honest, not to lie, not to beat one's wife, to bring up children and so forth; so we are going to do a little work on this subject, which will enable us to show that these values exist all the same, inscribed in an intelligible heaven although, of course, there is no God. In other words—and this is, I believe, the purport of all that we in France call radicalism—nothing will be changed if God does not exist; we shall rediscover the same norms of honesty, progress and humanity, and we shall have disposed of God as an out-of-date hypothesis which will die away quietly of itself. The existentialist, on the contrary, finds it extremely embarrassing that God does not exist, for there disappears with Him all possibility of finding values in an intelligible heaven. There can no longer be any good *a priori*, since there is no infinite and perfect consciousness to think it. It is nowhere written that "the good" exists, that one must be honest or must not lie, since we are now upon the plane where there are only men. Dostoevsky once wrote "If God did not exist, everything would be permitted"; and that, for existentialism, is the starting point. Everything is indeed permitted if God does not exist, and man is in consequence forlorn, for he cannot find anything to depend upon either within or outside himself. He discovers forthwith, that he is without excuse. For if indeed existence precedes essence, one will never be able to explain one's action by reference to a given and specific human nature; in other words, there is no determinism—man is free, man *is* freedom. Nor, on the other hand, if God does not exist, are we provided with any values or commands that could legitimize our behavior. Thus we have neither behind us, nor before us in a luminous realm of values, any means of justification or excuse. We are left alone, without excuse. That is what I mean when I say that man is condemned to be free. Condemned, because he did not create himself, yet is nevertheless at liberty, and from the moment that he is thrown into this world he is responsible for everything he does. The existentialist does not believe in the power of passion. He will never regard a grand passion as a destructive torrent upon which a man is swept into certain actions as by fate, and which, therefore, is an excuse for them. He thinks that man is responsible for his passion. Neither will an existentialist think that a man can find help through some sign being vouchsafed upon earth for his orientation: for he thinks that the man himself interprets the sign as he chooses. He thinks that every man, without any support or help whatever, is condemned at every instant to invent man. As Ponge has written in a very fine article, "Man is the future of man." That is exactly true. Only, if one took this to mean that the future is laid up in Heaven, that God knows what it is, it would be false, for then it would no longer even be a future. If, however, it means that, whatever man may now appear to be, there is a future to be fashioned, a virgin future that awaits him—then it is a true saying. But in the present one is forsaken.

As an example by which you may the better understand this state of abandonment, I will refer to the case of a pupil of mine, who sought me out in the following circumstances. His father was quarrelling with his mother and was also inclined to be a "collaborator"; his elder brother had been killed in the German offensive of 1940 and this young man, with a sentiment somewhat primitive but generous, burned to avenge him. His mother was living alone with him, deeply afflicted by the semi-treason of his father and by the death of her eldest son, and her one consolation was in this young man. But he, at this moment, had the choice between going to England to join the Free French Forces or of staying near his mother and helping her to live. He fully realized that this woman lived only for him and that his disappearance—or perhaps his death—would plunge her into despair. He also realized that, concretely and in fact, every action he performed on his mother's behalf would be sure of effect in the sense of aiding her to live, whereas anything he did in order to go and fight would be an ambiguous action which might vanish like water into sand and serve no purpose. For instance, to set out for England he would have to wait indefinitely in a Spanish camp on the way through Spain; or, on arriving in England or in Algiers he might be put into an office to fill up forms. Consequently, he found himself confronted by two very different modes of action; the one concrete, immediate, but directed towards only one individual; and the other an action addressed to an end infinitely greater, a national collectivity, but for that very reason ambiguous—and it might be frustrated on the way. At the same time, he was hesitating between two kinds of morality; on the one side the morality of sympathy, of personal devotion and, on the other side, a morality of wider scope but of more debatable validity. He had to choose between those two. What could help him to choose? Could the Christian doctrine? No. Christian doctrine says: Act with charity, love your neighbor, deny yourself for others, choose the way which is hardest, and so forth. But which is the harder road? To whom does one owe the more brotherly love, the patriot or the mother? Which is the more useful aim, the general one of fighting in and for the whole community, or the precise aim of helping one particular person to live? Who can give an answer to that *a priori*? No one. Nor is it given in any ethical scripture. The Kantian ethic says, Never regard another as a means, but always as an end. Very well; if I remain with my mother, I shall be regarding her as the end and not as a means: but by the same token I am in danger of treating as means those who are fighting on my behalf; and the converse is also true, that if I go to the aid of the combatants I shall be treating them as the end at the risk of treating my mother as a means.

If values are uncertain, if they are still too abstract to determine the particular, concrete case under consideration, nothing remains but to trust in our instincts. That is what this young man tried to do; and when I saw him he said, "In the end, it is feeling that counts; the direction in which it is really pushing me is the one I ought to choose. If I feel that I love my mother enough to sacrifice everything else for her—my will to be avenged, all my longings for action and adventure—then I stay with her. If, on the contrary, I feel that my love for her is not enough, I go." But how does one estimate the strength of a feeling? The value of his feeling for his mother was determined precisely by the fact that he was standing by her. I may say that I love a certain friend enough to sacrifice such or such a sum of money, for him, but I cannot prove that unless I have done it. I may say, "I love my mother enough to remain with her," if actually I have remained with her. I can only estimate the strength of this affection if I have performed an action by which it is defined and ratified. But if I then appeal to this affection to justify my action, I find myself drawn into a vicious circle.

Moreover, as Gide has very well said, a sentiment which is play-acting and one which is vital are two things that are hardly distinguishable one from another. To decide that I love my mother by staying beside her, and to play a comedy the upshot of which is that I do so—these are nearly the same thing. In other words, feeling is formed by the deeds that one does; therefore I cannot consult it as a guide to action. And that is to say that I can neither seek within myself for an authentic impulse to action, nor can I expect, from some ethic, formulae that will enable me to act. You may say that the youth did, at least, go to a professor to ask for advice. But if you seek counsel—from a priest, for example you have selected that priest; and at bottom you already knew, more or less, what he would advise. In other words, to choose an adviser is nevertheless to commit oneself by that choice. If you are a Christian, you will say, Consult a priest; but there are collaborationists, priests who are resisters and priests who wait for the tide to turn: which will you choose? Had this young man chosen a priest of the resistance, or one of the collaboration, he would have decided beforehand the kind of advice he was to receive. Similarly, in coming to me, he knew what advice I should give him, and I had but one reply to make. You are free, therefore choose—that is to say, invent. No rule of general morality can show you what you ought to do: no signs are vouchsafed in this world. The Catholics will reply, "Oh, but they are!" Very well; still, it is I myself, in every case, who have to interpret the signs. While I was imprisoned, I made the acquaintance of a somewhat remarkable man, a Jesuit, who had become a member of that order in the following manner. In his life he had suffered a succession of rather severe setbacks. His father had died when he was a child, leaving him in poverty, and he had been awarded a free scholarship in a religious institution, where he had been made continually to feel that he was accepted for charity's sake, and, in consequence, he had been denied several of those distinctions and honors which gratify children. Later, about the age of eighteen, he came to grief in a sentimental affair; and finally, at twenty-two—this was a trifle in itself, but it was the last drop that overflowed his cup—he failed in his military examination. This young man, then, could regard himself as a total failure: it was a sign—but a sign of what? He might have taken refuge in bitterness or despair. But he took it—very cleverly for him—as a sign that he was not intended for secular successes, and that only the attainments of religion, those of sanctity and of faith, were accessible to him. He interpreted his record as a message from God, and became a member of the Order. Who can doubt but that this decision as to the meaning of the sign was his, and his alone? One could have drawn quite different conclusions from such a series of reverses—as, for example, that he had better become a carpenter or a revolutionary. For the decipherment of the sign, however, he bears the entire responsibility. That is what "abandonment" implies, that we ourselves decide our being. And with this abandonment goes anguish. . . .

Feminist Ethics

The story of the rise of "feminism" in the United States is well known, and the story of the worldwide struggle for equal rights for women commands the headlines on a daily basis. This struggle is, with respect, of no philosophical interest. It is a political story, whose philosophical origins were established long ago, in Aristotle, in Thomas Aquinas, in John Locke and in Thomas Jefferson. (To remind yourself of those origins, leaf back in this volume to the summary of them submitted by Dr. Martin Luther King Jr. to his fellow clergy in Birmingham, Alabama, from his jail cell in that city; the ethical foundations of the Civil Rights movement also undergird the movement for the equality of women.) But in the course of the political movement, two new and interesting intellectual themes emerged, apart from the slow but inevitably successful struggle for legal and economic equality. One of them was psychological, an argument (championed early by Betty Friedan in The Feminine Mystique*) that in the male-dominated culture of the United States, women had assumed psychological and social attitudes which were false to their experience—they were suffering from what Marx would call "false consciousness," a belief that they were what they were not, and therefore that they did not have potential that they did. We will have no time to explore that theme, although its social consequences are still unfolding. The other was a frontal attack (eventually) on the very ruling values of Western philosophy, and that theme we cannot ignore.*

It started with Lawrence Kohlberg, a developmental psychologist who articulated what he took to be the "normal progression" of moral stages through the life cycle of the human being. For Kohlberg, the child who operates only at the level of fear and greed turns into the adolescent who derives all moral direction from the group and its rules, then becomes the adult who reasons like J. S. Mill in his ordinary moments but like Immanuel Kant, from the lofty perspective of autonomy and justice, at his best. Above all the adult learns to transcend all particular attachments, all emotions of love or loyalty, to become perfectly objective in judgment.

Carol Gilligan, carrying on research under his direction, noticed something wrong with the progression. Like, women didn't fit the pattern. Women retained particular loyalties to family and friends in spite of objectivity and quite without the necessity of appeal to "fiduciary relationships" (see Chapter 3, "The 'Lectric law Library's Legal Lexicon on Fiduciary/Fiduciary Duty"). They thought that individuals were more important than abstractions, relationships more important than rules, and caring more important than judging. (The change in perspective reminds us of the Confucian orientation to duties and obligations—first the family, those close to us, and these relationships shall serve as a model for all others.) Gilligan started wondering if our whole system of ethics was systematically biased toward a masculine interpretation of the social world, and eventually collected a series of studies of women's views of morality (Gilligan, In a Different Voice*, 1982). From her insights a literature has evolved, placing caring and relationship in the central position accorded autonomy and rationality by Kant. Rita Manning's article is a brief sample of that literature.*

From Rita Manning, *Just Caring*

An ethic of caring, as I shall defend it, includes two elements. First is a disposition to care. This is a willingness to receive others, a willingness to give the lucid attention to the needs of others which filling these needs appropriately requires. I see this disposition to care as nourished by a spiritual awareness similar to the awareness argued for by proponents of the women's spirituality movement. As Starhawk describes this awareness: "Immanent justice rests on the first principle of magic: all things are interconnected. All is relationship. Perhaps the ultimate ethic of immanence is to choose to make that relationship one of love . . . love for all the eternally self-creating world, love of the light and the mysterious darkness, and raging love against all that would diminish the unspeakable beauty of the world."

In addition to being sensitive to my place in the world and to my general obligation to be a caring person, I am also obligated to care for. (I am following Noddings in using "care for" to indicate caring as expressed in action.) In the paradigm case, caring for involves acting in some appropriate way to respond to the needs of persons, and animals, but can also be extended to responding to the needs of communities, values, or objects. My obligation to care for is limited by a principle of supererogation, which is necessary to keep an ethic of caring from degenerating into an ethics of total self-sacrifice. I shall argue that we are obligated to adopt this model of caring as far as we can in our moral deliberations. We are morally permitted and sometimes morally obliged to appeal to rules and rights. In Gilligan's idiom, we are required to listen to the voices of both care and justice. In what follows, I shall first fill in some of the details of this model. Specifically, I shall discuss what it is to care for someone or something and when we are obligated to care for. Next, I shall say something about the role of rules and rights in this model.

Caring

I have often wondered if taking a class in moral philosophy was the best way for students to become sensitive to moral concerns. It seemed to me that a better way would be to have students work in soup kitchens or shelters for the homeless. I am convinced that taking care of my children has made me more open to moral concerns. In taking care of the hungry, homeless, and helpless, we are engaged in caring for. In the standard case, caring for is immediate; it admits of no surrogates. When I directly care for some creature, I am in physical contact. Our eyes meet, our hands touch. Not every need can be met in this immediate way. In that case, I must accept a surrogate. Not every need can be met by individual action. In those cases, I must seek collective action. But when I can do the caring for myself, I ought to do so, at least some of the time. The need of the other may sometimes require that I do the caring for. If my child needs my attention, I cannot meet this need by sending her to a therapist. Even when the needs of the other do not require my personal attention, I must provide some of the caring for directly in order to develop and sustain my ability to care.

My day-to-day interactions with other persons create a web of reciprocal caring. In these interactions, I am obliged to be a caring person. I am free, to a certain extent, to choose when and how to care for these others. My choice is limited by my relationships with these others and by their needs. A pressing need calls up an immediate obligation to care for; roles and responsibilities call up an obligation to respond in a caring manner. In the first case, I am obligated (though this obligation can be limited by a principle of supererogation) to respond; in the second, I can choose, within limits, when and how to care.

A creature in need who is unable to meet this need without help calls for a caring response on my part. This response needn't always be direct. Sometimes it is better to organize a political response. (Many, for example, who are confronted on the street by homeless people are unsure about how to respond, convinced that their immediate response will not be enough, might even be counterproductive.) Certain relationships obligate me to provide direct caring for. When my daughter falls and asks me to "kiss it and make it better," I can't send her to my neighbor for the kiss.

My roles as mother, as teacher, as volunteer, put me in particular relationships to others. These roles require and sustain caring. My obligation to my infant children and my animals is to meet their basic needs for physical sustenance (food, shelter, clothing, health care) and for companionship and love. My obligation to my students is grounded on my roles as teacher and philosopher and their psychological needs to discover who they are and how they can live with integrity. Here I feel a connection with my students but also with teaching and philosophy. But if one of my students comes to me needing another kind of care, I may be obligated to provide it, though I may not be obligated to do so singlehandedly. My response depends on my ability to care for, my obligation to care for myself, and my sense of the appropriateness of the need and the best way to meet it.

In discharging obligations to care for that are based on role responsibility, I am conscious of my need to fill those roles conscientiously. The role of teacher, for example, requires a certain impartiality; the role of mother requires a fierce devotion to each particular child. But I am free, to a certain extent, to choose my roles. In adopting or reshaping roles, I should be sensitive to my need to be cared for as well as my capacity to care. In critiquing socially designed and assigned roles, we should aim for roles and divisions of roles that make caring more likely to occur.

Caring for can involve a measure of self-sacrifice. The rescuers of Jessica McClure who went without sleep for days, the parents of an infant who go without uninterrupted sleep for months, are involved in caring for. Caring for involves an openness to the one cared for. Caring for requires that I see the real need and that I satisfy it insofar as I am able. In satisfying it, I am sensitive not just to the need but to the feelings of those in need.

Caring for does not require that I feel any particular emotion toward the one cared for, but that I am open to the possibility that some emotional attachment may form in the caring for. Nor does it require that I have an ongoing relationship with the one cared for. I may meet the one cared for as stranger, though the caring for will change that.

Obviously, a model of caring along the lines I am defending must include an account of needs. I cannot offer a complete account here, but I would draw heavily from the biology, psychology, and other relevant social sciences in constructing such an account; there would be an essentially normative component as well. I want to begin by drawing a distinction between what I call subsistence needs and psychological needs. Subsistence needs will usually be needs that must be filled if physical existence is to continue. Psychological needs are needs that must be filled if human flourishing is to occur. Filling subsistence needs does not automatically benefit both the carer and the cared for. Rather, the carer is likely to feel burdened by filling such needs, though the recognition that one has filled such needs often creates a sense of virtue in the carer. I am reminded here of the ferocious demands for food that infants make on their parents with astonishing regularity. Filling psychological needs can often be more fulfilling. It is more likely to be done in a reciprocal relationship and in such a relationship filling psychological needs requires that both parties share the roles of carer and cared for. I needn't respond to every need. In choosing how and when to respond, I should consider the seriousness of the need, the benefit to the one needing care of filling this particular need, and the competing needs of others, including myself, that will be affected by my filling this particular need.

Objects of Care

I can care for persons, animals, values, institutions, and objects. My choice of objects of caring about should reflect my own need to be cared for and my capacity to care. But decisions about what to care for should not depend exclusively on my own needs and capacities. I should also be sensitive to the needs that summon the obligation to care for. If I understand my obligation to care for as following from the existence of need and helplessness, I should care for institutions, values, and practices that would diminish such needs. One might argue that we could virtually eliminate the need to care for by creating such institutions, values, and practices and hence undermine our capacity to care. But even in a perfectly just world, children would need care and people and animals would get sick. Furthermore, human needs include more than needs for physical sustenance. Human needs for companionship and intimacy would exist even in a world free from the horrors of war, homelessness, sickness, and disease.

Defense of a General Obligation to Care

The obligation to respond as carer when appropriate can be defended on three grounds. The first is the need. Here I would appeal to Peter Singer's principle, "if it is in our power to prevent something very bad happening without thereby sacrificing anything of comparable moral significance, we ought to do it."

The second is the recognition that human relationships require a continuous kind of caring. This caring involves three components: being receptive to the other, being accepting of the other, and being on-call for the other when s/he is in need. Unless we want to do away with human relationships, we must be open to the demands of caring that such relationships require. But caring in human relationships is, as human relationships are, reciprocal.

The third defense is that I cannot develop and sustain my ability to care unless I do some active caring. This is an empirical claim and we must look both to social science and to our own experience in evaluating it, but there is an obvious way in which caring for enhances our ability to care. When I make the real attempt to care for, I must understand the needs of the one cared for. I must also see how that one wants the needs to be addressed. This ability to notice needs and wants, to empathize as well as sympathize is developed through caring. Of course, one might ask why one should want to develop this capacity to care. It seems to me that the right response is to point out that human lives devoid of caring impulses and responses would be nasty, brutish, short, and lonely.

Limitation on Obligations to Care

I don't think that we are obligated to be like Mother Teresa. Mother Teresa care[d] for continuously. We can limit our obligation to care for by focusing on the defenses of this obligation. First, I have a *prima facie* obligation to care for when I come across a creature in need who is unable to meet that need without help, when my caring is called on as a part of a reciprocal relationship, or when indicated as part of my role responsibility. My actual obligation rests on the seriousness of the need, my assessment of the appropriateness of filling the need, and my ability to do something about filling it. But I must also recognize that I am a person who must be cared for and that I must recognize and respond to my own need to be cared for. The continuous caring for required to respond to needs for physical sustenance is, for most of us, incompatible with caring for ourselves. But not all caring for involves responding to physical needs. The caring for required to sustain relationships, which is usually reciprocal, can be a source of great strength to the person doing the caring for. Finally, allowing myself to suffer caring burnout also diminishes my ability to care for others in the future. I don't mean to argue that caring for requires no sacrifice. Indeed, where the need is great and my ability to meet it sufficient, I am required to sacrifice. But I am not required to adopt this as a form of life.

My obligation to care for is not an all-or-nothing thing. Being unable to care for now does not eliminate the possibility that I may be obligated to meet this need later. This is a general point about obligations. I might owe someone money and be unable to pay it back now, through no fault of my own. If I later come into a windfall, I am obligated to pay the money back then. In addition, there is no one right way to care for. My assessment of the appropriateness of the need, my ability to meet the need, and my sense of the most successful way of doing so provide some guidance here. Perhaps immediate caring for is the best way to meet a need in one case, and cooperative political activity the most successful way of meeting other needs. I would want to leave these kinds of choices up to the agent.

Rules and Rights

In my model, rules and rights serve three purposes. They can be used to persuade, to sketch a moral minimum below which no one should fall and beyond which behavior is condemned, and they can be used to deliberate in some cases.

My attention to rules and rights here does not reflect my unwillingness to make appeals to virtues and practices. I think it is fair to describe caring as a virtue. I do include other virtues and practices as fulfilling each of the three functions that rules and rights play in my model. We certainly can and do persuade by reminding others of virtues: "Would an honest man do that?" We likewise persuade by pointing to practices: "Native Americans don't have that kind of an attitude about the earth." Virtues and practices can serve as minimums: "I can see that you won't be doing me any favors, but at least give me the courtesy of an honest reply."

We don't live in a caring world. By that I mean that not everyone recognizes his or her obligation to care. Our society does not encourage the flourishing of this capacity, but undermines it in various ways. In a world infamous for its lack of caring, we need tools of persuasion to protect the helpless. This is one of the roles that rules and rights fill. We can reason in the language of rules with those who lack a sufficient degree of caring. If their natural sympathies are not engaged by the presence of suffering, we can attempt to appeal to reason: "How would you feel if you were in their place?" "What would be the consequences of such behavior on a large scale?" I am not convinced of the effect of such persuasion, and it is, I think, an empirical question whether such appeals would persuade where caring did not, but I suspect that such socially agreed on minimums could serve as persuasive appeals.

Rules and rights provide a minimum below which no one should fall and beyond which behavior is morally condemned. Rules provide a minimum standard for morality. Rights provide a measure of protection for the helpless. But on this level of moral discourse, morality is, like politics, the art of the possible. In the face of largescale selfishness and inattention, perhaps the best we can hope for is a minimum below which no one should fall and beyond which behavior is roundly condemned. But we shouldn't fool ourselves into thinking that staying above this minimum is a sufficient condition for being a morally decent person. I don't want to deny the importance of these socially agreed on minimums; in a less than perfect world, they provide some real protection. They are not, in principle, incompatible with caring but can, I think, encourage caring. Much caring requires collective action and without a shared sense of moral minimums it will be difficult to organize such collective action.

Elizabeth Wolgast, in *The Grammar of Justice*, argues against the claim that treating patients in a moral fashion is entirely a matter of respecting their rights. She points out that patients are often sick and in need of caring for. In this situation, she argues, we want doctors and other health-care workers to care for the patient. This involves far more than respecting rights. One could talk, I suppose, about a patient's right to be cared for, but as Wolgast points out, rights talk suggests a minimum below which the doctor should not fall, and in this case, we are less interested in the minimum than in the maximum. We want all our moral citizens to be open to the obligation to care for.

Rules and rights can also be used to deliberate under some conditions. Often we don't need to appeal to rules in deciding whom to care for and how to care for them. A creature's need and our ability to meet it identifies it as a candidate for caring for. We decide how to care for by appeal to the need, the strategies for meeting it, and the desires of the one in need about how best to meet the need. But when

I am not in direct contact with the objects of care, my actions cannot be guided by the expressed and observed desires of those cared for, and hence I might want to appeal to rules. In these cases, I must make assumptions about their desires. I shall assume that they do not wish to fall below some minimum. Rules that provide a minimum standard for acceptable behavior ought to be sensitive to the general desires and aims of creatures, so I may take these into account. I am also free to appeal to my needs for care and on that basis decide that I do not wish to violate some socially approved minimum standard of behavior. I can also appeal to rules and rights when care must be allocated. For example, in a hospital emergency room we must make sure that the needs of the first accident victim of the night do not cause us to ignore the later victims. Finally, since rules and rights can express a consensus about morally acceptable behavior, I should be sensitive to the expectations generated in the one cared for by the public recognition of such roles and rights. For example, suppose I want to make sure that my family and friends are happy and involved in the wedding of my son. I might be tempted to ignore the rules of etiquette in making sure that my guests are uniquely provided for. But if the mother of the bride feels slighted because I didn't treat her the way she expected to be treated (i.e., as the etiquette rules say you should treat the mother of the bride), then I haven't really responded to her in a caring manner.

One might argue here that meeting some expressed needs might violate the moral minimums in our society. I am willing to grant that this can happen. If it does, we must remember that the rules do not have a life of their own, but are guides. They help us to formulate a caring response because they speak to us of what most of us would want as a caring response in a similar situation. If the one needing care does not want the response suggested by the appropriate rule, we should listen to them very carefully and be willing to ignore the rule. For example, suppose someone wanted us to help him/her commit suicide. I suspect that ideally we could and should settle this kind of a case without appealing to rules. Instead, we should appeal to the facts of the case. Is the person terminally ill or merely depressed? These conditions require different remedies. In the first case, one might be doing the right thing to aid in the suicide. Here, one must count the cost to oneself, as well as the needs and desires of the one cared for. In the second case, we appeal beyond the expressed needs to the unexpressed needs. This person probably needs some other care. Here, we make every attempt to listen to this person, to understand his or her pain, but we also remind ourselves that suicide is the final option for dealing with pain. We make this decision, not by appeal to a rule, but by reminding ourselves of the times when we or someone we know came close to suicide. We remember how it felt and how it was resolved.

In some cases, though, I cannot respond as one caring. As I approach caring burnout, I can then appeal to rules and rights. I do not want my behavior to fall below some minimum standard, nor do I want the one in need of care to fall below some moral minimum.

In the ideal caring society with sufficient resources to meet needs and to provide for some sort of flourishing, each of us would spend roughly the same amount of time being cared for. We would experience this as children and as adults. Hence, we would be surrounded by a nexus of caring. We would be persons who cared for and were supported by a history of being cared for. We would be free, to some extent, to choose whom to care for because there would be others to provide for needs and for flourishing. We would not be totally free, because social roles would commit us to some responsibilities to care. It's not clear that rules and rights would play a very big part in this world, but this is certainly not the world in which we live.

The people in our world differ in their ability and their willingness to care for others. Since I am both a creature who can care and a creature who needs care, I would, if I were committed to caring, be faced with enormous needs for care while sometimes suffering from a lack of caring for myself. This is true even if we grant that the kind of caring (in particular, psychological caring) involved in reciprocal relationships sustains all parties in the relationship. But since such relationships don't come easily and naturally, I would have to spend some time and energy establishing a nexus of care to support myself. In creating and maintaining this nexus of care, I would be developing bonds and responsibilities of care.

But spending much of one's time getting one's own needs for care satisfied leaves little time for caring for others. At the same time, everyone else is in much the same boat. And the gross inequality in the distribution of resources means that many slip between the caring cracks and into dire need. This puts the caring person in a bind. Real need presents itself to a person who is often running a caring deficit of his or her own. Caring burnout results. The only way to effectively reduce caring burnout is to change cultural and social institutions toward a model of caring. This it not the path that our culture has taken. Instead we career from me-firstisms to paroxysms of guilt about the tremendous needs that have resulted. We make renewed commitments to care which are rejected as softheaded a generation later.

What are caring persons to do? Caring persons should try to respond to need by caring for, but they must pay attention to their own needs for care. They must navigate through an uncaring world without falling into total caring burnout. They should work for institutions, cultures, and practices that would reduce subsistence needs by redistributing resources and increasing the supply of caretakers, and they should encourage social change toward a culture of reciprocity in meeting psychological needs. But while struggling in our pre-caring world, caring persons are not obligated to care until they slip into caring burnout. This denies their own status as persons who deserve care and is counterproductive. It diminishes, in the long run, the amount of care they can provide. As they approach caring burnout, they should refill their care tanks by taking care of their own needs. During this period of renewal, they are still required to respect the moral minimums represented by rules and rights.

I haven't talked about what the rules and rights should be. In drafting a set of rules and rights, I should be sensitive to two considerations. The first is that rules and rights provide a moral minimum. The second is that rules and rights reflect a consensus about moral minimums. In this sense, morality is the art of the possible.

The morally preferred way to live is to appeal to caring. This suggests that rules and rights should reflect a sense of what counts as need, and a conception of flourishing, and a recognition of what would usually be accepted, by the ones cared for, as appropriate ways of responding to need and providing for flourishing. Notions of need and flourishing ought to be sensitive to empirical considerations about human nature, interaction, social organization, and so on, but they also have an irreducibly normative component. A defense of rules and rights would need to defend this normative component. We would also want rules and rights that would provide a climate for moral growth toward a caring society.

Rules and rights do play an important role in my ethics of caring, but we shouldn't forget that our primary responsibility is to care for. If this means that we are often unsure about just what to do, then we must live with this uncertainty. Discovering what to do requires that we listen carefully to the ones cared for. We should also recognize that it is often painful to be confronted by those in need, and even by those whom we could enrich. Appealing to rules provides a measure of security for ourselves, but we shouldn't allow it to distance us from the objects of care.

Environmentalism

Much of the history of the human race to this point, to paraphrase Marx, is the history of the exploitation and destruction of the natural world. In the foraging phase of our existence—about 40,000 years of the 50,000 that human beings just like us have been around—we destroyed nothing. We moved constantly and ate only what was immediately available, produced by Nature as a surplus, built fires with dead branches fallen from trees, and left no footprint on the earth at all. Of course we also developed no culture—no art, no traditions, no preserved language, no buildings, nothing at all. Not until we settled down did we start accumulating material goods and creating a recognizable human life.

When agriculture began, about 10,000 years ago, the troubles for the environment began. Once the Fertile Crescent was fertile; now it is desert. Once the Red Sea was lined with bustling ports, and you could ride across North Africa from Tunisia to Alexandria in the shade. Now they are desert. There was a change in the pattern of rainfall, yes; but did that change, for reasons unknown, turn forest and field into desert and destroy all human enterprise in those regions? Or was it the progressive deforestation, the removal of all the ancient forests, tree by tree, over several thousand years, that changed the climate? Wherever humans thrived in that ancient world is desert now. The exhaustion of the soil and the collapse of civilizations have gone hand in hand for most of our existence; not until the present century have we begun to think we could do something about it.

The environmental movement is primarily a phenomenon of the developed world. Only after survival is taken care of do we begin to think of preserving the natural world for non-survival purposes. The first tracts of nature preserved from exploitation anywhere were the forest reserves of the priests and the hunting lands of the nobility. Here in the United States, focus of Ethics in America concern, the environmental movement began in the same way, as wealthy hunters on the East Coast moved to put their hunting grounds under protection in the 1870s. (That is one reason why there is land to argue about today.) Through the twentieth century the movement enlisted scholars, biologists, bureaucrats, and the occasional President, to set up National Parks, National Forests, and eventually National Wilderness Areas.

All this was done before Rachel Carson published Silent Spring in 1962. The book, a careful tracking of the way in which pesticides were infiltrating the food chain and poisoning the birds, galvanized the nation. Suddenly nature was vulnerable. Suddenly we had to learn about watersheds, habitats, ecosystems, food chains and global warming. The transformation was profound, and the sequelae, through the activist 1960s, culminated in a national celebration of the natural world, Earth Day, April 22, 1970. Congress responded to the national mandate with legislation protecting our air, water, and coastlands; the political battle to protect the natural environment has been going on ever since. Like the political battle over equal rights, we leave this subject for a more appropriate work. But the environmental movement raised one question crucial for the way we do our ethics, and that we have to consider.

Are we the only beings worth valuing? Every author to this point in this volume has assumed that we are. They may have disagreed about what was worth valuing in us— our autonomy, our rationality, our happiness—but it's always been about us, not anything else. We have always been aware of "primitive" religions that gave Nature a value independent of human beings (see the selection by "Eagle Man,"), but the possibility of assigning independent value to the natural environment has not occurred to us. Yet the possibility has been around for awhile. The selection that follows is from Aldo Leopold, sometime naturalist, government hunter, professor of biology, whose modest little book, A Sand County Almanac, remains one of the best statements of the environmental perspective.

Aldo Leopold (1887–1948)

From Aldo Leopold, *Selections from A Sand County Almanac*

The Land Ethic

When god-like Odysseus returned from the wars in Troy, he hanged all on one rope a dozen slave-girls of his household whom he suspected of misbehavior during his absence.

This hanging involved no question of propriety. The girls were property. The disposal of property was then, as now, a matter of expediency, not of right and wrong.

Concepts of right and wrong were not lacking from Odysseus' Greece: witness the fidelity of his wife through the long years before at last his black-prowed galleys clove the wine-dark seas for home. The ethical structure of that day covered wives, but had not yet been extended to human chattels. During the three thousand years which have since elapsed, ethical criteria have been extended to many fields of conduct, with corresponding shrinkages in those judged by expediency only.

The Ethical Sequence

This extension of ethics, so far studied only by philosophers, is actually a process in ecological evolution. Its sequences may be described in ecological as well as in philosophical terms. An ethic, ecologically, is a limitation on freedom of action in the struggle for existence. An ethic, philosophically, is a differentiation of social from anti-social conduct. These are two definitions of one thing. The thing has its origin in the tendency of interdependent individuals or groups to evolve modes of co-operation. The ecologist calls these symbioses. Politics and economics are advanced symbioses in which the original free-for-all competition has been replaced, in part, by co-operative mechanisms with an ethical content.

The complexity of co-operative mechanisms has increased with population density, and with the efficiency of tools. It was simpler, for example, to define the anti-social uses of sticks and stones in the days of the mastodons than of bullets and billboards in the age of motors.

The first ethics dealt with the relation between individuals; the Mosaic Decalogue is an example. Later accretions dealt with the relation between the individual and society. The Golden Rule tries to integrate the individual to society; democracy to integrate social organization to the individual.

There is as yet no ethic dealing with man's relation to land and to the animals and plants which grow upon it. Land, like Odysseus' slave-girls, is still property. The land relation is still strictly economic, entailing privileges but not obligations.

The extension of ethics to this third element in human environment is, if I read the evidence correctly, an evolutionary possibility and an ecological necessity. It is the third step in a sequence. The first two have already been taken. Individual thinkers since the days of Ezekiel and Isaiah have asserted that the despoliation of land is not only inexpedient but wrong. Society, however, has not yet affirmed their belief. I regard the present conservation movement as the embryo of such an affirmation.

An ethic may be regarded as a mode of guidance for meeting ecological situations so new or intricate, or involving such deferred reactions, that the path of social expediency is not discernible to the average individual. Animal instincts are modes of guidance for the individual in meeting such situations. Ethics are possibly a kind of community instinct in-the-making.

The Community Concept

All ethics so far evolved rest upon a single premise: that the individual is a member of a community of interdependent parts. His instincts prompt him to compete for his place in that community, but his ethics prompt him also to co-operate (perhaps in order that there may be a place to compete for).

The land ethic simply enlarges the boundaries of the community to include soils, waters, plants, and animals, or collectively: the land.

This sounds simple: do we not already sing our love for and obligation to the land of the free and the home of the brave? Yes, but just what and whom do we love? Certainly not the soil, which we are sending helter-skelter downriver. Certainly not the waters, which we assume have no function except to turn turbines, float barges, and carry off sewage. Certainly not the plants, of which we exterminate whole communities without batting an eye. Certainly not the animals, of which we have already extirpated many of the largest and most beautiful species. A land ethic of course cannot prevent the alteration, management, and use of these "resources," but it does affirm their right to continued existence, and, at least in spots, their continued existence in a natural state.

In short, a land ethic changes the role of *Homo sapiens* from conqueror of the land-community to plain member and citizen of it. It implies respect for his fellow-members, and also respect for the community as such.

In human history, we have learned (I hope) that the conqueror role is eventually self-defeating. Why? Because it is implicit in such a role that the conqueror knows, *ex cathedra*, just what makes the community clock tick, and just what and who is valuable, and what and who is worthless, in community life. It always turns out that he knows neither, and this is why his conquests eventually defeat themselves.

In the biotic community, a parallel situation exists. Abraham knew exactly what the land was for: it was to drip milk and honey into Abraham's mouth. At the present moment, the assurance with which we regard this assumption is inverse to the degree of our education.

The ordinary citizen today assumes that science knows what makes the community clock tick; the scientist is equally sure that he does not. He knows that the biotic mechanism is so complex that its workings may never be fully understood.

That man is, in fact, only a member of a biotic team is shown by an ecological interpretation of history. Many historical events, hitherto explained solely in terms of human enterprise, were actually biotic interactions between people and land. The characteristics of the land determined the facts quite as potently as the characteristics of the men who lived on it.

Consider, for example, the settlement of the Mississippi valley. In the years following the Revolution, three groups were contending for its control: the native Indian, the French and English traders, and the American settlers. Historians wonder what would have happened if the English at Detroit had thrown a little more weight into the Indian side of those tipsy scales which decided the outcome of the colonial migration into the cane-lands of Kentucky. It is time now to ponder the fact that the cane-lands, when subjected to the particular mixture of forces represented by the cow, plow, fire, and axe of the pioneer, became bluegrass. What if the plant succession inherent in this dark and bloody ground had, under the impact of these forces, given us some worthless sedge, shrub, or weed? Would Boone and Kenton have held out? Would there have been any overflow into Ohio, Indiana, Illinois, and Missouri? Any Louisiana Purchase? Any transcontinental union of new states? Any Civil War?

Kentucky was one sentence in the drama of history. We are commonly told what the human actors in this drama tried to do, but we are seldom told that their success, or the lack of it, hung in large degree on the reaction of particular soils to the impact of the particular forces exerted by their occupancy. In the case of Kentucky, we do not even know where the bluegrass came from—whether it is a native species, or a stowaway from Europe.

Contrast the cane-lands with what hindsight tells us about the Southwest, where the pioneers were equally brave, resourceful, and persevering. The impact of occupancy here brought no bluegrass, or other plant fitted to withstand the bumps and buffetings of hard use. This region, when grazed by livestock, reverted through a series of more and more worthless grasses, shrubs, and weeds to a condition of unstable equilibrium. Each recession of plant types bred erosion; each increment to erosion bred a further recession of plants. The result today is a progressive and mutual deterioration, not only of plants and soils, but of the animal community subsisting thereon. The early settlers did not expect this: on the *cienegas* of New Mexico some even cut ditches to hasten it. So subtle has been its progress that few residents of the region are aware of it. It is quite invisible to the tourist who finds this wrecked landscape colorful and charming (as indeed it is, but it bears scant resemblance to what it was in 1848).

This same landscape was "developed" once before, but with quite different results. The Pueblo Indians settled the Southwest in pre-Columbian times, but they happened not to be equipped with range livestock. Their civilization expired, but not because their land expired.

In India, regions devoid of any sod-forming grass have been settled, apparently without wrecking the land, by the simple expedient of carrying the grass to the cow, rather than vice versa. (Was this the result of some deep wisdom, or was it just good luck? I do not know.)

In short, the plant succession steered the course of history; the pioneer simply demonstrated, for good or ill, what successions inhered in the land. Is history taught in this spirit? It will be, once the concept of land as a community really penetrates our intellectual life.

The Ecological Conscience

Conservation is a state of harmony between men and land. Despite nearly a century of propaganda, conservation still proceeds at a snail's pace; progress still consists largely of letterhead pieties and convention oratory. On the back forty we still slip two steps backward for each forward stride.

The usual answer to this dilemma is "more conservation education." No one will debate this, but is it certain that only the volume of education needs stepping up? Is something lacking in the *content* as well?

It is difficult to give a fair summary of its content in brief form, but, as I understand it, the content is substantially this: obey the law, vote right, join some organizations, and practice what conservation is profitable on your own land; the government will do the rest.

Is not this formula too easy to accomplish anything worth-while? It defines no right or wrong, assigns no obligation, calls for no sacrifice, implies no change in the current philosophy of values. In respect of land-use, it urges only enlightened self-interest. Just how far will such education take us? An example will perhaps yield a partial answer.

By 1930 it had become clear to all except the ecologically blind that southwestern Wisconsin's topsoil was slipping seaward. In 1933 the farmers were told that if they would adopt certain remedial practices for five years, the public would donate CCC labor to install them, plus the necessary machinery and materials. The offer was widely accepted, but the practices were widely forgotten when the five-year contract period was up. The farmers continued only those practices that yielded an immediate and visible economic gain for themselves.

This led to the idea that maybe farmers would learn more quickly if they themselves wrote the rules. Accordingly the Wisconsin Legislature in 1937 passed the Soil Conservation District Law. This said to farmers, in effect: *We, the public, will furnish you free technical service and loan you specialized machinery, if you will write your own rules for land-use. Each county may write its own rules, and these will have the force of law.* Nearly all the counties promptly organized to accept the proffered help, but after a decade of operation, *no county has yet written a single rule.* There has been visible progress in such practices as strip-cropping, pasture renovation, and soil liming, but none in fencing woodlots against grazing, and none in excluding plow and cow from steep slopes. The farmers, in short, have selected those remedial practices which were profitable anyhow, and ignored those which were profitable to the community, but not clearly profitable to themselves.

When one asks why no rules have been written, one is told that the community is not yet ready to support them; education must precede rules. But the education actually in progress makes no mention of obligations to land over and above those dictated by self-interest. The net result is that we have more education but less soil, fewer healthy woods, and as many floods as in 1937.

The puzzling aspect of such situations is that the existence of obligations over and above self-interest is taken for granted in such rural community enterprises as the betterment of roads, schools, churches, and baseball teams. Their existence is not taken for granted, nor as yet seriously discussed, in bettering the behavior of the water that falls on the land, or in the preserving of the beauty or diversity of the farm landscape. Land-use ethics are still governed wholly by economic self-interest, just as social ethics were a century ago.

To sum up: we asked the farmer to do what he conveniently could to save his soil, and he has done just that, and only that. The farmer who clears the woods off a 75 per cent slope, turns his cows into the clearing, and dumps its rainfall, rocks, and soil into the community creek, is still (if otherwise decent) a respected member of society. If he puts lime on his fields and plants his crops on contour, he is still entitled to all the privileges and emoluments of his Soil Conservation District. The District is a beautiful piece of social machinery, but it is coughing along on two cylinders because we have been too timid, and too anxious for quick success, to tell the farmer the true magnitude of his obligations. Obligations have no meaning without conscience, and the problem we face is the extension of the social conscience from people to land.

No important change in ethics was ever accomplished without an internal change in our intellectual emphasis, loyalties, affections, and convictions. The proof that conservation has not yet touched these foundations of conduct lies in the fact that philosophy and religion have not yet heard of it. In our attempt to make conservation easy, we have made it trivial.

Substitutes for a Land Ethic

When the logic of history hungers for bread and we hand out a stone, we are at pains to explain how much the stone resembles bread. I now describe some of the stones which serve in lieu of a land ethic.

One basic weakness in a conservation system based wholly on economic motives is that most members of the land community have no economic value. Wildflowers and songbirds are examples. Of the 22,000 higher plants and animals native to Wisconsin, it is doubtful whether more than 5 per cent can be sold, fed, eaten, or otherwise put to economic use. Yet these creatures are members of the biotic community, and if (as I believe) its stability depends on its integrity, they are entitled to continuance.

When one of these non-economic categories is threatened, and if we happen to love it, we invent subterfuges to give it economic importance. At the beginning of the century songbirds were supposed to be disappearing. Ornithologists jumped to the rescue with some distinctly shaky evidence to the effect that insects would eat us up if birds failed to control them. The evidence had to be economic in order to be valid.

It is painful to read these circumlocutions today. We have no land ethic yet, but we have at least drawn nearer the point of admitting that birds should continue as a matter of biotic right, regardless of the presence or absence of economic advantage to us.

A parallel situation exists in respect of predatory mammals, raptorial birds, and fish-eating birds. Time was when biologists somewhat overworked the evidence that these creatures preserve the health of game by killing weaklings, or that they control rodents for the farmer, or that they prey only on "worthless" species. Here again, the evidence had to be economic in order to be valid. It is only in recent years that we hear the more honest argument that predators are members of the community, and that no special interest has the right to exterminate them for the sake of a benefit, real or fancied, to itself. Unfortunately this enlightened view is still in the talk stage. In the field the extermination of predators goes merrily on: witness the impending erasure of the timber wolf by fiat of Congress, the Conservation Bureaus, and many state legislatures.

Some species of trees have been "read out of the party" by economics-minded foresters because they grow too slowly, or have too low a sale value to pay as timber crops: white cedar, tamarack, cypress, beech, and hemlock are examples. In Europe, where forestry is ecologically more advanced, the non-commercial tree species are recognized as members of the native forest community, to be preserved as such, within reason. Moreover some (like beech) have been found to have a valuable function in building up soil fertility. The interdependence of the forest and its constituent tree species, ground flora, and fauna is taken for granted.

Lack of economic value is sometimes a character not only of species or groups, but of entire biotic communities: marshes, bogs, dunes, and "deserts" are examples. Our formula in such cases is to relegate their conservation to government as refuges, monuments, or parks. The difficulty is that these communities are usually interspersed with more valuable private lands; the government cannot possibly own or control such scattered parcels. The net effect is that we have relegated some of them to ultimate extinction over large areas. If the private owner were ecologically minded, he would be proud to be the custodian of a reasonable proportion of such areas, which add diversity and beauty to his farm and to his community.

In some instances, the assumed lack of profit in these "waste" areas has proved to be wrong, but only after most of them had been done away with. The present scramble to reflood muskrat marshes is a case in point.

There is a clear tendency in American conservation to relegate to government all necessary jobs that private landowners fail to perform. Government ownership, operation, subsidy, or regulation is now widely prevalent in forestry, range management, soil and watershed management, park and wilderness conservation, fisheries management, and migratory bird management, with more to come. Most of this growth in governmental conservation is proper and logical, some of it is inevitable. That I imply no disapproval of it is implicit in the fact that I have spent most of my life working for it. Nevertheless the question arises: What is the ultimate magnitude of the enterprise? Will the tax base carry its eventual ramifications? At what point will governmental conservation, like the mastodon, become handicapped by its own dimensions? The answer, if there is any, seems to be in a land ethic, or some other force which assigns more obligation to the private landowner.

Industrial landowners and users, especially lumbermen and stockmen, are inclined to wail long and loudly about the extension of government ownership and regulation to land, but (with notable exceptions) they show little disposition to develop the only visible alternative: the voluntary practice of conservation on their own lands.

When the private landowner is asked to perform some unprofitable act for the good of the community, he today assents only with outstretched palm. If the act costs him cash this is fair and proper, but when it costs only forethought, open-mindedness, or time, the issue is at least debatable. The overwhelming growth of land-use subsidies in recent years must be ascribed, in large part, to the government's own agencies for conservation education: the land bureaus, the agricultural colleges, and the extension services. As far as I can detect, no ethical obligation toward land is taught in these institutions.

To sum up: a system of conservation based solely on economic self-interest is hopelessly lopsided. It tends to ignore, and thus eventually to eliminate, many elements in the land community that lack commercial value, but that are (as far as we know) essential to its healthy functioning. It assumes, falsely, I think, that the economic parts of the biotic clock will function without the uneconomic parts. It tends to relegate to government many functions eventually too large, too complex, or too widely dispersed to be performed by government.

An ethical obligation on the part of the private owner is the only visible remedy for these situations.

The Outlook

It is inconceivable to me that an ethical relation to land can exist without love, respect, and admiration for land, and a high regard for its value. By value, I of course mean something far broader than mere economic value; I mean value in the philosophical sense.

Perhaps the most serious obstacle impeding the evolution of a land ethic is the fact that our educational and economic system is headed away from, rather than toward, an intense consciousness of land. Your true modern is separated from the land by many middlemen, and by innumerable physical gadgets. He has no vital relation to it; to him it is the space between cities on which crops grow. Turn him loose for a day on the land, and if the spot does not happen to be a golf links or a "scenic" area, he is bored stiff. If crops could be raised by hydroponics instead of farming, it would suit him very well. Synthetic substitutes for wood, leather, wool, and other natural land products suit him better than the originals. In short, land is something he has "outgrown."

Almost equally serious as an obstacle to a land ethic is the attitude of the farmer for whom the land is still an adversary, or a taskmaster that keeps him in slavery. Theoretically, the mechanization of farming ought to cut the farmer's chains, but whether it really does is debatable.

One of the requisites for an ecological comprehension of land is an understanding of ecology, and this is by no means co-extensive with "education"; in fact, much higher education seems deliberately to avoid ecological concepts. An understanding of ecology does not necessarily originate in courses bearing ecological labels; it is quite as likely to be labeled geography, botany, agronomy, history, or economics. This is as it should be, but whatever the label, ecological training is scarce.

The case for a land ethic would appear hopeless but for the minority which is in obvious revolt against these "Modern" trends.

The "key-log" which must be moved [the metaphor is from lumbering—the breaking of a logjam by finding the log that anchors it] to release the evolutionary process for an ethic is simply this: quit thinking about decent land-use as solely an economic problem. Examine each question in terms of what is ethically and esthetically right, as well as what is economically expedient. *A thing is right when it tends to preserve the integrity, stability, and beauty of the biotic community. It is wrong when it tends otherwise.*

It of course goes without saying that economic feasibility limits the tether of what can or cannot be done for land. It always has and it always will. The fallacy the economic determinists have tied around our collective neck, and which we now need to cast off, is the belief that economics determines all land-use. This is simply not true. An innumerable host of actions and attitudes, comprising perhaps the bulk of all land relations, is determined by the land-users' tastes and predilections, rather than by his purse. The bulk of all land relations hinges on investments of time, forethought, skill, and faith rather than on investments of cash. As a land-user thinketh, so is he.

I have purposely presented the land ethic as a product of social evolution because nothing so important as an ethic is ever "written." Only the most superficial student of history supposes that Moses "wrote" the Decalogue; it evolved in the minds of a thinking community, and Moses wrote a tentative summary of it for a "seminar." I say tentative because evolution never stops.

The evolution of a land ethic is an intellectual as well as emotional process. Conservation is paved with good intentions which prove to be futile, or even dangerous, because they are devoid of critical understanding either of the land, or of economic land-use. I think it is a truism that as the ethical frontier advances from the individual to the community, its intellectual content increases.

The mechanism of operation is the same for any ethic: social approbation for right actions: social disapproval for wrong actions.

By and large, our present problem is one of attitudes and implements. We are remodeling the Alhambra with a steam-shovel, and we are proud of our yardage. We shall hardly relinquish the shovel, which after all has many good points, but we are in need of gentler and more objective criteria for its successful use.

Epilogue

Through the course of these pages, we have been in the presence of philosophers of many different traditions, methods, backgrounds, and beliefs. This collection contains devout pagans (Epictetus, Eagle Man); Catholics (St. Thomas Aquinas), Protestants (Immanuel Kant), Eastern Orthodox (Dostoevsky), Jews (Moses, Amos, Jesus), Muslims (Abu'l A'la Mawdudi), and convinced atheists (Epicurus, Hobbes, Sartre). There are Consequentialists (including Jeremy Bentham, who seems to think that most Deontologists are frauds), and Deontologists (including Immanuel Kant, who seems to think that most Consequentialists are corrupt). Yet we talk about the "philosophical approach to life," or "taking things philosophically," as if there were some unifying strand in the thought of the teachers whom we call "philosophers."

Even—or particularly—in the field of ethics, do we assume that there is unity beneath the apparent diversity. There is little to support this assumption in the pages of the current professional journals, where no message at all seems to emerge from the metaethical discussions of person and agency. Yet if we set aside the technical writings and look back to the beginning of the twentieth century and earlier, we can find three recurrent dispositions of thought that appear in all our writers from Plato to Rita Manning.

First among these dispositions is the *concern for the larger issues of human life and society.* Philosophy and ethics were designed at the outset to take on the most demanding and abstract problems that the human mind could devise. Only in the twentieth century do we encounter the sentiment that these disciplines are really not up to considering any problems larger than the meanings and logical relations of certain traditional philosophical terms. From Plato on, the philosophers have dealt with ethical dilemmas of war and peace, economic freedom and social welfare, political accountability and statesmanship—in short, all the issues taken up in this television course as a whole.

So there is commonality from the beginning in the breadth and the seriousness of the problems chosen for analysis by the ethical traditions. There is further commonality in the approach the great teachers of the traditions have taken to these problems, which we may call the *method of objective and systematic reasoning.* No matter what their metaphysical assumptions about the origin of humanity and the universe, all have assumed that human reason is entirely adequate to discover the outlines of the moral life. Even those most firmly convinced of the role of a supernatural power in the formation of law have held that the law can be known by humans and practiced by humans, and that human agency is essential for, and quite adequate to, the determination of policies that will implement the general provisions of human values and the moral law.

Finally, there is commonality of result. All philosophers who have taught ethics have taught about human happiness and moral obligation, and the relation between the two. There are strands of agreement on the treatment of this problem; preeminent among these strands is the one we may call *the conclusion that self-interest and moral obligation coincide*—or "honesty is the best policy" writ large. All philosophers worth our attention recognize the conceptual or *formal* distinction between "pursuing your own advantage" and "fulfilling your moral obligations"; they did not imagine that the two were the same by definition. But there is a surprising agreement on the *empirical* fact of convergence of those two courses of action. If you live your life as you ought to live it, fulfilling your duties to others and serving your community, you will be, in fact, and possibly to your surprise, happy. As might be expected, their explanations for this convergence differ.

The Utilitarians will point to the advantages to all and the general increase in welfare that is expected to follow from the free pursuit of self interest. The economic application of this reasoning, in the economist Adam Smith, became the basis of the economic arrangements for most of the contemporary Western world. Hence to pursue our self-interest is to promote the general welfare. Presupposed, of course, is a moral framework of respect for liberty, respect for private property, and a general good will toward our fellow humans. From the latter, we can derive the benefit to each from service to all (from a simple expectation of reciprocity—if you do good to others, they will naturally be inclined to do good unto you), and the benefits that flow to all when a society is able to command the services of all.

The contractarians also provide an explanation of the convergence of interest and morality. Rawls points to the probability of benefit to all in the fulfillment of the obligation to help the least advantaged; no one can fall very far below the average in welfare. He and all the contractarians can point to the enormous advantage to each individual that flows from the renunciation of the *unrestricted* pursuit of individual advantage in the "state of nature" in favor of the state of civil society.

A different kind of argument to the same conclusion is found in the Biblical tradition, and implicit also in the Christian members of the Moral Law tradition. Again and again the Prophets tell us that the only tolerable course of life is the one that conforms to the way of the Lord, and that the relapse into injustice will bring destruction in its wake. The way of the Lord is simple, and right, and leads to joy; the way of selfishness destroys individual and society both. Brought forward into the promises of Christianity, we find an extraordinarily simple and beautiful way of life being preached as the one sure Way to the Father in Heaven. Again, the way of love for others is the way to personal happiness.

But that result, reached in those ways, returns us to the beginning of the reader, and of the course, and of Philosophy. Where have we seen these two arguments before? Note that in both the contractarian and the religious traditions, the advantage to the individual that follows from the moral life is *indirect*. For the contractarians, the conclusion—that my own advantage follows from service to the community—amounts to a canny guess that if I subscribe to a set of rules, and to a police force that will enforce them, I am less likely to be victimized by those stronger than I, than if I take my chances on my own. For the religious tradition, that same conclusion follows from God's promise (or from a settled disposition of God observed from His treatment of my people in the past) that renunciation of personal gain results in eternal salvation—that is, short-term investments of pain have a good likelihood of producing very high long-term gains in happiness through supernatural agencies. We have seen precisely these calculations in the arguments presented by Glaucon and Adeimantus respectively in the opening of the second book of Plato's *The Republic* (see p. 17). Plato's brothers were arguing to

Socrates that the people who themselves are reputed to be just, and who advocate the choice of a moral life as beneficial to the individual who chooses, actually believe that "justice pays" *only* on one of those indirect justifications. They challenge Socrates to present an alternative to those justifications, remember? They challenge Socrates to show that the moral life is the happiest life for the individual who chooses it *in itself,* in its effect on the soul of the just person. And as we read, that is what Socrates did, or tried to do.

Did he succeed? His argument is a good one, not obviously flawed, engagingly presented, and even intuitively plausible—he's surely right, that the ravages of unsatisfiable desire are unpleasant, and that the contentment of one who has brought all desires under control is enviable. His argument is buttressed—illustrated, we might say, as with pictures in the text—by compelling portraits of the extremes of human success and failure. The entirely just philosopher condemned to die in prison is serene and happy; those of Plato's readers who had read his earlier account of Socrates' last conversation and death in the Athenian prison would recognize him as the model for that serenity. The entirely unjust despot, living in an unending cycle of terror, hatred, and violence, has had so many models in history that Plato did not need to supply specific examples. Yes, the argument is successful.

But we have never accepted it as valid, or if we have, we have not lived it. We began this series of readings with a telling passage from the historian Thucydides, presenting in the baldest terms the contrasting argument: that might is right, advantage is all, and morality is worthless. Time and again these contentions are accepted as unquestionably true by kings planning conquests, criminals planning "perfect" crimes, or corporate Chief Executive Officers planning to unload all their company's stock just before it tanks. Each expects to obtain only the advantages of the coup, and never to face retribution from the parties injured or to deal with the damage caused by his act to the ordered society in which he otherwise tries to live as a citizen. Time and again the ruthless advantage-seekers, tripped by their own *hubris,* come to grief and find themselves in jail, or in poverty, or alone, or all of the above. It happens often enough, anyway, to provide good moral tales for ethics teachers. But always some escape— enough, anyway, to provide hope to the next generation of inexperienced self-seekers. We have never been able to establish, to the satisfaction of the society as a whole for any length of time, that crime really does not pay and that happiness really does follow from a life of adherence to ethical principles.

And perhaps this is as it should be. Our human dignity does not reside ultimately in our correct belief or good behavior. As Kant and Jefferson point out, had God wanted us to believe and behave in certain ways, He could easily have equipped us with instincts that would have compelled us to do so. Instead we find that we are creatures of our own choices, condemned to be free. Our dignity resides in that freedom, and in the quality of reason we use to engage it, for better or for worse.

Suggestions for Further Reading

Comprehensive works on the history of philosophy:

COPLESTON, FREDERICK C. *A History of Philosophy*, in nine volumes. London: Burns, Oates and Washbourne, 1946–1975.

This is an excellent source, for everything. Very thorough.

HAMLYN, D. W. *A History of Western Philosophy*, in one volume. London: Penguin [Viking], 1987.

Necessarily condensed, but reflects the most recent scholarship.

JONES, W. T. *A History of Western Philosophy*, in two volumes. New York: Harcourt Brace and Co., 1952.

This is my favorite. Very readable, contains crucial passages for most authors, not too long. May be out of print, but your library should have it. Not as thorough as Copleston.

O'CONNOR, D. J., ed. *A Critical History of Western Philosophy*. London, and Glencoe, Illinois: Collier-Macmillan, 1964; Paperback, Basingstoke: Macmillan, 1985.

A different scholar for each chapter. What you lose in continuity of style you make up with diversity of scholarship.

RUSSELL, BERTRAND. *A History of Western Philosophy*, 2nd edition. London: Allen and Unwin, 1961.

Marvelous work by one of the greatest philosophers of the twentieth century. You may not agree with everything he says.

EDWARDS PAUL, ed. *The Encyclopedia of Philosophy* in eight volumes. New York and London: Collier-Macmillan, 1967.

Not historical, but a gold mine of information about individual philosophers, their place in history, and the development of the fields of philosophy. You might start with the entry on "Ethics."

Beyond these sources, there is no substitute for reading the philosophers themselves. They are all available, in several translations, in any library or university bookstore. Go to it.

Acknowledgments

The Scripture quotations are from the *Revised Standard Version Bible,* copyright 1946, 1952, 1971 by the Division of Christian Education of the National Council of the Churches of Christ in the USA, and are used by permission.

AQUINAS, THOMAS. *Treatise on Law.* Chicago: Regnery Gateway, Inc., 1979. Question 91, article 2, Question 94, art. 2, 5, and 6, Question 95, art. 1. Reprinted by permission of Regnery Gateway, Inc., Publishers.

ARISTOTLE. *Nicomachean Ethics* and *The Politics.* Translated and edited by W. D. Ross. The Oxford Translation of Aristotle, vol. 9. Oxford: Oxford University Press, 1925, pp. 935–37, 941–45, 952–59, 964–74, 1004–13, 1061, 1068–69, 1071–73, 1104–12, 1127–30. Reprinted by permission of Oxford University Press.

BENTHAM, JEREMY. *Principles of Morals and Legislation.* "A New Edition, corrected by the Author." Oxford: Oxford University Press, 1823, pp. 1–7, 17–20, 29–32.

CONFUCIUS. *The Book of Rites.* Translated by Constance Barnett. New York: Macmillan, © 1864.

DOSTOEVSKY, FYODOR MIKHAILOVIC. *Notes from Underground.*

EPICTETUS. *The Moral Discourses of Epictetus.* Edited with an introduction by Dr. Thomas Gould. New York: Washington Square Press, Inc., © 1964, pp. 5–8, 16–19, 52–56, 57. Reprinted by permission of Washington Square Press, a Pocket Book division of Simon & Schuster, Inc.

EPICURUS. *Epicurus: The Extant Remains.* Translated by Cyril Bailey. Oxford: Oxford University Press, 1926, pp. 83–93. Reprinted by permission of Oxford University Press.

HOBBES, THOMAS. *Leviathan.* Oxford: Oxford University Press, 1909, pp. 94–109.

JEFFERSON, THOMAS. *Social and Political Philosophy,* edited by John Somerville and Ronald Santoni. New York: Doubleday, 1963, pp. 239, 247. Published by Doubleday, a division of Bantam, Doubleday, Dell Publishing Group, Inc.

KANT, IMMANUEL. Reprinted with permission of Macmillan Publishing Company from *Foundations of the Metaphysics of Morals.* Translated by Lewis White Beck. Macmillan Publishing Company, © 1959, pp. 5–6, 9–14, 16–18, 29–34, 38–39, 45–47, 49, 51–55.

KING, MARTIN LUTHER, JR. "A Letter from a Birmingham Jail." In *Why We Can't Wait.* Copyright 1963 by Martin Luther King, Jr. pp. 76–95. Reprinted by permission of Harper & Row Publishers, Inc.

LEOPOLD, ALDO. *A Sand County Almanac*. New York: Oxford University Press, 1949, 1987, pp. 201–226.

LOCKE, JOHN. *Two Treatises of Civil Government*. Introduction by W. S. Carpenter. Everyman's Library Series. London: J. M. Dent & Sons, Ltd., 1924, 1975, pp. 118–24, 129–35, 154–55, 158–66, 179–82, 189–90, 195–96, 203. Reprinted by permission of J. M. Dent & Sons, Ltd., Publishers.

MANNING, RITA. "Just Caring." From *In a Different Voice* by Carol Gilligan. Indiana University Press, 1992, pp. 45–54.

MARX, KARL and Engels Frederick. *The Communist Manifesto*. Selections can be found at http://www.marxists.org/archive/marx/works/1848/communist-manifesto/ch01.htm.

MAWDUDI, ABU'L A'LA. *The Islamic Law and Constitution*. Translated by Khurshid Ahmad. Reprinted by permission of Kazi Publications, © 1955, 1960, pp. 131–132; 145–161.

MILL, JOHN STUART. "*On Liberty: In Three Essays*." Oxford: Oxford University Press, 1912, pp. 92–114.

MILL, JOHN STUART. *Utilitarianism*. London: Longmans, Green and Company, 1882, pp. 8–51.

PLATO, *Euthyphro, Apology, Crito*. Reprinted with permission of Macmillan Publishing Company. Translated by F. J. Church. Translation revised with an introduction and notes by Robert D. Cumming. © 1985 by Macmillan Publishing Company. © 1948, 1956, pp. 34–36, 46–48.

PLATO. *The Republic of Plato*. Translated by F. M. Cornford. Oxford: Oxford University Press, 1941, pp. 6–7, 9–12, 18–26, 42–53, 139–43, 268, 276–77, 282–83, 284–86, 296–98, 300–6. Reprinted by permission of Oxford University Press.

RAHULA, WALPOLA. *What the Buddha Taught*. New York: Grove/Atlantic Monthly Press, © 1959 edition Copyright renewed by W. Rahula, © 1987, pp. 45–50.

RAWLS, JOHN. Excerpted by permission of the publishers from A *Theory of Justice* by John Rawls, Cambridge, Massachusetts: Harvard University Press. © 1971 by the President and Fellows of Harvard College, pp. 11–15, 19–21, 60–64.

ROUSSEAU, JEAN-JACQUES. *Of the Social Contract*. New York: Nafner Publishing Co. © 1947.

ROYCE, JOSIAH. *Philosophy of Loyalty*. New York: Macmillan, Nafner Publishing Co. © 1947, pp. ___ 1908 and 1936, pp. 103–7, 110, 112, 116–21, 124–40.

THUCYDIDES. *Thucydides: The Peloponnesian War*. Translated by Rex Warner and with notes by M. I. Finley. Penguin Classics. London: Penguin, 1954, 1972. © Rex Warner, 1954, M. I. Finley, 1972, pp. 400–8. Reproduced by permission of Penguin Books Ltd.

SARTRE, JEAN-PAUL. "Existentialism is a Humanism". *Existentialism from Dostoevsky to Sartre*. Edited by Walter Kaufman. New York: New American Library, © 1975, pp. 345–369.

SARTRE, JEAN-PAUL. "Portrait of an Anti-Semite". *Existentialism from Dostoevsky to Sartre*. Edited by Walter Kaufman. New York: New American Library, © 1975, pp. 329–345.

SMITH, ADAM. *An Inquiry Into the Nature and Causes of the Wealth of Nations*. Methuen & Co., Ltd. 1776.

"The Four Noble Truths," *Thus Have I Heard: The Long Discourses of the Buddha: Digha Nikaya*. Translated by Maurice Walshe. Boston: Wisdom Publications, © 1987, pp. 344–349.

I would also like to thank Peter G. Murphy, University of South Carolina, Union; Michael Coste, Front Range Community College; Daniel Restaino, Sacramento City College; and Michael Anker, Contra Costa College for reviewing this book.